B E Y O N D
METHODOLOGY

W9-BGO-415

B E Y O N D
METHODOLOGY

*Feminist Scholarship as
Lived Research*

EDITORS

*Mary Margaret Fonow
Judith A. Cook*

INDIANA UNIVERSITY PRESS
Bloomington and Indianapolis

© 1991 by Indiana University Press

All rights reserved

No part of this book may be reproduced or utilized in any form or by
any means, electronic or mechanical, including photocopying and
recording, or by any information storage and retrieval system, without
permission in writing from the publisher. The Association of American
University Presses' Resolution on Permissions constitutes the only
exception to this prohibition.

The paper used in this publication meets the minimum requirements of American
National Standard for Information Sciences—Permanence of Paper for Printed
Library Materials, ANSI Z39.48-1984.

⊚ ™

Manufactured in the United States of America

Library of Congress Cataloging-in-Publication Data
Beynd methodology : feminist scolarship as lived research / Mary
Margaret Fonow, Judith A. Cook, editors.
p. cm.
Includes index.
ISBN 0-253-32345-2 (alk. paper). — ISBN 0-253-20629-4 (pbk.: alk.
paper)
1. Women—Research. 2. Feminism—Research. I. Fonow, Mary
Margaret. II. Cook, Judith A.
HQ1180.B49 1991
305.42'072—dc20   90-43508
                                                          CIP

4 5 6 7 01 00 99 98

CONTENTS

B E Y O N D
METHODOLOGY

1. BACK TO THE FUTURE

A Look at the Second Wave of Feminist Epistemology and Methodology

MARY MARGARET FONOW AND JUDITH A. COOK

Our collection of articles and corresponding analysis presents feminist episte-mological ideas as they exist at a "moment in time," capturing one point in the dynamic, ongoing development of feminist discourse about the conduct of inquiry. The same can be said about feminist influence on a number of method-ological techniques and approaches, extending the notion of method to encom-pass all phases of the research process. Our major purpose in assembling and presenting these articles is to enable a better understanding of epistemology and methodology in feminist research by viewing them from a sociology-of-knowledge perspective. We argue that through formulating an in-depth analy-sis in this area, it is possible to uncover some of the factors that stimulate or hamper feminist scholarship. By stepping back from the ideas contained in individual articles to integrate the whole, we find a common ground, an interdisciplinary plane on which feminist researchers in all fields can share their insights and experiences.

The need for this type of analysis comes from the limitations and strictures placed on feminist studies by a patriarchal academic and research infrastructure (Cook and Fonow, 1986). These constraints and reactions to them extend logically to social and political action, and a part of this is feminist attempts to transform the research process.

Another equally important impetus for this integrative perspective comes from the notion that the experience of oppression due to sexism can create a unique type of insight, involving the ability to penetrate "official" explanations and assumptions to grasp the underlying gender relations and their motor mechanisms. Both of these influences on feminist research—conditioned by patriarchal gender relations on the one hand, and a source of radical insight on the other—can be viewed as a way to approach each of the pieces included in this collection.

Two concepts appear frequently in our thinking and writing about trends in feminist research. The first is "epistemology," and by this we mean the study of assumptions about how to know the social and apprehend its meaning. The second concept, more familiar to most, is "methodology," by which we mean the study of actual techniques and practices used in the research process. The articles in this volume have been chosen because they represent the current state of the literature in both of these areas of feminist scholarship across a variety of fields. In history, philosophy, psychology, sociology, women's studies, and demography the feminist perspective has been used as a lens through which to view the process of inquiry and its social, historical, and political context.

We have argued elsewhere that feminist epistemology and methodology arise from a critique of each field's biases and distortions in the study of women (Cook, 1988b). We have demonstrated how the approaches used by feminist researchers working in different disciplines are fundamentally affected by critiques of the ways each field studies women and gender relations (Cook, 1983). Our survey of these issues in research published over a nine-year period in the field of sociology identified several underlying assumptions in the literature on feminist methods (Cook and Fonow, 1986). Some of these are included in four themes we feel run throughout the articles in this collection, as well as other works in this area. These are four aspects we encountered repeatedly, in different forms, although there are certainly others. The four themes that run throughout the works contained in this volume are: reflexivity; an action orientation; attention to the affective components of the research; and use of the situation-at-hand. We will discuss each theme with illustrations from the articles themselves as well as contemporary literature, and then discuss the interrelations of the four themes.

The Role of Reflexivity

A sociology-of-knowledge approach to feminist scholarship reveals the role of reflexivity as a source of insight (Cook and Fonow, 1986). By reflexivity we mean the tendency of feminists to reflect upon, examine critically, and explore analytically the nature of the research process. To some extent, this tendency toward reflection is part of a tradition of attention to what Abraham Kaplan (1964) refers to as "logic-in-use" or the actual occurrences that arise in the inquiry, idealized and unreconstructed. Emphasis on reflection also belongs to a tradition of reminiscence about fieldwork experiences by sociologists and anthropologists. Compare, for example, Daniels (1983), Gurney (1985), and Warren and Rasmussen (1977).

Yet feminist epistemology carries this tradition of reflection one step further by using it to gain insight into the assumptions about gender relations underlying the conduct of inquiry. This is often accomplished by a thorough-going review of the research setting and its participants, including an exploration of the investigator's reactions to doing the research. In fact, Kathryn Pyne Addelson argues in this collection that feminists may be in the best position to challenge the "cognitive authority" of traditional male social theorists. Arguing that misogyny is itself irrational, Addelson shows how feminist scholars can insist on a more rational science as one that takes into account, through critique and evaluation, the metaphysical commitments of the scientist as well as the social arrangements of doing science. The acknowledgment of metaphysical commitments as part of the content of scientific understanding opens the production of knowledge to a more fruitful scrutiny.

Consciousness Raising

One of the ways in which reflexivity is employed involves the concept of consciousness raising, a process of self-awareness familiar to those involved with the women's movement. Underlying much of the reflexivity found in feminist scholarship is the notion found in the earlier work of scholars such as W. E. B. DuBois (1969) and Paulo Friere (1970) that consciousness of oppression can lead to a creative insight that is generated by experiencing contradictions (often at life "rupture points"). Under ideal circumstances, transformation occurs, during which something hidden is revealed about the formerly taken-for-granted aspects of sexual asymmetry. Thus, in this model, previously-hidden phenomena which are apprehended as a contradiction can lead to one or more of the following: an emotional catharsis (discussed later in a section on the affective components of feminist research); an academic insight and resulting intellectual product; and increased politicization and corresponding activism.

For example, Patricia Hill Collins argues in this volume that it is the awareness of her marginal status as the "outsider within" that provides the black female intellectual with a unique black feminist standpoint from which to analyze self, family, and society. It is the "outsider within" who is more likely to challenge the knowledge claims of insiders, to acknowledge the discrepancy between insiders' accounts of human behavior and her own experiences and to identify anomalies. The most common anomalies involve the omission and distortion of facts and observations about the lives and experiences of black women. Collins suggests that there are a number of benefits of "outsider within" status that actually enhance the production of knowledge; these benefits include greater objectivity, ability to see patterns insiders are too immersed to see, and latent advantages of invisibility.

Consciousness raising is employed in at least three ways by the feminist scholars writing in this collection as well as by others in the field. The first way is through attention to the consciousness-raising effects of research on the researcher. Laurel Richardson's article in this collection talks about what happened to her sense of identity as a feminist researcher during the promotional tour for a book on affairs between single women and married men. Similarly, Liz Stanley and Sue Wise's article in this volume deals with the consciousness-raising effects of presenting their research on obscene phone calls to audiences of male colleagues.

Consciousness raising is also involved in discussions of ways in which the research process influences subjects of the inquiry. Some authors view the research act as an explicit attempt to reduce the distance between the woman researcher and female subjects. This is described by Joan Acker, Kate Barry, and Johanna Esseveld, who write about the experience of giving their work to their key informants for comments in order to encourage reciprocity. Attention to the ways in which research can bridge the gaps between isolated women in rural India who are victims of domestic violence is explored by Maria Mies in her analysis, translated for this volume, of feminist research in the so-called Third World.

Consciousness raising also plays a part in feminist methods as a central feature of research technique. This is found in a wide variety of instances. For example, consciousness raising is employed as a *a process that is studied* by feminists when women's lives are examined at "structural rupture points" in their biographies such as divorce, unemployment, occurrence of rape and physical abuse, coming out, and many other times when social actors commonly forge new aspects of their identities. Maria Mies's article in this volume discusses how studying women at these rupture points reveals aspects about them that might otherwise remain hidden. "Click moments" for both researcher and subject are often used as sources of creative insight that are transferred into the research process. Liz Stanley and Sue Wise speak of women's subordinate position as fostering a "double consciousness" through the contradictions that arise when women study women.

Another application of this method is through the *use of specific consciousness-raising techniques* such as role playing, rap groups, simulations, and psychodrama, in a more self-conscious, deliberate manner. These approaches have provided feminist researchers with a way to tap women's collective consciousness as a source of data and have provided participants in the research process with a way to confirm the experiences of women which have often been denied as real in the past (Reinharz, 1983). In this collection, Maria Mies describes her work in India with "Sangam's" or village women's groups which she organized into regional women's conferences with weekend retreats where women from many villages could stay overnight at the local college. The establishment of this communication and social network empowered the women and helped them deal more effectively with a case of woman battering that occurred during the fieldwork. Similarly, Thelma McCormack (1981) proposes the use of simulations to examine processes such as persuasion and problem-solving in a controlled laboratory setting designed to encourage subjects' role flexibility and freedom from their personal biographies. She notes that simulation techniques enable women to ignore history in formulating their behavior and that such a method generates effective responses among subjects that result in consciousness-raising.

Collaborative Scholarship

Reflexivity is also evident in feminist methodology through its emphasis on collaboration between women researchers (Cook, 1983). To some extent, this encouragement of collaboration is a reaction to the impetus for action discussed in a following section. But not only is collaboration a strategy for ameliorating the problems of scarce resources; there is also the expectation among some scholars that feminist collaboration will bring about a deeper intellectual analysis, an original approach to framing the questions, with a mind-set of innovation to deal with the gendered context of research. This has been described in an analysis of a feminist sociology seminar that grew into a community of gender scholars as members left graduate school and entered the profession (Richardson, Fonow and Cook, 1985).

In order to test whether women were more likely than men to coauthor scholarly publications, Kathryn B. Ward and Linda Grant, in an article included in this collection, analyzed patterns of authorship in more than 3,500 articles appearing in ten major sociology journals over a ten-year period. They found that being female and writing about gender increased the propensity to publish joint-authored rather than solo-authored work. They also found that coauthorship is least common in high-status mainstream national sociology journals, suggesting that feminists who prefer collaboration may in fact be at a disadvantage when the rewards of the academy are meted out.

Unexamined Stages of the Research Process

One final aspect of reflexivity occurs in regard to the typically "hidden" or unexamined stages of the research process. Feminists pay particular attention to these ignored phases of inquiry for a variety of reasons. First, women have been unfairly excluded from full participation in scholarship because of events that occur during such stages as obtaining funding or presenting their results to others (Cook and Fonow, 1986). In this collection Laurel Richardson discusses how negotiating the demands of the publicity tour associated with her book changed the ways she saw herself as a woman, a sociologist, a feminist, and a writer. Also in this volume, Liz Stanley and Sue Wise describe the reactions of their male scholarly audience to presentation of their work on homophobic obscene phone calls. Attention to ways in which gender and sexual asymmetry transform the initial topic formulation, presentation of results to colleagues, and marketing of feminist scholarship to lay audiences are ways feminists seek a better understanding of the political and social contexts of the production of knowledge. This understanding is then incorporated by researchers into the ways they think about research and plan for its products. It is this orientation toward action to which we now turn.

Action Orientation

Another feature of the feminist approach to research is the emphasis on action (Cook and Fonow, 1986). This action orientation is reflected in the statement of purpose, topic selection, theoretical orientation, choice of method, view of human nature, and definitions of the researcher's roles. This emphasis on action is something feminists share with other traditions of social thought such as Black Studies, Marxism, and Gay and Lesbian Studies. As more researchers attempt to implement an action approach to research, we begin to see a more critical reexamination and a more constructive reformulation of the action agenda in research.

Political Action

In feminist circles, the most common expression of action is found in intention: the aim of feminist research is liberation. This emancipatory impulse can be found in positions ranging from a radical insistence that the purpose of research is the total transformation of patriarchy and corresponding empowerment of women, to the more liberal insistence that specific attention be paid to the policy implications of research on women. At the more radical end of the continuum, Maria Mies continues to maintain that the intention and method of feminist research should be consistent with the political goals of the women's movement, and that research should be fully integrated into social and political action for the emancipation of women.

Writing in 1983, Mies proposed that "social change is the starting point of science, and in order to understand the content, form, and consequences of patriarchy, the researcher must be actively involved in the fight against it; one has to change something before it can be understood" (p. 125). Because intention alone does not guarantee outcome, feminist scholars must play active roles in the struggle for women's liberation in order to guard against the misuse of their theoretical and methodological innovations. In her new article in this volume, Mies uses her own scholarship to illustrate how political organizing through the women's movement can orient the researcher to the selection of research topics that serves the needs and interests of the majority of women. Participation in a common struggle may reduce distance between the researcher and researched, opening up the possibility that "knowledge-from-below" can influence the research process. Such activities force the individual to notice what was previously taken for granted. Methodologically, this implies a search for research techniques which take account of and record everyday processes, and which reduce the isolation between research participants.

Historical Perspectives on Action

Documenting and analyzing past struggles through the construction of individual and group histories can lead to the development of more sophisticated long-term strategies for social change. Verta Taylor and Leila Rupp, in this collection, discovered through oral history interviews with the women who had helped to sustain the women's movement during the forties and fifties that the strategies that enabled them to survive were the same strategies that limited their growth. They warn us that an uncritical examination of the past or a simplistic valorization of our feminist ancestors will not help contemporary feminism build a diverse grassroots women's movement. The face to face confrontations these researchers had with their foremothers led them to rethink and reevaluate not only their beliefs about the effectiveness of particular strategies for political and social change, but also some of their beliefs about the nature of feminist research.

Public Policy

The action orientation of feminist research is also reflected in more systemic ways through a focus on the policy implications of specific research findings. In

1979, Jean Lipman-Blumen (1979) argued for the necessity of developing research strategies and reporting styles appropriate for policy users. Research such as that of Ronnie Steinberg and Lois Haignere in this volume on different methods of measuring pay equity has helped to answer that earlier call for policy-ready research results. Lipman-Blumen also cautioned that the relationship between policy and feminist research is viewed differently by the various constituencies of social change research. While researcher, target groups, policy maker and community activist may all agree on the general goal of a specific piece of research, each operates out of a different set of traditions which may create obstacles in communicating research results and formulating policy. The formation of research teams composed of all four groups may be one way to transcend the barriers to cooperation and produce more useful research, perhaps one impetus for the collaborative nature of feminist scholarship, described in a later section.

Feminists enter the policy process in a variety of ways. One way is through the establishment of research and policy centers. The Women's Research and Education Institute (WREI) serves as the research arm of the Congressional Caucus for Women's Issues and publishes a directory of women's research centers around the country that link research on women to public policy. The National Council for Research on Women is an association representing fifty-seven centers and organizations that provide institutional resources for feminist research, policy analysis, and educational programs for women and girls.

Feminist researchers have been involved in social policy formation and implementation through research on comparable worth, domestic violence, rape, pornography, displaced homemakers, women and poverty, women's health issues, education, and employment. Our collection features a number of these important policy studies as examples of the potential ability of feminist research to change the lives of women. Ronnie Steinberg and Lois Haignere discuss the historical background and political implications of comparable worth research and evaluate two methods of measuring pay equity. Pauline B. Bart, Linda N. Freeman, and Peter Kimball demonstrate through the use of multivariate analysis that men and women have very different attitudes and opinions about pornography and that efforts to define community standards without acknowledging gender differences will not serve or protect women.

A concern for the quality of data used by policy makers has motivated some feminist researchers to critique the sex-based biases of official government statistics and develop better ways to operationalize concepts as they apply to women. According to Ruth Dixon-Mueller, distorted statistics that undercount Third World women's labor force participation in agricultural activities not only impede theoretical understanding of sex stratification but also lead to the creation and implementation of development plans that ignore or even harm women's interests. On the other hand, Christine E. Bose makes creative use of U.S. census data to develop a household resource model capable of testing a sophisticated reconceptualization of the integration of work and family life at the turn of the century, thus giving us a more multidimensional picture of the factors associated with women's gainful employment.

This type of empirical work demonstrates the point made by Toby Epstein Jayaratne and Abigail J. Stewart that carefully designed research grounded in feminist theory and ethics is more useful to understanding women's experiences than an allegiance to any one particular method as more "feminist" than another. A well crafted quantitative study may be more useful to policy makers and cause less harm to women than a poorly crafted qualitative one. In addition, as Lynn Weber Cannon, Elizabeth Higginbotham, and Marianne L. A. Leung argue, class and race bias are just as likely to manifest themselves in the more qualitative research strategies often preferred by feminists over purely quantitative designs. These authors describe the extra measures they had to take to ensure that their qualitative study of professional/managerial women included a representative sample of black respondents. Given the serious policy implications of much of feminist research, it is important to understand their conclusions that in order to study race one must be aware of class differences among black women and work actively to recruit working and lower class women so as not to bias the sample.

Another way in which action is emphasized in feminist research is found in the move away from the view of human nature as passive, always acted upon by outside forces beyond the individual's control, toward a view of the individual as actor capable of resisting pressures to conform (Cook, 1983). The assumption that women confront, resist, and challenge gender asymmetry in a myriad of different ways has oriented feminist researchers to search for signs of sabotage in every social setting. According to Patricia Hill Collins, a self-conscious black woman's everyday behavior can be a source of resistance and a form of activism. "People who view themselves as fully human, as subjects, become activists, no matter how limited the sphere of their activism may be."

Dilemmas of an Activist Stance

The action orientation of feminist research can create a number of ethical, political, and practical dilemmas. Because much of feminist research involves the personal and intimate lives of women and men, any intervention risks the possibility of disrupting relationships that are personally satisfying to the participants and perhaps materially necessary for survival.

Finch (1984) raises the question of ethics in feminist research when she questions the amount of control feminists are able to exert over the research process. Because women subjects identify more readily with women researchers, it may be too easy for subjects to reveal the intimate details of their lives. Feminists' attempts to reduce the power differential between themselves and those they research often employ equalitarian research techniques that generate trust. "Each interview can take on the aura of an intimate conversation and respondents can accept too eagerly what are rather flimsy guarantees of confidentiality" (p. 80). Since they are often not in a position to control how the data will be used, feminists must take extra precautions not to betray the trust so freely given. Even if individual interests can be protected, the collective interests of women are at stake, and the latter, according to Finch, may be much harder to secure. A feminist has a "special responsibility to anticipate whether research findings can be interpreted and used in ways quite different from her own intentions" (p. 83).

In a similar vein, Judith Stacey (1988) warns that ethnographic methods, often valued by feminists because they reduce the distance between the researcher and the researched and accord the respondent a more active role in the research process, may be more harmful to subjects than quantitative research methods. The emphasis on collaboration between researcher and researched masks the real power of the researcher, who has much greater control over the research process and product. Moreover, the researcher is free to leave the field at any time and is generally the final author of any account.

Joan Acker and her associates, in this volume, discuss the difficulties and dilemmas thay encountered when consciously attempting to apply feminist principles to the research process. They choose to examine the impact of women's entry or reentry into the paid labor force on the development of feminist consciousness because they saw the study of consciousness raising as being consistent with the emancipatory goals of the women's movement. A study of change could produce the kind of knowledge women themselves might use to challenge the status quo. Furthermore, they selected methods—repeated in-depth interviews over time—that were nonoppressive and reduced the social distance between researcher and researched. They discovered, however, that the researched actively resisted efforts to be included as equal partners in the researchers' efforts to interpret the broader implications of the changes they were experiencing. The researchers also discovered that studying change as a process was problematic, especially when research becomes a part of the change process. How can we distinguish the effects of returning to work from the consciousness-raising effects of participating in a feminist interviewing process? Which produced the change in consciousness?

Attention to the Affective Components of the Research Act

Another major feature of feminist epistemology is its refusal to ignore the emotional dimension of the conduct of inquiry. Feminist researchers often attend specifically to the role of affect in the production of knowledge. To some extent, this is an outgrowth of women's greater familiarity with the world of emotions and their meaning. At another level, however, this feature is also analyzed for the purposes of scholarship and innovation. Thus, this aspect of epistemology involves not only acknowledgment of the affective dimension of research, but also recognition that emotions serve as a source of insight or a signal of rupture in social reality (Cook, 1988a).

Caring and Emotionality

The notion that "women care" at both a practical and an interpersonal level is not a new idea (see, for example, Finch and Groves, 1983). Carol Gilligan's landmark research into male and female moral development found that caring is a major feature of how women view the world and resolve moral dilemmas (1982). Gilligan's research subjects showed great concern about protecting others from harm, and the question of "who gets hurt?" was often foremost in women's accounts. Similarly, this theme emerges in the writings of many feminist scholars, who describe their commitment to the welfare of their research subjects. This is evident in Verta Taylor and Leila Rupp's discussion of the decision-making process that led them to omit questions about lesbianism from their oral history interviews with elderly participants in the early women's rights movement.

Patricia Hill Collins (1989) eloquently argues elsewhere that black feminist thought represents the convergence of Afrocentric and feminist values through the creation of an alternative epistemology based on the ethic of caring. The ethic of caring, used to validate knowledge claims, includes an emphasis on individual uniqueness, the acceptance of the appropriateness of emotions in dialogue, and the cultivation of the capacity for empathy.

Many feminist scholars connect emotional intimacy between female respon-dents to the notion of reciprocity between the researcher and researched. Some of the authors in this collection discuss the difficult yet rewarding "transition to friendship" that occurs with informants. Joan Acker and her associates describe the difficulties and rewards of piercing the methodological dictum of noninvolvement with one's subjects. One of these benefits is the higher quality of information possible as a result of mutual disclosure. Others write about the therapeutic value of research for participants. For example, Maria Mies describes how the research she conducted on women's village organizations in the rural Indian state of Andhra Pradesh enabled the women to pool their "subjectivity and concern," something she calls "affectedness." This affectedness, in turn, is a result of victimization and conscientization and consists of a feeling of angry rebellion, a reaction that must be translated into action to avoid becoming self-defeating and demoralizing.

In another way, Liz Stanley and Sue Wise discuss how turning the obscene phone calls they were already receiving into a subject of inquiry became a way to manage sexism in their personal (i.e., home) environment. This willingness to admit to the therapeutic value of participation in the research process is somewhat novel and may represent a unique contribution of feminist epistemology.

Dealing with Negative Feelings

Also included in their discussion of emotions is a willingness to address what happens when the research act evokes negative reactions for the investigator and her subjects. Feminist scholars have steadfastly refused to ignore this dimension of their work. Thus, Verta Taylor and Leila Rupp in this volume address the issue of how to manage when one discovers that older "feminists" behave in what are considered "unenlightened" ways. They encountered this situation when leaders of the "between-waves" women's movement expressed negative opinions about lesbians and bisexuals, those from lower class backgrounds, and female militancy. Joan Acker and her colleagues also found that sharing their interpretations could be upsetting to women respondents, especially given large differences in class and educational background between the investigators and informants. As these authors point out, subjects have expectations regarding what it is like to be interviewed and they often want investigators to act accordingly.

Rather than ignoring the complexities of negotiating unpleasant interactions in the field, feminist epistemology involves explicit attention to these experiences, analysis of their meaning, and the incorporation of conclusions into further inquiry.

Attention to the affective components of inquiry represents an attempt among feminist scholars to restore the emotional dimension to the current conceptions of rationality. As the critical theorists of the Frankfurt School argued, the concept of reason in 20th century social science has been stripped of its affective content, so that objectivity and unemotionality came to be seen as interchangeable (Horkheimer, 1976). Feminist scholars, as Alison Jaggar (1989:164) argues, have attempted to rescue emotion from its discarded role in the creation of knowledge. Jaggar contends that feminist scholars as well as scholars from other oppressed groups have developed "outlaw emotions" that afford them the unique opportunity to create alternative epistemologies, ones that "would show how our emotional responses to the world change as we conceptualize it differently and how our changing emotional responses then stimulate us to new insights." Attention to these emotions becomes a part of the critical reflexivity, discussed earlier, that we believe characterizes feminist approaches to knowledge.

Use of the Situation at Hand

Feminist approaches to research are often characterized by an emphasis on creativity, spontaneity, and improvisation in the selection of both topic and method (Cook and Fonow, 1986). This includes the tendency to use already-given situations both as the focus of investigation and as a means of collecting data.

Concern with the Everyday Life World

There are a number of factors that inspire the willingness of feminists to try unconventional approaches. Theoretical advances in ethnomethodology, phenomenology, and dramaturgy have made it possible, as well as legitimate, to study the taken-for-granted, mundane features of everyday life. For women, these routine aspects of everyday life help to sustain gender inequality. Analysis of "common courtesies," linguistic practices, commercial advertisements, and even tombstone inscriptions have revealed the cultural norms and assumptions governing gender relations. This concern with the ordinary extends itself to the selection of research settings such as beauty parlors, children's playgrounds, weight watchers meetings, and shopping malls, and research topics such as volunteerism, meal preparation, and husband maintenance.[1]

Feminists seem particularly adept at recognizing the opportunities available in unforeseen settings to study otherwise-hidden processes. Once a researcher finds herself in a particular situation and recognizes the research potential in her surroundings, she may decide to make a study of it. For example, Laurel Richardson saw her book tour as an opportunity to study the impact of the "going public" process on her view of herself, her role as a researcher, and her feminist values.

Studying the situation at hand may also be seen as a way in which the feminist researcher manages her own experiences of sexism. The decision by Liz Stanley and Sue Wise to study obscene phone calls they received after their phone numbers were used in public ads for lesbian support groups was made as a way to cope with their sense of personal assault. They decided to terminate the study when they could no longer manage the antipathy they felt toward the male callers.

Another way in which an already-given situation becomes an opportunity for research is exemplified when the researcher actively intervenes in an ongoing event as a way to understand a particular process. The researcher changes the situation, then studies it. For example, Maria Mies's project teaming Third World women students with Dutch feminist groups arose from her experiences as developer and coordinator of a Women and Development program at the Institute of Social Studies in The Hague. After convincing her mostly male colleagues that "fieldwork" could be scholarship, Mies opened up her Women and Development course to nonminority women Dutch students for the first time. Interestingly, these students served as intermediaries between the Third World women students and the Dutch women's groups, arranging contacts and doing translation.

Utilizing the situation at hand is a methodological strategy that is well suited to circumstances in which nonreactive data gathering is essential. Often, the research subjects in an already-given setting have little control over the events either because they have already occurred or because they occurred for some reason other than research. It is unlikely, for example, that the obscene phone callers in the Stanley and Wise study would have been so honest about their prejudiced, violent feelings toward women and lesbianism in an interview or questionnaire situation.

Innovation as a Reaction to Exclusion

Exclusionary practices in field settings may limit the access of women researchers to records, people, or activities; therefore, feminists have to be particularly resourceful when it comes to getting around these obstacles. Mary Margaret Fonow (1980) found it necessary to arrange interviews with female Steelworkers Union convention delegates in the women's restrooms when union officials barred her access to the convention floor. Hacker (1980) was able to use the obstacles she encountered as a major source of data in her study of agribusiness and its impact on women and minority workers. Her analysis suggests ways to fight fire with fire when one encounters resistance from gatekeepers in the field. While all good field researchers need to know how to maneuver around obstacles, we believe that women, especially feminist investigators, face special problems when they occupy the role of "low-caste stranger" (Daniels, 1967) and when their topics are perceived as controversial.

The ability of feminists to transform the situation at hand into a research opportunity may be a survival mechanism. The under-representation of women in traditional research institutions and the lack of adequate funds for feminist researchers forces feminists to be very opportunistic in their choice of topic, setting, and method (Cook and Fonow, 1986). It may also be the case that those scholars who juggle multiple roles select situations at hand as a way to conserve scarce resources. Children's play groups, Little League, PTA, and other everyday settings in the lives of women loom large as potential sources of insight and innovation.

Summary and Integration

These four trends do not constitute an exhaustive list, nor are the categories entirely separable. In some cases the situation at hand is itself a political action; in others, emotional reactions of the researcher and her subjects are themselves the object of reflection. Yet these four features run like threads throughout the articles in this volume and elsewhere, indicating some degree of cohesiveness in outlook.

All the themes are connected to the subordinate nature of women's status in the research enterprise and the larger society. First, the process of reflection is seen as enlightening due to women's oppressed position that enables a view from the "bottom up," and stems from women's capacity to deal with inequality through intimate knowledge of their oppressors. Second, political action is by its very definition tied to women's disadvantageous location in the social class hierarchy. Third, the emotional context of research experiences may be heightened when "rupture points" provide a locus for analysis given the volatile nature of life experiences such as rape, divorce, discrimination, and unemployment. Finally, scholars with lesser access to research resources (money, research assistants, office space, support staff) turn more frequently to their immediate (at hand) environment for topics and research settings. It is thus possible to relate women's societal and professional positions to the kinds of research they produce and the ways they produce it.

These features of feminist research also reflect the position of feminism in today's research institutions. Although there are some outlets for publication, many mainstream journals are suspicious of feminist epistemological assumptions, especially if they are accompanied by qualitative methodologies.

Finally, since we began this review asserting that feminist research is molded by historical and cultural conditions, it is important to identify these conditions as well as their implications. While this is rightly a subject for a separate study, there are several current trends that come to mind. An important set of influences are those in today's climate of social science research. Many of the issues that confront women today—poverty, violence against women, sexism— are not "fundable" research topics at federal or foundation levels. The decline of available funding for research is one trend which has surely hampered feminist inquiry. At another level, the co-optation of feminist research agendas to the paler topics of "research on" rather than "research for" women has done little to direct attention to epistemological considerations. The current emphasis on computer technology can also be viewed as having an impact on feminist research, given the location of such technology within institutional settings that may exclude feminists, and given the types of questions that are more appropriate to statistical approaches.

At the same time, it would have been impossible to collect these articles and perform this survey if a tradition of feminist attention to epistemological and methodological questions had not been already in existence. Even within a hostile academic environment, feminist scholars have repeatedly turned to issues that plague their investigations. Without a critique well enough developed to allow investigators to innovate and revise, there would be no impetus for the on-going development of feminist thought in regard to inquiry. Perhaps socialization of today's scholars in a historical climate of social movement activity over the past two decades has helped feminist academics to question the status quo they encounter in the research enterprise. The necessary critical impetus can only continue to develop if we insist on the inclusion of feminist epistemological and methodological insights within our individual disciplines, and this goal can be achieved by the application of the reader's "critical lens" to articles such as those presented here. It is our goal that this volume serve such a purpose.

NOTE

1. All of these are actual research topics or settings of master's or doctoral thesis work pursued by feminist scholars who were part of a graduate sociology of gender class at Ohio State University (Richardson et al., 1985).

REFERENCES

Collins, Patricia Hill (1989). The social construction of black feminist thought. *Signs 14*, 745–73.

Cook, Judith A. (1983). An interdisciplinary look at feminist methodology: Ideas and practice in sociology, history, and anthropology. *Humboldt Journal of Social Relations 10,* 127–52.

——— (1988a). Who "mothers" the chronically mentally ill? *Family Relations 37,* 42–49.

——— (1988b). Integrating feminist epistemology and qualitative family research. *Qualitative Family Research Network Newsletter 2,* 3–5.

Cook, Judith A., and Mary Margaret Fonow (1984). Am I my sister's gatekeeper? Cautionary tales from the academic hierarchy. *Humanity and Society 8,* 442–52.

——— (1986). Knowledge and women's interests: Issues of epistemology and methodology in feminist sociological research. *Sociological Inquiry 56,* 2–29.

Daniels, Arlene (1967). The low-caste stranger in social research. In G. Sjoberg (ed.), *Ethics, Politics and Social Research.* Cambridge: Schenkman.

——— (1983). Self-deception and self-discovery in fieldwork. *Qualitative Sociology 6,* 195–214.

DuBois, W. E. B. (1969). *The souls of black folks.* New York: New American Library.

Finch, Janet (1984). "It's great to have someone to talk to": The ethics and politics of interviewing women. In C. Bell and H. Roberts (eds.), *Social Researching: Politics, Problems, Practice.* London: Routledge and Kegan Paul.

Finch, Janet, and Dulcie Groves, (eds.) (1983). *A labour of love: Women, work and caring.* London: Routledge and Kegan Paul.

Fonow, Mary Margaret (1980). Feminism and union participation: The case of women steelworkers. Paper presented at the annual meeting of the American Sociological Association, New York.

Freire, Paulo (1970). *The pedagogy of the oppressed.* New York: Herder and Herder.

Gilligan, Carol (1982). *In a different voice.* Cambridge: Harvard University Press.

Gurney, J. N. (1985). Not one of the guys: The female researcher in a male dominated setting. *Qualitative Sociology 8,* 42–62.

Hacker, Sally (1980). Technological change and women's role in agribusiness. *Human Services in the Rural Environment, Jan-Feb.,* 6–14.

Horkheimer, Max (1976). The end of reason. In Andrew Arato and Eike Gebhardt (eds.), *The essential Frankfurt school.* Oxford: Basil Blackwell.

Jaggar, Alison (1989). Love and knowledge: Emotion in feminist epistemology. In Alison Jaggar and Susan R. Bordo (eds.), *Gender/body/knowledge.* New Brunswick: Rutgers University Press.

Kaplan, Abraham (1964). *The conduct of inquiry: Methodology for behavioral science.* San Francisco: Chandler Publishing Co.

Lipman-Blumen, Jean (1979). The dialectic between research and social policy. In J. Lipman-Blumen and J. Bernard (eds.), *Sex roles and social policy.* Beverly Hills: Sage Publishers.

McCormack, Thelma (1981). Good theory or just theory? Toward a feminist philosophy of social science. *Women's Studies International Quarterly 4,* 1–12.

Mies, Maria (1983). Towards a methodology for feminist research. In G. Bowles and R. Klein (eds.), *Theories of women's studies.* Boston: Routledge and Kegan Paul.

Reinharz, Shulamit (1983). Experiential analysis: A contribution to feminist research. In G. Bowles and R. Klein (eds.), *Theories of women's studies.* Boston: Routledge and Kegan Paul.

Richardson, Laurel, Mary Margaret Fonow, and Judith A. Cook (1985). From gender seminar to gender community. *Teaching Sociology 12*(3).

Stacey, Judith (1988). Can there be a feminist ethnography? *Women's Studies International Forum 11,* 21–27.

Warren, C., and P. K. Rasmussen, (1977). Sex and gender in field research. *Urban Life 6,* 349–69.

2. THE MAN OF PROFESSIONAL WISDOM

KATHRYN PYNE ADDELSON

1. Cognitive Authority and the Growth of Knowledge

Most of us are introduced to scientific knowledge by our schoolteachers, in classrooms and laboratories, using textbooks and lab manuals as guides. As beginners, we believe that the goal of science is "the growth of knowledge through new scientific discoveries."[1] We believe that the methods of science are the most rational that humankind has devised for investigating the world and that (practiced properly) they yield objective knowledge. It seems to us that because there is only one reality, there can be only one real truth, and that science describes those facts. Our teachers and our texts affirm this authority of scientific specialists.

The authority of specialists in science is not per se an authority to command obedience from some group of people, or to make decisions on either public policy or private investment. Specialists have, rather, an epistemological or cognitive authority: we take their understanding of factual matters and the nature of the world within their sphere of expertise as knowledge, or as the definitive understanding. I don't mean that we suppose scientific specialists to be infallible. Quite the contrary. We believe scientific methods are rational because we believe that they require and get criticism of a most far-reaching sort. Science is supposed to be distinguished from religion, metaphysics, and superstition *because* its methods require criticism, test, falsifiability.

Our word "science" is ambiguous. Is it a body of knowledge, a method, or an activity? Until recently, many Anglo-American philosophers of science ignored science as an activity and applied themselves to analyzing the structure of the body of knowledge which they conceived narrowly as consisting of theories, laws, and statements of prediction. To a lesser degree, they spoke of "scientific method," conceived narrowly as a set of abstract canons. With such an emphasis, it is easy to assume that it is theory and method which give science its authority. It is easy to assume that researchers' cognitive authority derives from their use of an authoritative method and that they are justified in exercising authority only within the narrow range of understanding contained in the theories and laws within their purview. Everyone knew, of course, that "scientific method" had been developed within a historical situation; but commitment to abstract canons led philosophers to put aside questions of how

Reprinted from Sandra Harding and Merrill B. Hintikka (eds.), *Discovering Reality*, 165–86. Copyright 1983 by Kathryn Pyne Addelson.

particular methods were developed, came to dominate, and (perhaps) were later criticized and rejected.[2] Everyone believed that it is an essential characteristic of scientific knowledge that it *grows*, and that new theories are suggested, tested, criticized, and developed. But the narrow focus on knowledge as theories and laws, and the emphasis on analyzing their abstract structure or the logical form of scientific explanation, led philosophers to neglect asking how one theory was historically chosen for development and test rather than another.[3] Most important, philosophers did not ask about the social arrangements through which methods and theories came to dominate or to wither away. Although the "rationality of science" is supposed to lie in the fact that scientific understanding is the most open to criticism of *all* understanding, a crucial area for criticism was ruled out of consideration: the social arrangements through which scientific understanding is developed and through which cognitive authority of the specialist is exercised.

Within the past twenty years, many scientists, historians, and philosophers have begun to move away from the abstract and absolutist conceptions of theory and method. The work which has reached the widest audience is Thomas Kuhn's *The Structure of Scientific Revolutions*. Two major changes in analytic emphasis show in his work. First, Kuhn focuses on science as an activity. Second, given this focus, he construes the content of scientific understanding to include not only theories and laws but also metaphysical commitments, exemplars, puzzles, anomalies, and various other features. Altering the focus to activity does lead one to ask some questions about rise and fall of methods and theories, and so Kuhn could make his famous distinction between the growth of knowledge in normal science and its growth in revolutionary science. However, he makes only the most limited inquiry into social arrangements in the practice of science. And, although he says that under revolutionary science, proponents of the old and the new paradigms may engage in a power struggle, he does not explicitly consider cognitive authority.[4] Yet the power struggle in a period of revolutionary change is over which community of scientists will legitimately exercise cognitive authority—whose practices will define the normal science of the specialty and whose understanding will define the nature of the world which falls within their purview. To take cognitive authority seriously, one must ask seriously after its exercise, as embodied in social arrangements inside and outside science.

Within the activity of science in the United States today, researchers exercise cognitive authority in various ways.[5] One major way is within the specialties themselves. In accord with the norm of the "autonomy of science," researchers develop hypotheses and theories, discover laws, define problems and solutions, criticize and falsify beliefs, make scientific revolutions. They have the authority to do that on matters in their professional speciality: microbiologists have authority on questions of viruses and demographers, on questions of population changes, though within a specialty some have more power to exercise cognitive authority than others. Researchers have authority to revise the history of ideas in their field, so that each new text portrays the specialty as progressing by developing and preserving kernels of truth and rooting out error and superstition, up to the knowledge of the present.

Researchers also exercise cognitive authority outside their professions, for scientific specialists have an authority to define the true nature of the living and non-living world around us. We are taught their scientific understanding in school. Public and private officials accept it to use in solving political, social, military, and manufacturing problems. The external authority follows the lines of the internal authority. Experts are hired and their texts adopted according to their credentials as specialists in the division of authority-by-specialty within science. But because, within specialties, some people have more power than others, many people never have a text adopted and most never serve as expert advisors.

If we admit Kuhn's claim that metaphysical commitments are an integral part of scientific activity, then we see that scientific authority to define the nature of the world is not limited to the laws and theories printed in boldface sentences in our textbooks. Metaphysical commitments are beliefs about the nature of the living and non-living things of our world and about their relations with us and with each other. In teaching us their scientific specialties, researchers simultaneously teach us these broader understandings. Speaking of Nobel Prize winners in physics from the time of Roentgen to Yukawa, Nicholas Rescher says,

> The revolution wrought by these men in our understanding of nature was so massive that their names became household words throughout the scientifically literate world. (Rescher, 1978, p. 27)

The Darwinian revolution, even more thoroughgoing, changed the metaphysics of a world, designed by God in which all creatures were ordered in a great chain of being, to a world of natural selection. These scientific breakthroughs weren't simply changes in laws, hypotheses, and theories. They were changes in scientists' understanding of the categories of reality, changes in the questions they asked, the problems they worked with, the solutions they found acceptable. After the revolution, the changed understanding defined "normal science."

I will use the notion of cognitive authority to argue that making scientific activity more rational requires that criticizing and testing social arrangements in science be as much a part of scientific method as criticizing and testing theories and experiments. In doing this, I will talk a little more about how cognitive authority is exercised within professional specialties (part 2). To make my case, I assume (with Kuhn) that metaphysical commitments are an essential part of scientific understanding and that greater rationality in science requires criticizing such commitments. I give a number of examples in part 3. Part 4 considers whether social arrangements within the sciences limit criticism of scientific understanding. I suggest that prestige hierarchies, power within and without the scientific professions, and the social positions of researchers themselves affect which group can exercise cognitive authority. Thus these features of social arrangements play a major role in determining which metaphysical commitments come to dominate, thus what counts as a legitimate scientific problem and solution. In the end, they affect how we all understand the nature of our world and our selves.

2. Cognitive Authority, Autonomy, and Certified Knowledge

Philosophy of science texts, as well as the *New York Times*, talk of "science" and "scientific knowledge" as if there were one unified activity and one stock of information. But, as we all know, there are many scientific specialties, each with its own Ph.D. program. Members of each specialty or subspecialty certify and criticize their own opinions in their own journals and at their own professional meetings. Each specialist shows excellence by climbing the prestige ladder of the specialty.

Only some of the many people who work within a research specialty have epistemological authority within it. Barbara Reskin remarks,

> The roles of both student and technician are characterized by lower status and by a technical division of labor that allocates scientific creativity and decision making to scientists and laboratory work to those assigned the role of technician or student. (Reskin, 1978, p. 20)[6]

The role division justifies assigning credit to the chief investigator, but its most important effect is on communication. Technicians and students work on the chief investigator's problems in ways he or she considers appropriate.[7] They rarely communicate with other researchers through conferences or journal articles or by chatting over the WATS line. They are not among the significant communicators of the specialty.

Researchers who *are* significant communicators set categories for classifying their subjects of study, and they define the meaning of what is taking place. With the aid of physicists, chemists define what chemical substance and interaction are. Microbiologists categorize viruses and molecules and explain the significance of electron microscopes. These are different from the understandings we all have of the physical and chemical parts of our world *as we live in it*. We choose honey by taste, smell, and color, not by chemical composition, and we meet viruses in interactions we know as flus and colds.[8]

Scientific understandings appear in hypotheses, laws, and theories, but they presuppose metaphysics and methodology. Thomas Kuhn mentions the importance of metaphysics, using physical science in the seventeenth century as an example:

> [Among the] still not unchanging characteristics of science are the . . . quasi-metaphysical commitments that historical study so regularly displays. After about 1630, for example, and particularly after the appearance of Descartes' immensely influential scientific writings, most physical scientists assumed that the universe was composed of microscopic corpuscles and that all natural phenomena could be explained in terms of corpuscular shape, size, motion, and interaction. That nest of commitments proved to be both metaphysical and methodological. As method-

ological, it told them what ultimate laws and fundamental explanations must be like: laws must specify corpuscular motion and interaction, and explanation must reduce any given natural phenomenon to corpuscular action under these laws. More important still, the corpuscular conception of the universe told scientists what many of their research problems should be (Kuhn, 1970, p. 41)

The seventeenth century scientists also made metaphysical assumptions which most contemporary scientists share. They assumed that because there is *one* reality, there can be only one correct understanding of it. That metaphysical assumption, disguised as a point of logic, took root in western thought more than two millennia ago, when Parmenides said being and thinking are the same; that which exists and that which can be thought are the same. From that maxim, he concluded that the reality which is the object of knowledge, and not mere opinion, is one and unchanging. Differ though they might about the nature of reality, both Plato and Aristotle shared the metaphysical assumption that the object of scientific knowledge is the one essential, intelligible structure of the one reality. Contemporary scientists share an analogous metaphysical assumption when they presuppose that reality is known through universal laws and predictions, which give the correct description of the world. All admit, of course, that in its present state, scientific knowledge is partial, suffering from inaccuracies, and so on. But, they say, this incompleteness and error is what is to be corrected by the scientific method. In principle the scientific enterprise is based on the metaphysical premises that because there is one reality, there must be one, correctly described truth. This premise is the foundation of the cognitive authority of scientific specialists. The specialist offers the correct understanding of reality while the lay person struggles in the relativity of mere opinion.

In some specialties, researchers deal with living subjects which may have their own understanding of what is going on. But the researcher's understanding is scientifically definitive. Donna Haraway reports on the 1938 field studies of rhesus monkeys done by Clarence Ray Carpenter, an outstanding scientist in his day (Haraway, 1978, p. 30). The studies were designed to answer questions about dominance and social order. Researchers observed an "undisturbed" group for a week as a control, then removed the "alpha-male" (the dominant male in terms of priority access to food and sex). Carpenter found that without the alpha male, the group's territory was restricted relative to other groups and intra-group conflict and fights increased. As the next two males in order of dominance were removed, social chaos seemed to result. Upon returning the males, researchers observed that social order was restored.

"Alpha male" is obviously a technical term. But understanding primate subjects in terms of dominance and competition is Carpenter's definition of the situation, not the rhesus monkeys'—and not the understanding of their former keepers or the man in the street either, for Carpenter was making scientific discoveries. Underlying Carpenter's definition of the primate interactions is a metaphysics. Haraway puts the understanding this way.[9]

True social order must rest on a balance of dominance, interpreted as the foundation of cooperation. Competitive aggression became the chief form that organized other forms of social integration. Far from competitions and cooperation being mutual opposites, the former is the precondition of the latter—on physiological grounds. If the most active (dominant) regions, the organization centers, of an organism are removed, other gradient systems compete to restablish organic order: a period of fights and fluidity ensues. (Haraway, 1978, p. 33)

The metaphysics clearly enters into questions asked—from "Which male is dominant?" to "What happens to social order when the dominant males are removed?"

If we look at scientific research this way, then theories and explanations can be taken as *the conventional understandings among significant communicators in a scientific specialty of the interactions of researchers with the subjects of the field of study, and of the interactions of those subjects among themselves and with their environments* (whether natural, social, or laboratory).[10]

The conventional understandings are published in journals and presented at conferences, and the significant communicators of the specialty criticize and alter the understandings, correct hypotheses, expand theories and explanations—as part of the process of certifying the knowledge. Some of the understandings are shown to be false in the process. Others emerge as pretty certainly true. Eventually, conventional understandings are ritualized in college texts. To use other language:

> The community's paradigms (are) revealed in its textbooks, lectures, and laboratory exercises. By studying them and by practicing with them, the members of the corresponding community learn their trade. (Kuhn, 1970, p. 43)

Through the textbooks and lectures, and through advice to government and industry, the conventional understandings are passed on to the rest of us as part of the exercise of the specialist's external authority.

3. Metaphysical Commitments and the Growth of Scientific Knowledge

Within a specialty, certified knowledge consists at any given time of the conventional understandings of researchers not only about the subjects and instruments of their fields of study but about metaphysics, methodology, and the nature of science itself. Scientific discovery and the extension of certified knowledge may therefore sometimes arise from a change in understandings of metaphysics, methodology, and the appropriate questions to ask rather than changes in theories, methods, or instruments. The example of functionalist metaphysics in some of the life sciences and social sciences indicates how knowledge has grown as a result of such changes as widespread sharing of a metaphysics across disciplines. Clarence Ray Carpenter's work is an example.

Concurrent with the sharing of a metaphysics, there may be differences in the understanding of that metaphysics. These differences seem important to the criticism which leads to scientific advance; my example here is Robert K. Merton's theory of deviance.

Finally, although a metaphysics may be shared across disciplines, a single discipline may contain quite different and competing metaphysical commitments. The interactionist theory of deviance in sociology illustrates this and shows how a difference in metaphysics may lead to a difference in scientific questions asked. The interactionist example also indicates that the scientific questions asked may not merely define factual problems, they may also define *social problems*. This raises serious questions about the epistemological authority we grant to research specialists and leads to the analysis of power and cognitive authority in part 4.

In our own day, advance of knowledge in the life sciences has included a change in metaphysics. The historian of science, Donna Haraway, says,

> Between World War I and the present, biology has been transformed from a science centered on the organism, understood in functionalist terms, to a science studying automated technological devices, understood in terms of cybernetic systems. (Haraway, 1979, p. 207)

Haraway does not talk about metaphysical changes. But the change she mentions involves a move to a new metaphysics, one based not on the organism and a physiological paradigm but on "the analysis of information and energy in statistical assemblages," a "communication revolution."

> A Communication revolution means a retheorizing of natural objects as technological devices properly understood in terms of mechanism of production, transfer, and storage of information. . . . Nature is structured as a series of interlocking cybernetic systems, which are theorized as communications problems. (Haraway, 1979, pp. 222–23)

Individual specialties which share a metaphysics change on a widespread basis when there is a metaphysical change of this sort, and scientific knowledge grows by leaps and bounds. For example, the "communication revolution" made possible the revolutionary discoveries in genetics after the second World War. Those discoveries in turn gave plausibility and prestige to the communications metaphysics. This is one way in which metaphysics spreads.

Clarence Ray Carpenter worked under the earlier metaphysics (based on the organism) in his rhesus monkey studies I mentioned above. He conceived social space to be like the organic space of a developing organism, and he shared functionalist metaphysical presuppositions which were current. Haraway remarks,

> Functionalism has been developed on a foundation of organismic metaphors, in which diverse physiological parts of subsystems are coordinated into a harmonious, hierarchical whole. (Haraway, 1978, p. 40)

Carpenter himself was important in the cross-disciplinary spread of metaphysics. Haraway says that, theoretically, Carpenter "tied the interpretations of the laboratory discipline of comparative psychology and sex physiology to evolutionary and ecological field biology centered on the concepts of population and community" (Haraway, 1978, p. 30)

Functionalism (in various forms) was also the metaphysics of some of the most progressive work done in sociology and anthropology during Carpenter's time, and even today it underlies some respected work in those fields. Sociologist Robert K. Merton was a significant communicator in sociology. In an essay written in 1949, he remarks on the widespread use of the "functional approach":

> The central orientation of functionalism—expressed in the practice of interpreting data by establishing their consequences for larger structures in which they are implicated—has been found in virtually all the sciences of man—biology and physiology, psychology, economics, and law, anthropology and sociology. (Merton, 1949, p. 47)

In this essay, Merton reviews literature in the social sciences and he clarifies the notion of function—relying on the use of the concept in other fields:

> Stemming in part from the native mathematical sense of the term, (the sociological) usage is more often explicitly adopted from the biological sciences, where the term function is understood to refer to the "vital or organic processes considered in the respects in which they contribute to the maintenance of the organism." (Merton, 1949, p. 23)

Merton insists that he is only borrowing a *methodological framework* from the biological sciences. In fact, the framework carries with it a metaphysics—as the change in life sciences reported by Haraway shows. This widespread use of metaphysics confirms its truth, through the internal authority of specialists.[11] It changes dominant world views in a society through the external authority of specialists.

Although a generally functionalist metaphysics was widely shared between the two World Wars, it is more accurate to speak of *varieties* of functionalism. Some of the varieties arose (or were clarified) through metaphysical criticism of earlier varieties.[12] I'll use one of Robert K. Merton's criticisms as an example.

In "Social Structure and Anomie" (originally published before World War II), Merton developed a theory of deviance in which he criticized an earlier, widely held metaphysics:

> A decade ago, and all the more so before then, one could speak of a marked tendency in psychological and sociological theory to attribute the faulty operation of social structures to failures of social control over man's imperious biological drives. The imagery of the relations between man and society implied by this doctrine is as clear as it is questionable. In the beginning, there are man's biological impulses which see full expression. And then, there is the social order,

essentially an apparatus for the management of impulses. . . . Nonconformity with the demands of a social structure is thus assumed to be anchored in original nature. It is the biologically rooted impulses which from time to time break through social control. And by implication, conformity is the result of a utilitarian calculus or of unreasoned conditioning. (Merton, 1949, p. 125)

Haraway calls this "management of impulses" perspective the "body politic" view, and she indicates that Clarence Ray Carpenter (and many others) held it.[13] So, for that matter, did Freud and Aristotle.[14] In criticizing this metaphysics, Merton advanced knowledge in a way that was both scientifically enlightened and morally humane.

As a functionalist, Merton does suppose that deviance indicates faulty operation of the social structure. His metaphysics assumes social structures and functions exist in a way that makes them suitable for use in scientific explanation. But social structures are not understood as functioning to restrain biological impulses. Using monetary success goals in American culture as his example, he considers how people in different social positions adapt to those goals. He notes that rates of some kinds of deviance are much higher in the underclasses than in the upper classes. Rather than saying that some members of the underclasses are driven by ungoverned impulses, he suggests they are responding normally to problematic social conditions they face. They accept the goal of monetary success but have little opportunity to achieve it through legitimate, institutionally approved means. So some choose innovative means to reach the goal—perhaps becoming criminally deviant as bank robbers. Others, unable to take the strain, may retreat and become "psychotics, autistics, pariahs, outcasts, vagrants, vagabonds, tramps, chronic drunkards, and drug addicts."[15] But it's not due to "ungoverned" impulses." Rather, the cause is that "some social structures exert a definite pressure on certain persons in the society to engage in nonconformist rather than conformist conduct" (Merton, 1949, p. 125).

Conformist conduct, in Merton's view, is conduct within an institution which serves a positive function in the society. It's not simply that being a banker is approved and being a bank robber is disapproved. Banking is an institution which contributes to the stability of our society. Bank robbing undermines stability, running a danger of destroying the vital processes necessary to maintenance of our social organism. In this regard, Merton says,

> Insofar as one of the most general functions of social structure is to provide a basis for predictability and regularity of social behavior, it becomes increasingly limited in effectiveness as these elements of the social structure become dissociated. At the extreme, predictability is minimized and what may be properly called anomie or cultural chaos supervenes (Merton, 1949, p. 149)

Scientific knowledge grew by Merton's criticism of one variety of functionalism. This "pluralism" of metaphysics seems as important as the sharing of metaphysics. For example, within sociology, functionalists compete with the tradition called interactionism, whose adherents assume that human society must be explained in terms of acting units which themselves have interpretations of the world. Interactionist Herbert Blumer criticizes functionalist metaphysics in this way:

> Sociological thought rarely recognizes or treats human societies as composed of individuals who have selves. Instead, they [sic] assume human beings to be merely organisms, with some kind of organization, responding to forces that play upon them. Generally, though not exclusively, these forces are lodged in the make-up of the society as in the case of "social system" . . .
>
> . . . Some conceptions, in treating societies or human groups as "social systems" regard group action as an expression of a system, either in a state of balance or seeking to achieve balance. Or group action is conceived as an expression of the "functions" of a society or a group. . . . These typical conceptions ignore or blot out a view of group life or of group action as consisting of the collective or concerted actions of individuals seeking to meet their life situations. (Blumer, 1967, pp. 143–44)

The interactionist theory of deviance, quite different from Merton's functionalist theory, offers a good case in which to see how a different metaphysics influences the questions asked.

In 1963, Howard Becker's *Outsiders* was published, marking the emergence of what was misleadingly called the "labeling" theory of deviance. In an interview about the development of the theory, Becker said, "The theory, and it really was a pretty rudimentary theory, wasn't designed to explain why people robbed banks but rather how robbing banks came to have the quality of being deviant" (Debro, 1970, p. 167). Merton looked for the *cause* of deviant behavior (as did the "management of impulses" functionalists he criticized) and found the cause in "social structures exerting a definite pressure on some people." Becker asked about deviant behavior as behavior under *ban,* and so he asks about who does the banning, how the ban is maintained, and what effect the ban has on the activity itself.[16] On the basis of interactionist metaphysics, he doesn't assume that deviance is something there for the natural scientific eye to discern. Whether something is deviant or normal in a society is a question of perspective and power within the society. Although bank robbers and marijuana smokers may be considered deviant by "the population at large," that is, in the dominant opinion, the deviants themselves have their own perspective on the matter, and within their perspective, most aren't much interested in looking for the alleged *causes* of their activities so that they can be cured.

The interactionist criticism brings out an important connection between metaphysics, scientific questions, and social problems.[17] Bank robbing, pot smoking, and homosexuality are social problems in the eyes of certain segments of our population, not others. Becker and other sociologists in the interactionist tradition have argued that social problems don't exist for the neutral scientific eye to discern any more than deviance does. Something is a social problem or not depending on one's social position and perspective. It is often a political question—as is the question of what function a social institution serves. In fact, "the function of a group or organization (is sometimes) decided in political conflict, not given in the nature of the organization" (Becker, 1973, p. 7).

The examples I've given in this section indicate that metaphysical commitments have been important to scientific criticism and the growth of knowledge. In some cases at least, they may enter into the definition of a social problem and its solution.

Functionalist metaphysics was widely accepted in the natural sciences before World War II when Merton formulated his anomie. Functionalist sociologists offered a theory of society that was coherent with then current understandings in biology. This isn't simply a case of a "pseudoscience" (sociology) putting on the trappings of a "real science" (biology), for any biological specialty dealing with social organisms requires a theory of society and social behavior.[18] Rather, the sociological case shows that metaphysical understandings in the natural sciences help define the human world in which social problems are categorized and dealt with. In the Merton example, labeling theorist criticism indicates that the cognitive authority of science supported one set of political positions over another by that definition of the human world. This happened not by abuse of authority but by the normal procedures in the normal social arrangements of science. The time has now come to ask more explicitly how those social arrangements influence scientific criticism and the growth of knowledge.

4. Cognitive Authority and Power

In part 2, I suggested that the conventional understandings of significant communicators in science are the definitive understandings of the nature of the world within their spheres of expertise. In part 3, I suggested that metaphysical commitments are important to the growth of knowledge. In those sections, I spoke as though any researcher with the appropriate certificates of training could serve as a significant communicator, and the reader might think that if one group exercised greater cognitive authority it was on meritocratic or purely rational grounds: their theories and commitments have been shown to withstand test and criticism better than those of their competitors. I believe it is a valuable feature of the scientific enterprise that rational criticism is a factor in determining which group exercises cognitive authority. However, social arrangements are factors as well, and to the degree that we refuse to acknowledge that fact, we limit criticism and cause scientific work to be less rational than it might be. In this section, I shall indicate some social factors which may be relevant, and then I'll close with an example of how scientific understanding has been improved by recent criticisms which did take social arrangements into account.

First, let me take up questions of prestige. The sciences differ in prestige, physics have more than economics, and both having more than educational psychology. Specialties in a science too differ in prestige, experimental having more than clinical psychology, for example. Prestige differences affect researchers' judgments on which metaphysical and methodological commitments are to be preferred. Carolyn Wood Sherif remarks on the "prestige hierarchy" in psychology in the 1950s:

> Each of the fields and specialties in psychology sought to improve its status by adopting (as well and as closely as stomachs permitted) the perspectives, theories, and methodologies as high on the hierarchy as possible. The way to "respectability" in this scheme has been the appearance of rigor and scientific inquiry, bolstered by highly restricted notions of what science is about. (Sherif, 1979, p. 98)

Many philosophers of science have not only taken prestige hierarchies to be irrelevant to scientific rationality; they have accepted the hierarchies themselves and in doing so have shared and justified "highly restricted notions of what science is about." This failing was blatant in the work of logical positivists and their followers, for they constructed their analysis of scientific method to accord with an idealization of what goes on in physics, and they discussed the "unity of science" in a way that gave physics star status.[19]

Within specialties, researchers differ in prestige, so that some have access to positions of power while others do not. Some teach in prestigious institutions and train the next generations of successful researchers. Researchers judge excellence in terms of their own understandings of their field, of which problems are important, of which methods are best suited to solving them. Researchers in positions of power can spread their understandings and their metaphysical commitments. Consider the primatology example in part 3.

Because Robert Yerkes held influential positions, he was able to give an important backing to Clarence Ray Carpenter's career, helping Carpenter to compete successfully for the positions and funding needed to do his research. Haraway says of Carpenter,

> From his education, funding, and social environment, there was little reason for Carpenter to reject the basic assumptions that identified reproduction and dominance based on sex with the fundamental organizing principles of a body politic. (Haraway, 1978, p. 30)

Yerkes shared the "body politic" metaphysics. In helping Carpenter, he was helping spread his own metaphysical commitments.

The question is not whether top scientists in most fields produce some very good work but rather the more inportant question whether other good work, even work critical of the top scientists, is not taken seriously because its proponents are not members of the same powerful networks and so cannot exercise the same cognitive authority. The question is made particularly difficult because, by disregarding or downgrading competing research, the "top scientists" cut off the resources necessary for their competition to develop really good work. In most fields it is next to impossible to do research without free time, aid from research assistants, secretaries, craftsmen, custodians, and in many cases, access to equipment.

Some very influential philosophers of science have insisted that criticism is an essential part of scientific method and that criticism requires that there be competing scientific theories.[20] Accepting that as an abstract canon, one might philosophically point out that Yerkes should have encouraged more competition and (if one became particularly moralistic) that he should have been more careful about showing favoritism and bias. But it would be a mistake to describe Yerkes as showing favoritism and bias. As a matter of fact, he did much to set the practice of researchers investigating unpopular subjects and reaching unpopular results in the interests of scientific freedom and research in "pure science." But he made his judgments according to his own understanding of scientific research. Any researcher must do that. Researchers are also the judges of which competing theories it makes sense to pursue or to encourage others in pursuing. If this seems to result in bias, the way to correct it is not by blaming individual researchers for showing favoritisms because they depart from some mythical set of abstract canons. The way to begin to correct it is to broaden rational criticism in science by requiring that both philosophers of science and scientists understand how prestige and power are factors in the way cognitive authority is exercised.

So far, I have talked about influences on the exercise of cognitive authority with the scientific professions. Many people have observed that there are outside influences on scientific research—funding, for example. Given legally dominant understandings of capitalism in the United States, many people consider it proper for private business to fund research on problems that need solving for reasons of economic competition and expansion. Most of us considered it appropriate that public agencies in a democracy should fund research to help solve social problems of the moment (as do private philanthropic foundations for the most part). If we think of science as a stock of knowledge embodied in theories, then the problem of funding does not seem to be a problem having to do with rationality and criticism in science. Instead it may appear to be a question of political or other outside interference with the autonomy of the researchers, at worst preventing them from setting their own problems to investigate.[21] If we use the notion of cognitive authority, however, we may see that the question of funding indeed has to do with scientific rationality and with the content of our scientific understanding of the world.

Metaphysical commitments of a science tell scientists what many of their research problems should be (Kuhn, 1970, p. 41). As we saw from the Merton-Becker example, a difference in metaphysics may bring a difference in *what the problem is taken to be*. In that case, it was a difference between explaining why people rob banks and explaining how robbing banks comes to have the quality of being deviant (Debro, 1970, p. 167). Because problems investigated by a tradition are related to the metaphysical and methodological commitments of its researchers, some understandings of nature will have a better chance for support than others.[22] Those researchers will have a better opportunity to exercise cognitive authority and to help others of their metaphysical persuasion rise in the ranks. They will write the texts and serve as advisors and use their external authority to popularize their metaphysical outlook. So funding influences the content of science at a given historical moment and it influences the way we all come to understand the world.

The influence goes beyond the question of which of a number of competing traditions are to be rewarded. Arlene Daniels traces some of the ramifications in discussing Allan Schnaiberg's remarks on obstacles to environmental research. She says,

> Schnaiberg shows us how unpopular socioenvironmental research is within establishment contexts. The science industries won't pay for it, the research foundations won't sanction it. Rewards in the academic market place depend on quick payoffs; accordingly, independent researchers there cannot wait for results that require large expenditures of time in unfunded research. (Daniels, 1979, p. 38–39)

This means not only that some existing metaphysical and methodological traditions will flourish while others are passed over. It means that potentially fruitful metaphysics and methods won't get a chance for development at all because social arrangements in the scientific professions and the influence of funding work against them.

So far, I've suggested that social arrangements within the scientific professions, and between those professions and the larger society, involve factors relevant to the exercise of cognitive authority in the sciences and thus to the content of scientific understanding. Are the professional and social life experiences of researchers also relevant to their metaphysical commitments? This is an extremely interesting question because of the quite general assumption in the United States that there is a privileged definition of reality which scientists capture, a main assumption underlying the authority we give them. Feminists in nearly every scientific field have questioned that assumption.[23] I questioned it from an interactionist perspective in discussing Merton, above. Let me give two suggestive examples here.

The anthropologist E. Ardener suggests that because of their social experience, men and women conceptualize their societies and communities differently (Ardener, 1972). In most societies, men more frequently engage in political activities and public discourse and have the definitional problem of bounding their own society or community off from others. Models suited to the usual women's experience aren't the object of public discourse and so when circumstances call for it, women will use men's models, not their own.

Ethnographers tend to report the male models for three reasons, according to Ardener. They are more accessible to the researcher. Male models are the officially accepted ones in the ethnographer's home society. And they accord with the metaphysical and theoretical outlook of functionalism which, in the past, many ethnographers have held. Milton reports Ardener's claim this way:

> Ethnographers, especially those who have adopted a functionalist approach, tend to be attracted to the bounded models of society, with which they are presented

mainly by men and occasionally by women. These models accord well with functionalist theory and so tend to be presented as *the* models of society. (Milton, 1979, p. 48)

We need not accept Ardener's claims as gospel truth to realize that we *cannot* accept without test the empirical assumption that a specialist's social experience has no significant effect on his or her scientific understanding of the world.

Nor can we accept without test the empirical hypothesis that the long training and isolating, professional experience of scientific specialists has no significant effect on their scientific understanding. The sociologist Vilhelm Aubert says,

> Members of society have, through their own planning and their own subsequent observations, verifications, and falsifications, built up a cognitive structure bearing some resemblances to a scientific theory. . . . But . . . social man behaves only in some, albeit important, areas in this purposive way. Any attempt, therefore, to stretch the predictability criterion beyond these areas—their limits are largely unknown—may result in a misrepresentation of the nature of human behavior. This danger is greatly increased by the origin of most social scientists in cultures which heavily stress a utilitarian outlook, and by their belonging even to the subcultures within these, which are the main bearers of this ethos. A sociology produced by fishermen from northern Norway or by Andalusian peasants might have been fundamentally different. The leading social scientists are people with tenure and right of pension. (Aubert, 1965, p. 135)

The leading physicists, biologists, and philosophers of science are also people with tenure and right of pension. They live in societies marked by dominance of group over group. As specialists, they compete for positions at the top of their professional hierarchies which allow them to exercise cognitive authority more widely. Out of such cultural understandings and social orderings, it is no wonder that we get an emphasis on predictive law and an insistence that the currently popular theories of a specialty represent the one, true, authoritative description of the world. It is no wonder that our specialists continually present us with metaphysical descriptions of the world in terms of hierarchy, dominance, and competition. The wonder is that we get any development of our understanding at all.

But we do. Scientific understanding does seem to grow (in however ungainly a fashion) and our knowledge does seem to "advance" (however crabwise).

In our own century, scientific knowledge has often seemed to grow at the expense of wisdom. However, the corrective isn't to dismiss science as hopelessly biased and wrongheaded and return to some kind of folk wisdom. We can't get along without science any more. The corrective seems rather to ferret out all the irrationalities we can find in scientific activity and to expand our understanding of what science and scientific rationality are. To do this, we should acknowledge metaphysical commitments as part of the content of scientific understanding and thus open them to scrutiny and criticism by specialist and non-specialist alike. Feminist criticism offers a very instructive example here. In the past ten years, political feminists have given lay criticisms of much of our scientific metaphysics. Other feminists have gained specialist training and brought the lay criticisms to bear on technical theories within their fields.[24] This was possible because sexism is a political issue at the moment and funding, journals, etc., are available for this sort of research and criticism. I am suggesting that we should institutionalize this sort of criticism and make it an explicit part of "scientific method." We should also try using the notion of cognitive authority and expanding the range of the criteria of scientific rationality and criticism so that it includes social arrangements within the scientific professions.

If we expand the range of criticism, I believe that philosophers of science and scientists as well will find themselves advocating change in our social system. This would not result in a sudden illegitimate politicization of science or an opening of the floodgates of irrationality. Quite the contrary. Because they have cognitive authority our scientists already *are* politicized. It is the *unexamined* exercise of cognitive authority within our present social arrangements which is most to be feared. Illegitimate politicization and rampant irrationality find their most fruitful soil when our activities are mystified and protected from criticism.

NOTES

Research for this paper was supported in part by a grant from the National Endowment for the Humanities and by the Mellon Foundation grant to the Smith College Project on Women and Social Change. I am very grateful for criticism or advice I received from Howard Becker, Donna Haraway, Arlene Daniels, Sandra Harding, Vicky Spelman, Helen Longino, Kay Warren, Noretta Koertge, Arnold Feldman, and members of two seminars I taught in the Northwestern University sociology department, Fall 1980.

I have previously published under the name Kathryn Pyne Parsons.

1. The quoted remark is from Cole (1979, p 6n).

2. Instead, philosophers criticized each other's versions of the abstract canons. Positivist Rudolf Carnap was particularly painstaking at criticizing his own and other positivists' analyses of the structure of scientific theories. See, for example, Carnap (1956). Karl Popper also devoted time and energy to criticizing the positivists. See, for example, Popper (1965).

3. At the beginning of the "new wave" in philosophy of science, N. R. Hanson did ask after the choosing of new theories, but he did so by discussing the logic of discovery and the ways in which theories that groups of scientists develop are constrained by their patterns of conceptual organization rather than by asking after constraints in the social arrangements within which scientific understanding is developed and criticized. See Hanson (1958).

4. It is there implicitly, however, particularly in his wonderful discussion of science texts.

5. Whether or not a group has authority regarding something depends on social arrangements in the society in which they form a group, thus my restriction to "the

United States today." I should make more severe restrictions because there are sub-groups in the U.S.A. which don't grant "scientists" much authority. We do through our public and major private educational systems, however.

6. One doesn't usually think of artisans as part of science, but one physicist said of his university's craftsmen, "The gadgets they produce for us are just crucial. The reason the work the department does is internationally competitive with major research centers all over the world is in part due to the capabilities of the people in the machine shop. Some of the research simply could not be done without them." *Contact*, August 1980, page 8 (University of Massachusetts, Amherst, publication).

7. Within the hierarchical social relations of the research group, the chief in-vestigator has authority to command obedience from technicians, students, secretaries, and the like. I'm not concerned with that sort of authority in this chapter.

8. My remark about honey may still be true, but due to changes in the food industry consequent to the "growth of scientific knowledge," we are learning to choose foods by applying the chemist's categories to lists of ingredients on packages at the supermarket.

9. Haraway doesn't explicitly talk about metaphysics in her paper, and in fact she may use the term in a more limited way than I do. (personal communication)

10. In fields like history or archeology, researchers themselves interact with non-living material, not with the (formerly living) subjects of study, but their theories and explanations represent the researchers' conventional understandings of those subjects.

11. Merton himself says, "The prevalence of the functional outlook is in itself no warrant for its scientific value, but it does suggest that cumulative experience has forced this orientation upon the disciplined observers of man as biological organism, psycholog-ical actor, members of society and bearer of culture" (Merton, 1949, p. 47). A whole metaphysic and theory of science underlies that remark, as the reader may see by comparing my remarks and those of other authors in part 4 of this chapter. For example, Merton hints that scientific observation and laboratory and field experience "force" the outlook, while some authors I report on in part 4 suggest social experience in the professions and the specialists' society are major influences.

12. Haraway (1978) also indicates that other researchers in the life sciences later criticized the metaphysics, from the standpoint of other varieties of functionalism.

13. See Haraway (1978).

14. See Elizabeth V. Spelman's paper in this volume for an illuminating discussion of the view as Aristotle held it.

15. Merton (1949, p. 142). Merton's theory of deviance is broader and more complex than I am representing it here. I am selecting features for a dual purpose: to show the criticism of the "uncontrolled impulse" view and to contrast with the interactionist theory I give below.

16. Becker himself does not speak of behavior under *ban*. That conceptualization is David Matza's (1969).

17. See Spector (1977) for a discussion of social problems.

18. Philip Green (1981) discusses this issue in criticizing sociobiologists' theories. See also the introduction and several of the essays in Addelson (n.d.).

19. Some philosophers of science have insisted that the methods of the physical sciences aren't suitable for historical sciences—see, for example, the whole *Verstehen* controversy (Collingwood, 1946) as a classic source. For social sciences generally see Winch (1958).

20. See Popper (1965) and Feyerabend (1970).

21. George H. Daniels suggests that the rise of the ideal of pure scientific research in the late nineteenth century led to conflicts with democratic assumptions in 'The Pure-Science Ideal and Democratic Culture,' *Science* 156 (1967). 1699–1705. My discussion here displays the other side of the conflict.

22. I'm not claiming here that stating a problem in a certain way entails that you'll have a certain metaphysics, or even determines it in some unidirectional way. My point is about the ranges of theories and traditions available at a historical moment and which of them will receive encouragement and support.

23. See, for example, Millman (1975) and Sherman (1979).
24. Feminist criticism may seem, more obviously politicized than, say, Yerkes's or Merton's or Becker's criticisms I discussed above, but I think that is because feminists themselves insist on the political connections.

REFERENCES

Addelson, Kathryn Pyne, and Martha Ackelsberg: (n.d.), *An Endless Waterfall: Studies on Women and Social Change,* forthcoming.

Ardener, E.: 1972. "Belief and the Problem of Women," in J. S. LaFontaine (ed.), *The Interpretation of Ritual* (London: Tavistock).

Ardener, E.: 1975, "The Problem Revisited," in S. Ardener (ed.), *Perceiving Women* (London: Malaby Press).

Aubert, Vilhelm: 1965, *The Hidden Society* (New Jersey: Bedminster Press).

Becker, Howard S.: 1973, *Outsiders* (New York: The Free Press).

Blumer, H.: 1967, "Society as Symbolic Interaction," in J. Manis and B. Mattzer (eds.), *Symbolic Interaction* (Boston: Allyn and Bacon).

Carnap, Rudolf: 1956, "The Methodological Character of Theoretical Concepts," in H. Feigl and N. Scriven (eds.), *Minnesota Studies in the Philosophy of Science,* Vol. 1 (Minneapolis: University of Minnesota Press).

Cole, Jonathan R.: 1979, *Fair Science, Women in the Scientific Community* (New York: The Free Press).

Cole, J., and S. Cole: 1973, *Social Stratification in Science* (Chicago: University of Chicago Press).

Collingwood, R. G.: 1946, *The Idea of History* (Oxford: Oxford University Press).

Daniels, Arlene: 1979, "Advocacy Research: Providing New Wares for the Free Marketplace of Ideas," in Sociology's Relations with the Community (Calgary: University of Calgary Colloquium Proceedings).

Debro, Julius: 1970, "Dialogue with Howard S. Becker," *Issues in Criminology* 5 (2, Summer).

Feyerabend, P.: 1970, "Against Method," in M. Radner and S. Winokur (eds), *Minnesota Studies in the Philosophy of Science,* Vol. 4 (Minneapolis: University of Minnesota Press).

Green, Philip: 1981, *The Pursuit of Inequality* (New York: Pantheon Books).

Hanson, N. R.: 1958, *Patterns of Discovery* (Cambridge: Cambridge University Press).

Haraway, Donna: 1978, "Animal Sociology and a Natural Economy of the Body Politic," Parts 1 and 2, *Signs* 4, 21–60.

———: 1979, "The Biological Enterprise: Sex, Mind and Profit from Human Engineering to Sociobiology," *Radical History Review,* Spring-Summer special issue, 206–237.

Kuhn, T.: 1970, *The Structure of Scientific Revolution,* second edition (Chicago: University of Chicago Press).

Matza, David: 1969, *Becoming Deviant* (Englewood Cliffs, N.J.: Prentice Hall).

Merton, Robert K.: 1949, *Social Theory and Social Structure* (Glencoe, Illinois: The Free Press).

Millman, M., and R. Kanter: 1975, *Another Voice* (New York: Anchor Press/ Doubleday).

Milton, Kay: 1979, "Male Bias in Anthropology," *Man, The Journal of the Royal Anthropological Institute, London,* N.S. 14, 40–54.

Mullins, N. C.: 1973, *Science: Some Sociological Perspectives* (New York: Bobbs-Merrill Co.).

Popper, Karl: 1965, *Conjectures and Refutations: The Growth of Scientific Knowledge,* second edition (New York: Basic Books).

Rescher, Nicholas: 1978, *Scientific Progress* (Pittsburgh: University of Pittsburgh Press).

Reskin, Barbara F.: 1978, "Sex Differentiation and the Social Organization of Science," *Sociological Inquiry* 48 (3–4).

Sherif, Carolyn Wood: 1979, "Bias in Psychology," Julia A. Sherman and Evelyn Torton Beck (eds.), *The Prism of Sex: Essays in the Sociology of Knowledge* (Madison: University of Wisconsin Press), 93–124.

Sherman, Julia A., and Evelyn Torton Beck (eds.): 1979, *The Prism of Sex: Essays in the Sociology of Knowledge* (Madison: University of Wisconsin Press).

Spector, Malcolm: 1977, *Constructing Social Problems* (Menlo Park, Calif.: Cummings Publishing Company).

Winch, Peter: 1958, *The Idea of a Social Science and Its Relation to Philosophy* (New York: Humanities Press).

3. LEARNING FROM THE OUTSIDER WITHIN

The Sociological Significance
of Black Feminist Thought

PATRICIA HILL COLLINS

Black women have long occupied marginal positions in academic settings. I argue that many Black female intellectuals have made creative use of their marginality—their "outsider within" status—to produce Black feminist thought that reflects a special standpoint on self, family, and society. I describe and explore the sociological significance of three characteristic themes in such thought: (1) Black women's self-definition and self-valuation; (2) the interlocking nature of oppression; and (3) the importance of Afro-American women's culture. After considering how Black women might draw upon these key themes as outsiders within to generate a distinctive standpoint on existing sociological paradigms, I conclude by suggesting that other sociologists would also benefit by placing greater trust in the creative potential of their own personal and cultural biographies.

Afro-American women have long been privy to some of the most intimate secrets of white society. Countless numbers of Black women have ridden buses to their white "families," where they not only cooked, cleaned, and executed other domestic duties, but where they also nurtured their "other" children, shrewdly offered guidance to their employers, and frequently became honorary members of their white "families." These women have seen white elites, both actual and aspiring, from perspectives largely obscured from their Black spouses and from these groups themselves.[1]

On one level, this "insider" relationship has been satisfying to all involved. The memoirs of affluent whites often mention their love for their Black "mothers," while accounts of Black domestic workers stress the sense of self-affirmation they experienced at seeing white power demystified—of knowing that it was not the intellect, talent, or humanity of their employers that supported their superior status, but largely just the advantages of racism.[2] But on another level, these same Black women knew they could never belong to their white "families." In spite of their involvement, they remained "outsiders."[3]

This "outsider within" status has provided a special standpoint on self, family, and society for Afro-American women.[4] A careful review of the emerging Black feminist literature reveals that many Black intellectuals, especially those in touch with their marginality in academic settings, tap this standpoint in producing distinctive analyses of race, class, and gender. For example, Zora Neal Hurston's 1937 novel, *Their Eyes Were Watching God*, most certainly reflects

Reprinted from Social Problems, Vol. 33, No. 6 (December 1986), S14-S32. © 1986 by the Society for the Study of Social Problems, Inc.

her skill at using the strengths and transcending the limitations both of her academic training and of her background in traditional Afro-American community life.[5] Black feminist historian E. Frances White (1984) suggests that Black women's ideas have been honed at the juncture between movements for racial and sexual equality and contends that Afro-American women have been pushed by "their marginalization in both arenas" to create Black feminism. Finally, Black feminist critic Bell Hooks captures the unique standpoint that the outsider within status can generate. In describing her small-town Kentucky childhood, she notes, "living as we did—on the edge—we developed a particular way of seeing reality. We looked both from the outside in and from the inside out . . . we understood both" (1984:vii).

In spite of the obstacles that can confront outsiders within, such individuals can benefit from this status. Simmel's (1921) essay on the sociological significance of what he called the "stranger" offers a helpful starting point for understanding the largely unexplored area of Black female outsider within status and the usefulness of the standpoint it might produce. Some of the potential benefits of outsider within status include (1) Simmel's definition of "objectivity" as "a peculiar composition of nearness and remoteness, concern and indifference" (2) the tendency for people to confide in a "stranger" in ways they never would with each other; and (3) the ability of the "stranger" to see patterns that may be more difficult for those immersed in the situation to see. Mannheim (1936) labels the "strangers" in academia "marginal intellectuals" and argues that the critical posture such individuals bring to academic endeavors may be essential to the creative development of academic disciplines themselves. Finally, in assessing the potentially positive qualities of social difference, specifically marginality, Lee notes, "for a time this marginality can be a most stimulating, albeit often a painful, experience. For some, it is debilitating . . . for others, it is an excitement to creativity" (1973:64).[6]

Sociologists might benefit greatly from serious consideration of the emerging cross-disciplinary literature that I label Black feminist thought, precisely because, for many Afro-American female intellectuals, "marginality" has been an excitement to creativity. As outsiders within, Black feminist scholars may be one of many distinct groups of marginal intellectuals whose standpoints promise to enrich contemporary sociological discourse. Bringing this group—as well as others who share an outsider within status vis-á-vis sociology—into the center of analysis may reveal aspects of reality obscured by more orthodox approaches.

In the remainder of this essay, I examine the sociological significance of the Black feminist thought stimulated by Black women's outsider within status. First, I outline three key themes that characterize the emerging cross-disciplinary literature that I label Black feminist thought.[7] For each theme, I summarize its content, supply examples from Black feminist and other works that illustrate its nature, and discuss its importance. Second, I explain the significance these key themes in Black feminist thought may have for sociologists by describing why Black women's outsider within status might generate a distinctive standpoint vis-á-vis existing sociological paradigms. Finally, I discuss one general implication of this essay for social scientists: namely, the potential usefulness of identifying and using one's own standpoint in conducting research.

Three Key Themes in Black Feminist Thought

Black feminist thought consists of ideas produced by Black women that clarify a standpoint of and for Black women. Several assumptions underlie this working definition. First, the definition suggests that it is impossible to separate the structure and thematic content of thought from the historical and material conditions shaping the lives of its producers (Berger and Luckmann, 1966; Mannheim, 1936). Therefore, while Black feminist thought may be recorded by others, it is produced by Black women. Second, the definition assumes that Black women possess a unique standpoint on, or perspective of, their experiences and that there will be certain commonalities of perception shared by Black women as a group. Third, while living life as Black women may produce certain commonalities of outlook, the diversity of class, region, age, and sexual orientation shaping individual Black women's lives has resulted in different expressions of these common themes. Thus, universal themes included in the Black women's standpoint may be experienced and expressed differently by distinct groups of Afro-American women. Finally, the definition assumes that, while a Black women's standpoint exists, its contours may not be clear to Black women themselves. Therefore, one role for Black female intellectuals is to produce facts and theories about the Black female experience that will clarify a Black woman's standpoint for Black women. In other words, Black feminist thought contains observations and interpretations about Afro-American womanhood that describe and explain different expressions of common themes.

No one Black feminist platform exists from which one can measure the "correctness" of a particular thinker; nor should there be one. Rather, as I defined it above, there is a long and rich tradition of Black feminist thought. Much of it has been oral and has been produced by ordinary Black women in their roles as mothers, teachers, musicians, and preachers.[8] Since the civil rights and women's movements, Black women's ideas have been increasingly documented and are reaching wider audiences. The following discussion of three key themes in Black feminist thought is itself part of this emerging process of documentation and interpretation. The three themes I have chosen are not exhaustive but, in my assessment, they do represent the thrust of much of the existing dialogue.

The Meaning of Self-Definition and Self-Valuation

An affirmation of the importance of Black women's self-definition and self-valuation is the first key theme that pervades historical and contemporary statements of Black feminist thought. Self-definition involves challenging the political knowledge-validation process that has resulted in externally-defined, stereotypical images of Afro-American womanhood. In contrast, self-valuation stresses the content of Black women's self-definitions—namely, replacing externally-derived images with authentic Black females images.

Both Mae King's (1973) and Cheryl Gilkes's (1981) analyses of the importance of stereotypes offer useful insights for grasping the importance of Black women's self-definition. King suggests that stereotypes represent externally-defined, controlling images of Afro-American womanhood that have been central to the dehumanization of Black women and the exploitation of Black women's labor. Gilkes points out that Black women's assertiveness in resisting the multifaceted oppression they experience has been a consistent threat to the status quo. As punishment, Black women have been assaulted with a variety of externally-defined negative images designed to control assertive Black female behavior.

The value of King's and Gilkes's analyses lies in their emphasis on the function of stereotypes in controlling dominated groups. Both point out that replacing negative stereotypes with ostensibly positive ones can be equally problematic if the function of stereotypes as controlling images remains unrecognized. John Gwaltney's (1980) interview with Nancy White, a 73-year-old Black woman, suggests that ordinary Black women may also be aware of the power of these controlling images in their everyday experiences. In the following passage, Ms. White assesses the difference between the controlling images applied to Afro-American and white women as being those of degree, and not of kind:

> My mother used to say that the black woman is the white man's mule and the white woman is his dog. Now, she said that to say this: we do the heavy work and get beat whether we do it well or not. But the white woman is closer to the master and he pats them on the head and lets them sleep in the house, but he ain't goin' treat neither one like he was dealing with a person. (1980:148)

This passage suggests that while both groups are stereotyped, albeit in different ways, the function of the images is to dehumanize and control both groups. Seen in this light, it makes little sense, in the long run, for Black women to exchange one set of controlling images for another even if, in the short run, positive stereotypes bring better treatment.

The insistence on Black female self-definition reframes the entire dialogue from one of determining the technical accuracy of an image to one stressing the power dynamics underlying the very process of definition itself. Black feminists have questioned not only what has been said about Black women, but the credibility and the intentions of those possessing the power to define. When Black women define themselves, they clearly reject the taken-for-granted assumption that those in positions granting them the authority to describe and analyze reality are entitled to do so. Regardless of the actual content of Black women's self-definitions, the act of insisting on Black female self-definition validates Black women's power as human subjects.

The related theme of Black female self-valuation pushes this entire process one step further. While Black female self-definition speaks to the power dynamics involved in the act of defining images of self and community, the theme of Black female self-valuation addresses the actual content of these self-definitions. Many of the attributes extant in Black female stereotypes are actually distorted renderings of those aspects of Black female behavior seen as most threatening to white patriarchy (Gilkes, 1981; White, 1985). For example, aggressive Afro-American women are threatening because they challenge white patriarchal definitions of femininity. To ridicule assertive women by labeling them Sapphires reflects an effort to put all women in their place. In their roles as central figures in socializing the next generation of Black adults, strong mothers are similarly threatening, because they contradict patriarchal views of family power relations. To ridicule strong Black mothers by labelling them matriarchs (Higginbotham, 1982) reflects a similar effort to control another aspect of Black female behavior that is especially threatening to the status quo.

When Black females choose to value those aspects of Afro-American womanhood that are stereotyped, ridiculed, and maligned in academic scholarship and the popular media, they are actually questioning some of the basic ideas used to control dominated groups in general. It is one thing to counsel Afro-American women to resist the Sapphire stereotype by altering their behavior to become meek, docile, and stereotypically "feminine." It is quite another to advise Black women to embrace their assertiveness, to value their sassiness, and to continue to use these qualities to survive in and transcend the harsh environments that circumscribe so many Black women's lives. By defining and valuing assertiveness and other "unfeminine" qualities as necessary and functional attributes for Afro-American womanhood, Black women's self-valuation challenges the content of externally-defined controlling images.

This Black feminist concern—that Black women create their own standards for evaluating Afro-American womanhood and value their creations—pervades a wide range of literary and social science works. For example, Alice Walker's 1982 novel, *The Color Purple*, and Ntozake Shange's 1978 choreopoem, *For Colored Girls Who Have Considered Suicide*, are both bold statements of the necessity for Black female self-definition and self-valuation. Lena Wright Myers's (1980) work shows that Black women judge their behavior by comparing themselves to Black women facing similar situations and thus demonstrates the presence of Black female definitions of Afro-American womanhood. The recent spate of Black female historiography suggests that self-defined, self-valuating Black women have long populated the ranks of Afro-American female leaders (Giddings, 1984; Loewenberg and Bogin, 1976).

Black women's insistence on self-definition, self-valuation, and the necessity for a Black female-centered analysis is significant for two reasons. First, defining and valuing one's consciousness of one's own self-defined standpoint in the face of images that foster a self-definition as the objectified "other" is an important way of resisting the dehumanization essential to systems of domination. The status of being the "other" implies being "other than" or different from the assumed norm of white male behavior. In this model, powerful white males define themselves as subjects, the true actors, and classify people of color and women in terms of their position vis-á-vis this white male hub. Since Black women have been denied the authority to challenge these definitions, this model consists of images that define Black women as a negative other, the virtual antithesis of positive white male images. Moreover, as Brittan and Maynard (1984:199) point out, "domination always involves the objectification of the dominated; all forms of oppression imply the devaluation of the subjectivity of the oppressed."

One of the best examples of this process is described by Judith Rollins (1985). As part of her fieldwork on Black domestics, Rollins worked as a domestic for six months. She describes several incidents where her employers treated her as if she were not really present. On one occasion while she sat in the kitchen having lunch, her employers had a conversation as if she were not there. Her sense of invisibility became so great that she took out a pad of paper and began writing field notes. Even though Rollins wrote for 10 minutes, finished lunch, and returned to work, her employers showed no evidence of having seen her at all. Rollins notes,

> It was this aspect of servitude I found to be one of the strongest affronts to my dignity as a human being . . . These gestures of ignoring my presence were not, I think, intended as insults; they were expressions of the employers' ability to annihilate the humanness and even, at times, the very existence of me, a servant and a black woman. (1985:209)

Racist and sexist ideologies both share the common feature of treating dominated groups—the "others"—as objects lacking full human subjectivity. For example, seeing Black women as obstinate mules and viewing white women as obedient dogs objectifies both groups, but in different ways. Neither is seen as fully human, and therefore both become eligible for race/gender specific modes of domination. But if Black women refuse to accept their assigned status as the quintessential "other," then the entire rationale for such domination is challenged. In brief, abusing a mule or a dog may be easier than abusing a person who is a reflection of one's own humanness.

A second reason that Black female self-definition and self-valuation are significant concerns their value in allowing Afro-American women to reject internalized, psychological oppression (Baldwin, 1980). The potential damage of internalized control to Afro-American women's self-esteem can be great, even to the prepared. Enduring the frequent assaults of controlling images requires considerable inner strength. Nancy White, cited earlier, also points out how debilitating being treated as less than human can be if Black women are not self-defined. She notes, "Now, you know that no woman is a dog or a mule, but if folks keep making you feel that way, if you don't have a mind of your own, you can start letting them tell you what you are" (Gwaltney, 1980:152). Seen in this light, self-definition and self-valuation are not luxuries—they are necessary for Black female survival.

The Interlocking Nature of Oppression

Attention to the interlocking nature of race, gender, and class oppression is a second recurring theme in the works of Black feminists (Beale, 1970; Davis, 1981; Dill, 1983; Hooks, 1981; Lewis, 1977; Murray, 1970; Steady, 1981).[9] While different socio-historical periods may have increased the saliency of one or another type of oppression, the thesis of the linked nature of oppression has long pervaded Black feminist thought. For example, Ida Wells Barnett and Frances Ellen Watkins Harper, two prominent Black feminists of the late 1800s, both spoke out against the growing violence directed against Black men. They realized that civil rights held little meaning for Black men and women if the right to life itself went unprotected (Loewenberg and Bogin, 1976:26). Black women's absence from organized feminist movements has mistakenly been attributed to a lack of feminist consciousness. In actuality, Black feminists have possessed an ideological commitment to addressing interlocking oppression yet have been excluded from arenas that would have allowed them to do so (Davis, 1981).

As Barbara Smith points out, "the concept of the simultaneity of oppression is still the crux of a Black feminist understanding of political reality and . . . is one of the most significant ideological contributions of Black feminist thought" (1983:xxxii). This should come as no surprise since Black women should be among the first to realize that minimizing one form of oppression, while essential, may still leave them oppressed on other equally dehumanizing ways. Sojourner Truth knew this when she stated, "there is a great stir about colored men getting their rights, and not colored women theirs, you see the colored men will be masters over the women, and it will be just as bad as before" (Loewenberg and Bogin, 1976:238). To use Nancy White's metaphors, the Black woman as "mule" knows that she is perceived to be an animal. In contrast, the white woman as "dog" may be similarly dehumanized, and may think that she is an equal part of the family when, in actuality, she is a well-cared-for pet. The significant factor shaping Truth's and White's clearer view of their own subordination than that of Black men or white women is their experience at the intersection of multiple structures of domination.[10] Both Truth and White are Black, female, and poor. They therefore have a clearer view of oppression than other groups who occupy more contradictory positions vis-á-vis white male power—unlike white women, they have no illusions that their whiteness will negate female subordination, and unlike Black men, they cannot use a questionable appeal to manhood to neutralize the stigma of being Black.

The Black feminist attention to the interlocking nature of oppression is significant for two reasons. First, this viewpoint shifts the entire focus of investigation from one aimed at explicating elements of race or gender or class oppression to one whose goal is to determine what the links are among these systems. The first approach typically prioritizes one form of oppression as being primary, then handles remaining types of oppression as variables within what is seen as the most important system. For example, the efforts to insert race and gender into Marxist theory exemplify this effort. In contrast, the more holistic approach implied in Black feminist thought treats the interaction among multiple systems as the object of study. Rather than adding to existing theories by inserting previously excluded variables, Black feminists aim to develop new theoretical interpretations of the interaction itself.

Black male scholars, white female scholars, and more recently, Black feminists like Bell Hooks, may have identified one critical link among interlocking systems of oppression. These groups have pointed out that certain basic ideas crosscut multiple systems of domination. One such idea is either/or dualistic thinking, claimed by Hooks to be "the central ideological component of all systems of domination in Western society" (1984:29).

While Hooks's claim may be somewhat premature, there is growing scholarly support for her viewpoint.[11] Either/or dualistic thinking, or what I will refer to as the construct of dichotomous oppositional difference, may be a philosophical lynchpin in systems of race, class, and gender oppression. One fundamental characteristic of this construct is the categorization of people, things, and ideas in terms of their difference from one another. For example, the terms in dichotomies such as black/white, male/female, reason/emotion, fact/opinion, and subject/object gain their meaning only in *relation* to their difference from their oppositional counterparts. Another fundamental characteristic of this construct is that difference is not complementary in that the halves of the dichotomy do not enhance each other. Rather, the dichotomous halves are different and inherently opposed to one another. A third and more important characteristic is that these oppositional relationships are intrinsically unstable. Since such dualities rarely represent different but equal relationships, the inherently unstable relationship is resolved by subordinating one half of each pair to the other. Thus, whites rule Blacks, males dominate females, reason is touted as superior to emotion in ascertaining truth, facts supercede opinion in evaluating knowledge, and subjects rule objects. Dichotomous oppositional differences invariably imply relationships of superiority and inferiority, hierarchical relationships that mesh with political economies of domination and subordination.

The oppression experienced by most Black women is shaped by their subordinate status in an array of either/or dualities. Afro-American women have been assigned the inferior half of several dualities, and this placement has been central to their continued domination. For example, the allegedly emotional, passionate nature of Afro-American women has long been used as a rationale for their sexual exploitation. Similarly, denying Black women literacy—then claiming that they lack the facts for sound judgment—illustrates another case of assigning a group inferior status, then using that inferior status as proof of the group's inferiority. Finally, denying Black women agency as subjects and treating them as objectified "others" represents yet another dimension of the power that dichotomous oppositional constructs have in maintaining systems of domination.

While Afro-American women may have a vested interest in recognizing the connections among these dualities that together comprise the construct of dichotomous oppositional difference, that more women have not done so is not surprising. Either/or dualistic thinking is so pervasive that it suppresses other alternatives. As Dill points out, "the choice between identifying as black or female is a product of the patriarchal strategy of divide-and-conquer and the continued importance of class, patriarchal, and racial divisions, perpetuates such choices both within our consciousness and within the concrete realities of our daily lives" (1983:136). In spite of this difficulty, Black women experience oppression in a personal, holistic fashion and emerging Black feminist perspectives appear to be embracing an equally holistic analysis of oppression.

Second, Black feminist attention to the interlocking nature of oppression is significant in that this view implicitly involves an alternative humanist vision of societal organization. This alternative world view is cogently expressed in the following passage from an 1893 speech delivered by the Black feminist educator, Anna Julia Cooper:

> We take our stand on the solidarity of humanity, the oneness of life, and the unnaturalness and injustice of all special favoritisms, whether of sex, race, country, or condition . . . The colored woman feels that woman's cause is one and universal; and that . . . not till race, color, sex and condition are seen as accidents, and not the substance of life; not till the universal title of humanity to life, liberty, and the pursuit of happiness is conceded to be inalienable to all; not till then is woman's lesson taught and woman's cause won—not the white women's nor the black woman's, nor the red women's, but the cause of every man and of every woman who has writhed silently under a mighty wrong. (Loewenberg and Bogin, 1976:330–31)

I cite the above passage at length because it represents one of the clearest statements of the humanist vision extant in Black feminist thought.[12] Black feminists who see the simultaneity of oppression affecting Black women appear to be more sensitive to how these same oppressive systems affect Afro-American men, people of color, women, and the dominant group itself. Thus, while Black feminist activists may work on behalf of Black women, they rarely project separatist solutions to Black female oppression. Rather, the vision is one that, like Cooper's, takes its "stand on the solidarity of humanity."

The Importance of Afro-American Women's Culture

A third key theme characterizing Black feminist thought involves efforts to redefine and explain the importance of Black women's culture. In doing so, Black feminists have not only uncovered previously unexplored areas of the Black female experience, but they have also identified concrete areas of social relations where Afro-American women create and pass on self-definitions and self-valuations essential to coping with the simultaneity of oppression they experience.

In contrast to views of culture stressing the unique, ahistorical values of a particular group, Black feminist aproaches have placed greater emphasis on the role of historically specific political economies in explaining the endurance of certain cultural themes. The following definition of culture typifies the approach taken by many Black feminists. According to Mullings, culture is composed of

> the symbols and values that create the ideological frame of reference through which people attempt to deal with the circumstances in which they find themselves. Culture . . . is not composed of static, discrete traits moved from one locale to another. It is constantly changing and transformed, as new forms are created out of old ones. Thus culture . . . does not arise out of nothing: it is created and modified by material conditions. (1986a:13).

Seen in this light, Black women's culture may help provide the ideological frame of reference—namely, the symbols and values of self-definition and self-valuation—that assist Black women in seeing the circumstances shaping race, class, and gender oppression. Moreover, Mullings's definition of culture suggests that the values which accompany self-definition and self-valuation will have concrete, material expression: they will be present in social institutions like church and family, in creative expression of art, music, and dance, and, if unsuppressed, in patterns of economic and political activity. Finally, this approach to culture stresses its historically concrete nature. While common themes may link Black women's lives, these themes will be experienced differently by Black women of different classes, ages, regions, and sexual preferences as well as by Black women in different historical settings. Thus, there is no monolithic Black women's culture—rather, there are socially-constructed Black women's cultures that collectively form Black women's culture.

The interest in redefining Black women's culture has directed attention to several unexplored areas of the Black female experience. One such area concerns the interpersonal relationships that Black women share with each other. It appears that the notion of sisterhood—generally understood to mean a supportive feeling of loyalty and attachment to other women stemming from a shared feeling of oppression—has been an important part of Black women's culture (Dill, 1983:132). Two representative works in the emerging tradition of Black feminist research illustrate how this concept of sisterhood, while expressed differently in response to different material conditions, has been a significant feature of Black women's culture. For example, Debra Gray White (1985) documents the ways Black slave women assisted each other in childbirth, cared for each other's children, worked together in sex-segregated work units when pregnant or nursing children, and depended on one another when married to males living on distant farms. White paints a convincing portrait of Black female slave communities where sisterhood was necessary and assumed. Similarly, Gilkes's (1985) work on Black women's traditions in the Sanctified Church suggests that the sisterhood Black women found had tangible psychological and political benefits. [13]

The attention to Black women's culture has stimulated interest in a second type of interpersonal relationship: that shared by Black women with their biological children, the children in their extended families, and with the Black community's children. In reassessing Afro-American motherhood, Black feminist researchers have emphasized the connections between (1) choices available to Black mothers resulting from their placement in historically specific political economies, (2) Black mothers' perceptions of their children's choices as compared to what mothers thought those choices should be, and (3) actual strategies employed by Black mothers both in raising their children and in dealing with institutions that affected their children's lives. For example, Janice Hale (1980) suggests that effective Black mothers are sophisticated mediators between the competing offerings of an oppressive dominant culture and a nurturing Black value-structure. Dill's (1980) study of the childrearing goals of Black domestics stresses the goals the women in her sample had for their children and the strategies these women pursued to help their children go further than they themselves had gone. Gilkes (1980) offers yet another perspective on the power of Black motherhood by observing that many of the Black female political activists in her study became involved in community work through their role as mothers. What typically began as work on behalf of their own children evolved into work on behalf of the community's children.

Another dimension of Black women's culture that has generated considerable interest among Black feminists is the role of creative expression in shaping and sustaining Black women's self-definitions and self-valuations. In addition to documenting Black women's achievements as writers, dancers, musicians, artists, and actresses, the emerging literature also investigates why creative expression has been such an important element of Black women's culture.[14] Alice Walker's (1974) classic essay, "In Search of Our Mothers' Gardens," explains the necessity of Black women's creativity, even if in very limited spheres, in resisting objectification and asserting Black women's subjectivity as fully human beings. Illustrating Walker's thesis, Willie Mae Ford Smith, a prominent gospel singer featured in the 1984 documentary, "Say Amen Somebody," describes what singing means to her. She notes, "it's just a feeling within. You can't help yourself . . . I feel like I can fly away. I forget I'm in the world sometimes. I just want to take off." For Mother Smith, her creativity is a sphere of freedom, one that helps her cope with and transcend daily life.

This third key theme in Black feminist thought—the focus on Black women's culture—is significant for three reasons. First, the data from Black women's culture suggest that the relationship between oppressed people's consciousness of oppression and the actions they take in dealing with oppressive structures may be far more complex than that suggested by existing social theory. Conventional social science continues to assume a fit between consciousness and activity; hence, accurate measures of human behavior are thought to produce accurate portraits of human consciousness of self and social structure (Westkott, 1979). In contrast, Black women's experiences suggest that Black women may overtly conform to the societal roles laid out for them, yet covertly oppose these roles in numerous spheres, an opposition shaped by the consciousness of being on the bottom. Black women's activities in families, churches, community institutions, and creative expression may represent more than an effort to mitigate pressures stemming from oppression. Rather, the Black female ideological frame of reference that Black women acquire through sisterhood, motherhood, and creative expression may serve the added purpose of shaping a Black female consciousness about the workings of oppression. Moreover, this consciousness is not only shaped through abstract, rational reflection, but also is developed through concrete rational action. For example, while Black mothers may develop consciousness through talking with and listening to their children, they may also shape consciousness by how they live their lives, the actions they take on behalf of their children. That these activities have been obscured from traditional social scientists should come as no surprise. Oppressed peoples may maintain hidden consciousness and may not reveal their true selves for reasons of self-protection.[15]

A second reason that the focus on Black women's culture is significant is that it points to the problematic nature of existing conceptualizations of the term "activism." While Black women's reality cannot be understood without attention to the interlocking structures of oppression that limit Black women's lives, Afro-American women's experiences suggest that possibilities for activism exist even within such multiple structures of domination. Such activism can take several forms. For Black women under extremely harsh conditions, the private decision to reject external definitions of Afro-American womanhood may itself be a form of activism. If Black women find themselves in settings where total conformity is expected, and where traditional forms of activism such as voting, participating in collective movements, and officeholding are impossible, then the individual women who in their consciousness choose to be self-defined and self-evaluating are, in fact, activists. They are retaining a grip over their definition as subjects, as full humans, and rejecting definitions of themselves as the objectified "other." For example, while Black slave women were forced to conform to the specific oppression facing them, they may have had very different assessments of themselves and slavery than did the slaveowners. In this sense, consciousness can be viewed as one potential sphere of freedom, one that may exist simultaneously with unfree, allegedly conforming behavior (Westkott, 1979). Moreover, if Black women simultaneously use all resources available to them—their roles as mothers, their participation in churches, their support of one another in Black female networks, their creative expression—to be self-defined and self-valuating and to encourage others to reject objectification, then Black women's everyday behavior itself is a form of activism. People who view themselves as fully human, as subjects, become activists, no matter how limited the sphere of their activism may be. By returning subjectivity to Black women, Black feminists return activism as well.

A third reason that the focus on Black women's culture is significant is that an analytical model exploring the relationship between oppression, consciousness, and activism is implicit in the way Black feminists have studied Black women's culture. With the exception of Dill (1983), few scholars have deliberately set out to develop such a model. However, the type of work done suggests that an implicit model paralleling that proposed by Mullings (1986a) has influenced Black feminist research.

Several features pervade emerging Black feminist approaches. First, researchers stress the interdependent relationship between the interlocking oppression that has shaped Black women's choices and Black women's actions in the context of those choices. Black feminist researchers rarely describe Black woman's behavior without attention to the opportunity structures shaping their subjects' lives (Higginbotham, 1985; Ladner, 1971; Myers, 1980). Second, the question of whether oppressive structures and limited choices stimulate Black women's behavior characterized by apathy and alienation, or behavior demonstrating subjectivity and activism, is seen as ultimately dependent on Black women's perceptions of their choices. In other words, Black women's consciousness—their analytical, emotional, and ethical perspective of themselves and their place in society—becomes a critical part of the relationship between the working of oppression and Black women's actions. Finally, this relationship between oppression, consciousness, and action can be seen as a dialectical one. In this model, oppressive structures create patterns of choices which are perceived in varing ways by Black women. Depending on their consciousness of themselves and their relationships to these choices, Black women may or may not develop Black-female spheres of influence where they develop and validate what will be appropriate, Black-female sanctioned responses to oppression. Black women's activism in constructing Black-female spheres of influence may, in turn, affect their perceptions of the political and economic choices offered to them by oppressive structures, influence actions actually taken, and ultimately alter the nature of oppression they experience.

The Sociological Significance of Black Feminist Thought

Taken together, the three key themes in Black feminist thought—the meaning of self-definition and self-valuation, the interlocking nature of oppression, and the importance of redefining culture—have made significant contributions to the task of clarifying a Black women's standpoint of and for Black women. While this accomplishment is important in and of itself, Black feminist thought has potential contributions to make to the diverse disciplines housing its practitioners.

The sociological significance of Black feminist thought lies in two areas. First, the content of Black women's ideas has been influenced by and contributes to on-going dialogues in a variety of sociological specialties. While this area merits attention, it is not my primary concern in this section. Instead, I investigate a second area of sociological significance: the process by which these specific ideas were produced by this specific group of individuals. In other words, I examine the influence of Black women's outsider within status in academia on the actual thought produced. Thus far, I have proceeded on the assumption that it is impossible to separate the structure and thematic content of thought. In this section, I spell out exactly what form the relationship between the three key themes in Black feminist thought and Black women's outsider within status might take for women scholars generally, with special attention to Black female sociologists.

First, I briefly summarize the role sociological paradigms play in shaping the facts and theories used by sociologists. Second, I explain how Black women's outsider within status might encourage Black women to have a distinctive standpoint vis-á-vis sociology's paradigmatic facts and theories. I argue that the thematic content of Black feminist thought described above represents elements of just such a standpoint and give examples of how the combination of sociology's paradigms and Black women's outsider within status as sociologists directed their attention to specific areas of sociological inquiry.

Two Elements of Sociological Paradigms

Kuhn defines a paradigm as the "entire constellation of beliefs, values, techniques, and so on shared by the members of a given community" (1962:175). As such, a paradigm consists of two fundamental elements: the thought itself and its producers and practitioners.[16] In this sense, the discipline of sociology is itself a paradigm—it consists of a system of knowledge shared by sociologists—and simultaneously consists of a plurality of paradigms (e.g., functionalism, Marxist sociology, feminist sociology, existential sociology), each produced by its own practitioners.

Two dimensions of thought itself are of special interest to this discussion. First, systems of knowledge are never complete. Rather, they represent guidelines for "thinking as usual." Kuhn (1962) refers to these guidelines as "maps," while Schutz (1944) describes them as "recipes." As Schutz points out, while "thinking as usual" is actually only partially organized and partially clear, and may contain contradictions, to its practitioners it provides sufficient coherence, clarity, and consistency. Second, while thought itself contains diverse elements, I will focus mainly on the important fact/theory relationship. As Kuhn (1962) suggests, facts or observations become meaningful in the context of theories or interpretations of those observations. Conversely, theories "fit the facts" by transforming previously accessible observations into facts. According to Mulkay, "observation is not separate from interpretation; rather these are two facets of a single process" (1979:49).

Several dimensions of the second element of sociological paradigms—the community formed by a paradigm's practitioners—are of special interest to this discussion. First, group insiders have similar worldviews, acquired through similar educational and professional training, that separate them from everyone else. Insider worldviews may be especially alike if group members have similar social class, gender, and racial backgrounds. Schutz describes the insider worldview as the "cultural pattern of group life"—namely, all the values and behaviors which characterize the social group at a given moment in its history. In brief, insiders have undergone similar experiences, possess a common history, and share taken-for-granted knowledge that characterizes "thinking as usual."

A second dimension of the community of practitioners involves the process of becoming an insider. How does one know when an individual is really an insider and not an outsider in disguise? Merton suggests that socialization into the life of a group is a lengthy process of being immersed in group life, because only then can "one understand the fine-grained meanings of behavior, feeling, and values . . . and decipher the unwritten grammar of conduct and nuances of cultural idiom" (1972:15). The process is analogous to immersion in a foreign culture in order to learn its ways and its language (Merton, 1972; Schutz, 1944). One becomes an insider by translating a theory or worldview into one's own language until, one day, the individual converts to thinking and acting according to that worldview.

A final dimension of the community of practitioners concerns the process of remaining an insider. A sociologist typically does this by furthering the discipline in ways described as appropriate by sociology generally, and by areas of specialization particularly. Normal foci for scientific sociological investigation include: (1) determining significant facts; (2) matching facts with existing theoretical interpretations to "test" the paradigm's ability to predict facts; and (3) resolving ambiguities in the paradigm itself by articulating and clarifying theory (Kuhn, 1962).

Black Women and the Outsider Within Status

Black women may encounter much less of a fit between their personal and cultural experiences and both elements of sociological paradigms than that facing other sociologists. On the one hand, Black women who undergo sociology's lengthy socialization process, who immerse themselves in the cultural pattern of sociology's group life, certainly wish to acquire the insider skills of thinking in and acting according to a sociological worldview. But on the other hand, Black women's experienced realities, both prior to contact and after initiation, may provide them with "special perspectives and insights . . . available to that category of outsiders who have been systematically frustrated by the social system" (Merton, 1972:29). In brief, their outsider allegiances may militate against their choosing full insider status, and they may be more apt to remain outsiders within.[17]

In essence, to become sociological insiders, Black women must assimilate a standpoint that is quite different from their own. White males have long been the dominant group in sociology, and the sociological worldview understandably reflects the concerns of this group of practitioners. As Merton observes, "white male insiderism in American sociology during the past generations has largely been of the tacit or de facto . . . variety. It has simply taken the form of patterned expectations about the appropriate . . . problems for investigation" (1972:12). In contrast, a good deal of the Black female experience has been spent coping with, avoiding, subverting, and challenging the workings of this same white male insiderism. It should come as no surprise that Black women's efforts in dealing with the effects of interlocking systems of oppression might produce a standpoint quite distinct from, and in many ways opposed to, that of white male insiders.

Seen from this perspective, Black women's socialization into sociology represents a more intense case of the normal challenges facing sociology graduate students and junior professionals in the discipline. Black women become, to use Simmel's (1921) and Schutz's terminology, penultimate "strangers."

> The stranger . . . does not share the basic assumptions of the group. He becomes essentially the man who has to place in question nearly everything that seems to be unquestionable to the members of the aproached group . . . To him the cultural patterns of the approached group do not have the authority of a tested system of recipes . . . because he does not partake in the vivid historical tradition by which it has been formed. (Schutz, 1944:502)

Like everyone else, Black women may see sociological "thinking as usual" as partially organized, partially clear, and contradictory, and may question these existing recipes. However, for them, this questioning process may be more acute, for the material that they encounter—white male insider-influenced observations and interpretations about human society—places white male subjectivity at the center of analysis and assigns Afro-American womanhood a position on the margins.

In spite of a lengthy socialization process, it may also be more difficult for Afro-American women to experience conversion and begin totally to think in and act according to a sociological worldview. Indeed, since past generations of white male insiderism has shaped a sociological worldview reflecting this group's concerns, it may be self-destructive for Black women to embrace that worldview. For example, Black women would have to accept certain fundamental and self-devaluing assumptions: (1) white males are more worthy of study because they are more fully human than everyone else; and (2) dichotomous oppositional thinking is natural and normal. More importantly, Black women would have to act in accordance with their place in a white male worldview. This involves accepting one's own subordination or regretting the accident of not being born white and male. In short, it may be extremely difficult for Black women to accept a worldview predicated upon Black female inferiority.

Remaining in sociology by doing normal scientific investigation may also be less complicated for traditional sociologists than for Afro-American women. Unlike Black women, learners from backgrounds where the insider information and experiences of sociology are more familiar may be less likely to see the taken-for-granted assumptions of sociology and may be more prone to apply their creativity to "normal science." In other words, the transition from student status to that of a practitioner engaged in finding significant facts that sociological paradigms deem important, matching facts with existing theories, and furthering paradigmatic development itself may proceed more smoothly for white middle-class males than for working-class Black females. The latter group is much more inclined to be struck by the mismatch of its own experiences and the paradigms of sociology itself. Moreover, those Black women with a strong foundation in Black women's culture (e.g., those that recognize the value of self-definition and self-valuation, and that have a concrete understanding of sisterhood and motherhood) may be more apt to take a critical posture toward the entire sociological enterprise. In brief, where traditional sociologists may see sociology as "normal" and define their role as furthering knowledge about a normal world with taken-for-granted assumptions, outsiders within are likely to see anomalies.

The types of anomalies typically seen by Black female academicians grow directly from Black women's outsider within status and appear central in shaping the direction Black feminist thought has taken thus far. Two types of anomalies are characteristically noted by Black female scholars. First, Black female sociologists typically report the omission of facts or observations about Afro-American women in the sociological paradigms they encounter. As Scott points out, "from reading the literature, one might easily develop the impression that Black women have never played any role in this society" (1982:85). Where white males may take it as perfectly normal to generalize findings from studies of white males to other groups, black women are more likely to see such a practice as problematic, as an anomaly. Similarly, when white feminists produce generalizations about "women," Black feminists routinely ask "which women do you mean?" In the same way that Rollins (1985) felt invisible in her employer's kitchen, Afro-American female scholars are repeatedly struck by their own invisibility, both as full human subjects included in sociological facts and observations, and as practitioners in the discipline itself. It should come as no surprise that much of Black feminist thought aims to counter this invisibility by presenting sociological analyses of Black women as fully human subjects. For example, the growing research describing Black women's historical and contemporary behavior as mothers, community workers, church leaders, teachers, and employed workers, and Black women's ideas about themselves and their opportunities reflects an effort to respond to the omission of facts about Afro-American women.

A second type of anomaly typically noted by Black female scholars concerns distortions of facts and observations about Black women. Afro-American women in academia are frequently struck by the difference between their own experiences and sociological descriptions of the same phenomena. For example, while Black women have and are themselves mothers, they encounter distorted versions of themselves and their mothers under the mantle of the Black matriarchy thesis. Similarly, for those Black women who confront racial and sexual discrimination and know that their mothers and grandmothers certainly did, explanations of Black women's poverty that stress low achievement motivation and the lack of Black female "human capital" are less likely to ring true. The response to these perceived distortions has been one of redefining distorted images—for example, debunking the Sapphire and Mammy myths.

Since facts or observations become meaningful in the context of a theory, this emphasis on producing accurate descriptions of Black women's lives has also refocused attention on major omissions and distortions in sociological theories themselves. By drawing on the strengths of sociology's plurality of sub-disciplines, yet taking a critical posture toward them, the work of Black feminist scholars taps some fundamental questions facing all sociologists. One such question concerns the fundamental elements of society that should be studied. Black feminist researchers' response has been to move Black women's voices to the center of the analysis, to study people, and by doing so, to reaffirm human subjectivity and intentionality. They point to the dangers of omission and distortion that can occur if sociological concepts are studied at the expense of human subjectivity. For example, there is a distinct difference between conducting a statistical analysis of Black women's work, where Afro-American women are studied as a reconstituted amalgam of reseracher-defined variables (e.g., race, sex, years of education, and father's occupation), and examining Black women's self-definitions and self-valuations of themselves as workers in oppressive jobs. While both approaches can further sociological knowledge about the concept of work, the former runs the risk of objectifying Black women, of reproducing constructs of dichotomous oppositional difference, and of producing distorted findings about the nature of work itself.

A second question facing sociologists concerns the adequacy of current interpretations of key sociological concepts. For example, few sociologists would question that work and family are two fundamental concepts for sociology. However, bringing Black feminist thought into the center of conceptual analysis raises issues of how comprehensive current sociological interpretations of these two concepts really are. For exmple, labor theories that relegate Afro-American women's work experiences to the fringe of analysis miss the critical theme of the interlocking nature of Black women as female workers (e.g., Black women's unpaid domestic labor) and Black women as racially-oppressed workers (e.g., black women's unpaid slave labor and exploited wage labor). Examining the extreme case offered by Afro-American women's unpaid and paid work experiences raises questions about the adequacy of generalizations about work itself. For example, Black feminists' emphasis on the simultaneity of oppression redefines the economic system itself as problematic. From this perspective, all generalizations about the normal workings of labor markets, organizational structure, occupational mobility, and income differences that do not explicitly see oppression as problematic become suspect. In short, Black feminists suggest that all generalizations about groups of employed and unemployed workers (e.g., managers, welfare mothers, union members, secretaries, Black teenagers) that do not account for interlocking structures of group placement and oppression in an economy are simply less complete than those that do.

Similarly, sociological generalizations about families that do not account for Black women's experience will fail to show how the public/private split shaping household composition varies across social and class groupings, how racial/ethnic family members are differentially integrated into wage labor, and how families alter their household structure in response to changing political economies (e.g., adding more people and becoming extended, fragmenting and becoming female-headed, and migrating to locate better opportunities). Black women's family experiences represent a clear case of the workings of race, gender, and class oppression in shaping family life. Bringing undistorted observations of Afro-American women's family experiences into the center of analysis again raises the question of how other families are affected by these same forces.

While Black women who stand outside academia may be familiar with omissions and distortions of the Black female experience, as outsiders to sociology, they lack legitimated professional authority to challenge the sociological anomalies. Similarly, traditional sociological insiders, whether white males or their nonwhite and/or female disciples, are certainly in no position to notice the specific anomalies apparent to Afro-American women, because these same sociological insiders produced them. In contrast, those Black women who remain rooted in their own experiences as Black women—and who master sociological paradigms yet retain a critical posture toward them—are in a better position to bring a special perspective not only to the study of Black women, but to some of the fundamental issues facing sociology itself.

Toward Synthesis: Outsiders Within Sociology

Black women are not the only outsiders within sociology. As an extreme case of outsiders moving into a community that historically excluded them, Black women's experiences highlight the tension experienced by any group of less powerful outsiders encountering the paradigmatic thought of a more powerful insider community. In this sense, a variety of individuals can learn from Black women's experiences as outsiders within: Black men, working-class individuals, white women, other people of color, religious and sexual minorities, and all individuals who, while from social strata that provided them with the benefits of white male insiderism, have never felt comfortable with its taken-for-granted assumptions.

Outsider within status is bound to generate tension, for people who become outsiders within are forever changed by their new status. Learning the subject matter of sociology stimulates a reexamination of one's own personal and cultural experiences; and, yet, these same experiences paradoxically help to illuminate sociology's anomalies. Outsiders within occupy a special place—they become different people, and their difference sensitizes them to patterns that may be more difficult for established sociological insiders to see. Some outsiders within try to resolve the tension generated by their new status by leaving sociology and remaining sociological outsiders. Others choose to suppress their difference by striving to become bonafide, "thinking as usual" sociological insiders. Both choices rob sociology of diversity and ultimately weaken the discipline.

A third alternative is to conserve the creative tension of outsider within status by encouraging and institutionalizing outsider within ways of seeing. This alternative has merit not only for actual outsiders within, but also for other sociologists as well. The approach suggested by the experiences of outsiders within is one where intellectuals learn to trust their own personal and cultural biographies as significant sources of knowledge. In contrast to approaches that require submerging these dimensions of self in the process of becoming an allegedly unbiased, objective social scientist, outsiders within bring these ways of knowing back into the research process. At its best, outsider within status seems to offer its occupants a powerful balance between the strengths of their sociological training and the offerings of their personal and cultural experiences. Neither is subordinated to the other. Rather, experienced reality is used as a valid source of knowledge for critiquing sociological facts and theories, while sociological thought offers new ways of seeing that experienced reality.

What many Black feminists appear to be doing is embracing the creative potential of their outsider within status and using it wisely. In doing so, they move themselves and their disciplines closer to the humanist vision implicit in their work—namely, the freedom both to be different and to be part of the solidarity of humanity.

NOTES

I wish to thank Lynn Weber Cannon, Bonnie Thornton Dill, Alison M. Jaggar, Joan Hartman, Ellen Messer-Davidow, and several anonymous reviewers for their helpful comments about earlier drafts of this paper. Correspondence to: Department of Afro-American Studies, University of Cincinnati, ML 370, Cincinnati, OH 45221.

1. In 1940, almost 60 percent of employed Afro-American women were domestics. The 1970 census was the first time this category of work did not contain the largest segment of the Black female labor force. See Rollins (1985) for a discussion of Black domestic work. .

2. For example, in *Of Women Born: Motherhood as Experience and Institution*, Adrienne Rich has fond memories of her Black "mother," a young, unstereotypically slim Black woman she loved. Similarly, Dill's (1980) study of black domestic workers reveals Black women's sense of affirmation at knowing that they were better mothers than their employers, and that they frequently had to teach their employers the basics about children and interaction in general. Even though the Black domestic workers were officially subordinates, they gained a sense of self-worth at knowing they were good at things that they felt mattered.

3. For example, in spite of Rich's warm memories of her Black "mother," she had all but forgotten her until beginning research for her book. Similarly, the Black domestic workers in both Dill's (1980) and Rollins's (1985) studies discussed the limitations that their subordinate roles placed on them.

4. For a discussion of the notion of a special standpoint or point of view of oppressed groups, see Hartsock (1983). See Merton's (1972) analysis of the potential contributions of insider and outsider perspectives to sociology. For a related discussion of outsider within status, see his section "Insiders as 'Outsiders' " (1972:29–30).

5. Hurston has been widely discussed in Black feminist literary criticism. For example, see selected essays in Walker's (1979) edited volume on Hurston.

6. By stressing the potentially positive features of outsider within status, I in no way want to deny the very real problem this social status has for large numbers of Black women. American sociology has long identified marginal status as problematic. However, my sense of the "problems" diverge from those espoused by traditional sociologists. For example, Robert Park states, "the marginal man . . . is one whom fate has

condemned to live in two societies and in two, not merely different but antagonistic cultures (1950:373)." From Park's perspective, marginality and difference themselves were problems. This perspective quite rationally led to the social policy solution of assimilation, one aimed at eliminating difference, or if that didn't work, pretending it was not important. In contrast, I argue that it is the meaning attached to difference that is the problem. See Lorde (1984:114–23 and passim) for a Black feminist perspective on difference.

7. In addition to familarizing readers with the contours of Black feminist thought, I place Black women's ideas in the center of my analysis for another reason. Black women's ideas have long been viewed as peripheral to serious intellectual endeavors. By treating Black feminist thought as central, I hope to avoid the tendency of starting with the body of thought needing the critique—in this case sociology—fitting in the dissenting ideas, and thus, in the process, reifying the very systems of thought one hopes to transform.

8. On this point, I diverge somewhat from Berger and Luckmann's (1966) definition of specialized thought. They suggest that only a limited group of individuals engages in theorizing and that "pure theory" emerges with the development of specialized legitimating theories and their administration by full-time legitimators. Using this approach, groups denied the material resources to support pure theorists cannot be capable of developing specialized theoretical knowledge. In contrast, I argue that "traditional wisdom" is a system of thought and that it reflects the material positions of its practitioners.

9. Emerging Black feminist research is demonstrating a growing awareness of the importance of including the simultaneity of oppression in studies of Black women. For example, Paula Giddings's (1984) history of Afro-American women emphasizes the role of class in shaping relations between Afro-American and white women, and among Black women themselves. Elizabeth Higginbotham's (1985) study of Black college women examines race and class barriers to Black women's college attendance. Especially noteworthy is the growing attention to Black women's labor market experiences. Studies such as those by Dill (1980), Rollins (1985), Higginbotham (1983), and Mullings (1986b) indicate a new sensitivity to the interactive nature of race, gender, and class. By studying Black women, such studies capture the interaction of race and gender. Moreover, by examining Black women's roles in capitalist development, such work taps the key variable of class.

10. The thesis that those affected by multiple systems of domination will develop a sharper view of the interlocking nature of oppression is illustrated by the prominence of Black lesbian feminists among Black feminist thinkers. For more on this, see Smith (1983), Lorde (1984), and White (1984:22–24).

11. For example, African and Afro-American scholars point to the role dualistic thinking has played in domestic racism (Asante, 1980; Baldwin, 1980; Richards 1980). Feminist scholars note the linkage of duality with conceptualizations of gender in Western cultures (Chodorow, 1978; Keller, 1983; Rosaldo, 1983). Recently, Brittan and Maynard, two British scholars, have suggested that dualistic thinking plays a major role in linking systems of racial oppression with those of sexual oppression. They note that there is an implicit belief in the duality of culture and nature. Men are the creators and mediators of culture—women are the manifestations of nature. The implication is that man develop culture in order to understand and control the natural world, while women, being the embodiment of forces of nature, must be brought under the civilizing control of men. . . . This duality of culture and nature . . . is also used to distinguish between so-called higher nations or civilizations and those deemed culturally backward. . . . Non-European peoples are conceived of as being nearer to nature than Europeans. Hence, the justification . . . for slavery and colonialism. (1984:193–94).

12. This humanist vision takes both religious and secular forms. For religious statements, see Andrews's (1986) collection of the autobiographies of three nineteenth-century Black female evangelical preachers. For a discussion of the humanist tradition in Afro-American religion that has contributed to this dimension of Black feminist thought,

see Paris (1985). Much of contemporary Black feminist writing draws on this religious tradition but reframes the basic vision in secular terms.

13. During a period when Black women were widely devalued by the dominant culture, Sanctified Church members addressed each other as "Saints." During the early 1900s, when basic literacy was an illusive goal for many Blacks, Black women in the Church not only stressed education as a key component of a sanctified life, but supported each other's efforts at educational excellence. In addition to these psychological supports, the Church provided Afro-American women with genuine opportunities for influence, leadership, and political clout. The important thing to remember here is that the Church was not an abstract, bureaucratic structure that ministered to Black women. Rather, the Church was a predominantly female community of individuals in which women had prominent spheres of influence.

14. Since much Black feminist thought is contained in the works of Black women writers, literary criticism by Black feminist critics provides an especially fertile source of Black women's ideas. See Tate (1983) and Christian (1985).

15. Audre Lorde (1984:114) describes this conscious hiding of one's self as follows: "in order to survive, those of us for whom oppression is as American as apple pie have always had to be watchers, to become familiar with the language and manners of the oppressor, even sometimes adopting them for some illusion of protection."

16. In this sense, sociology is a special case of the more generalized process discussed by Mannheim (1936). Also, see Berman (1981) for a discussion of Western thought as a paradigm, Mulkay (1979) for a sociology of knowledge analysis of the natural sciences, and Berger and Luckmann (1966) for a generalized discussion of how everyday knowledge is socially constructed.

17. Jackson (1974) reports that 21 of the 145 Black sociologists receiving doctoral degrees between 1945 and 1972 were women. Kulis et al. (1986) report that Blacks comprised 5.7 percent of all sociology faculties in 1984. These data suggest that historically, Black females have not been sociological insiders, and currently, Black women as a group comprise a small portion of sociologists in the United States.

REFERENCES

Andrews, William L. (ed.)
 1986 Sisters of the Spirit. Bloomington, IN: Indiana University Press.
Asante, Molefi Kete
 1980 "International/intercultural relations." Pp. 43–58 in Molefi Kete Asante and Abdulai S. Vandi (eds.), Contemporary Black Thought. Beverly Hills, CA: Sage.
Baldwin, Joseph A.
 1980 "The psychology of oppression." Pp. 95–110 in Molefi Kete Asante and Abdulai S. Vandi (eds.), Contemporary Black Thought. Beverly Hills, CA: Sage.
Beale, Frances
 1970 "Double jeopardy: to be Black and female." Pp. 90–110 in Toni Cade (ed.), The Black Woman. New York: Signet.
Berger, Peter L., and Thomas Luckmann
 1966 The Social Construction of Reality. New York: Doubleday.
Berman, Morris
 1981 The Reenchantment of the World. New York: Bantam.

Brittan, Arthur, and Mary Maynard
    1984   Sexism, Racism and Oppression. New York: Basil Blackwell.
Chodorow, Nancy
    1978   The Reproduction of Mothering. Berkeley, CA: University of California Press.
Christian, Barbara
    1985   Black Feminist Criticism: Perspectives on Black Women Writers. New York: Pergamon.
Davis, Angela
    1981   Women, Race and Class. New York: Random House.
Dill, Bonnie Thornton
    1980   " 'The means to put my children through': child-rearing goals and strategies among Black female domestic servants." Pp. 107–23 in LaFrances Rodgers-Rose (ed.), The Black Woman. Beverly Hills, CA: Sage.
    1983   "Race, class, and gender: prospects for an all-inclusive sisterhood." Feminist Studies 9:131–50.
Giddings, Paula
    1984   When and Where I Enter . . . the Impact of Black Women on Race and Sex in America. New York: William Morrow.
Gilkes, Cheryl Townsend
    1980   " 'Holding back the ocean with a broom': Black women and community work." Pp. 217–31 in LaFrances Rodgers-Rose (ed.), The Black Woman. Beverly Hills, CA: Sage.
    1981   "From slavery to social welfare: racism and the control of Black women." Pp. 288–300 in Amy Smerdlow and Helen Lessinger (eds.), Class, Race, and Sex: The Dynamics of Control. Boston: G. K. Hall.
    1985   " 'Together and in harness': women's traditions in the sanctified church." Signs 10:678–99.
Gwaltney, John Langston
    1980   Drylongso, a Self-portrait of Black America. New York: Vintage.
Hale, Janice
    1980   "The Black woman and child rearing." Pp. 79–88 in LaFrances Rodgers-Rose (ed.), The Black Woman. Beverly Hills, CA: Sage.
Hartsock, Nancy M.
    1983   "The feminist standpoint: developing the ground for a specifically feminist historical materialism." Pp. 283–310 in Sandra Harding and Merrill Hintikka (eds.), Discovering Reality. Boston: D. Reidel.
Higginbotham, Elizabeth
    1982   "Two representative issues in contemporary sociological work on Black women." Pp: 93–98 in Gloria T. Hull, Patricia Bell Scott, and Barbara Smith (eds.), But Some of Us Are Brave. Old Westbury, NY: Feminist Press.
    1983   "Laid bare by the system: work and survival for Black and Hispanic women." Pp. 200–15 in Amy Smerdlow and Helen Lessinger (eds.), Class, Race, and Sex: The Dynamics of Control. Boston: G. K. Hall.
    1985   "Race and class barriers to Black women's college attendance." Journal of Ethnic Studies 13:89–107.
Hooks, Bell
    1981   Ain't I a Woman: Black Women and Feminism. Boston: South End Press.
    1984   From Margin to Center. Boston: South End Press.
Jackson, Jacquelyn
    1974   "Black female sociologists." Pp. 267–98 in James E. Blackwell and Morris Janowitz (eds.), Black Sociologists. Chicago: University of Chicago Press.
Keller, Evelyn Fox
    1983   "Gender and science." Pp. 187–206 in Sandra Harding and Merrill Hintikka (eds.), Discovering Reality. Boston: D. Reidel.

King, Mae
 1973 "The politics of sexual stereotypes." Black Scholar 4:12–23.
Kuhn, Thomas S.
 1970 The Structure of Scientific Revolutions. 2d Edition. Chicago: [1962] University of Chicago Press.
Kulis, Stephen, Karen A. Miller, Morris Axelrod, and Leonard Gordon
 1986 "Minority representation of U.S. departments." ASA Footnotes 14:3.
Ladner, Joyce
 1971 Tomorrow's Tomorrow: The Black Woman. Garden City, NY: Anchor.
Lee, Alfred McClung
 1973 Toward Humanist Sociology. Englewood Cliffs, NJ: Prentice-Hall.
Lewis, Diane
 1977 "A response to inequality: Black women, racism and sexism." Signs 3:339–61.
Loewenberg, Bert James, and Ruth Bogin (eds.)
 1976 Black Women in Nineteenth-Century Life. University Park, PA: Pennsylvania State University.
Lorde, Audre
 1984 Sister Outsider. Trumansburg, NY: The Crossing Press.
Mannheim, Karl
 1954 Ideology and Utopia: An Introduction to the Sociology of Knowledge. [1936] New York: Harcourt, Brace & Co.
Merton, Robert K.
 1972 "Insiders and outsiders: a chapter in the sociology of knowledge." American Journal of Sociology 78:9–47.
Mulkay, Michael
 1979 Science and the Sociology of Knowledge. Boston: George Allen & Unwin.
Mullings, Leith
 1986a "Anthropological perspectives on the Afro-American family." American Journal of Social Psychiatry 6:11–16.
 1986b "Uneven development: class, race and gender in the United States before 1900." Pp. 41–57 in Eleanor Leacock and Helen Safa (eds.), Women's Work, Development and the Division of Labor by Gender. South Hadley, MA: Bergin & Garvey.
Murray, Pauli
 1970 "The liberation of Black women." Pp. 87–102 in Mary Lou Thompson (ed.), Voices of the New Feminism. Boston: Beacon Press.
Myers, Lena Wright
 1980 Black Women: Do They Cope Better? Englewood Cliffs, NJ: Prentice-Hall.
Paris, Peter J.
 1985 The Social Teaching of the Black Churches. Philadelphia: Fortress Press.
Park, Robert E.
 1950 Race and Culture. Glencoe, IL: Free Press.
Rich, Adrienne
 1976 Of Woman Born: Motherhood as Experience and Institution. New York: Norton.
Richards, Dona
 1980 "European mythology; the ideology of 'progress'." Pp. 59–79 in Molefi Kete Asante and Abdulai S. Vandi (eds.), Contemporary Black Thought. Beverly Hills, CA: Sage.
Rollins, Judith
 1985 Between Women, Domestics and Their Employers. Philadelphia: Temple University Press.
Rosaldo, Michelle Z.
 1983 "Moral/analytic dilemmas posed by the intersection of feminism and social science." Pp. 76–96 in Norma Hann, Robert N. Bellah, Paul Rabinow, and

William Sullivan (eds.). Social Science as Moral Inquiry. New York: Columbia University Press.

Schutz, Alfred
1944   "The stranger: an essay in social psychology." American Journal of Sociology 49:499–507.

Scott, Patricia Bell
1982   "Debunking sapphire: toward a non-racist and non-sexist social science." Pp. 85–92 in Gloria T. Hull, Patricia Bell Scott, and Barbara Smith (eds.), But Some of Us Are Brave. Old Westbury, NY: Feminist Press.

Simmel, Georg
1921   "The sociological significance of the 'stranger'." Pp. 322–27 in Robert E. Park and Ernest W. Burgess (eds.), Introduction to the Science of Sociology. Chicago: University of Chicago Press.

Smith, Barbara (ed.)
1983   Home Girls: A Black Feminist Anthology. New York: Kitchen Table, Women of Color Press.

Steady, Filomina Chioma
1981   "The Black woman cross-culturally: an overview." Pp. 7–42 in Filomina Chioma Steady (ed.), The Black Woman Cross-culturally. Cambridge, MA: Schenkman.

Tate, Claudia
1983   Black Women Writers at Work. New York: Continuum.

Walker, Alice (ed.)
1974   "In search of our mothers' gardens." Pp. 231–43 in. In Search of Our Mothers' Gardens. New York: Harcourt Brace Jovanovich.

Walker, Alice
1979   I Love Myself When I Am Laughing . . . A Zora Neal Hurston Reader. Westbury, NY: Feminist Press.

Westkott, Marcia
1979   "Feminist criticism of the social sciences." Harvard Educational Review 49:422–30.

White, Deborah Gray
1985   Art'n't I a Woman? Female Slaves in the Plantation South. New York: W. W. Norton.

White, E. Frances
1984   "Listening to the voices of Black feminism." Radical America 18:7–25.

4. WOMEN'S RESEARCH OR FEMINIST RESEARCH?

The Debate Surrounding Feminist Science and Methodology

MARIA MIES

Translation by Andy Spencer

Many women had fought for the establishment of Women's Seminars at universities and for the acceptance of women's themes as subject matter for doctoral dissertations. In attempting this they encountered the open resistance of most male and also some female professors. They realized not only that the universities are bastions of male dominion, but also that the supposedly objective sciences are blind to women's issues. In this situation the "Methodological Postulates" became something akin to the stumblingblock which divided minds, not only the minds of male or female scholars, but also those of women representing different theoretical positions. Some welcomed the essay as a basis for committed feminist social science; others saw in it a manifesto of feminist propaganda.[1]

My present attempt to answer the criticisms made of my "Methodological Postulates" is set not only against the background of my own experience with this approach, but also against that of further and deeper reflection. I would like to stress that this rejoinder is therefore not concerned with the continuation of a purely academic discourse which has as its goal the accumulation of knowledge, but is rather an interim report on feminist praxis and research.

In the following I will therefore comment initially on the main points of the criticisms and then detail how I have worked with this methodological approach in order to further develop it in the direction of a feminist theory of science.

Before I come to the individual criticisms, a general introductory remark: The main body of reactions to the "Postulates" remained at the level of theoretical arguments. That is to say, the Postulates were much discussed, much quoted but, it seems to me, little tested. The discussion often followed the well-trodden paths of contemplative academic discourse which is fueled by claim and counter-claim and not by new findings made on the basis of new experiences. This procedure accords with the verbal tradition of the universities where it is a matter of "beating" one's opponent with the "best argument." It runs contrary, however, to the intended direction of feminist science and research as I formulated it in the introductory thesis of the Postulates. The necessity of searching for new methods and a new concept of research will only arise when women in the universities transform the sciences into a means by which to fight women's oppression and exploitation and want to change the status quo. If they do not want to do that (and there are many women who do not want to), if they want to make of women's issues debating-material for the Academy, then the whole dispute over a new initiative for theory and methodology becomes irrelevant. For such a debate can only repeat the old antagonisms between the different theories of science (e.g., critical theory versus positivism).

The Postulates, however, are concerned with producing a different relationship between science and social movements, in our case the women's movement. The aim of the women's movement is not just the study but the overcoming of women's oppression and exploitation. It is for this reason that the present-day relationship (in which science is viewed as apolitical) must itself be revolutionized. Such a revolutionizing cannot be carried out solely within the realms of purely scientific self-reflection, as Critical Theory has attempted it, not even if that theory calls itself "Marxist" or even "feminist." To this revolutionizing there belongs a social movement.

In my opinion, many of those who responded, either positively or negatively, to this approach have not understood that it is concerned with this revolutionizing. Although this initiative was expressly thought of as an invitation for experimentation and further discussion, it has been misunderstood by a number of women as a "model" or as a catalog of methodological recipes. Instead of personally working on the further development of this methodological initiative, many have used it solely in the accepted manner, as a source of quotations with which to either legitimize or defame feminist research. Whether consciously or unconsciously, they are thereby contributing to a renewed academicization of the whole complex of problems, which is precisely what the Postulates wanted to lead away from.

The criticism of the "Methodological Postulates for Women's Studies" centers above all else on the following problem areas:

- The relationship between the women's movement and women's research (politics and science)
- Research methods
- The relationship between action and research
- The relationship between researcher and research object

The Relationship between the Women's Movement and Women's Research or between Politics and Science

Although all women critics admit, either implicitly or explicitly, that women's research only became possible because of the women's movement, many deal with the relationship between the two areas in the following order:

First comes science, then politics; first women's research, then the women's movement. That this order sets the actual historical movement, the chronology of events, on its head, seems to escape the critics. They treat the relationship between the women's movement and women's research in the usual ahistorical, abstract way, as is expected of the dominant positivistic understanding of science. The clearest example of this is the essay by A. Bleich, U. Jansz, and S. Leyendorf: "In Praise Of Reason" (1980), wherein the authors take the motto in Postulate Four of my essay ("In order to understand a thing, one must change it") and simply dualistically invert it: "In order to change the world, one must know it." By so doing they uncritically adopt the dominant concept of knowledge and science which, ostensibly neutral and more-or-less autonomous, hovers "above" politics. They are against a politicization of science and therefore reject the idea that women's research must become a part of the emancipatory processes of praxis.

Without further ado they then connect this approach with Stalinism by alluding to the Lysenko Affair,[2] in which a scientific disagreement was decided, with Stalin's support, "not with arguments but with the help of political power" (Bleich et al., 1980).

I ask myself what happened to the authors' much-vaunted "objectivity" and "logic" when they wrote this. When was it ever a concern of Stalin's to further emancipatory and humanizing processes? And where are women so strongly represented in universities or politics that they can exercise power? To warn of "abuse of power" by a handful of feminist scientists is patently absurd when seen against the real backdrop of the extremely small representation of women in politics and science. A consistent argument of the men who control all the power centers of the world is that the oppressed who rebel want to exercise "power."

This whole argumentation is rooted in the postivistic understanding of the relationship between science and politics. The women authors are of the opinion that science and scientific theories are areas free of politics and power. In science it is a matter of "perception," in politics of "power." They have indeed to accede that one needs "power" in order to establish women's research in the universities, but when it is established, or so they argue, when it comes down to the research, then it is "arguments" and not "power" which are called for. Here it is clear that the relationship between science and politics is not only viewed in the wrong order, as noted above, but also as mechanical and additive. Political movements remain outside the doors of science, which is defined as an apolitical, neutral no-man's-land. It does not seem to be clear to the authors that the paradigm from which they apparently draw their arguments is political precisely because it claims to be "objective," "value-free," "scientific."

While these authors clearly stress the primacy of (contemplative) science over the women's movement, other critics view this position and the one represented in the "Methodological Postulates" as "complementary" (Ruitenberg, Blom, van de Brink, and de Coole, 1981). Others believe that it is a matter of two overly-precisely formulated extreme positions within the same theoretical paradigm, which differ only gradually and quantitatively. The "truth" is to be found somewhere in the middle between the positions of Maria Mies and the authors of "In Praise of Reason." They warn, above all, of over-meticulousness in the application of the Postulates and of the generality of such terms as "Political affiliation," "affectedness and concern (Betroffenheit)," and "the women's movement." They believe that violence would be done to the nuances and shades, to the pluralistic diversity of women's experience and women's research, through the use of such general formulations. The Postulates lead to an uncritical usage of such terms, to dogmatism and to an underestimation of the differences between women (Komter and Mossink, 1980; Göttner-Abendroth, 1983).

I should like to stress, to the contrary, that the definitions of the relationship between the women's movement and women's research, as outlined in the "Methodological Postulates" and in the contribution of Bleich, Jansz and Leyendorff, are two qualitatively different initiatives which have been derived from different understandings of politics and science. To view one initiative as scientific and the other as propagandistic is to avoid the heart of the problem. We are dealing with political and epistemological concepts fundamentally different in their tendencies, which cannot be simply linked one to the other, pluralistically and additively, according to the motto, "A bit of feminism, a bit of positivism." It is no accident that the criticism was ignited principally by Postulate Four, "Participation in social actions and struggles, and the integration of research into these processes, further implies that the change of the status quo becomes the starting point for a scientific quest. The motto for this approach could be: In order to understand a thing, one must change it." It is precisely this last sentence which points in a direction wholly opposed to the dominant scientific paradigm. While dominant science views things as static, dualistically ahistorical, mechanical, and additive, feminist science, which has not lost sight of its political goal, strives for a new view of the whole societal constellation in which things appear as historical, contradictory, linked to each other, and capable of being changed. Feminist science does not hover, all-knowing like God our Father or Goddess our Mother, over the women's movement; it is a part of this movement or it is nothing.

The determination of the relationship between politics and science, women's movement and women's research, depends upon the determination of the goal of scientific (and political) activity. For the authors of "In Praise of Reason" it is the acquisition of knowledge which is the unequivocal goal of science. This knowledge should, in turn, lead to an understanding of reality. In order to be able to correctly understand reality, however, "scientific activity" should be "as objective as possible" (Bleich, Jansz, and Leyendorff, 1980). They criticize the emphasis placed upon subjectivity in many contributions to the debates on women's research and believe that due to individual preference such an approach would lead to distorted results. Feminist research would be transformed into an instrument of propaganda and degenerate into an ideology. True (faithful to reality) insight is, however, assured the researchers who concern themselves with "objectivity," "rationality," "logic," and the "power of abstraction." They criticize (in my opinion, rightly so) the fact that many in the women's movement view rationality, logic, and powers of abstraction as masculine qualities and emotionality as feminine. Yet with the simple condemnation of this attitude, they are passing over the central problem here, namely that they employ the terms rationality, logic, power of abstraction, entirely uncritically as universal and timeless criteria for understanding reality, without enquiring as to their roots in European bourgeois thought (cf. Böhme, 1980). It is for this reason that these terms contribute less today to the exposure than to the veiling of sexist and capitalist control (cf. Gerrits, 1980).

Because many of the critics do not question the validity of the theoretical-scientific foundation upon which they base their thought—be it positivism or logical empiricism, be it structuralism or structuralistic Marxism à la Althusser—but instead equate it with science itself, they consciously or unconsciously criticize the "Methodological Postulates" with that understanding of science as the criterion.

Even Heide Göttner-Abendroth, in her criticism of the "Methodological Postulates" and in her own approach is, in the final analysis, bound to this scientific paradigm. She does indeed regard involvement and commitment as important conditions for critical women's research, but only at the "prescientific level," for the intuitive formulation of an insight-producing study. At the narrowly-defined "scientific level" the problem to be studied is then formulated scientifically and investigated in a methodologically systematic manner—in our case using the methodology of women's research (isn't this a case of the cat biting its own tail?). Also at this level there should take place an ideologically critical discussion of the state of research in the field and, above all, a defining of the central concepts and construction of a theory. In a third step the theory should again be mediated back into the social context.

This three-step process corresponds exactly with the conventional understanding of science. That which always remains open to question in this approach remains open in Heide Göttner-Abendroth's work, namely the question of the mediation among these steps and, moreover, the question as to how the scientific-theoretical insight gained is to be channeled back into the social context.

In conventional science, this lies outside the realm of responsibility of the scientist (Ulrike Büchner calls this the Oppenheimer effect). Heide Göttner-Abendroth ends up in essentially the same position. No word of the women's movement from which, at one time, this whole thing started. Is that accidental? I do not believe so, because if women's research wants only to introduce the theme "woman" into dominant science, cut off as it is from political praxis, instead of besieging science in its ivory tower, then it is cutting itself off from the women's movement and will become an interminable "scientific discourse," an end in itself.

If we understand feminist research and science as part of the historical movement out of which it has emerged, then it is, in my view, impossible to cling to the dichotomy between thought and action, science and politics. We are then left with no alternative but to question contemplative science, which veils power and exploitation, as something which divides historical reality into separate areas and sets it upon its head. To fight for the involvement of more women in the scientific organizations and for the integration of women's issues into the existing disciplines cannot be our only goal. It is much more a matter of creating an alternative scientific paradigm which supports emancipatory movements and does not limit them as dominant science does.[3]

The attempt to create a new definition of science from within the context of the women's movement, a feminist science, necessarily leads to a new definition of the whole constitution of society, to a new definition of the relationship between humankind and nature, between women and men, humans and work, a new definition of the relationship with one's own body, a new definition which excludes exploitation. The "other view" which we cast over reality from the perspective of our own subjective experience shows us not only that we women do not appear in the dominant view of the world and science, but also that this whole view is wrong, wrong because it continually leaves in darkness and detaches from societal processes those who are exploited and ruled over: women, colonies, nature. In order to maintain this darkness in the minds of the oppressed, it is necessary to divide people into "working," "active" (hands) and "thinking" (brain) parts on the one hand and "natural," i.e. unconsciously functioning (stomach, heart) parts on the other. I believe that feminist science can have no interest in this division. It is, moreover, in the position to progress from an analysis of the smallest of the above-mentioned relationships, namely that with one's own body or that between man and woman, to an analysis of global relations, since in all of these relationships one finds similar structures of authority, power, and exploitation. The analysis of violence against women which grew out of the work done at women's shelters opened up access not only to an understanding of structural violence in the Western welfare states (cf., Frauenhaus Köln, 1980 [Women's Shelter Cologne]; Bolder, Lütkes, Möller, and Seppelfricke, 1981), but also to an analysis of the exploitation of the Third World. This other total perspective on societal reality is, however, only possible when we radically think through our own involvement, i.e. when we comprehend that the "small," ever-different relationships in which we experience exploitation and oppression (or release) are linked with the "big" material and historical (and not just ideological) relationships.

Research Methods

The criticism of the "Methodological Postulates" also extended to the research methods (in the narrow sense) linked with this initiative. It concentrated, on the one hand, on the emphasis on the category of personal experience and, on the other, on the preference, imputed to me, for "soft" i.e. qualitative ("feminine") as opposed to "hard" i.e. quantitative ("masculine") methods.

Geertje Thomas-Lycklama concedes that personal experiences, which are important in creating awareness of women's oppression have no place among the so-called hard methods used almost exclusively in sociology and economics. On the other hand, she believes that women's research cannot forego the use of quantitative methods, statistics, etc. (1979). Some criticize my essay because they believe that many women, after reading it, will content themselves with simply listing their own experiences and those of other women without making any attempt at analysis or interpretation (Bleich, Jansz, and Leyendorff, 1980; Wiemann, 1980; Ruitenberg, Blom, van de Brink, and de Coole, 1981). I can agree in part with the contention that the mere description of mostly individual experiences does not add up to a scientific treatment of a problem. It is correct that many women remain mired in the describing of experiences. In my view, however, the reason for this lies not in intellectual laziness, as the critics suspect, but in a superficial, individualistic, and deterministic concept of experience. Experience is often equated with personal experience, with the atmosphere, the feelings which a woman has in a certain situation. In my opinion, however, experience means taking real life as the starting point, its subjective concreteness as well as its societal entanglements. We should not forget that the challenge to begin with our own experience arose out of our frustration at the realization that women's lives, their history, their struggles, their ideas constitute no part of dominant science. The introduction of the category of experience or the "subjective factor" into science corresponded with the slogan, "The personal is political." The forced subordination of this subjective factor to a concept of science which equates objectivity with truth is accepted by women to the same small degree as they themselves have access to this science. If we do not want to consent to our own scientific nonbeing, then we must have a basis upon which we can stand, from which we can be sure of reality, and from which we can judge theories opposed to our own. To begin with, that basis is none other than subjective experience, our own critical self-reflection on it and the resultant practice. According to my understanding, however, this term denotes more than specific, momentary, individual involvement. It denotes the sum of the processes which individuals or groups have gone through in the production of their lives; it denotes their reality, their history.

Moreover, it should be pointed out that even logical-empirical science relies upon the concept of experience, of empiricism, to verify its own results. In contrast to the feminist researcher, however, the researcher from this school consciously disregards his own concrete experience of life as well as all historical experience. Empiricism for him is the testing of hypotheses in laboratory situations. Research does not take place directly within life's processes but "afterward," i.e. when the "research objects" have been detached from their real-life surroundings and broken down into their constituent parts. This empirical research is forever engaged in the dissection of corpses.

In feminist research we counter this alienated concept of empiricism with the old and new concept of experience as it determined the knowledge of all women and men who are still involved in material life and production processes (e.g., the knowledge of the midwives earlier). This concept includes our experience of our own bodies as well as our experience with the environment. It mediates between internal and external matters.

The criticism that the category of experience is aligned with the "soft" methods and that these methods merely oppose the "hard," "masculine" i.e. quantitative methods, misses the real problem. The real problem lies in the fact that scientific research methods are instruments for the structuring of reality. This reality is presently structured in such a way that only that which is quantifiable qualifies as "real."

My criticism of quantifying methods is not directed against every form of statistics but at its claim to have a monopoly on accurately describing the world. Statistics, too, derives its definitions of women from the prevailing sexist ideology. They are based almost exclusively on the image of woman constructed during the rise of capitalism during the nineteenth century, namely that of a housewife dependent upon a male "provider" (cf. Bock and Duden, 1977). The fact that this image does not correspond with the experience of the majority of women of the world has caused the statisticians to change their definition hardly at all. It would be naïve to believe that statistical procedures are free of certain ideologies which stabilize the power relations.[4] On the contrary, they serve to legitimize and universalize them because they give the stamp of "truth" to the definitions which lie at their base. Since everybody knows that male scientists are of the opinion that women all over the world are housewives, (like their own wives), they are considered housewives in science (Machewski, 1979), and the policies designed for them will treat them as such, irrespective of their social reality. Moreover, we should not forget that the so-called soft, qualitative methods were also developed as instruments for the exercise of dominion, namely in the field of ethnology which arose in conjunction with colonialism. The difference between quantitative and qualitative methods lies, in my view, in the fact that the qualitative methods, despite ideological distortion, do not break living connections in the way that quantitative methods do. It is in this sense that I regard them as more useful for women's research.

The Relationship between Action and Research

A further stumblingblock was the challenge to replace contemplative spectator research with active involvement in emancipatory actions and the integration of research into such movements and actions. Since this was illustrated using the example of an action research project in the women's shelter in Cologne, several critics came to the conclusion that I should like to restrict women's research to similar actions and action research. Yet they certainly have an extremely specific preconception of action and action research. An "action" in their sense of the term usually means a narrowly defined set of aims of a particular group fighting against a social injustice, for example, discrimination. Their preconception of action research is similarly narrow and pragmatic.

Understood by this is the mostly planned intervention in social relations, usually with the cooperation and control of the authorities and accompanied by scientists, a form of social engineering.

My criticism of this kind of action research seems to have escaped the critics. But against this background it is understandable that some of them want to make a distinction between "consciousness-raising" research and action research (Komter and Mossink, 1980) or that they believe that there are many areas of women's research, e.g. historical research, which cannot be reduced to an action research model. One does not need a theory to undertake an action, just "anger" (Komter and Mossink, 1980). In my opinion, the separation of praxis from theory is here being furthered. For otherwise the critics would surely have grasped the fact that not every "action" is de facto emancipatory practice, but that an "action" will frequently end in circular, fruitless activism and further, that it can provide no thoroughgoing change in consciousness if it is not translated into an ongoing praxis.

In fact, many feminists believe that in order to overcome women's oppression it will suffice for change to take place in the consciousness of as many women (and men) as possible. They often overlook the fact that women and men are bound by existing social relationships which do not simply change as consciousness does. We know today, for example, that many women lose their jobs, even in the universities, despite their supposedly emancipatory consciousness (cf. the documentation of Kruttwa-Schott, Jurczyk, and Gravenhorst). Or they remarry in order to ensure their financial situation. These examples make it clear that the separation of consciousness raising from the struggle for an alternative to oppressive conditions (that is to say, the power structure) leads to a dead end. If women forego the opportunity to construct alternative institutions or organizations, which is to say centers of opposition, during their consciousness-raising processes and their research, then they have no other option but to adapt once more to the male power structures. The construction of such centers of opposition does not, however, transpire through enlightenment alone but demands praxis, i.e. struggle, a movement.

In calling for an integration of research and science in an emancipatory praxis process, I do not have in mind a particular action or action research model in the above-mentioned surface and activist sense. It is much more a matter of the reunification of life and thought, action and knowledge, change and research. I can imagine no freedom for women without this reunification. This is not to say that every single women's research project must have direct relation to an action. Nor does it mean that feminist researchers themselves must everywhere attempt to introduce some kind of action. In my postscript to the English version of the essay I said that researchers are indeed able to join with social movements but are rarely in a position to initiate such movements. The integration of research into emancipatory processes also calls, naturally, for theory work, for work in libraries and archives, and also for the study of history. However, in contrast to dominant science, this theory work is not an end in itself but remains linked with the social movement for the liberation of women.

The achievement of such a reunification, using examples from my own experience of praxis and research, is illustrated below.

The Relationship of Researcher to Research Object

The criticism of the "Methodological Postulates for Women's Research" concerned itself not only with the essay itself. It was also directed at the reception of this essay by different women who, in the opinion of the critics, had applied in an all too undifferentiated and uncritical fashion the First Postulate, that women's research should give up the indifferent, supposedly neutral spectator attitude toward research objects and replace it with a conscious partiality based on a partial identification.

Geertje Thomas-Lycklama wrote,

> It is already difficult for Dutch researchers to identify, even partially, with, for example, women farmers from Hintertupfingen or working girls in a cookie factory. It will be even more difficult for Western researchers to partially identify with the poorest and most oppressed women of the developing countries. Skin color, the speaking of another language, etc., play an important role among the factors which stand in the way of an identification. (1979, p. 15)

From the German discussions of women's research, we too are aware of the problem which Geertje Thomas is here addressing. Some maintain that the postulate of partial identification can only be realized if like study like. According to this belief, nonmothers could not carry out research on mothers, nor white women on black women, professors on students, attorneys on battered women, educated women on uneducated women, women who have not been raped on women who have, etc.

This concept of partial identification leads to the following viewpoints: (1) Identification with the "research object," "empathy," and an attainment of the "inner-view of the oppressed" are not viewed as partial identification but as total identification. (2) The relationship of researcher to research object is not understood as a material one but as a strictly moral (or psychic) one. To identify with other, above all poorer, less privileged, women is viewed as a moral appeal. The relationship arises only nominally from the insight into one's own contradictory levels of being and consciousness and those of the "other" women. "Identification" in this instance usually means dropping down to the level of the "others" (poorer, more exploited etc.), or "de-classing" oneself, as it is termed in leftist jargon. This "identification" can easily lead to the desire to idealistically leap over the real, existing societal relations by means of a kind of representative politics. This leads to (3), wherein the actual differences in power which exist among women are ignored and therefore cannot be employed productively, i.e. used for the liberation of women.

Partial identification does not mean, however, that I attempt to "become like" the "other" women, since this is not possible. Nor does it mean that I identify totally with my respective "role" (mother, professor, attorney, student, etc.); that is not necessary because we are of course much more than just these roles. The problem is not that some women have more power and some less, but rather how to most positively employ in the struggle against women's exploitation and oppression the qualitatively and quantitatively different power potentials of women involved in the research process.

Contribution to a Feminist Understanding of Science

The discussion of the criticisms of the "Methodological Postulates for Women's Research" clearly shows that at issue here is a different understanding of science from the one we find in the dominant scientific paradigm. We initially called this alternative understanding "feminist" because the political aim of our efforts is most clearly expressed in this term. This goal is the overcoming of women's exploitation and oppression. Initially we criticized the dominant paradigm from the perspective of this feminist understanding of science. It is not enough, however, to remain at the level of pure criticism of science. We must also attempt to arrive at a positive determination of that which we understand to be feminist science. Some basic elements of this determination have already been formulated in the Postulates, but they need to be deepened and extended. In order to do this, a further discussion of several central terms is necessary. The terms "affectedness and concern" and "partial identification" are central terms of the new feminist initiative. These terms form a logical whole, i.e. the one follows from the other.

Since the extension and deepening of the theoretical foundations (that is to say, the "creation of theory") are born, above all, out of the reflection on praxis processes, I should like to begin here by reporting on the experiences which I myself had with this methodological approach between 1978 and 1981. I shall restrict myself to two examples: (1) My experiences with a research project which I carried out among rural Indian women for the International Labor Organization, Geneva, and (2) the experiences which I have had as coordinator of the "Women and Development" program at the Institute of Social Studies, the Hague.

First Example: The Rural Women Workers of Nalgonda, or: The Reconciliation of Research with the Women's Movement.

The general problem complex which occupied me as I formulated my project proposal was the concern with getting to the root of the relationship between capitalist development and patriarchal structures. I was especially interested in probing into the effects which market-economic (capitalist) developments have on poor rural women in the Third World. The project was carried out in 1978–79 in two areas of the Indian state of Andhra Pradesh among home workers around the small city of Narsapur (cf. Mies, 1982) and among rural workers in the Nalgonda district. In the following I will concentrate only on the experiences which we—my two Indian women coworkers and myself—had with the latter group.[5]

In order to reconcile research with the women's movement, I had consciously chosen an area where there was already a movement, a movement of poor farmers organized by a rural development organization.[6] This movement had already begun to organize the women into their own village groups or "Sangams." We therefore made contact with these people, described the project, and asked if we could carry it out in several villages.

Both the organizers and the women received us with great openness. The women even wanted for us to be able to see every village where there was a women's Sangam—something which proved impossible because of time restraints. After this contact had been established it became a matter of getting a "view from below" of the normal, everyday reality of these women. Researchers in Third World villages usually make contact with the poor through village leaders or other rich and influential people. They live in the houses of these people and receive most of their information from them and not from the poor themselves.

We decided to share, as far as possible, the living conditions of the rural women workers. We lived in their settlements, some of the time in a hut which had been placed at our disposal and the rest of the time together with the women. We fetched water from the well as they did, cooked our food in the same way, slept on the clay ground like them, and, like them, had to relieve ourselves in an open field since there were none of the amenities of civilization in these villages. We also accompanied the women as they worked in the fields and took part in some of the work ourselves, even if only "for fun." In this way we established a relationship between them and us from the outset. Without such a relationship no research would have been possible. Through this participation in their life, we also learned more about the division of labor according to gender, more about working hours, wages, exploitation, patriarchal structures, and the women's forms of resistance than we could have had we followed the usual research methods.

Alongside this direct participation in their lives we also carried out many discussions. Sometimes they were unplanned; sometimes we organized group discussions in which not only did we probe the connections between the lives of these women and their subjective opinions about them, but they also carried out their research on us. They wanted to know whether we were married, had children, what we did during menstruation, whether all the women in my country wore trousers, why we were doing this research, what a woman rural worker earned in my country, whether the people there also ate rice, etc. All communication took place in the Telugu language which my coworkers spoke. I knew only a little Telugu, but the language barrier was not the greatest of problems in this form of reciprocal research. For these poor women our presence in their village was an event. Every evening after work they came and sat with us behind our huts where we were undisturbed by the men who otherwise continually attempted to speak for the women. Since they usually sang while working in the fields and we were interested in their songs, these after-work meetings usually ended with singing and dancing. We thereby learned that these women still had their own culture, independent of that of the men. Moreover, we attempted to pass on to the women as soon as possible the results of our work, which meant during the course of the research process itself. Toward the end of the research phase in this area we arranged, together with the organizers of the movement, several weekend camps for the rural women workers. Through these camps we hoped not only that women from other villages would discover something about us and our research, but above all that women from the individual village-Sangams, who to this point were organized only at the village level, would be able to exchange their experiences with women from other villages, i.e. that they would carry out "research" among themselves. This was the first time that these hardworking women had had a free weekend for themselves, unmolested by children and husbands. Most of the camps were held at a college in a small town where the women could also spend the night. The exchange between the women took the form of role-playing exercises, testimonies, songs, and original poetry, which were then discussed.[7] We in turn reported on our experiences or showed slides which we had made as part of our research.

The women were so enthusiastic about these regional women's conferences that they wanted to make them monthly occurrences. The organizers thought that would be asking too much and were afraid that the men would rebel. The women, however, insisted that these camps should take place regularly. When I visited the women again at the end of 1980 they had already arranged 13 such conferences. It is possible that the women would have started these conferences without our involvement, but our research project and our initiative represented an important stimulus for the rural women's movement at a time when the groups were not yet able by themselves to get beyond the village horizon.

Our results were put to further use when the report on this organization was translated into Telugu and made available for discussion by one of our Indian coworkers who today organizes similar educational events for poor rural women on a larger scale. In addition, the report was published in English in Delhi in the feminist journal *Manushi*. That such a reconciliation of research with the women's movement leads to very different, much richer theoretical and political insights than the usual form of research only became clear to me after the fact, when I heard how the rural working women used these conferences not only for discussion but also for the solution of class and man-woman problems besetting them, e.g. the problem of violent men. Whereas, during our first year there, male violence was treated more or less as an everyday thing which women simply had to accept, one year later it was being hotly debated in the whole area, by women and by men.

The impetus for this was the fact that a certain Mrs. Rukamma, who also played an important role in the women's Sangams, was regularly beaten by her husband after she returned home from the women's meetings. Because the women now had a communications network and an organization of their own and because their consciousness had changed over the course of time, they now said, "Enough is enough. The beatings must stop." They began by discussing the matter in their women's groups and came to a conclusion: "If a man and a woman cannot live together in peace, then the man must leave the hut, since the hut belongs to the woman. Our workplace is there, we cannot leave. The men can easily go to the city." This resolution was then discussed in the whole region, and finally the men had to get involved in the argument. Some men claimed that one should not make a great deal out of the matter since it is something private between husband and wife. The women, however, said that it was not at all a private matter if Mrs. Rukamma could not come to their meetings without being beaten afterward.

These women had still never heard anything of feminism and were naturally unaware of the slogan, "the personal is political." Yet they recognized the truth of this slogan from their own experiences, their own praxis, and group reflection on it. Yet more, they immediately translated their realization into action. They put out the following call: If this man does not apologize, he will receive no more food or water from any woman in the village. He ultimately excused himself not only before his wife, but also before the women's group.

The insight which I have gained from this story is the following: Not only had we carried out some research, but also our Indian sisters, in addition, had succeeded in integrating it into their movement. The existence of an autonomous women's organization, the reciprocal exchange of their experiences with patriarchal authority, their anger, affectedness, concern, and commitment, and not least the creation of a communications network through the periodic women's conferences, gave the women so much courage and strength that they could tackle a taboo topic like violence against women. The interesting thing for me is that they went about it in a different way from what we in the women's shelter movement were used to. These rural working women recognized that it was primarily a matter of securing the woman's means of subsistence, i.e. her hut and her workplace. Therefore they said, "The man must go!" We, on the other hand, fetch the battered women from their apartments and give them protection in the women's shelters. They usually have to search for a long time before finding another apartment.

By acting as they did, the Indian rural working women imparted to me the important political and theoretical insight that even we cannot solve the problem of male violence if the material basis for a woman's existence, i.e. her apartment primarily, is not better secured. Would it not also be possible here to fight for the forced eviction of a violent man from an apartment instead of making the woman and children leave? Should we not be leading a political struggle to gain for women control of their homes, instead of exhausting our strength in endless hours of voluntary social work?

This brings me to the second essential theoretical insight which I gained from this form of research, namely, the importance of an autonomous women's organization. Contradicting the claim of the Left that an autonomous women's organization will divide "class loyalty," these women have shown me that just the opposite is true. The women use their organization not only in the struggle against the violence of their own husbands but also against their landlords. The strength of the class of rural workers and poor farmers was doubled through the women's organization.

It would never have been possible for me to gain either of these insights by way of conventional research methods.

Second Example: "Fieldwork in Women's Studies," Holland, 1979–81.

After the conclusion of my field research in India, I received an offer from the Institute of Social Studies (ISS) in the Hague to generate and coordinate a new study and research program with the title "Women and Development." I accepted this offer.[8]

In order to translate the "Methodological Postulates" into praxis and to make available to women students from the Third World who participated in the "Women and Development" program a field of teaching and research outside that of the contemplative academic teaching of the ISS, I entered into the teaching schedule a course with the title "Fieldwork in Holland." This field-work took the form of small groups of Third World women coming into contact with Dutch women's groups which were working on a project or participating in a movement. The aim of this attempt was to confront the women from the Third World with the problems of women in so-called developed countries, to make the theoretical knowledge which they had gained from their studies refer to "real life," for them to enter into reciprocal learning and research processes with Dutch women's groups, for all of them to reflect as a group on these new experiences, and, if possible, to conceptualize brief, communal plans of action.

There were some difficulties and struggles linked with this two-year experiment. In order to integrate the "Fieldwork" into the regular ISS study plan, the status quo had to be disrupted in many ways. The Institute recognized only theoretical courses of study without practical components. Considerable struggles were required to make it clear to the academic authorities that "Fieldwork" could be a worthwhile experiment. Since they (overwhelmingly men—there were only three women among sixty colleagues!) could have nothing against experiments—especially in such an "unserious" matter as women's studies— they allowed us (i.e. my students, my predecessor Mia Berden, who has since retired, and myself) to go ahead.

At the same time I myself was a stranger in Holland and was reliant upon Dutch women to arrange the contact between the Third World women and Dutch women's groups. In order to facilitate this another change in the status quo was required: I opened up the "Women and Development" class to Dutch women students. This too had never happened at the Institute. This innovation was initially received unenthusiastically but was "endured" for the above reasons. In this way we attained two things: First, there were more women in the class, i.e. more "presence," and that also meant more "power" than we would have had otherwise; second, there was now a personal and direct connection between women from the Third World and Dutch feminists interested in the Third World. Many of the artificial barriers jealously maintained in usual scientific enterprise between people who do indeed have something in common or want to have were broken down, for example, the barrier between women engaged in science and women "outside" and the barrier between women "developed" and "underdeveloped" countries. The Dutch women students played an essential mediatory role in this fieldwork. They themselves belonged to feminist groups or arranged the contact with women's groups and interpreted for the Third World women. It should also be mentioned that in the execution of this "Fieldwork" there were not only successes but also some frustrations and failures.

They were due, in part, to a lack of time—there were only three months available for the "Fieldwork"—and to organizational problems, but also to other forms of resistance to the initiative. For example, one group in the first year (1979) wanted to make contact with unionized women workers. Mia Berden provided a good contact with a leading woman in the FNV, the Dutch labor union organization, who was responsible for women's concerns. She was greatly interested in working together with the women students from the Third World who, in turn, were highly motivated to discover how women workers in Holland live, which problems they have as workers and as women, and so forth. Despite this motivation, no contact with Dutch workers was possible before the end of the course. The students went through the official, institutional channels, i.e. through the union bureaucracy. They thereby discovered that the apparatus is hermetically sealed against the outside world and that women have very little say in its running, that even the contacted official could do nothing without her boss, and that there was considerable resistance on the part of the leading union men to such a direct contact between union women and "other" women. Despite their frustration at not coming face to face with a Dutch woman worker, regardless of all their attempts, the students did gain essential insights. They now understood that they would never get near the women via such a bureaucratic "view from above." They had never dreamed that a labor union in a developed country would be such a hermetically sealed, impenetrable, male-dominated power structure. In none of their countries would they have experienced the difficulties that they did in Holland. Everywhere would it have been possible to reach the people to whom one wanted to speak, if not through official channels then certainly through unofficial ones. Admittedly, the "Fieldwork" had not led to the expected results, but instead it had confronted the students with the reality of patriarchal-bureaucratic structures as scarcely any other method could do.

Between 1979 and 1981 the women students of the ISS worked together with the following Dutch groups: The Women's Project in "DePijp," Amsterdam; the Turkish women's group "Schildershage," the Hague; the Surinamian-Dutch Women's Group ANS, the Hague; the women in the Industry Association FNV, the Hague; the Women's Health Center, Utrecht; the Open School for Women, Amsterdam; the Single Parenthood Group, resp. the BOM-Mothers, Amsterdam; a group of Women against Fascism, Rotterdam; and the Latin American workgroup V.K.W., Utrecht.

Meeting with "other affected women," in this case with Dutch women, opened up a new horizon of thought for the women from the Third World, a new perspective on their own societal reality, through that of a world of prejudices, pre-judgments, so-called scientific insights and of universally held norms which prove to be at the very least relative when not genuinely mystifying.

To these mystifications belong, for example, the following opinions:

The cultural differences between women from the Third World and the "First World" are so great that there can scarcely be any similarities between these two groups. Or: The major problem facing Western women is the man-woman issue; that facing Third World women, however, is poverty. Or: Questions of sexuality and of one's own body can indeed be discussed by European women but are taboo for women from the Third World because they are too constrained by tradition. Or: The different experiments undertaken by feminists to reshape human relations would only frighten away women from the Third World, since they still hold true to an unequivocal and fixed concept of family.

After the "Fieldwork" with the Utrecht health collective, several women said: "We now understand that the whole talk about women from the 'Third' and from the 'First World' being so different is only a trick to keep us separated. We have ascertained that women here have the same problems with men as we do, sometimes even worse. The so-called cultural differences are indeed there but we also have much in common in questions of sexuality and man-woman relationships."

A woman from the Philippines who had worked with the "BOM-Mothers" of Amsterdam said: "I always believed that Western values and Western institutions were good for the West but not for us. Now I have seen that Western values do not function in the West either. For example, the nuclear family, which I had learnt was functional for a modern society, no longer functions here and gives women nothing."

For a woman from the Philippines it was initially impossible to comprehend that women might indeed want to have children, but no husband. Yet after she had worked with these women, after they had talked together during this process, she understood why these women do not want to have husbands and what actually goes on between men and women in these small families here. This knowledge gained through experience led her to the insight that the small family does not even work for women here. It was an essential experience for her and the other women to see that repression and violence against women have not disappeared in an affluent, developed society, but have simply assumed different forms from those in their own countries. For example, they recognized what a fetter romantic love is for European women. Asiatic and African women are psychically much less dependent upon "love" than we. They began to comprehend that much of what they had learned in their universities about the progress of modern societies was simply untrue. This knowledge awakened in them a new critical consciousness with regard to many of the theories which had been presented to them.

Some of the most important insights gained from the two-year attempt at applying the "Methodological Postulates" within the "Fieldwork" are as follows:[9]

1. In contrast to the dominant scientific paradigm, various forms of knowledge were suited to the "Fieldwork" and not just one form (so-called scientific). These included practical, everyday knowledge, political knowledge and political "skills," self-recognition (insight into one's own strengths and weaknesses), critical knowledge (the ability to critique ideologies, to demystify), theoretical knowledge (the ability to relate empirical findings to theoretical statements), social knowledge (the ability to relate to others, to recognize social conditions and develop social relationships with "others"; to recognize that individuals live in certain relationships with each other and with their material, social, and historical environment).

Since they are linked together, all of these forms of knowledge are necessary for an emancipatory research and learning process, not just one which, once set, then claims primacy over all the others as the "scientific" knowledge. In "Fieldwork" the artificially constructed barriers which usually exist among the different forms of knowledge (usually erected along the lines delimiting the academic disciplines) were broken through and there arose something akin to a total view of reality.

2. This was possible because the research and learning situation was not a laboratory situation, but a real-life, everyday situation. The problems to be studied were defined by the Third World women and the Dutch women together. In this way it became clear to both which questions were important and which were not. The questions as the students had initially envisioned them had to be modified after contact with the Dutch women.

3. The confrontation with "other women" and the reality of their lives caused many questions to arise in the minds of the Third World women, questions about themselves, the situation of women in their countries, their institutions and value systems, areas which were previously largely taboo, e.g. one's own body, sexuality, etc. At first this confrontation initiates a process of un-learning, i.e. a critical testing of that which the women had previously regarded as "normal," "natural," "correct," "universal," and which had been presented to them at school and university as scientifically proven. They saw that the reality of the "other women's" lives did not correspond to their institutionally acquired knowledge.

4. The Third World as well as the Dutch women brought their "affected-ness," i.e. their subjectivity and concern, into the research situation. This did not hinder the research process but rather furthered it because it sharpened and extended perceptions and prompted new questions. The research situation was a reciprocal one: Two groups of "other women" encountered each other and not only researched each other but plunged ever deeper into an investigation of that which constitutes the essence of women's exploitation and repression.

5. This reciprocal research was possible because, in contrast to the dominant understanding of science, the research situation did not represent a power

relationship. The women from the Third World were indeed students, but in this situation the "privilege" was neutralized on account of their coming from underdeveloped, poor countries.

This combination of contradictions led to important insights on both sides: The Dutch women saw that not all women in the Third World are "poor" and that despite "underdevelopment," Third World women were freer in some respects than they themselves.

Conversely, the women from the Third World saw that capitalist development of material riches and the supposedly progressive small family do not free women but have instead made them profoundly more dependent.

6. This new perspective also had the tendency to lead to another view of the totality of society. A new perspective on the totality of society means, however, that we bring relationships to light which previously remained in darkness. That is to say, when we speak of women, we must speak of men; when we study poverty, we must study wealth; when we speak of the Third World, we must speak of the "First World." In dominant science one of the two sides is always left in darkness. Feminist science, alternatively, must concern itself with both sides because the one conditions the other. This became clear to me by extension in the "Fieldwork."

7. The fieldwork also broke through the cultural-relativist mystification according to which we here are so very different from the people in Africa or Asia, for example. How often do we hear from well-intentioned people that we are in no position to say what is good for Indian or Filipino women, since their culture is so very different from ours? What might be good for us is by no means good for other cultures. Through the reciprocal research in the fieldwork it was clearly established that it is not culture which separates us, but rather the fact that there are simply different manifestations of patriarchal man-woman relations and that these differences are stressed above all by those who want to maintain these relations.

8. During this reciprocal research and learning process a new concept of intersubjectivity arose. Intersubjective comparability is the reality of criterion of empirical, analytical science. It is to be achieved by excluding subjective elements from the research process wherever possible. What emerges is certainly not "objectivity" in the sense of truth to reality, but rather total fetishism and alienation.

Intersubjectivity in the sense of feminist research was developed in the "Fieldwork" through the application of the principles of double consciousness and partial identification. The criticized tendency to total identification which is usually moralistically and paternalistically motivated could not arise in this situation. That was attributable, in part, to the fact that no one side could derive any kind of material advantage from the relationship, there was nobody who wanted to "help" the others.

The attempt at a total identification was also excluded by the fact that the "otherness" in this meeting of "other women" led to a new view of oneself. The women from the Third World began to discover themselves and their society in distancing themselves from it. This dialectic process which consists of one being able to observe oneself from outside is, in my opinion, identical to that which is indicated by the term double consciousness. The outside in this case is not, however, some imaginary reality, but rather the real, living other woman who is looking at me, trying to understand me, posing unusual questions. The outside, therefore, consists of another "ensemble of social relations" and that also means that a total identification, even if it were to be attempted, is not possible. For despite all the empathy, all the understanding, the others remain "others."

On the other hand, the reciprocal research process led to the women's ability to discuss among themselves the most strongly taboo questions of sexuality and their relations with men. On this point they ascertained that, despite all of the different cultural manifestations, all women share a common affectedness, that there are not only differences but also commonalities between different groups of women. This recognition led to the ISS women students' referring to themselves from that point on as the "Feminists from the 'Third World' " and coining the slogan,

Culture divides us
Struggle unites us

During the reciprocal research and learning process, there arose new questions on both sides and a great theoretical curiosity to understand how things had come to be the way they are today. Furthermore, this experience led the women from the Third World to devise concrete plans of action and project ideas as to how to implement in their own countries that which they had experienced and how they could promote international contact among women.[10]

Against the background of these experiences, it is now also possible for us to come to an expanded and more profound understanding of the terms "partial identification" and "affectedness and concern."

The concept of partial identification means first that we proceed from our own contradictory state of being and consciousness. That is to say, not only do the "other" women have a problem, but I do, too. It means, further, that I no longer want to repress this contradiction. This enables recognition of that which binds me to the "other women" as well as that which separates me from them. Binding us are the experiences of women all over the world of repression, sexism, and exploitation. Partial identification means in addition that I also recognize what separates us. At the level of appearances that might be rooted in such traits as skin color, language, education, etc. (cf. Thomas-Lycklama, 1979). Yet in these appearances we see simply a manifestation of the power relations according to which the whole of society is structured; the appearances are not the actual relations. Under the rule of capital those are commodity and market relations which will, as a last resort, be created and maintained through the use of direct violence. Partial identification, which begins with a double consciousness, means, therefore, that we as researchers are aware of the objective structures within which we live and work.

When, for example, I carried out the ILO research project among rural Indian women workers, I found myself initially in a de facto commodity and power relationship with these women. I was being paid to do this research and to deliver some corresponding goods, namely research results. For their part, the rural women workers could not come to Germany and carry out research on us here. They were fully aware of the asymmetry of this relationship. This material relationship, mediated through the capitalistic connection between exploitation and world markets, could not be overcome through a short research visit and an idealistic attempt at identification with these poor women. Both groups of women involved in this research project recognized this. That was the first thing.

The other, however, was that that which had brought us together on the one hand and separated us on the other, namely class, imperialism, skin color, language, and education, was not total, but that there was a level at which we as women were similarly affected by patriarchal relationships and that there was room in this research process to talk with each other about this common experiential perspective. This level does of course lie deeper than the appearance level of cultural, economic, political differences. Because this level exists, women are in a position to communicate with each other as people across the different barriers. Labeling alone creates no communication. It arranges people together as if they were things. Partial identification is hence possible if we reject the total claim on our existence as a commodity, as exchange value, if we do not sublimate to commodity relations that part in us where we are afflicted and affected in our human beingness. We will thereby move into a position from which to recognize also the affectedness of the "other" women which perhaps finds expression in other forms.

Partial identification therefore makes possible the necessary closeness to the others as well as the necessary distance from myself.

Communication at this deeper level will, however, only be possible when women begin with their own affectedness and concern. This concept was also criticized by some as undifferentiated, monolithic. It is, therefore appropriate to define it more precisely.

It was in the search for an answer to the question of what binds us with battered women that the concept of "affectedness" arose. It designates much (something which was not clear to us at the outset):

1. "Affectedness" refers to the victim and object status of oppressed, humiliated, exploited beings who have become the target of violence and repression. That is to say, they have been directly affected at one time by aggression, injustice, discrimination. They are victims. When talk is of "the affected" in normal usage, it is usually only this level of meaning which is implied. The "affected" are "the others," not me myself (as a rule). From this understanding of affectedness there arises the moralistic and paternalistic fussing with which the "affected" are often treated by the "un-affected." They usually become renewed objects of "assistance" (social work, development help, Caritas) for which they are expected to be thankful. We, however, had all been directly affected ourselves at some time by male violence.

2. Also denoted by the concept of affectedness and concern is the conscious reflection in the mind on this condition, the shock and outrage at it. That is to

say, we are not dealing here with a mechanical stimulus-response scheme, but expressed in the concept of affectedness and concern is a quality of feeling which contains something akin to rebellion or anger. A first inner detaching from the victim status takes place through critical self-reflexivity and rebellion, a distancing, even if it is initially only at the emotional level. It begins the break with the continuity of the normal misery. It is difficult to say when the moment of the inner break has come and also what effect this inner detaching has on us. In the case of the women who came into the women's shelter, we found that the point in time was reached when they realized that they would lose their self-respect as human beings if they did not turn away, at least inwardly, from their tormentors. In my own case this point came only after I had gone away and been confronted by "other" women (in India). In the case of the ISS students it was similar. They discovered their own affectedness and therewith the gradual distancing from their normal women's misery only after meeting with the Dutch women. It is probably only possible for us to specify this point if the status quo has already been changed and we have completed the break with continuity.

3. The state of being affected and concerned and the perspective of critical self-reflexivity mean, additionally, becoming conscious. That is to say, the victims who began to rebel against their victim status are searching for explanations, for the causes of this situation. The dialectic movement within the victim who initially distances herself from her object status leads necessarily to criticism and analysis, and that means to the search for theoretical underpinnings for the bad status quo and for a liberation from it. Affectedness and concern mean then that the victims think their anger through to the end and emerge capable of action.

4. Affectedness only becomes a concept which transcends victim status when those affected do not remain at the level of simply coming to consciousness. Their societal being is far from being altered on account of that alone. In order to alter this, the dialectical movement in the one affected must press toward action. It cannot remain at the level of emotional outrage, of coming to consciousness, of criticism and analysis. If it does, it will inevitably end in resignation and regression.

Within the concept of affectedness all of these levels of meaning are at least implicitly present: being hurt and affected, outrage and anger, criticism and analysis, motivation for action, whatever else "the others" might experience that leads finally to the conviction that a change in the whole structure of society is needed. In this sense the term embraces several central fundamentals of a feminist theory of cognition.

The debate as to feminist research and methodology is not closed. I have tried to give answers to several questions; many have remained open. But if we want to move forward with the women's movement, or more precisely, if we do not want to lose that for which we have already fought, then it is important to understand that feminist research cannot simply be inserted into or added onto the old scientific paradigm, a scientific paradigm that everywhere splits up living unities into life and thought, politics (morality) and science, and which implies the dominion over women, primitive peoples, and other races. If we want to arrive at a new paradigm, a new horizon of thought and action in which these divided and subjugated parts coexist in a living, which is to say integrated, relationship, then we must "go beyond" the old paradigm, transcend it. But this cannot be a going beyond in thought alone, in a permanent academic discourse. A new horizon of thought must be one which—at least this applies to us as women—can be and then indeed is experienced. Without a change of position in the concrete sense, without praxis, without a change in the status quo, no new horizon will become visible. It is here especially that the confrontation with "other" women helps.

This does not mean that this going beyond is always a stroll in the park and that we experience no defeats along the way. The defeats are, however, only of consequence if we conclude from them that the entire undertaking of uniting politics and science, life, thought, and struggle, is the wrong track to take because it is no longer possible. Such a "turn" has to end with deadly consequences, either in resignation or prostitution in the dominant academic or political house of men. I see this happening above all in the different attempts being made to academicize women's studies, or in the giving up of feminist fundamentals—after they have first been set up as boogey men—(e.g., the way in which Sibylle Plogstedt deals with the concept of autonomy, cf. *Courage*, 1983), in order to enamor oneself of the existing institutions and organizations. We women must know that such opportunism is not worth it; it does not even guarantee us survival, much less a respectable existence.

We have a very old problem, and for its solution we need much patience and true radicalism. That also means, however, that we can afford to stay composed during times of defeat. The women's movement, often now pronounced dead by disappointed women, does not collapse because one action meets with no success. This applies particularly to our topic. Instead of making a "turn" to long rejected positions in the hope of perhaps still being able to find a place in the increasingly scarcer flesh-pots in the academic house of men, I regard it as more realistic to continue on the path embarked upon, especially now, as the house of men is beginning to crash in at the corners anyhow, as the cleverest men themselves move out and in their search for new horizons of thought and action look hopefully over at our "feminist" islands.

NOTES

1. The Dutch debate took place chiefly in the *Tijdschrift voor Vrouwenstudies*, in issues 2 and 3 (1980), 6 (1981), and 9 (1982). The first version of this present contribution was published in issue 9 (1982) in Dutch.

2. With Stalin's help, the dispute over genetics between the classical biologists and the Russian agronomist Lysenko was decided in Lysenko's favor. Later, however, Lysenko's theory was found to be incorrect.

3. Cees Hamelink draws a clear distinction between repressive and emancipatory research. Among the theories of science which are legitimized by repressive research he includes positivism or logical empiricism (cf. Cees Hamelink, "New Structure of International Communication: The Role of Research." ISS Occasional Paper No. 87, July, 1981).

4. I was able to see how lacking in objectivity supposedly neutral statistics could be during my research on the lace makers in India: The 150,000 to 200,000 of these women who worked at home were not even entered into the district census under the rubric "worker" or "home-worker." They were hidden away in the number of "nonworkers" which also included housewives. Yet these statistically nonexistent women annually created goods with a value of millions! (cf. Mies, 1982).

5. The comprehensive report on the research appeared as an ILO (Geneva) publication in 1986, "Indian Women in Subsistence and Agricultural Labour." A depiction of the organization of these women can be found in C. v. Werlhof, M. Mies, and V. Bennholdt-Thomsen, *Women, the Last Colony*, London: ZED Books, 1988.

6. This organization is called "Comprehensive Rural Operations Service Society" (CROSS). It is a politically independent organization and is also supported by "Brot für die Welt" (Bread for the World).

7. The method used here was a creative evolution of the method of Paulo Freire.

8. Within the framework of this program, a woman from the Third World can complete a fifteen-month period of study with a concentration in "Women and Development" and graduate as a Master of Development.

9. The experiences of the two-year experiment in implementing the new methodological initiatives were brought together in a report: Mia Berden and Maria Mies, "Experimenting With a New Methodological Approach: 'Fieldwork,'" in *Women's Studies*, Institute of Social Studies, 1979–81, The Hague: ISS, 1981.

10. A further activity which grew out of the "Fieldwork" was the founding by the ISS students of their own women's group and later an international network which they named "Insisterhood." Through the organization, which also sends out a newsletter, they try to maintain the contact and exchange with women after they have returned to their own countries.

REFERENCES

Berden, Mia, and Maria Mies. "Experimenting With a New Methodological Approach: 'Fieldwork,'" in Women's Studies, Institute of Social Studies, 1979–81. The Hague: Institute of Social Studies, 1981.

Bleich, Anet, Ulla Jansz, and Selma Leyendorff. "Lof der Rede," in Tijdschrift voor Vrouwenstudies, vol. 1, 2/1980.

Bock, Gisela, and Barbara Duden. "Arbeit aus Liebe—Liebe als Arbeit," in Gruppe Berliner Dozentinnen, ed., Frauen und Wissenschaft, Beiträge zur Berliner Sommeruniversität für Frauen 1976. Berlin: Courage-Verlag, 1977.

Böhme, Gernot. Alternativen der Wissenschaft. Frankfurt am Main: Suhrkamp, 1980.

Bolder, Barbara, Anne Lütkes, Carola Möller, and Rita Seppelfricke. "Frauenhaus Köln, Politische Arbeit oder Dienstleistung für den Sozialstaat?" in Alternative 139, 24, October 1981.

Frauenhaus Köln. Nachrichten aus dem Ghetto Liebe. Frankfurt am Main: Verlag Jugend und Politik, 1980.

Geisel, Beatrix. "Mitarbeit oder Verweigerung?" in Frankfurter Rundschau 1/25/84.

Gerrits, Corrie. "De Slaap van de Rede verwekt Monsters," in Tijdschrift voor Vrouwenstudies, vol. 1, 4/1980.

Göttner-Abendroth, Heide. "Wissenschaftstheoretische Positionen in der Frauenforschung," in Halina Bendkowski and Brigitte Weishaupt, eds. Was Philosophinnen denken: Eine Dokumentation. Zürich: Amman, 1983. Pp. 253ff.

Hamelink, Cees. "New Structure of International Communication: The Role of Research," Occasional Paper No. 87. The Hague: Institute of Social Studies, 1981.

Komter, Aafke, and Marijke Mossink. "Kennis of verandering: de wankele balans tussen wetenschap en politiek" in Tijsschrift voor Vrouwenstudies, vol. 1, 3/1980.

Machewski, Werner. "Socialweetenschappelijke methoden en hun vooronderstellingen over het ondersoeksobjekt," in Psychologie en maatschappij. Amsterdam: SUA, 1979. Reprinted in Methodologie, Theorie Feminisme. Utrecht: 1980.

Mies, Maria. "Methodische Postulate zur Frauenforschung: Dargestellt am Beispiel der Gewalt gegen Frauen," in Beiträge zur feministischen Theorie und Praxis, vol. 1, no. 1, Munich: 1978. Pp. 41–63.

———. "Methodische Postulate zur Frauenforschung," in Heksenkollege, verlagsboek over Vrouwen, wetenschap en kultuur. Nijmegen: University of Nijmegen, 1978.

———. "Towards a Methodology of Women's Studies," ISS Occasional Paper No. 77. The Hague: Institute of Social Studies, 1979.

———. "Hausfrauen produzieren für den Weltmarkt, die Spitzenmacherinnen von Narsapur," in Die Peripherie, 7, 1981/82.

———. The Lace Makers of Narsapur: Indian Housewives in the World Market. London: ZED Press, 1982.

———. "Towards a Methodology of Feminist Research," in Gloria Bowles and Renate Duelli Klein, eds. Theories of Women's Studies. London: Routledge & Kegan Paul, 1983.

———. Indian Women in Subsistence and Agricultural Labour. Geneva: International Labour Organization, 1986.

Plogstedt, Sibylle, "Wenn Autonomie zum Dogma wird," in Courage, December, 1983.

Ruitenberg, Christa, Stine Blom, Anja van de Brink, and Bookje de Coole. "Feministisch Onderzoek" (Paper). Utrecht: 1981.

Thomas-Lycklama, Geertje. "Feminisme en Wetenschap," Inaugural Lecture, Landbouwhogeschool Wageningen, 1979.

Werlhof, Claudia v., Maria Mies, and Veronika Bennholdt-Thomsen. Women, the Last Colony. London: ZED Press, 1988.

5. Quantitative and Qualitative Methods in the Social Sciences

Current Feminist Issues and Practical Strategies

TOBY EPSTEIN JAYARATNE AND
ABIGAIL J. STEWART

Within the last decade, the feminist research community has engaged in a dialogue concerning the use of quantitative versus qualitative methods in social research. Much of this debate has concerned the claim that quantitative research techniques—involving the translation of individuals' experience into categories predefined by researchers—distort women's experience and result in a silencing of women's own voices. Advocates of qualitative methods have argued that individual women's understandings, emotions, and actions in the world must be explored in those women's own terms. Defenders of quantitative methods in turn have worried that qualitative methods often include few safeguards against the operation of researcher biases and that abandonment of all aspects of traditional methodology may carry political and scholarly costs. In addition, some have pointed out that although quantitative methods can be and have been used to distort women's experience, they need not be. Although feminist advocates in this debate have generally embraced qualitative methods, they have expressed a range of views on the use of quantitative research, from condemning quantitative methods wholesale to promoting research which incorporates aspects of both qualitative and quantitative methods (Birke, 1986; Healy and Stewart, in press; Jayaratne, 1983).

The purpose of this essay is to review the evolution of this dialogue, to evaluate several issues which continue to be problematic in this literature, and to propose productive and practical strategies for feminist researchers concerned with these issues. In particular, this essay will emphasize the value of quantitative methods as effective tools to support feminist goals and feminist ideologies, while rejecting those traditional research procedures which are antithetical to feminist values.

We believe that much of the feminist debate about qualitative and quantitative research has been sterile and based on a false polarization. Moreover, as we will show below, solutions offered for methodological problems have frequently been either too general or too constraining to be realistically incorporated into research activity. Finally, much of the discussion of feminist methodology is really a discussion of basic epistemological issues (for example, the validity of various forms of knowledge); the dialogue is, therefore, fundamental but relatively esoteric and inaccessible. This nonempirical basis for discussion makes translation of the feminist philosophical perspective into testable research questions or acceptance by many researchers impractical. Given this state of affairs, we think a more practical, less abstract analysis of this topic is overdue. We hope the formulation of some pragmatic and useful recommendations for conducting feminist research will allow a variety of options and strategies to those who wish their empirical research to be consistent with feminist values.

The Feminist Methodology Dialogue

Feminist Criticism

The initial dialogue on feminist methodology originated from feminist criticism of traditional quantitative research. This criticism, as well as later advocacy of alternative feminist procedures, has been abundant since the late 1960s and has focused on a broad range of issues (Keller, 1982; Roberts, 1981). DuBois (1983) succinctly defined the basic issue by stating, "we literally cannot see women through traditional science and theory" (p. 110).

Specific criticisms of this research have included

1. The selection of sexist and elitist research topics (Cook and Fonow, 1984; Frieze, Parsons, Johnson, Ruble, and Zellman, 1978; Grady, 1981; Jayaratne, 1983; Scheuneman, 1986) and the absence of research on questions of central importance to women (see Parlee, 1975; Roberts, 1981)
2. Biased research designs, including selection of only male subjects (Grady, 1981; Lykes and Stewart, 1986)
3. An exploitative relationship between the researcher and the subject (Jayaratne, 1983; Mies, 1983; Oakley, 1981; Reinharz, 1979; Stanley and Wise, 1983) and within research teams (Birke, 1986; Harding, 1987)
4. The illusion of objectivity, especially associated with the positivist approach (Bleier, 1984; Jayaratne, 1983; Lykes and Stewart, 1986; Stanley and Wise, 1983; Wallston, 1981)
5. The simplistic and superficial nature of quantitative data (Jayaratne, 1983)
6. Improper interpretation and overgeneralization of findings (Jayaratne and Kaczala, 1983; Lykes and Stewart, 1986; Westkott, 1979), including the use of person-blame explanations and application to women of theory tested on exclusively male subjects
7. Inadequate data dissemination and utilization (Jayaratne, 1983; Tangri and Strasburg, 1979). Mies (1983) nicely sums up these criticisms by noting a fundamental contradiction between methodological theories which are currently accepted in the social sciences and the goals of the feminist community.

Many classic studies in social science may be analyzed now in terms of these criticisms. For example, Milgram's (1974) famous studies of "obedience," in which participants were led to believe they were administering painful shocks to another person (actually a "stooge" of the experimenter) in the name of "teaching," may be considered in light of these issues.

First, Milgram's definition of "obedience" (following the experimenter's instructions) relied on the rather abstract authority of the "scientist" and ignored both economic and personal safety factors which may in fact motivate "obedience" among those without power. In addition, if participants generally assumed that the experimental situation was one in which nothing dangerous or harmful could "really" happen, the relevance of that situation to real-world "obedience" contexts (e.g., war) is unclear. Second, *all* of Milgram's studies involved a male victim or "learner" and a male experimenter. In addition, most of his studies included only white, male, well-educated subjects in New Haven, Connecticut (although one study was conducted with 40 female subjects of unknown age, occupation, social class, or other characteristics, and some experiments apparently included industrial workers and unemployed persons).

Third, the entire research design depended on maximizing the hierarchical distance between experimenter and research participants; in addition, the experimenter actually deceived the participants throughout the experiment. At the end, a "debriefing" was held, in which "at the very least every subject was told that the victim had not received dangerous electric shocks" (p. 24). In addition, Milgram reports that both obedient and disobedient subjects were told that their behavior in the experiment was "normal" and acceptable. It is noteworthy that although Milgram did feel compelled to address subjects' worries about their own behavior (in his role as psychologist and authority), he did not feel compelled to account for his behavior (in exposing them to a stressful situation, in lying to them, etc.).

Fourth, the "indicators" selected for analysis were thoroughly "objective," for example, the actual voltage of the current, apparently administered to the stooge "learner" by the research participant. Similarly, fifth, analysis of the data was conducted in the most quantitative terms; thus, the participants' beliefs about their actions, and their feelings in the situation, were often not assessed at all. When such attitudes were measured, they too were assessed in highly quantitative terms: "the experimental subjects were asked to indicate on a 14-point scale just how nervous or tense they felt at the point of maximun tension" (p. 41).

Sixth, despite the rather narrow definition of "obedience" and the limited range of people included as research participants, Milgram believed that

> the essence of obedience consists in the fact that a person comes to view himself [*sic*] as the instrument for carrying out another person's wishes, and he therefore no longer regards himself as responsible for his actions. Once this critical shift of viewpoint has occurred in the persons, all of the essential features of obedience follow. . . . The question of generality, therefore, is not resolved by enumerating

all the manifest differences between the psychological laboratory and other situations but by carefully constructing a situation that *captures the essence of obedience* . . . [italics added] (Milgram, 1974, p. xii)

The critical question, of course, is how we know that the "essence of obedience" has indeed been captured. Although Milgram invokes an internal, self-definitional process as accounting for "obedience," he does not in fact assess directly any aspect of that process. Moreover, although he explores a number of contextual factors affecting rates of obedience, he concludes—without proof—that the "essence" of it is captured in all variants of the experimental paradigm. Hornstein (1988), in a completely different context, has argued that in general shifts toward quantification in psychology have accompanied burial of the question of the link between the measure and what is being measured. Thus, just as intelligence came to be thought of as that which intelligence tests measure, so too obedience comes to be defined as that which the obedience paradigm assesses.

Clearly, then, the feminist criticisms of traditional research practice are relevant not only to some social science research, but to many of the most respected and significant "landmark" studies.

Sources of Feminist Criticism

The specific feminist criticisms of traditional methodology derive from at least three sources. First, criticism has resulted from negative personal experiences with traditional research (for example, see Weisstein, 1977). Thus, Reinharz (1979), in describing the disillusionment she felt when participating in a research study at Columbia University, states that there were enormous discrepancies between her idealized version of research and her actual day-to-day experiences on and observations of this research project. She judged research procedures to be deceptive, dishonest, and disruptive, in violation of principles she believed should apply.

A second source of criticism is political, stemming from a concern that existing methodologies support sexist, racist, and elitist attitudes and practices and therefore negatively affect peoples' lives. For example, Unger (1981) states that "it is time to reexamine our methodologies. We need to know not only how many significant differences between the sexes exist, but the extent to which psychological studies contribute to the sexual reality with which we deal" (p. 652). Research which only documents differences between the sexes offers no understanding of why those differences exist or how such differences may be attenuated and therefore may reinforce (or create) the public's preconceived and sexist attitudes.

Thus, for example, Eccles and Jacobs (1986) report that media coverage of social scientists' research on sex differences in math ability results in differential parental encouragement of boys and girls equally gifted in math. The importance of this fact is underlined by Eccles and Jacobs's documentation of the power of parental encouragement of children's math efforts as a key predictor of children's performance over time.

In another example in a different area, Yllo (1988) documents the damage done by research reporting that husbands and wives are equally likely to engage in "violent acts," when that research was used as an excuse not to provide services to battered women. Later "clarifications" revealed the nontrivial fact that there were large sex differences in the tendency to resort to violence in self-defense and in the amount of physical harm inflicted by the violence. As a final example, many researchers have suggested (see, e.g., Lott, 1981; Morawski, 1985) that the study of "masculinity" and "femininity," as well as later studies of "androgyny," both reflect and create sex-role norms and standards by which individuals judge themselves and each other.

A third source of feminist criticism is philosophical and is based on a general rejection of positivism, its claim that science is value neutral, and that the scientific method protects against contamination of findings by "subjectivity" (see Wittig, 1985). Thus, for example, Unger (1983) argues that

> the ideological framework of positivist empiricism defines the relationship between researcher and subject as an impersonal one. The logic of these methods (and even their language) prescribes prediction and control. It is difficult for one who is trained in such a conceptual framework to step beyond it and ask what kind of person such a methodology presupposes. (p. 11)

Many feminist critics have argued that the person "presupposed" is a male scientist trained to ignore or mistrust feelings and subjectivity (see, for example, Keller, 1985).

Partly because the accepted methods of research in the social sciences have been quantitative, the focus of all three kinds of feminist criticism has been on quantitative research.[1] Some feminists have argued that the issue of quantitative versus qualitative methods reflects the relationship between gender and science (Keller, 1978). Keller, along with many others, such as Oakley (1981) and Bernard (1973), has suggested that most scientists are men and that, as a result, the masculine values of automony, separation, distance, and control are embodied in traditional quantitative research.

Feminist Support for Qualitative Methods

In response to these criticisms, some feminist researchers recognized the need to discover or develop research methodologies consistent with feminist values (Mies, 1983) that could be advocated for general use in the social sciences. The methodology which they embraced was primarily qualitative. It was promoted for numerous reasons, often parallelling the reasons for rejection of quantitative methods. Running through much of this enthusiasm for qualitative methods has been an understanding that many aspects of women's experience have not yet been articulated or conceptualized within social science. A deep suspicion of quantitative methods as having concealed women's real experience has motivated much preoccupation with, and advocacy of, qualitative methods as methods which permit women to express their experience fully and in their own terms. Thus, for example, Smith (1974/1987) argues that social scientists' methods must permit respondents to describe the world as they experience it.

> There are and must be different experiences of the world and different bases of experience. We must not do away with them by taking advantage of our privileged speaking to construct a sociological version which we then impose upon them as their reality. We may not rewrite the other's world or impose upon it a conceptual framework which extracts from it what fits with ours. Our conceptual procedures should be capable of explicating and analyzing the properties of their experienced world rather than administering it. Their reality, their varieties of experience must be an unconditional datum. (p. 93)

One frequent source of enthusiasm for qualitative methods stems from their potential to offer a more human, less mechanical relationship between the researcher and "the researched." For example, Oakley (1981) suggests that "the goal of finding out about people through interviewing is best achieved when the relationship of interviewer and interviewee is nonhierarchical and when the interviewer is prepared to invest his or her own personal identity in the relationship" (p. 41). For Oakley, the process of "collecting data" which will, according to traditional social science ideals, be transformed into numbers should be replaced by a process of "interviewing women," in which "personal involvement is more than dangerous bias—it is the condition under which people come to know each other and to admit others into their lives" (p. 58).

Feminists', as well as others', advocacy and use of qualitative methods has not generally been welcomed in the social sciences. Despite the argument that qualitative methods provide more accurate and valid information about respondents' experience, use of qualitative methods, and especially qualitative feminist research, often produces strong negative reactions in the mainstream academic community (Cook and Fonow, 1984; DuBois, 1983; Healy and Stewart, in press; Reinharz, 1979), primarily because it is thought to be "unscientific" or politically motivated, and therefore overtly biased. As DuBois (1983) states, "feminist scientists and scholars will continue to be charged with bias, advocacy, subjectivity, ideologizing, and so on" (p. 112).[2] Penalties for the use of these methods have ranged from publication rejections and the consequent development of alternative, lower-prestige publication outlets (see Lykes and Stewart, 1986) to difficulty getting tenure.

An Inclusive Feminist Perspective

Over time, though, feminist theorists and researchers have increasingly distinguished between qualitative methods and a feminist approach to social science research, thus deemphasizing the critical focus on quantification. For example, Stanley and Wise (1983) have argued that "methods in themselves aren't innately anything" (p. 159). They point out that although "positivist methods and world views are objectionable, sexist even, . . . what should be objected to about them isn't quantification or their use of statistical techniques" (p. 159). Instead, the ways in which research participants are treated and the care with which researchers attempt to represent the lived experience of research participants are of more central concern. In fact, in reviewing recent discussions of feminist methods, Harding (1987) argues that

> feminist researchers use just about any and all of the methods, in this concrete sense of the term, that traditional androcentric researchers have used. Of course, precisely how they carry out these methods of evidence gathering is often strikingly different. (p. 2)

She concludes, "it is not by looking at research methods that one will be able to identify the distinctive features of the best of feminist research" (p. 3).

An inclusive viewpoint on methods, which appears to be increasingly accepted in feminist research circles, takes the form of promoting the value and appropriate use of both qualitative and quantitative methods as feminist research tools. The emphasis here is on using methods which can best answer particular research questions, but always using them in ways which are consistent with broad feminist goals and ideology. Thus, the feminist debate on these issues can be seen to have evolved from one defined by opposition to all aspects of mainstream research to an argument for use of a broad range of methods in pursuit of research reflecting feminist values and goals. Thus, Jayaratne (1983) and Wittig (1985) have argued that both types of methods can be effectively utilized by feminists and can be implemented in ways which are consistent with feminist values. Procedures commonly used in quantitative research which are inconsistent with feminist values can be altered without abandoning the quantitative strategies which can be beneficial to feminists. Moreover, combining methods, sometimes termed "triangulation" (see Denzin, 1978; Jick, 1979) permits researchers to "capture a more complete, holistic, and contextual portrayal . . ." (Jick, p. 603). As Jick points out, "the effectiveness of triangulation rests on the premise that the weaknesses in each single method will be compensated by the counter-balancing strengths of another" (p. 604).

Yllo (1988) is most persuasive in making this case with respect to research on marital rape. As she points out, the true nature of marital rape cannot be captured in statistics; the experience of violent victimization at the hands of a loved one in an act grotesquely similar to and totally different from an act of love cannot be conveyed in traditional questionnaire or survey format. Thus, Yllo conducted (along with her colleague; see Finkelhor and Yllo, 1985) extensive qualitative interviews with a sample of women who volunteered to be in a study of marital rape. She points out that this analysis yielded a new typology of marital rape (p. 32).

> I learned a great deal about wife abuse from those 50 women that the quantitative data on over 2,000 couples could not begin to reveal. My talks with battered women made clear to me that I am a part of what I am studying. . . . Being aware of this makes a difference in how I understand the problem. (p. 34)

On the other hand, Yllo points out that associations which are powerfully significant to an individual woman cannot be understood in terms of their generality without careful survey research.

For example, we found that a large portion of the marital rape victims had also been sexually abused as children. We cannot discover the extent of the relationship between child sexual abuse and marital rape unless we construct a controlled study using a representative sample. It may be that child sexual abuse is no more common among marital rape victims than among other women. But, only by comparing marital rape victims with nonvictims could we come to any adequate conclusions. (p. 35)

Current Issues in the Feminist Methodology Literature

Although there seems to be increasing consensus in the feminist community that quantitative methods are legitimate research tools and that methods should be chosen based on an appropriate fit with the research question, there remain at least three conceptual areas in discussions of feminist methodology where the dialogue remains problematic. First are definitional difficulties with the terms "quantitative," "qualitative," "method" and "methodology." Second is the tendency of many authors to take an essentialist position, which assumes that female researchers feel comfortable, and are competent using only certain "female" methods. The third problem concerns the epistemological issue of objectivity/subjectivity, a continuing central focus for debate.

Definitional Issues

A number of terms used in the feminist methodology dialogue have different implicit or explicit definitions, resulting in some confusion. This difficulty is particularly apparent with regard to the distinction between "methods" and "methodology" and between "quantitative" and "qualitative" processes. Researchers considering the merits of an argument must, therefore, be careful to assess the precise definitions being proposed or implied. Harding (1987) has recently suggested one set of distinctions among terms. She identifies "methods" as particular procedures used in the course of research (e.g., interviews), "methodology" as a theory of how research is carried out or the broad principles about how to conduct research and how theory is applied (e.g., survey research methodology or experimental methodology), and "epistemology" as a theory of knowledge (e.g., the "scientific method" which aims to establish the truth-value of various propositions). It follows from these definitions that first, quantitative and qualitative "methods" are simply specific research procedures; second, "feminist methodology" or a "feminist perspective on methodology" must be taken to refer to a much broader theory of how to do feminist research. There may, then, be a "feminist methodology" without any particular feminist "methods." In the last section of this paper, we will propose some particular strategies for conducting "feminist research"; this will be, then, a discussion of feminist methodology, but will involve use of a variety of existing quantitative and qualitative methods or procedures.

Besides distinguishing methods and methodology, we also distinguish historical from logical associations between specific procedures and specific ideologies. For example, quantitative methods have been associated historically with sexist and antifeminist attitudes. We propose that although quantitative research may have been used in the past to obscure the experience of women, it need not always be used in that way. That is, the association is an historical one but not a logical one. Similarly, we propose that although some feminist researchers use qualitative methods to reveal important aspects of women's experience, there is no guarantee that they always will be used to do so.

However, despite the prevalence of these historical associations, there may be some absolute constraints or limitations associated with each type of method. Thus, for example, quantitative methods may never provide the kind of richly textured "feeling for the data" that qualitative methods can permit. As Healy and Stewart (in press) indicate, "Kotre (1984) argues that *only* qualitative analysis can accurately capture the complex pattern of an individual life without violating the integrity of the life or dehumanizing the individual" (p. 3). This observation underlies some feminist enthusiasm for incorporating a contextual perspective in research, indicated by qualitative methods. However, it can also be argued that multivariate statistical analyses of large data sets may provide the most truly "contextual" analyses of people's experience. This is because certain multivariate statistical procedures allow the incorporation of a large number of contextual variables, permitting the simultaneous testing of elaborate and complex theoretical models. It has been argued that such analysis is more "ecologically valid" (Bronfenbrenner, 1977).

One common stereotype of qualitative methods is that they are unsystematic and thus unscientific. Clearly such methods can be unsystematic, but they need not be. Hornstein (in press) is able to spell out detailed procedures for a "phenomenological approach to the study of lives." She describes three stages in the researchers' analysis of a phenomenological account. In the first stage the researcher is "attempting to uncover the structure of an experience," and therefore "takes each bit of the subject's report and scrutinizes it to uncover its meaning." She points out that "crucial to this process is a way of thinking termed *imaginal variation,* in which a given feeling, thought, or outcome is compared with other possibilities" (pp. 6–7). The second stage of analysis involves construction of "analytic categories" that emerge from the themes identified in the first stage. "To the greatest extent possible, one strives to allow the categories to emerge from the data themselves, rather than from a preconceived theoretical or empirical framework" (p. 7). Finally, the researcher attempts to describe the relationships among the various categories in order to identify the "pattern" or "structure" of the experience—the ways in which the elements combine to create a unified whole (p. 8). This approach is wholly qualitative and rigorously systematic. Similarly, Gerson (1985) applies Glaser and Strauss's (1967) "constant comparative method" to interviews with a relatively small sample of women in a way which is qualitative, aimed at theory development, and systematic.

Thus, we would distinguish between methods which are systematic and methods which are quantitative. Quantification, in a strict sense, only refers to the transformation of observations (by a researcher or participant) into numbers. It can occur in the context of unsystematically collected data, and it need not occur in the context of systematically collected data. It may permit one form of systematic analysis, but it also permits unsystematic, ad hoc analyses. Thus, while historical associations between quantitative and systematic methods can be documented, logical associations between them are debatable, suggesting that a feminist methodology cannot ultimately be tied to either qualitative or quantitative methods.

An additional difficulty with the terms "quantitative" and "qualitative" is that they have frequently been used to refer to an absolute methodological dichotomy (Healy and Stewart, in press), so that the entire research process or methodology is characterized as discretely quantitative or qualitative. However, if we think of a research project as involving a group of separate procedures or methods, it is useful to reconceptualize each procedure as located on a qualitative to quantitative continuum (Healy and Stewart). Thus, not only can specific research procedures be more or less quantitative or qualitative, but the entire research approach, made up of these separate procedures, may also be characterized in these relative terms.

"Essentializing" the Issue: What Is "Women's Research?"

Although it is our view that many feminist critiques of traditional quantitative methods have considerable merit and that qualitative research is often more consistent with feminist values, we also believe that many authors incorrectly base their criticisms on what we term "the different voice" perspective. This perspective, represented in Gilligan's *In A Different Voice* (1982), emphasizes the difference between the male voice, which defines the self in terms of distinctness and separation from others, and the female voice, which defines the self in terms of connections and relationships. Numerous discussions of feminist methodology have applied this essentialist view to the quantitative and qualitative dialogue (for example, see Davis, 1985, and Sheuneman, 1986) concluding that the female voice is, in fact, qualitative. Furthermore, this view has emphasized the differences between qualitative and quantitative research, regarding the former as subjective, relevant, and descriptive and the latter as objective, irrelevant, and superficial.

In general, those who take an essentialist position believe that women are more able than men to study issues of importance to women. According to Mies (1983), because of women's personal experience with oppression they "are better equipped than their male counterparts to make a comprehensive study of the exploited groups" (p. 121). While we generally agree that women, on the average, *should* have a better understanding of issues important to feminists, it is unclear whether this *is*, in fact the case, and, if it is true in general, under what circumstances it is true. Overall, evidence in support of the essentialist position is lacking, and thus a more cautious approach to evaluating this belief is appropriate. Moreover, differences among women are ignored and rendered invisible by this exclusive focus on inter-sex differences.

The essentialist view is exemplified by two beliefs found in the literature or raised as issues for discussion in the feminist community. One belief about women researchers is that they take a more "contextual" approach. Thus, for example, Gilligan (1982) suggests that where men see individuals arranged in hierarchies, women see a web of interconnected relationships. Scheuneman (1986) argues that this tendency toward a contextual perspective (which is, indeed, a frequently voiced feminist research value; see, e.g., Smith, 1974/ 1987) will lead women to use multivariate research designs. However, no evidence for this belief is presented, and it runs counter to the stereotype of women as fearful and avoidant of complex statistics (see below).

A second essentialist belief expressed in some feminist literature is that women researchers are more likely to study issues important to feminists. Interestingly, in an analysis of articles published in personality and social psychology between 1963 and 1983, Lykes and Stewart (1986) found that "female authorship was uncorrelated with the sex-typing of research topics, age of subjects, analysis of sexes separately, inclusion of gender as an aspect of the research question, discussion of sex roles, or interpretation of gender differences" (p. 400). Thus, there is no automatic association between gender of researcher and research methods used.

We suggest several problems with the essentialist position, in addition to the lack of empirical support. First, it amounts to wishful thinking by confusing an ideal with reality. In other words, although essentialist beliefs appear consistent with feminist values, they may have no basis in fact. The underlying values expressed in this literature could, however, function more usefully as ideals. For example, DuBois's (1983) call for a wholistic (contextual and non-linear) approach, is clearly stated as an ideal we must develop and use. Second, these beliefs about women's use of research methods confuse *women's* and *feminists'* beliefs. Although there is no evidence that either women or feminists might conduct research in this way, it is certainly more likely that feminists, rather than women in general, would do this, since it is consistent with feminist values. To hold essentialist views about all women is to stereotype all women as feminists. It is too easy to forget that most women researchers (including feminist researchers) are primarily trained and socialized as traditional quantitative methodologists and, despite any interest in alternative procedures, it is far more likely than not that they will carry out their research largely using traditional methods and methodologies (Lykes and Stewart, 1986).

There is one additional belief concerning women's approach to science which is sometimes a focus for discussion not only among feminists, but in the public media as well. This is the stereotype of women as math anxious or as avoiding the acquisition of advanced math skills. Evidence indicates that females, beginning in high school, express more negative attitudes toward math than males, although the sex difference does not appear to be large (Eccles, 1984). Moreover, examination of average sex differences obscures equally important intra-sex differences among women. Nevertheless, Eccles suggests that anxiety may ultimately influence some women's academic choices. It can handicap women in their entrance to numerous professions, including the social sciences. Despite the evidence to support this view, it is not necessarily the case that those women who do enter social science professions and who may not therefore be "typical" of "all" women in a number of ways—with their current reliance on quantitative methods—are seriously handicapped by math anxiety. However, if women scientists *are* more suspicious or uncomfortable with mathematical analyses, they may be disadvantaged professionally. Advanced statistical procedures used in quantitative research may make publication more likely, and, as Cook and Fonow (1984) suggest, agencies may be more willing to fund research projects which propose sophisticated statistical techniques.

Although all women need not learn advanced mathematical or statistical skills, such skills are advantageous to feminist researchers for a number of reasons. First, although these skills are more or less appropriate for use in various disciplines,[3] in research in the social sciences they are used consistently and effectively as research tools. Furthermore, whether or not one intends to use these skills in one's own research, it is important that feminist researchers obtain adequate statistical or mathematical knowledge in order to evaluate and critique research which does use such tools. Given the abundance of research with an antifeminist message, it is absolutely critical that feminist researchers understand the methods behind such research, so that their critiques will be cogent.

A second reason for feminist researchers to have knowledge of statistical and mathematical principles is in their application to both qualitative and quantitative research. Without a basic understanding of the functioning of these principles in research procedures such as design, sample selection, data interpretation, and generalization, both qualitative and quantitative research can result in erroneous and misleading findings. However, more damaging than inaccurate results is the potential for others to generalize from one example of inferior research motivated by feminist values and to stereotype all feminist research as being politically motivated and biased, exactly the charge feminists make of traditional research. When feminist research is poorly done, it is not only difficult to defend the charge of bias, but it makes it increasingly difficult to defend quality feminist research as well.

Perhaps the clearest example of research claiming to be "qualitative" which has been problematic for feminists is Hite's study on women's sexuality and love relationships, which resulted in two well-publicized books (Hite, 1976, 1987). Her work—not associated with any traditional academic discipline or setting—has been prominently identified as feminist, both by her and by some of the media; it thereby reflects on all research by feminists. One difficulty with this work is that, while it strongly supports the feminist call for more qualitative, in-depth study of women's lives, it violates some very basic methodological principles, thus jeopardizing the validity of its conclusions. Although there are numerous examples which could be targeted for criticism, one stands out in particular. In *Women and Love* (Hite, 1987) Hite distributed approximately 100,000 questionnaires, 4,500 being returned. In spite of her attempt to justify the representativeness of her sample, it is clear that it is a highly self-selected sample[4] and not representative of the U.S. female population, which she implies it is. Because of the unknown nature of the sample, it is inaccurate to draw *any* conclusions about what U.S. women in general may believe. Nevertheless, such conclusions are intended in this volume. Although, as feminists, we might wish to believe in the truth of her findings, we must recognize the fact that her data simply cannot answer questions about how most American women feel about love. At most, we can only say that some women feel this way.

Despite the strength of this criticism, it is not a single methodological flaw which most concerns us, but rather the contribution which this research makes to the stereotype of feminists as biased researchers. The negative press which this type of research received, primarily for its shoddy methodology (see, for example, Tavris, 1987, and Ferguson, 1987), detracts from its message and contributes to the stereotype of feminists as incapable of sophisticated and valid research. If Hite had used proper methodological procedures (even just better sampling methods), and the book were still attacked for its feminist message (which undoubtedly it would have been), at least it could have been defended. Instead, we are faced with guilt by association. For example, one review which appeared in the *Wall Street Journal* (Ferguson, 1987) stated that the book

> serves up the kind of buncombe we have come to expect from "feminist scholarship": the bloated generalization, the bizarre pseudoethnology masquerading as a critique of "patriarchy," the sure-handed dismissal of tradition and history, and above all, the free-floating indeterminate malice. (p. 13)

It is important to note here that there are many examples of careful, rigorous qualitative research to set against the Hite studies. Unfortunately, none of them is likely to attract the level of media attention that her research did. Detailed consideration of the signs which distinguish excellent qualitative research may help make this point clearer. Gerson (1985) conducted a qualitative study of different patterns of work and family life among contemporary young women. In a thoughtful appendix to the monograph describing her findings, Gerson explained that "the research questions called for an exploratory study" (p. 240), which was based on "open-ended, in-depth interviews with a carefully targeted sample of women" (p. 241). She explained her sampling procedure in detail, spelling out the biases and limitations of the sample (pp. 241–45). She concluded that "the insights and conclusions of this analysis can and, I hope will be applied to and tested among other groups of women in different social environments and of other races and age cohorts" (p. 243). Perhaps most important, in the body of the text itself, Gerson pointed to the proper use of her findings: "They should be considered in the context of corroborative findings from larger, more representative samples" (p. 217). Research like this does indeed stand

> the best chance of avoiding the Scylla of qualitative research that is descriptively rich, but lacks analytic precision, and the Charybdis of quantitative research that is causally precise, but lacks the data necessary to uncover processes or answer the critical questions. (Gerson, 1985, p. 241)

The Issue of Objectivity

What Is the Issue?

A frequent theme in feminist criticism of social science research is the negative consequences of professional obsessiveness with "scientific objectivity," which is in turn associated (historically, though not logically) with quantification. Feminist criticisms have focused on several important points: (1) apparently "objective" science has often been sexist (hence, not "objective") in its purposes and/or its effects (see, for example, DuBois, 1983; Sherif, 1979/1987); (2) glorification of "objectivity" has imposed a hierarchical and controlling relationship upon the researcher-researched dyad (Keller, 1978; Fee, 1983; Arditti, 1980); and (3) idealization of objectivity has excluded from science significant personal subjectively-based knowledge and has left that knowledge outside of "science" (Unger, 1983; Wallston, 1981). This last point makes it clear that leaving the subjective outside of science also leaves it unexamined. Thus, Harding (1987), has recently concluded that

> the best feminist analysis . . . insists that the inquirer her/himself be placed in the same critical place as the overt subject matter, thereby recovering the entire research process for scrutiny in the results of research. (p. 9)

It may be, then, that an important source of the sexist (and racist and classist) bias in traditional "objective" research is the fact that the personal and subjective—which inevitably influences many aspects of the research process—were exempt from analysis (see Hubbard, 1978; Unger, 1983).

For some feminists a "truly feminist social science" originates "from women's experience of women's reality" (Stanley and Wise, 1983, p. 165; see also Smith, 1974/1987). Some believe that this perspective implies the exclusion of the concept of objectivity in the research process. It is clear, nevertheless, that most contemporary feminists reject any notion that objectivity should be renounced as a goal altogether. Although absolute objectivity is not possible (even if it were desirable), the pursuit of some types of objectivity, as a goal, does have potential to protect against several forms of bias. For example, a researcher who has an investment in a particular theory may tend to use methods that are likely to produce supportive findings. However, the use of certain research procedures generally accepted in the social sciences mitigate against such biased results. An illustration of this safeguard is representative sampling techniques. Such techniques do not permit a researcher to generalize from a sample of selected respondents who are likely to exhibit the researcher's pet hypothesis. Thus, while many feminists wish to incorporate subjective elements into the research process, they also reject the notion that the process must be entirely subjective. As Rose (1982) states, "feminist methodology seeks to bring together subjective and objective ways of knowing the world" (p. 368). Furthermore, Birke (1986) notes that the association of objectivity with masculinity has sometimes led feminists to reject objectivity and to glorify subjectivity in opposition to it. While it is necessary to revalue the subjective . . . we do ourselves a disservice if we remove ourselves from objectivity and rationality; we then simply leave the terrain of rational thought . . . to men, thus perpetuating the system which excluded us in the first place. (p. 157)

There is, then, increasing recognition that the use of particular methods and procedures does not automatically confer objectivity, just as inclusion of analysis of one's personal subjective experience does not preclude it. With no necessary connection between (qualitative and quantitative) methods and (objective vs. subjective) outcomes, there is no substitute for a reflexive social science conducted by reflective social scientists (Harding, 1987; Unger, 1983).

Dangers of Apparent Objectivity

Despite our recognition of the legitimate use of objective methods, there are realistic dangers of poor quality antifeminist research disguised as good, quantitative and, thus, "objective" research. An example of such research which required a strong feminist critique and reinterpretation is work by Benbow and Stanley on math achievement (1980, 1983). This study, which made headlines in major newspapers[5] throughout the country, supported the view that girls were innately less capable of math achievement than boys. A study assessing the negative impact of this research (Jacobs and Eccles, 1985) concluded that

one of the major effects of popular media coverage of the research report was that it changed the "social desirability" climate. Before the media coverage, it was popular to espouse a belief in equal math abilities of males and females. After the media coverage it was "okay" to say that males are better than females in math. (p. 24)

Numerous problems with this research have been pointed out (for example, see Eccles and Jacobs, 1986; Fennema, 1981), and many are violations of basic principles for conducting quantitative research. Most important, the research failed adequately to examine the roles of values and attitudes in girls' math performance (see Eccles and Jacobs, 1986), which reasonably may have explained the sex difference in performance. Although these critiques did not receive as much press coverage as the original Benbow and Stanley article, such critical analysis of traditional objective research is essential in the feminist and academic community and requires a thorough knowledge of basic research and statistical procedures. Thus, there is a very practical need for feminists to acquire such knowledge if we are even to attempt to counter the effects of such harmful, "objective" work.

Benefits and Uses of Traditional Research Methods

Although this example illustrates the damage which this kind of research can do, as feminists we must also consider any potential benefits which our own use of "objectivity" can bring. The greatest benefit of apparent objectivity lies in its power to change political opinion. Thus, traditional research methods can be used to our advantage to change sexist belief systems or to support progressive legislation. Two examples of the uses of statistics attest to its power. First, as noted in Jayaratne (1983), prior to the court decision of *Griggs v. Duke Power Company* (1971), which was argued under Title VII of the Civil Rights Act of 1964, sex discrimination could be substantiated in court only if one could prove intent on the part of the defendant. The decision resulting from this case, however, was that discrimination could be demonstrated by presenting statistics which show a different and unfair impact on a racial, sex, or other group covered by Title VII. This decision set a new course for discrimination suits.

In a second example, a study of maternal death rates in Chicago (Siefert and Martin, 1988) documented a much higher rate among black than white women, as well as a rate for black women higher than that in many Third World countries. In specific response to this study (Wolinsky, 1986; Wolinsky and Franchine, 1986), a new program was initiated by the Illinois health commissioner and the Chicago Health Department ($35 million allocated) to ensure that pregnant women get prenatal care.

An additional benefit derived from the use of "objective" methods in research lies in their ability to provide tests of theories. Thus, statistics can be a practical tool in the evaluation of feminist theories, since such analysis can identify the most effective strategies for implementing feminist goals. This remains an imperative task if feminists are going to correctly target problem areas for change or effectively direct our energies toward change.

A Feminist Perspective on Methodology

In much of the feminist methodology literature the critical questions ask for the definition of the "feminist perspective" on research. We believe that there is now some consensus on the answer to this question. Thus, there is general concurrence in recent writing on feminist methodology that there can be no single, prescribed method or set of research methods consistent with feminist values, although there are methods antithetical to such values.

> The idea that there is only "one road" to the feminist revolution, and only one type of "truly feminist" research, is as limiting and as offensive as male-biased accounts of research that have gone before. (Stanley and Wise, 1983, p. 26)

There is, then, no substitute for each researcher making independent assessments about the appropriateness of a given method for a given research question and purpose, as well as about the competence of the execution of the research method used. Feminist researchers must be critical of both quantitative and qualitative research which is used against women and must be able to marshal the richest and most persuasive evidence in the service of women.

We believe that the focus of feminist dialogue on "methods," and particularly on qualitative versus quantitative methods, obscures the more fundamental challenge of feminism to the traditional "scientific method" (see also DuBois, 1983). That challenge really questions the epistemology, or theory of knowledge, underlying traditional science and social science, including the notion that science is, or can be, value free. It is appropriate and timely now to move the focus of the feminist methodology dialogue from definition to implementation. With such an enormous task ahead of us, as feminist researchers attempting to undo decades of sexist and elitist research, to continue the debate between quantitative and qualitative research at this point in the dialogue wastes our valuable time and effort.

Strategies for Practical Implementation of a Feminist Perspective in Social Science Research

Many significant contributions to the literature on feminist methodology are so abstract that the solutions they propose cannot be easily or practically implemented, let alone understood by those without knowledge of epistemology. Feminist researchers must develop realistic and pragmatic strategies which allow for implementation of the feminist perspective. The following specific procedures are examples of such strategies. They derive both from the above discussions of qualitative and quantitative methods, and from those research values explicitly found in the feminist methodology literature. We would like to emphasize, parenthetically, the importance of researchers selecting or developing other procedures which they can effectively implement. Thus, researchers need to consider practical issues such as the time, effort, money and other resources available to the research staff. It is our belief that *any*, even a limited, attempt at increasing the feminist value of research is worthwhile.

1. *When selecting a research topic or problem, we should ask how that research has potential to help women's lives and what information is necessary to have such impact.* The desire to conduct research can either stem from a general theoretical interest in a subject matter (e.g., beliefs about rape), or from a specific political perspective (e.g., how can research help to decrease the incidence of rape). Although ultimately the goal should always be political, theoretical research can also be important to feminists (Jayaratne, 1983). Whatever the origins of the research topic, it is important to determine, specifically, the kind of information which will be most useful and will have the most positive impact on women's lives. One research goal is not always better or more appropriate for a given problem. For example, if a researcher is interested in helping battered women, legitimate research goals might vary from increasing public understanding of their plight to influencing legislation.

2. *When designing the study, we should propose methods that are both appropriate for the kind of question asked and the information needed and*

which permit answers persuasive to a particular audience. Once a researcher knows the research goal or question and what information is necessary, the types of methods needed in the research should be clear. This view has been stated frequently in the feminist literature (DuBois, 1983; Jayaratne, 1983; Healy and Stewart, in press; Scheuneman, 1986; Wallston, 1981). As a general guideline, if the research goal is descriptive of individual lives and designed to promote understanding of a particular viewpoint of the subjects, more qualitative methods may be appropriate. If the goal is to document the operation of particular relationships between variables (e.g. how a government policy affects women), more quantitative methods may be useful. For example, if a researcher is interested in investigating the lives of homeless women, there are numerous approaches she can take. If her goal is to influence legislation to offer employment training to these women, the most persuasive case may involve gathering statistics on women whose job training led to employment and permanent housing. However, if the goal is to help the public to understand these women, in-depth interviews and narrative accounts might be most appropriate.

3. *In every instance of use of either qualitative and quantitative methods or both, we should address the problems associated with each approach.* Thus, if using qualitative methods, we must be aware of methodological problems of poor representation and overgeneralization. Alternatively, if using quantitative methods, we must consciously and actively incorporate feminist values into the procedures. Because quantitative methods have historically exploited women and excluded feminist values, those using such methods should be particularly aware of these problems. (Examples can be found above, in the section on feminist criticism.)

4. *Whenever possible, we should use research designs which combine quantitative and qualitative methods.* This approach, termed a "mixed method," has been advocated by numerous authors as a way to offset the disadvantages of one method with the strengths of the other (Denzin, 1978; Healy and Stewart, in press; Jick, 1979). This strategy suggests the value of acquiring knowledge of both methods. Although this combination of methods is not always possible or even practical, it should result in a more powerful research product, that is, one which not only effectively tests theory but also is convincing.

5. *Whether the research methods are quantitative or qualitative, it is critical that procedures be bias-free or sex-fair.* Not only will such research better test theory or more accurately communicate the research goal, but such research should be more influential on policymakers and the public. In fact, because feminist research tends to be suspect already, it is especially critical that procedures be free from apparent contaminating bias. (See Grady, 1981, for examples of methods to minimize bias.)

6. *We should take the time and effort to do quality research.* This means learning and using a variety of appropriate research skills, rather than taking short cuts which are more expedient. (See Jayaratne, 1983, p. 151, for a discussion of the abundance of "quick and dirty research" in social science.)

7. *When interpreting results, we should ask what different interpretations, always consistent with the findings, might imply for change in women's lives.* We should consider interpretations that imply the most effective interventions for improving women's lives. For example, victim-blaming interpretations tend to result in individual intervention strategies, whereas situational/ environmental interpretations can often yield more effective political strategies for change.

8. *We should always attempt some political analysis of the findings.* We should make an effort to explore how policy change suggested by research results might positively affect women's lives. This goal is not always clear from the findings and must be made explicit, when possible.

9. *Finally, as much as possible (given a realistic assessment of the frantic pace of academic life), we should actively participate in the dissemination of research results.* The importance of dissemination cannot be overstressed, since it is the goal of feminist research to make a difference in women's lives. If research is not "advertised" it will not have an impact, either on policymakers or on the public.

In conclusion, we would like to reemphasize that we view these strategies, combined with others discussed in the feminist literature, as a contribution to a dialogue focusing on the practical application of feminist theory in social research. Such dialogue can best advance feminist goals by producing research which not only positively affects women's lives, but also makes the research endeavor itself an exciting, relevant, and profitable experience for the researcher.

NOTES

1. It should be pointed out that criticism of quantitative methods has a long history which extends beyond the feminist community (Healy and Stewart, in press; Hornstein, 1988; Mies, 1983).

2. For example, the first author of this essay was told in her first year of graduate school (not at her present academic institution) that the faculty were concerned about her ability to conduct objective research because of her political (i.e., feminist) views.

3. See Hacker (1983) for an example of a discipline where mathematics is over-emphasized.

4. Not only is her return rate profoundly low, but the highly personal and lengthy nature of the questionnaire would result in a sample of women to whom this subject is unusually salient, such as women who are unhappy in their love relationships.

5. Popular media coverage of this research included headlines such as "Do Males Have a Math Gene?" in *Newsweek* (Williams & King, 1980) and "The Gender Factor in Math: A New Study Says Males May Be Naturally Abler Than Females" in *Time* (The Gender Factor, 1980).

REFERENCES

Arditti, R. (1980). Feminism and science. In R. Arditti, P. Brennan, and S. Cavrale, eds., *Science and liberation*. Boston: South End.

Benbow, C. P., and J. Stanley (1980). Sex differences in mathematical ability: Fact or artifact? *Science*, 210, 1262–64.

——— (1983). Sex differences in mathematical reasoning ability: More facts. *Science*, 222, 1029–31.

Bernard, J. (1973). My four revolutions: An autobiographical history of the ASA. In J. Huber ed., *Changing women in a changing society*. Chicago: University of Chicago Press.

Birke, L. (1986). *Women, feminism and biology*. New York: Methuen.

Bleier, R. (1984). *Science and gender*. New York: Pergamon.

Bronfenbrenner, U. (1977). Toward an experimental ecology of human development. *American Psychologist*, 32, 513–29.

Cook, J. A., and M. M. Fonow (1984). Am I my sister's gatekeeper? Cautionary tales from the academic hierarchy. *Humanity and Society*, 8, 442–52.

Davis, L. V. (1985). Female and male voices in social work. *Social Work*, 32, 106–113.

Denzin, N. K. (1978). *The research act*. New York: McGraw Hill.

DuBois, B. (1983). Passionate scholarship: Notes on values, knowing and method in social science. In G. Bowles and R. D. Klein, eds., *Theories of women's studies*, pp. 105–116. Boston: Routledge & Kegan Paul.

Eccles, J. (1984). Sex differences in mathematics participation. In M. Steinkam and M. Maehr, eds., *Advances in motivation and achievement*, pp. 93–137, vol. 2. Greenwich, Conn: JAI Press.

Eccles, J. S., and J. E. Jacobs (1986). Social forces shape math attitudes and performance. *Signs*, 11, 367–89.

Fee, E. (1983). Women's nature and scientific objectivity. In M. Lowe and R. Hubbard, eds., *Women's nature: Rationalizations of inequality*, pp. 9–28. New York: Pergamon.

Fennema, E. (1981). Women and mathematics: Does research matter? *Journal for Research in Mathematics Education*, 12, 380–85.

Ferguson, A. (1987). She says it's a dog's life in a man's world. *Wall Street Journal*, Nov. 13, p. 13.

Finkelhor, D., and K. Yllo, (1985). *License to rape: Sexual abuse of wives*. New York: Free Press.

Frieze, I. H., J. E. Parsons, P. B. Johnson, D. N. Ruble, and G. L. Zellman (1978). *Women and sex roles: A social psychological perspective*. New York: W. W. Norton.

The gender factor in math: A new study says males may be naturally abler than females. (1980). *Time*, Dec. 15, p. 57.

Gerson, K. (1985). *Hard choices*. Berkeley: University of California Press.

Gilligan, C. (1982). *In a different voice*. Cambridge, Mass.: Harvard University Press.

Glaser, B., and A. Strauss (1976). *The discovery of grounded theory*. Chicago: Aldine.

Grady, K. E. (1981). Sex bias in research design. *Psychology of Women Quarterly*, 5, 628–36.

Griggs v. Duke Power Company (1971), 401 US 424.

Hacker, S. (1983). Mathematization of engineering: Limits on women and the field. In J. Rothschild, *Machina ex dea: Feminist perspectives on technology*. New York: Pergamon.

Harding, S. (1987). Introduction. Is there a feminist method? In S. Harding, ed., *Feminism and methodology*, pp. 1–14. Bloomington: Indiana University Press.

Healy, J. M., Jr., and A. J. Sewart, (in press). On the compatibility of quantitative and qualitative methods for studying individual lives. In A. J. Stewart, J. M. Healy, Jr., and D. Ozer, eds., *Perspectives on personality: Theory, research, and interpersonal dynamics*, vol. 3. Greenwich, Conn.: JAI Press.

Hite, S. (1976). *The Hite report*. New York: Macmillan.

———. (1987). *Women and love*. New York: Alfred Knopf.

Hornstein, G. A. (1988). Quantifying psychological phenomena: Debates, dilemmas, and implications. In J. G. Morawski, ed., *The rise of experimentation in American psychology*. New Haven: Yale University Press.

———. (In press). Painting a portrait of experience: The phenomenological approach to the study of lives. In A. J. Stewart, J. M. Healy, Jr., and D. J. Ozer, eds., *Perspectives in personality: Approaches to studying lives*. Greenwich, Conn.: JAI Press.

Hubbard, R. (1978). Have only men evolved? In R. Hubbard, M. S. Henifin, and B. Fried, eds., *Women look at biology looking at women*. Cambridge: Schenkman.

Jacobs, J., and J. S. Eccles (1985). Gender differences in math ability: The impact of media reports on parents. *Educational Researcher*, 14, 20–25.

Jayaratne, T. E. (1983). The value of quantitative methodology for feminist research. In G. Bowles and R. Duelli Klein, eds., *Theories of women's studies*, pp. 140–61. Boston: Routledge & Kegan Paul.

Jayaratne, T. E., and C. M. Kaczala (1983). Social responsibility in sex difference research. *Journal of Educational Equity and Leadership*, 3, 305–316.

Jick, T. D. (1979). Mixing qualitative and quantitative methods: Triangulation in action. *Administrative Science Quarterly*, 24, 602–610.

Keller, E. F. (1978). Gender and science. *Psychoanalysis and contemporary thought*, 1, 409–433.

———. (1982). Feminism and science. *Signs*, 7, 589–602.

———. (1985). *Reflections on gender and science*. New Haven, Conn.: Yale University Press.

Kelly, A. (1978). Feminism and research. *Women's Studies International Quarterly*, 1, 225–32.

Kotre, J. (1984). *Outliving the self*. Baltimore: Johns Hopkins University.

Lott, B. (1981). A feminist critique of androgyny: Toward the elimination of gender attributions of learned behavior. In C. Mayo and N. Henley, eds., *Gender and nonverbal behavior*, pp. 171–80. New York: Springer-Verlag.

Lykes, M. B., and A. J. Stewart (1986). Evaluating the feminist challenge to research in personality and social psychology: 1963–1983. *Psychology of Women Quarterly*, 10, 393–412.

Mies, M. (1983). Towards a methodology for feminist research. In G. Bowles and R. Duelli Klein, *Theories of women's studies*, pp. 117–39. Boston: Routledge & Kegan Paul.

Milgram, S. (1974). *Obedience to authority*. New York: Harper.

Morawski, J. (1985). The measurement of masculinity and feminity: Engendering categorical realities. *Journal of Personality*, 53, 196–223.

Oakley, A. (1981). Interviewing women: A contradiction in terms. In H. Roberts, ed., *Doing feminist research*, pp. 30–61. Boston: Routledge & Kegan Paul.

Parlee, M. B. (1975). Psychology: Review essay. *Signs*, 1, 119–38.

Reinharz, S. (1979). *On becoming a social scientist*. San Francisco: Jossey-Bass.

Roberts, H., ed. (1981). *Doing feminist research*. Boston: Routledge & Kegan Paul.

Rose, H. (1982). Making science feminist. In E. Whitelegg et al., eds., *The changing experience of women*. Oxford: Martin Robinson.

Scheuneman, J. D. (1986). The female perspective on methodology and statistics. *Educational researcher*, 15, 22–23.

Sherif, C. W. (1987). Bias in psychology. In S. Harding, ed., *Feminism and methodology*, pp. 37–56. Bloomington: Indiana University Press. (Reprinted from J. A. Sherman and E. T. Beck, eds., (1979). *The prism of sex*. Madison: University of Wisconsin Press.)

Siefert, K., and Martin, L. D. (1988). Preventing black maternal mortality: A challenge for the 90s. *Journal of Primary Prevention*, 9, 57–65.

Smith, D. E. (1987). Women's perspective as a radical critique of sociology. In S. Harding, ed., *Feminism and methodology*, pp. 84–96. Bloomington: Indiana University Press. (Reprinted from *Sociological Inquiry*, 1974, 44, 7–13.)

Stanley, L., and S. Wise (1983). *Breaking out: Feminist consciousness and feminist research*. London: Routledge & Kegan Paul.

Stasz Stoll, C. (1974). *Female and male: Socialization, social roles and social structure*. New York: Brown.

Tangri, S. S., and G. L. Strasburg (1979). Can research on women be more effective in shaping policy? *Psychology of Women Quarterly*, 3, 321–43.

Tavris, C. (1987). Method is all but lost in the imagery of social-science fiction. *Los Angeles Times*, Nov. 1, p. V5.

Unger, R. K. (1981). Sex as a social reality: Field and laboratory research. *Psychology of Women Quarterly*, 5, 645–53.

———. (1983). Through the looking glass: No wonderland yet! (The reciprocal relationship between methodology and models of reality). *Psychology of Women Quarterly*, 8, 9–32.

Wallston, B. (1981). What are the questions in psychology of women? A feminist approach to research. *Psychology of Women Quarterly*, 5, 597–617.

Weisstein, N. (1977). How can a little girl like you teach a great big class of men? the chairman said, and other adventures of a woman in science. In S. Ruddick and P. Daniels, eds., *Working it out*, pp. 241–50. New York: Pantheon.

Westkott, M. (1979). Feminist criticism of the social sciences. *Harvard Educational Review*, 49, 422–30.

Williams, D. A., and P. King (1980). Do males have a math gene? *Newsweek*, Dec. 15, p. 73.

Wittig, M. (1985). Metatheoretical dilemmas in the psychology of gender. *American Psychologist*, 40, 800–812.

Wolinsky, H. (1986). Program targets maternal deaths. *Chicago Sun-Times*, August 11, p. 22.

Wolinsky, H., and P. Franchine (1986). Black maternal deaths here 4 times U.S. level. *Chicago Sun-Times*, Aug. 8, p. 3.

Yllo, K. (1988). Political and methodological debates in wife abuse research. In K. Yllo, ed., *Feminist perspectives on wife abuse*, pp. 28–50. Newbury Park, N.J.: Sage.

6. Race and Class Bias in Qualitative Research on Women

Lynn Weber Cannon,
Elizabeth Higginbotham, and
Marianne L. A. Leung

Exploratory studies employing volunteer subjects are especially vulnerable to race and class bias. This article illustrates how inattention to race and class as critical dimensions in women's lives can produce biased research samples and lead to false conclusions. It analyzes the race and class backgrounds of 200 women who volunteered to participate in an in-depth study of Black and White professional, managerial, and administrative women. Despite a multiplicity of methods used to solicit subjects, White women raised in middle-class families who worked in male-dominated occupations were the most likely to volunteer, and White women were more than twice as likely to respond to media solicitations or letters. To recruit most Black subjects and address their concerns about participation required more labor-intensive strategies involving personal contact. The article discusses reasons for differential volunteering and ways to integrate race and class into qualitative research on women.

Feminist research has relied heavily on qualitative methodologies (Cook and Fonow, 1986; Grant, Ward, and Rong, 1987; Roberts, 1981; Stacey and Thorne, 1985; Ward and Grant, 1985). In-depth qualitative studies can reveal much about social processes that women experience, but like all research methods, they have limitations. Prominent among them are the relatively small and homogeneous samples that constitute the subjects of each study. While in-depth analysis of small homogeneous samples is a key to discovering the unique quality of subjects' lives, if this approach is used repeatedly on the same population, it can block discovery of the diversity of human experience. Although qualitative research on women has accumulated useful data in many substantive areas, too often the emergent body of knowledge excludes women of color and working-class women (Zinn, Cannon, Higginbotham, and Dill, 1986).

Correcting this imbalance in feminist scholarship requires theoretical conceptualizations that include all dimensions of inequality, more complex research designs, and strategies that confront the obstacles to the incorporation of diverse groups of women. This article discusses the obstacles to integrating race and class into qualitative research on women and offers some solutions to the problem. It reports the sampling strategy for an in-depth study of Black and

Reprinted from *GENDER & SOCIETY*, Vol. 2 No. 4, December 1988 449–462, © 1988 Sociologists for Women in Society.

White professional, managerial, and administrative women and the obstacles to achieving a sample balanced by the race and class background of the subjects and the gender composition of their occupations.

We found that White women working in male-dominated occupations who were raised in middle-class families volunteered more often than any other group. We suggest that this difference is due to the higher concentration of White women of middle-class origins in the population of middle-class women and to fewer obstacles to their participation in research projects. In order to get Black women to participate, we had to use more labor-intensive recruitment strategies, such as verbal contact, usually face-to-face, with Black women researchers or other Black women working with the research team. Interviews also took more time to complete because of interruptions and canceled appointments. When Black women felt assured that the research was worthwhile, they were eager to participate.

This article discusses the sample selection for a study designed to control race and class background. The subjects were women employed full-time as professionals, managers, and administrators; the methodology used was in-depth interviews. We report here the problems we faced in subject recruitment and the strategies we used to produce a heterogeneous sample. Our study suggests that researchers who are committed to incorporating subjects of different races and classes in their qualitative research designs must be prepared to allow more time and money for subject recruitment and data collection.

The Study

The study explores the relationship of race, class, and gender inequality to the general well-being and mental health of full-time employed professional, managerial, and administrative women in the United States. Data were collected with face-to-face, focused, life-history interviews, lasting two to three hours each.

We wanted a sample of 200 Black and White professionals, managers, and administrators from the Memphis, Tennessee, metropolitan area. As is the case with many studies of women, there was no way to randomly sample the specific population of concern. We employed a quota sample structured by three dimensions of inequality: race and class background of the respondent and the gender composition of her occupation. We dichotomized the three dimensions, creating an eight-cell, $2 \times 2 \times 2$ design. Each cell contained twenty-five cases, a sample size large enough to allow statistical estimates of the relationships of the three major independent variables with other variables in the study.

Study Parameters

We restricted the study to women born between 1945 and 1960 who were 25–40 years old at the time of the interview, because their formal education took place at a time when greater funds and opportunities were available for working-class and Black women to attend college. Seeking to examine institutional supports for upward mobility through college attendance (e.g., the role of high school counselors and teachers), we restricted the study to full-time employed college graduates who had gone to college immediately or within two years of finishing high school. Because we wanted to compare Black and White women raised in middle-class and working-class families, we excluded nurses (a popular occupation for mobile working-class women but rarely the choice of women from middle-class families) and physicians (few working-class women can secure funds needed to cover years of medical education). Because many White teachers but few Black teachers in the area are employed in the private sector, we limited the sample of primary and secondary school teachers to those employed in the public schools.

Our interest in investigating how class background manifests itself in the lives of middle-class women required that our sample include women in the full range of middle-class positions (e.g., professionals, managers, and administrators). The sample included women in each of three primary relations of control over the working class: political (supervision), economic (ownership), and ideological (mental labor), in order to shed light on issues such as the nature of social interactions across class lines (Braverman, 1974; Ehrenreich and Ehrenreich, 1979; Poulantzas, 1974; Vanneman and Cannon, 1987). The study also examines how women of different races, from different class backgrounds, and with different support networks manage these across-class contacts.

Since professional networks tend to be homogeneous and insular, we set quotas for the proportions of professionals, managers, and administrators, and within each of those broad categories, for specific occupations. To match regional representation, the design called for 60 percent professionals and 40 percent managers and administrators in the male-dominated occupations, and 76 percent professionals and 24 percent managers and administrators in the female-dominated occupations. Within each gender-composition category, we selected particular occupations for inclusion in the sample, based on their regional proportions among professionals, managers, and administrators.

Finally, subjects were selected to minimize confounding race or class background with their occupations. A growing body of evidence indicates that in addition to gender segregation in the labor force, substantial race segregation occurs as well (National Committee on Pay Equity, 1987). Given the structural relations among race, class, and occupation, we could easily draw a sample of upwardly mobile working-class or Black women who are concentrated in the specific occupations that are more open to them (e.g., public school teaching, social work). To avoid the confounding of race, class background, and occupation, we selected subjects so that each race and class background category contained women from the same or closely related occupations. For example, in the category of male-dominated professionals, the sample includes equal numbers of Black and White lawyers raised in working-class and middle-class families. Subjects were also classified into three age groupings defined by birth cohort (1956–1960, 1951–1955, and 1945–1950) to prevent overrepresentation of any age group in a race, class background, or specific occupational category.

Every few weeks, volunteers who met all study parameters were sorted according to all of the stratifying variables (race, class, gender composition of occupation, professional versus managers and administrators, specific occupation, and age category). We then randomly selected subjects to interview from each pool.

Recruitment of Subjects

Less Labor-Intensive Outreach Strategies

The first subject recruitment strategies we employed were less labor intensive. These strategies, quite common in sociological and psychological research, consisted mainly of letters to organizations and individuals known to fit the study criteria, and announcements in the local media (radio programs, daily newspaper, a business daily magazine, and so on) describing the study and asking for volunteers.

All forty-six women's organizations that were listed in the public library's most recent list and were likely to include members eligible for the study received letters. This included both professional organizations such as the American Society of Certified Public Accountants and social organizations such as the National Council of Negro Women. The letters asked that organizations inform their members of the study and offered to send study team members to speak to their groups if they so desired. Individuals interested in participating in the study received a personal letter containing a general description of the study and describing the criteria for inclusion in it (i.e., age 25–40; direct route to college degree; full-time employed professional, manager, or administrator). Regarding the three major independent variables in the study, the letter indicated our interest in studying the life histories of Black and White women in male- and female-dominated occupations. The letter did not mention social class.

Volunteers completed a one-page information form and returned it to the authors' university. Since the women knew the eligibility criteria, the sampling frame included almost all of the volunteers.

Less labor-intensive strategies reached more White than Black subjects. As Table 1 reveals, we recruited 22.9 percent of the Whites but only 3.7 percent of the Blacks through the media (see columns 3 and 6). Letters to occupational groups garnered 31.2 percent of the Whites and 13.4 percent of the Blacks. In all, these strategies reached 74.1 percent of the White but only 38.8 percent of the Black women volunteers.

More Labor-Intensive Outreach Strategies

After tracking the characteristics of the women who responded to letters and media solicitations, we started using more labor-intensive strategies to recruit other categories of women. Those strategies included personal presentations to women's organizations' meetings, snowball techniques of calling individuals to recommend others for the study, and identifying special newsletters to receive advertisements.

Table 1 Success of Subject Recruitment by Race and Class Origins

	Black			White		
Type of Strategy	Working Class 49% (N = 84)	Middle Class 51% (N = 50)	Total Black 100% (N = 134)	Working Class 32.3% (N = 86)	Middle Class 67.7% (N = 180)	Total White 100% (N = 266)
Less labor intensive mass media	6.0 (5)	—	3.7 (5)	27.9 (24)	20.6 (37)	22.9 (61)
occupational mailing lists	14.2 (12)	12.0 (6)	13.4 (18)	23.2 (20)	35.0 (63)	31.2 (83)
other mailings	20.2 (17)	24.0 (12)	21.7 (29)	18.6 (16)	20.6 (37)	20.0 (53)
subtotal	40.4	36.0	38.8	69.7	76.2	74.1
More labor intensive organizational presentations	6.0 (5)	4.0 (2)	5.2 (7)	4.7 (4)	2.2 (4)	3.0 (8)
snowball technique	53.6 (45)	60.0 (30)	56.0 (75)	25.6 (22)	21.6 (39)	22.9 (61)
subtotal	59.6 (50)	64.0 (32)	61.2 (82)	30.3 (26)	23.8 (43)	25.9 (69)
Total	100 (84)	100 (50)	100 (134)	100 (86)	100 (180)	100 (266)

NOTE: For each item, the top row of figures represents percentages; the numbers in parentheses indicate the number of subjects.

Most Black women (61.2 percent) were recruited through labor-intensive strategies such as presentations at meetings and, most often, through word-of-mouth snowball techniques. We recruited over half (56 percent) of the Black volunteers through direct contact by project staff or by other Black women professionals who either participated in the study themselves and recommended other names to their interviewer or worked with the project staff from the beginning of the study to recruit volunteers.

Class Background and Outreach Strategies

Despite a strong race effect, class background did not influence the success of the recruitment strategies (see columns 1, 2, 4, and 5). Within each race, every recruitment strategy was about equally likely to reach subjects from working- and middle-class backgrounds. The one exception is the 11.8 percent greater likelihood of reaching White middle-class as opposed to White working-class volunteers through occupational mailing lists. Such a difference may have resulted from greater concentrations of women of middle-class origins in the particular occupations for which we had mailing lists.

Race and Class Background of the Volunteers

After nine months of subject recruitment, 400 women employed as professionals, managers, and administrators had volunteered to participate in the study. Of the total, 134 or 33.5 percent were Black, and 266 or 66.5 percent were White. According to the 1980 census, Black women constituted 25.3 percent of the women employed as professionals, managers, or administrators in the Memphis Standard Metropolitan Statistical Area (U.S. Bureau of the Census 1983). Since Black women's concentration in the middle class had not greatly increased during the period from 1980 to 1985 (Higginbotham, 1987), we felt that Black women had volunteered at a rate consistent with—and perhaps slightly higher than—their representation in the population under study. However, we used different recruitment strategies to achieve these roughly equivalent rates of volunteering among Black and White women. Had we not employed different strategies, our sample would have been disproportionately White.

There were 170 volunteers with working-class origins, and 230 with middle-class origins. The class origins of these professional and managerial women differed significantly for Blacks and Whites. Of the 400 volunteers, 180 (45.0 percent) were Whites raised middle class, 86 (21.5 percent) were Whites raised working class, 84 (21.0 percent) were Blacks raised working class, and 50 (12.5 percent) were Blacks raised middle class.

Although our data do not permit a thorough examination of the issue, two factors seem likely to have produced a pool of volunteers that was heavily weighted to White women who had come from and stayed in the middle class, and among Black women, to the upwardly mobile. These factors are the race and class background of the population of middle-class women employed full-time and the structural and social psychological factors restricting Black women's participation in this kind of research.

Population Parameters

Our sample was not random; so we cannot infer directly from these data that two-thirds of the Black middle-class women were upwardly mobile while two-thirds of White middle-class women were born into the middle class. However, these proportions are plausible, since the extent of intraclass mobility from the working class to the professional-managerial class in the United States has never been high (Coleman and Rainwater, 1978; Ryan and Sackrey, 1984; Vanneman and Cannon, 1987).

At first glance, a sample with one-third of its Whites upwardly mobile might seem to overrepresent that group. But the post-World War II era (especially between the late 1950s and the early 1970s) brought the greatest increase in the size of the professional-managerial class (Vanneman and Cannon, 1987). In addition, the economic boom of the 1960s and early 1970s, coupled with the breakdown of racial barriers, nearly doubled the size of the Black middle-class population, a larger increase than for Whites (Cannon, 1984). Consequently, after World War II and for the first time in American history, the Black class structure began to approximate the White class structure (Vanneman and Cannon, 1987; Wilson, 1978).

It was the "baby-boom" generation educated in the 1960s and 1970s who benefited most from post-World War II changes and who are the subjects of our study. They reached college age just as the civil rights movement brought down legal segregation and a strong economy provided the financial support for college attendance among large numbers of Black and working-class youth. Thus we feel confident that the proportions of upwardly mobile volunteers in our sample approximate their prevalence in the population.

Obstacles to Participation

Some social psychological and structural factors militated against Black women's participation. These factors were skepticism about the purpose of the research, worries about protection of anonymity, and structural obstacles such as less free time. Dominant-group women have less reason than minority-group women to suspect that they or members of their group will be exploited in research (Zinn, 1979). As a result, White women in this study were more than twice as likely to respond to letters or media solicitations, but personal contact was usually required to recruit Black subjects. The contact enabled Black women to gain the assurances they needed that neither they nor others would be exploited by the research process or its products.

We expected that the Black women might also be apprehensive about participating, since the request came from researchers at a predominantly White educational institution. Anticipating many of these concerns, we devised research strategies to minimize their impact. For example, we made explicit in every communication about the study that the coprincipal investigators for the study were a Black and a White woman, that the research team was biracial, and that we sought both Black and White subjects. We also sent Black members of the research team to speak to exclusively Black groups, White members to speak to exclusively White groups, and a biracial team to speak to every group that had both Black and White women. Only Black interviewers interviewed Black subjects, and White interviewers interviewed White subjects.

Despite the above precautions, more Black than White women required additional assurance, especially about guarantees of anonymity. Many Black middle-class subjects were highly visible in the community as, for example, the only or one of a few bank vice presidents, newscasters, university administrators, library branch directors, or judges. White women in similar positions were more numerous, if not in a single firm, at least throughout the city. The Black women were more likely to ask for specific details, for example, about how we would refer to them in any future reports, before they felt comfortable about the protection of their anonymity.

In addition, it became clear that these Black middle-class women had less free time than the White middle-class women to devote to activities like participation in social research. Even though there were no racial differences in marital status in the final sample, 65 percent of the Black women had children, and 65 percent of the White women had no children. It was more difficult to schedule and complete interviews with Black volunteers. They had less free time to devote to the project, were often unable to complete the interview in one sitting, and were more likely to cancel scheduled interviews because of unforeseen circumstances. We did not interpret these actions as reflecting resistance to the project or the interview because these women continued to express an interest in participation, and almost all did in fact complete the interview.

Female-Dominated Occupations

Although we cannot be sure of the population distribution across class origins of the middle-class women, census data do indicate the gender-composition of the female middle-class labor force. In the Memphis SMSA, 55 percent of the women professionals, managers, and administrators worked in female-dominated occupations. The volunteers for our study, however, came mainly from male-dominated occupations—57 percent of the Black (N = 76) and 56 percent (N = 148) of the White women volunteers.

Many women in female-dominated occupations also appeared to have less control over their time and less free time. Scheduling and completing interviews with women teachers, for example, was more difficult than with lawyers or administrators who could block out time during the work day while secretaries held their calls. Thus in the cases of both Black women and women in female-dominated occupations, greater persistence was required to recruit subjects, to schedule, and to complete interviews. These structural realities meant that the White interviewers completed their interviews sooner than the Black interviewers. White interviewers were then able to facilitate the work of Black project team members by assisting with transcriptions, coding, and other activities.

Biased Samples—Biased Results

Although we have only begun to analyze the data from the study, we have already identified several areas in which we would have made false inferences had we not attended to the race and class background of the middle-class women. For example, we investigated the level of social supports that women received in making the transition from high school to college (Cannon, Higginbotham, and Leung, 1987; Newsome, 1986). The working-class women received far less financial support and information from family. Since the typical Black woman volunteer for our study was raised in a working-class family, while the typical White volunteer was raised in a middle-class family, had we not attended to the class background of the women as well as their race, we would have concluded that these middle-class Black women had received far less family support than White women. Such a conclusion could easily have fueled a "cultural deficit" interpretation. Had we not interviewed Black women raised in middle-class families and White women from the working-class, we would have neglected a small but theoretically significant segment of professional and managerial women. Failing to recognize their experiences could greatly distort our conclusions about how they had reached their current occupations and class position.

Conclusions

Since qualitative research frequently involves face-to-face contact between researcher and subject, open-ended rather than closed-ended questions, unstructured rather than structured interview schedules, samples are typically small. To generate theory, it is much more useful if the small samples under study are relatively homogeneous, since extreme diversity makes the task of identifying common patterns almost impossible. Unfortunately, as a result, much of the newly emerging scholarship on women excludes women of color and working-class women of all races. For example, in her review of research on women's occupational experiences, Harkess (1985) reports that the most commonly studied group of women workers is still white-collar workers, and that even among them, women working in male-dominated spheres receive the most attention, despite the fact that the majority of women still work in female-dominated occupations (Dill, Cannon, and Vanneman, 1987; Reskin, 1984).

Feminist research in sociology and psychology is replete with caveats like that reported in a study that sampled White undergraduate students at a private university to identify "generational differences in women's attitudes toward the female role in society." The authors, Slevin and Wingrove (1983), state, "Selection of subjects this way avoided the complexities of analysis which would have been introduced by racial and regional differences" (p. 611). Chodorow's (1978) study, *The Reproduction of Mothering*, drew criticism for "trying to explain the perpetuation of a certain kind of mothering—middle class, psychologically oriented, and achievement oriented (husbands and sons toward careers, mothers and daughters toward perfect children)—in short, the hothouse tending of two or three offspring in an isolated nuclear family" (Lorber, 1981, p. 485).

For some researchers, issues of race or class never surface until the research is completed. Hertz (1986) stated in her recent book, *More Equal Than Others: Women and Men in Dual-Career Marriages*, "Although this was not a deliberate sampling strategy, all respondents were Caucasian" (p. 217). However, the exclusion of other groups frequently takes place despite feminist researchers' awareness of the importance of the many dimensions of inequality.

In some cases, feminist researchers make politically motivated decisions to exclude particular groups from research. In her powerful study, *Father-Daughter Incest*, Herman (1981) took account of dominant-culture views of minority families and the potential for misuse of results in her decision to exclude minority women:

> All of the informants [40 women] were white. We made the decision to restrict the interviewing to white women in order to avoid even the possibility that the information gathered might be used to fuel idle speculation about racial differences. (p. 68)

While such deliberate exclusion might be protective, the pervasiveness of exclusionary practices produces a cumulative impact on the empirical generalizations that constitute the elements of feminist theory. As a result, the prevailing literature, which seems to identify particular "social realities," merely represents White and middle-class experiences. The social realities of other groups, such as minorities and the working classes, become relegated to side issues in the field (Zinn et al., 1986).

NOTE

This article is a revision of an earlier work presented at the Annual Meeting of the Southern Sociological Society, New Orleans, April 1986. The research was supported by National Institute of Mental Health Grant MH38769, coprincipal investigators Lynn Weber Cannon and Elizabeth Higginbotham. We wish to thank Margaret Andersen and Steve McNamee for comments on an earlier draft. We also appreciate the comments of Judith Lorber and two anonymous reviewers.

REFERENCES

Braverman, H. 1974. *Labor and Monopoly Capital*. New York: Monthly Review Press.
Cannon, L. Weber. 1984. "Trends in Class Identification Among Blacks from 1952 to 1978." *Social Science Quarterly* 65:112–26.

Cannon, L. Weber, E. Higginbotham, and M. L. A. Leung, 1987. "Race and Class Bias in Research on Women: A Methodological Note." Working Paper 5. Center for Research on Women, Memphis State University, Memphis, TN.

Chodorow, N. 1978. *The Reproduction of Mothering*. Berkeley: University of California Press.

Coleman, R. P., and L. Rainwater. 1978. *Social Standing in America: New Dimensions of Class*. New York: Basic Books.

Cook, J. A., and M. M. Fonow. 1986. "Knowledge and Women's Interests: Issues of Feminist Epistemology and Methodology in Feminist Sociological Research." *Sociological Inquiry* 56:2–29.

Dill, B. Thorton, L. Weber Cannon, and R. Vanneman. 1987. "Race and Gender in Occupational Segregation." Pp. 13–70 in *Pay Equity: An Issue of Race, Ethnicity, and Sex*. Washington, DC: National Committee on Pay Equity.

Ehrenreich, B., and J. Ehrenreich. 1979. "The Professional-Managerial Class." Pp. 5–45 in *Between Labor and Capital*, edited by P. Walker. Boston: South End Press.

Grant, L., K. B. Ward, and X. L. Rong. 1987. "Is There an Association between Gender and Methods in Sociological Research?" *American Sociological Review* 52:856–62.

Harkess, S. 1985. "Women's Occupational Experience in the 1970's: Sociology and Economics." *Signs: Journal of Women in Culture and Society* 10:495–516.

Herman, J. 1981. *Father-Daughter Incest*. Cambridge, MA: Harvard University Press.

Hertz, R. 1986. *More Equal Than Others: Women and Men in Dual-Career Marriages*. Berkeley: University of California Press.

Higginbotham, E. 1987. "Employment for Professional Black Women in the Twentieth Century." Pp. 73–91 in *Ingredients for Women's Employment Policy*, edited by C. Bose and G. Spitze. Albany: SUNY Press.

Lorber, J. 1981. "On *The Reproduction of Mothering*: A Debate." *Signs: Journal of Women in Culture and Society* 6:482–86.

Miller, D. 1977. *Handbook of Research Design and Social Measurement*. 3rd edition. New York: David McKay.

National Committee on Pay Equity. 1987. *Pay Equity: An Issue of Race, Ethnicity and Sex*. Washington, DC: National Committee on Pay Equity.

Newsome, Y. 1986. "Class Obstacles to Higher Education: An Examination of the High School Experiences of Black Professional Women." Master's thesis, Memphis State University, Memphis, TN.

Poulantzas, N. 1974. *Classes in Contemporary Capitalism*. London: New Left Books.

Reskin, B. F. 1984. "Sex Segregation in the Workplace." Pp. 1–12 in *Gender at Work: Perspectives on Occupational Segregation and Comparable Worth*. Washington, DC: Women's Research and Education Institute of the Congregational Caucus for Women's Issues.

Roberts, H. 1981. *Doing Feminist Research*. Boston: Routledge & Kegan Paul.

Ryan, J., and C. Sackrey. 1984. *Strangers in Paradise: Academics from the Working Class*. Boston: South End Press.

Slevin, K. F., and C. R. Wingrove. 1983. "Similarities and Differences among Three Generations of Women in Attitudes toward the Female Role in Contemporary Society." *Sex Roles* 9:609–24.

Stacey, J., and B. Thorne. 1985. "The Missing Feminist Revolution in Sociology." *Social Problems* 32:301–16.

U.S. Bureau of the Census. 1983. "Detailed Population Characteristics: Tennessee." *U.S. Census of the Population, 1980*. Washington, DC: U.S. Government Printing Office.

Vanneman, R., and L. Weber Cannon. 1987. *The American Perception of Class*. Philadelphia: Temple University Press.

Ward, K. B., and L. Grant. 1985. "The Feminist Critique and a Decade of Published Research in Sociology Journals." *Sociological Quarterly* 26:139–57.

Wilson, W. J. 1978. *The Declining Significance of Race*. Chicago: University of Chicago Press.

Zinn, M. Baca. 1979. "Field Research in Minority Communities: Ethical, Methodological, and Political Observations by an Insider." *Social Problems* 27:209–19.

Zinn, M. Baca, L. W. Cannon, E. Higginbotham, and B. Dill. 1986. "The Cost of Exclusionary Practices in Women's Studies." *Signs: Journal of Women and Culture in Society* 11:290–303.

7. RESEARCHING THE WOMEN'S MOVEMENT

We Make Our Own History, But Not Just As We Please[1]

VERTA TAYLOR AND LEILA J. RUPP

When in the course of our research on the American women's rights movement in the 1940s and 1950s we telephoned a woman whom we knew to have been an active feminist in this period, we found that she was delighted that we were studying a forgotten stage of the movement, but that she was adamant about the differences between feminists then and now. "We were not like the young bra-burners and lesbians of today," she told us. As participants in the contemporary women's movement, we were taken aback. But we soon came to realize that, despite our expectations as feminists that researching the women's movement would provide us the quintessential opportunity to integrate our politics and research, we would have to set aside some of our own assumptions and political ideals. Only in this way could we truly understand the movement that survived the antifeminist climate of the years between 1945 and the early 1960s.[2]

We had undertaken this research knowing that both the scholarly and popular literature had assumed that the women's movement died in 1920—or shortly thereafter—and was not resurrected until the mid–1960s. Had we not been feminists, we might never have looked any further at the period characterized as "the bleak and lonely years" (Sochen, 1973). Our research originated in curiosity about the fate of women who had, during the Second World War, worked for what they termed "full citizenship" for women. Although we suspected that these women had not been converted or overwhelmed by "the feminine mystique" in the 1950s, we did not set out to prove that a women's rights movement existed. We did, however, find the period between the end of the war and what we have come to call the "resurgence" of the women's movement a particularly fascinating one, since it followed on the heels of a war that had brought women into areas previously reserved for men and preceded the emergence of a large and active women's movement, yet is traditionally characterized as a period of extreme domesticity for American women. Only in the course of our research did we begin to think of the organizations and individuals working for women's rights as a social movement, and this was originally because the women themselves saw their activity in this way. As Linda Gordon suggests, "[i]f you listen quietly and intently to the people who appear in your historical source material, it sometimes happens that they begin to speak to you." She warns against smothering their voices with preformed questions that come from either "methodological or political determinism" (Gordon, 1978, pp. 129–30).

What we found ultimately was not the kind of movement that contemporary feminists would be eager to claim. We discovered a continuance phase of the women's movement that we term "elite-sustained." This was not a broadly-based grassroots movement, but a small movement of elite women: primarily white, middle or upper class, well-educated professional women who had developed a commitment to feminism in the early decades of the twentieth century. They did not attempt to mobilize diverse groups of women, nor did they seek alliances with other movements for social change. Some used McCarthyite tactics to try to win support for their goals, and the movement as a whole saw labor as an enemy and the civil rights movement as a competitor. Feminists developed strategies and pursued goals consistent with their interests and with the structure of their movement. Their three primary objectives were passage of the Equal Rights Amendment, increased representation of women in policy-making positions, and recognition of women's history.

In the contemporary American women's movement, women of color, working-class women, and Jewish women have initiated a critique of the race, class, and cultural bias of a movement that defines only a limited set of goals, those that have traditionally been defined by the interests of white middle-class women, as appropriate for a movement focusing on gender inequality. We are entirely in sympathy with this critique, but this did not lead us to broaden our definition of the women's rights movement in the 1950s. We believe that it is essential to portray as accurately as possible the history of a relatively encapsulated stage of the movement in order to understand better what could befall the movement in the future. Although the portrait of the movement that emerged from our research was not one that suited our feminist tastes, we heeded the warning of Charles Tilly, who points out that it "takes confidence, even arrogance, to override a group's own vision of its interests in life" (Tilly, 1978, p. 61). Thus we attempted to analyze those interests and to understand why "feminism" and "women's rights" had come to have such narrow applications.

By training, one of us is a sociologist and the other a historian, and we are both feminists who are active in the women's movement. We found that cross-disciplinary collaboration had a great many advantages and one disadvantage. We believe that the disciplines of sociology and history have a great deal to contribute to each other, since history is too often atheoretical and sociology ahistorical. In fact, it seems to us that some of the best work in both disciplines has a cross-disciplinary character. In terms of methodology, we were able to make use of sociological perspectives on and experience in interviewing and historical approaches to documentary analysis. In addition, we found that the process of familiarizing ourselves with the literature, theories, and methods of each other's disciplines, and then discussing the assumptions and modes of research in both fields, expanded our understanding of the research process.

On the other hand, we met resistance in some quarters to our attempt to construct a truly cross-disciplinary approach to this research. When we applied to the National Endowment for the Humanities for a basic research grant to fund the research, we were told to play down the sociology and present a straight-forward traditional historical narrative. Although we did receive the grant, our final draft of the proposal looked quite different from the first. We also found, in presenting our research and submitting the manuscript of our book to a press, that historians were dubious about the usefulness of our social movement framework. Traditional historical monographs look quite different from sociological ones, and combining a sociological framework and a historical narrative was not simple.

This research, more than any work either of us had done previously, required what Liz Stanley and Sue Wise refer to as "breaking out" or moving beyond the limitations of any one of the discourses of sociology, history, and feminism (Stanley and Wise, 1983b). To make clear what we mean by this, we are going to discuss the research perspective that guided our work, the data-gathering process, and the political implications of our research on the post–1945 women's rights movement.

The Research Perspective

Feminist scholars have for some time argued that, from the perspective of women, the theories, models, and assumptions of the traditional academic disciplines are woefully inadequate (Millman and Kanter, 1975; Eichler, 1980; Bernard, 1981; Spender, 1981; Roberts, 1981; Smith, 1974). It is only recently, however, that feminists have enlarged the critique of "scientific objectivity" to argue that it is not merely the content of the traditional disciplines that is problematic, but the methods that have been used to gather knowledge about women as well (Daniels, 1975; Cook and Fonow, 1986; Bowles and Duelli Klein, 1983; Stanley and Wise, 1983b; DiIorio, 1980; Reinharz, 1983). In seeking to correct the androcentrism of traditional research, feminist social scientists have emphasized the importance of qualitative and descriptive studies, a closer link between the researcher and the researched, participant observation and experiential analysis, action research, acknowledging the role of values in research, and a whole host of techniques that are, in short, more contextual and subjective (Gould, 1980; DiIorio, 1980; Reinharz, 1983; Stanley and Wise, 1983a; Oakley, 1981; Rubin, 1976; Krieger, 1983; Lowe and Hubbard, 1983).

For us, feminist research implies a perspective, rather than any specific methodologies, in which women's experiences, ideas, and needs are viewed as valid in their own right, and in which androcentricity—and its theoretical and empirical constructions—no longer serves as the "objective" frame of reference against which all human experience is compared (Bowles and Duelli Klein, 1983; Stanley and Wise, 1983b; Cook and Fonow, 1986). There are three major ways that traditional approaches to the study of social movements reflect an androcentric vision of social life that we think has led scholars to overlook the women's rights movement in the post–1945 period: an emphasis on male-dominated movements, the prevalence of official views of social movements, and the tendency to differentiate sharply between social movements and established institutions.

First, most of the research on social movements from which the major theoretical positions in the field have been derived focuses on predominantly male-dominated movements (Wood and Jackson, 1982). Women's historians have begun to explore the role of gender in the establishment and structure of women's institutions as well as in women's historical participation in protests, demonstrations, strikes, social reform, and revolutionary activity; and recent sociological accounts of the civil rights, antiwar, and other New Left movements of the 1960s as well as of the contemporary women's movement make clear that gender inequality plays a major part in structuring the nature and style of women's participation in social movements (Graham, 1977; Smith-Rosenberg, 1971; Berg, 1978; Freedman, 1979; Evans, 1979; Freeman, 1975; Banks, 1981; Ferree and Hess, 1985). Yet the major theoretical perspectives on social movements still fail to incorporate gender as a major social process affecting the nature, style, and strategic choices of social movements. We believe that there is a need for work which, by focusing on women's lives and interests as well as men's, contributes to the reappraisal of conventional theories and ultimately to the development of more general nonsexist theories of social movements (Eichler, 1983).

A second reason that historians and sociologists have overlooked the feminist movement in this period of history is because they have adopted what Elliott Currie and Jerome Skolnick describe as a "managerial" or administrative perspective (Currie and Skolnick, 1972). The field of collective behavior and social movements has its roots in nineteenth-century European antidemocratic theories that saw social protest and rebellion as something to be controlled, managed, or contained in order to preserve the existing class structure and social fabric (Bramson, 1961). This underlying bias, although modified to some extent in modern approaches to social movements, still shows up in the tendency of sociologists and historians to accept "official" definitions of social movement activity and to discredit the beliefs, ideas, and strategies of participants engaged in collective action.

Perhaps unwittingly, historians and sociologists have accepted the popular and official view, perpetuated by the mass media, of the post–1945 period as devoid of an organized feminist movement. One of the principal tactics used by dominant groups, whose interests tend to be reflected in the established mass media, to constrain or "manage" the spread of social movements is to refuse to recognize a movement's existence, thereby limiting its access to the resources it needs to mobilize (Molotch, 1979). Just because established institutions fail to accord legitimacy to a social movement does not mean that it cannot manage to survive or, as has been assumed of the women's rights movement in our period, that it does not exist.

The third bias blurring our ability to see feminist activity in the post–1945 period is built into the way in which the boundaries of the field of collective behavior and social movements have been drawn historically. Until recently, collective behavior and social movements have been sharply distinguished from routine or established social life. Whereas conventional organizations and forms of social behavior are viewed as largely rational, orderly, preplanned, organized, and guided by self-restraint, behavior in crowds and social movements is seen, in contrast, as emotional, disorderly, spontaneous, disorganized, and impulsive. Drawing a sharp and exaggerated contrast between collective behavior and social movements, on the one hand, and established social behavior, on the other, obviously functions to discredit the actions and ideas of challenging groups.

Scholars have increasingly argued that these characterizations of collective behavior and social movements are generally inaccurate (Perry and Pugh, 1978; Quarantelli and Weller, 1974; Miller, 1985). The important point for us is that, if group behavior does not conform to the stereotypes set forth, then it has often fallen outside the boundaries of the field. Women have been much less likely to be aggressive and to use disruptive and confrontational tactics in pursuit of their aims. Instead, they have developed a style of participation in social movements—the temperance, abolition, child welfare, settlement house, and peace movements, for example—that can be seen as a natural extension of their traditional roles as nurturers and guardians of morality (Bernard, 1981). It is not surprising, then, that since the style and structural form of women's activism in the post–1945 period did not conform to the traditional stereotypes associated with collective behavior and social movements, scholars have overlooked the women's rights movement in this period. Contrary to the stereotypes, the movement was comprised of preexistent as well as emergent groups; established organizations, including the National Woman's Party, the National Federation of Business and Professional Women's Clubs, and other professional and service organizations of women made up the core of the movement.

We began our work with the assumption that the research questions dictated by the traditional theories of social movement scholars might not be the most revealing, but we did not completely abandon the conceptual tools of the field. Our analysis of the women's movement was guided by resource mobilization theory. The major premise of the resource mobilization perspective is that movements among long-standing aggrieved groups form not because of significant shifts in their objective circumstances, but because of long-term changes in group resources, organization, and the opportunities available to them for collective action (McCarthy and Zald, 1977; Jenkins, 1983).

Two important factors pointed to resource mobilization theory as an appropriate perspective from which to approach our analysis of the women's rights movement. First, this was not a historical period in which rising levels of discontent among masses of women could be taken as the central factor accounting for the movement. Women, confronted with increased demands in the realm of both work and family, were discontented, but women's grievances were not new and cannot alone explain the shape of feminist activism. In fact, most of the individuals active in this period were drawn to the feminist movement during or just subsequent to the suffrage struggle, and they were not themselves the women experiencing increasing tension between labor force participation, on the one hand, and childbearing and rearing, on the other.

Second, resource mobilization theory helped us to explain both why these women remained committed to the movement and why the movement remained small, isolated, and elite. To understand those factors that shape the strategies, growth, and success of any movement, the resource mobilization perspective directs our attention to a movement's internal dynamics—or the ways it organizes to manage its human and material resources—as well as to factors external to the movement—the support and constraint of the larger society. This "open-system" approach, which views the outcomes of movements as critically shaped by the larger political environment, contrasts sharply with the traditional "closed-system" model of social movement development that assumes that movements pass through a standard evolutionary "life cycle" from emergence to decline (Jenkins, 1983). By arguing for the continuity of the women's movement throughout a period in which scholars have refused to recognize its existence, our research makes a case for a model of movement development that departs from the view of invariant cycles of movement growth and decline.

Our feminist perspective, then, led us to new questions about the existence of a women's right movement in our period. By making use of sociological frameworks of social movements, we developed an analysis that challenged traditional androcentric views and proposed a new model of movement organization and strategy—an elite-sustained movement—that might be common to movements mobilizing for survival and continuance.

The Data-Gathering Process

Although our research was guided by premises drawn from resource mobilization theory, our overall approach was inductive. We did not prepare a series of questions and categories of analysis derived from the theory and then apply the data to them. Rather, we used the resource mobilization perspective to guide us in understanding the evidence we gathered about activity on behalf of women's rights. Perhaps we should emphasize that there is nothing exclusively feminist about using an inductive approach. One of us was, in fact, trained in a mainstream sociological research center, the Disaster Research Center, that produced "applied" as well as basic research and relied heavily on field research, interactive methods of data-gathering, inductive approaches, and qualitative analysis.

Data for our study were gathered over a five-year period through various methods and from a wide range of sources. Our data-gathering and analysis were guided by two principal questions. We looked first to see if there were organizations concerned with women's rights. Then we asked what kinds of relationships, if any, existed among the various groups and organizations. We first analyzed documentary material in public and private archival collections, which included pamphlets, newspaper clippings, official and unofficial organizational documents and correspondence, personal letters, and diaries. The second source of data was open-ended, semi-structured, tape-recorded interviews with members of the most central groups and with selected informants who provided a general overview of feminist activism in the period.

Women's historians emphasize the importance of sources that allow us to delve into women's consciousness, particularly personal letters and diaries (Lerner, 1979). Blanche Wiesen Cook has criticized the traditional historical perspective that dismisses the personal and emotional as irrelevant to history. Prior to the most recent wave of women's history, Cook herself, she tells us, paid little attention to the personal correspondence of women involved in the peace movement, which she was studying. "Whenever I came across a love letter by Lillian Wald," she writes, "I would note 'love letter,' and move on" (Cook, 1977, p. 44). Like most contemporary women's historians, as well as other social historians, we were interested in the personal aspects of women's lives and relied heavily on personal sources in researching the women's rights movement in this period.

In the data-gathering process, we found that the aspect most influenced by our feminist perspective was the interviewing. Although our funding agency preferred that we use interviews only to fill in gaps in the written record, we undertook them not only to obtain information missing in the documentary sources, but also to check the validity of our sources and interpretations. We knew from our preliminary analysis of the archival sources that our work would challenge previous assumptions in a fundamental way, so the interviews became a critical test of our analysis. From the interviews we wanted to ascertain the goals and strategies of feminists; the ways the women themselves defined their own activity in this period in relation to the larger history of the women's movement; the nature and strength of relationships among the various groups and individuals; the methods of feminist survival in a social climate opposed to feminism and social reform and characterized by intense anti-Communism; and the kinds of internal problems the movement faced and the way these may have contributed to the movement's inability to mobilize large numbers of women. We treated interviewees as informants, or experts, and utilized an open-ended format in order to allow new questions to emerge in the course of the interview. All of the interviews were tape recorded and transcribed.

Ann Oakley characterizes interviewing women, at least from a feminist perspective, as a "contradiction in terms" because it involves "objectifying your sister" (Oakley, 1981, p. 41). Traditional guidelines for interviewing, she suggests, assume that the interview situation is a one-way hierarchical process between interviewer and subject; advise interviewers to adopt an objective, noninvolved stance; and view interviews as a noninteractive means to a pre-established end. We found that not only would a "proper" interview have been impossible with the women in our study, but that it might not have yielded the most useful kind of data.

From the twelve figures from the movement that we interviewed, we needed to obtain large amounts of data, so the average interview lasted four to six hours. Many of these women, who ranged in age from their mid-sixties to early eighties, were reliving major events of their pasts, some of them reflecting on them for the first time. In all but one case, both of us conducted the interviews—despite the traditional rules of interviewing that prescribe only one interviewer—partly because of a discipline-based division of labor: one of us had extensive interview experience, and the other had worked with the documentary sources. As it turned out, the intensity and the energy of the women we interviewed would have exhausted either of us by herself; we found ourselves having to take turns conducting the interviews.

Most of the women we interviewed were retired, and we had to travel considerable distances to interview them. Sometimes a close friend of the interviewee participated in the interview. In many cases, the interview became a kind of social event, involving food and general conversation. Not surprisingly, some of the most sensitive information was shared during these activities, not when the tape recorder was running. Clearly, we did not treat these women as subjects in the traditional sense. Nor did they refrain from asking us questions about our research, our lives, and the contemporary women's movement. Our interviews were really more like structured conversations, although the "experts" did most of the talking. We learned a great deal, but we also shared our thoughts about the contemporary women's movement as well as our preliminary observations about the movement in the forties and fifties.

Ultimately, this kind of interview situation posed only one major dilemma for us. When we began this research, one of our objectives was to determine what role, if any, women's relationships might have played in sustaining women's involvement in the movement. We found, however, that in cases in which women had long-term companions and might have been lesbians, we were unable to inquire directly about the nature of their relationships. In some cases, the women made derogatory remarks about lesbians in the contemporary women's movement. For the most part, it was clear to us that asking about lesbianism—even in a general rather than personal way—would have been imposing contemporary conceptions and violating the atmosphere of the interaction. Barbara Levy Simon, in her book *Never Married Women*, describes a similar dilemma. In fact, her attempt to initiate questions about sexual activity with her older women interviewees broke their rapport and, in at least one case, led to a request that she leave the house (Simon, 1987).

Ultimately we relied on a woman who is now a lesbian-feminist scholar and had had some contact with the women's movement in earlier decades for perceptions about women's relationships in the movement. Our experience with this aspect of the interviewing represented one of the contradictions embedded in a feminist approach to research. Although our feminist perspective led to our interest in the role of women's relationships during an earlier stage of the movement, our feminist approach to interviewing—especially our respect for the interviewees and our attempt to learn about their world in their terms—did not allow us to impose our own definitions in framing questions about lesbians and the women's movement.

We see a similar contradiction in some of the feminist literature advocating action or experiential research that is designed to improve the status of women and calls for both the elimination of distance between the researcher and researched and for collaboration on the research project. German sociologist Maria Mies, for example, reports on the activities of an "action group" of sociologists who fought for a shelter for battered women while undertaking a research project with—not just on—the women who sought shelter. Mies admits, however, that it was not always easy to get egalitarian participation: "It was difficult to get [the women who came to the shelter] to understand gradually that women's liberation rather than social welfare and charity was the aim of the action group" (Mies, 1983, p. 131). Likewise, Shulamit Reinharz, who advocates a similar collaborative process that she calls "experiential analysis," notes that she experienced "community pressure to act like a conventional researcher and do the work myself rather than ask for extensive collaboration" (Reinharz, 1983, p. 184). As these examples make clear, some of the tenets that have come to be associated with "feminist methodology," like the normal science model, impose requirements on the participants that do not always meet their needs and expectations.

We found, then, that the actual methods we used did not differ significantly from those used by sensitive social historians and qualitative sociologists. In an early draft of our book, we entitled one section of the introduction "The Research Process: A Feminist Methodology." In the course of our work, however, we came to believe that there is not a distinctive feminist methodology but rather a feminist perspective on the research process.

Political Implications

As feminists, we believe that research on the women's movement in an earlier stage of its history has implications for our own involvement in the contemporary movement. As first, we felt compelled to explain to our classes and in public lectures that feminism in the forties and fifties seemed anachronistic, old-fashioned, in contrast to feminism in more recent years. But by 1985, we realized that feminism as an anachronism no longer needed explaining to the student-age population: they, too, thought of feminism as out-of-date, the province of women in their thirties or forties. This realization made us think in a new way about the relationship of young women to the contemporary movement.

In addition, when we began this project, we found ourselves thinking that we were studying the survival of the women's movement in the fifties in order to learn how to survive the eighties. We learned, in the course of our research, that the movement in the post–1945 period could teach us about survival, but the lessons were not exactly the ones that we expected when we first undertook this work. For the nature of the movement may have allowed it to survive, but that survival imposed serious costs at the time and, to the extent that the movement in the 1950s affected the resurgent movement of the 1960s, burdened the movement with a legacy of race and class limitation. The ERA, the central goal of the movement in the 1950s, symbolizes this connection, since it played such a central role at one point, in dividing supporters of the women's movement and, in later years, in serving as a rallying cry for the entire movement.

Perhaps the most immediate application of this research concerns the tension between organizational maintenance and recruitment in the women's movement. We found that the movement was able to survive, and feminists were able to sustain their commitment to feminism, by building a supportive community that valued feminism, required high levels of commitment, was held together by personal relationships, and was based to a large extent on ties from the days of the suffrage movement. All of these characteristics helped to create a close-knit world in which participation in the women's rights movement was possible, but they also meant that women not already committed to feminism would be unlikely to be recruited to the movement.

To proclaim oneself a feminist might earn one the epithet "kook" or "freak," one of the women we interviewed told us. Nothing in the social climate of the fifties made adherence to such an ideology attractive to the unconverted. Participation in the movement also required high levels of commitment. The majority of women in the movement had the affluence and/or occupational flexibility to participate in movement activities. Because they were predominantly in their fifties, sixties, seventies, or even eighties, and because a large proportion were single or widowed, they did not have the kind of family responsibilities that would have stood in the way of active involvement. But the high level of commitment expected meant that women in lower income brackets, with more typical job or family responsibilities, would have had difficulty participating in the movement.

Likewise, the role of personal relationships in holding the movement together meant that women outside the networks of already-committed feminists were unlikely to be recruited. The role of suffrage ties, in particular, as a bond among movement members meant that young women, who had no attachment to the suffrage struggle, would feel out of place in the movement. One of the women we interviewed had become involved in the women's movement in the 1940s when she was in her thirties, which qualified her as a young member. At the same time that she described the wonderful feeling of meeting supportive women who shared her feminist convictions, she characterized these women as "hatchet-faced" and "old fuddy-duddies." If even a woman as delighted to find feminist support as she felt a gulf between herself and the older women in the movement, what hope of recruiting younger women could there have been?

We concluded, then, that the very factors that helped to maintain the women's rights movement in a hostile social climate contributed to keeping the movement small, elite, and isolated. And when we looked around us at the women's movement in our own community, we saw that the tension between maintenance and recruitment was not just an issue of historical interest. As the media proclaims the advent of the "post-feminist generation," the cohort that came to feminism in the late sixties and early seventies grows older, and younger women come to believe that the women's movement has done its work, we see the same tension in operation. How do we create an environment in which we can sustain our feminist commitment and continue our involvement in the women's movement without shutting ourselves away from women not already interested in feminism? We do not have an answer, but we believe that awareness of the dilemma is essential. From this perspective, we found it encouraging, rather than discouraging, when the local radical feminist collective finally decided to give up its house, the maintenance of which required all of the energy, time, and money of the collective. The house was a haven for already-committed feminists, but was not an effective space in which to recruit new women to the cause, and we saw the admittedly very painful decision as a positive sign of change with the times rather than failure.

Our study also had implications for the contemporary movement by making us look at the history of the women's movement in a different way. We believe that the traditional emphasis on the death of the movement in 1920 and its rebirth in the 1960s overlooks the continuity of the movement from its origins in the 1840s to the present. Although the movement has reached its peak of activity and influence during periods in which other kinds of social protest flourished, it has also, we are convinced, continued to exist in other periods as well. But it has taken different shapes at different times, and a conception of the movement based on its contemporary form will not do for a historical analysis of the movement.

We have already suggested that the movement in the post–1945 period did not conform to contemporary feminist expectations for the women's movement. Not only was this a small movement of elite women, but it was also a movement that made little attempt to form coalitions with other social movements. One of the striking characteristics of the membership of the movement was the lack of consensus on all issues other than women's rights. Democrats and Republicans, liberals and conservatives, integrationists and segregationists, unionists and anti-unionists, anti-McCarthyites and supporters of McCarthy all worked together within the women's movement. What this meant was that the movement took no positions on issues other than women's rights, but sometimes engaged in activities that contemporary feminists would find reprehensible. For example, movement organizations sometimes used McCarthyite tactics to try to win support for the ERA—in particular by accusing opponents of siding with the Communist Party, which disapproved of the amendment—even though the movement for the most part did not support McCarthy and his followers. Or, to take another example, movement groups tried to "piggy-back" on the success of the emerging civil rights movement by complaining that legislation prohibiting discrimination on the basis of race, religion, or national origin left out only white, Christian, native-born women and therefore treated them unfairly.

Understanding why this elite-sustained movement developed the goals and strategies that it did helps us to understand the relationship between internal movement dynamics and the larger external environment. We used the contemporary critique of the race, class, and cultural bias of the movement to explore the process by which the movement came to define certain issues as "women's rights" and to exclude others as racial, class, or cultural issues. We recognize that the women we have studied were not the only women active on behalf of women in the post–1945 period; women in the National Council of Negro Women, the Women's Bureau of the Department of Labor, the Women's Bureau of the United Auto Workers Union, the Communist Party, the peace movement, and the birth control movement, to name only a few, were also working to improve the lives of women. But, we argue, the women's movement (we use the term "women's rights movement" to emphasize this) had come to mean something more narrow by this time; to participants, women in these other organizations, and the wider public, it referred to the heirs of the suffrage tradition who were identified for the most part as feminists and advocated what had traditionally been defined as "women's rights." Only if we understand the role that the elite-sustained stage of the movement played in the survival of feminism and in making connections to the newly-resurgent movement in the mid–1960s, can we understand its legacy, both negative and positive, for subsequent rounds of mobilization.

Researching the women's movement has been a process of intellectual and political growth for both of us. We learned a great deal about each other's disciplines, and our ideas about the relationship of feminist research to the methodologies and perspectives of history and sociology evolved in unexpected ways. To return to the conversation with which we began this paper, we learned that the process of researching the women's movement as feminists was not as predictable as we expected. Our feminist convictions shaped our research in critical ways, but our research findings also affected our conception of feminism. And some of the contradictions of feminist research led us to a new appreciation of some of the methodologies and perspectives of nonfeminist (or not explicitly feminist) research in our disciplines. Rather than throwing out the proverbial baby with the bathwater, feminist researchers today, we believe, can apply a feminist perspective that will make good use of existing approaches and develop new ones where they are needed.

NOTES

1. Our subtitle paraphrases Karl Marx, who wrote: "Men make their own history, but they do not make it just as they please; they do not make it under circumstances chosen by themselves, but under circumstances directly encountered, given, and transmitted from the past." Karl Marx, "The Eighteenth Brumaire of Louis Napoleon," originally published 1852, in *Karl Marx: Selected Works*, vol. 1 (Moscow: Progress Publishers, 1969).

2. We are full coauthors and have listed our names here in reverse alphabetical order. This article is based on our experience researching and writing *Survival in the Dol-*

drums: The American Women's Rights Movement, 1945 to the 1960s (New York: Oxford University Press, 1987). We are grateful to the following institutions for financial support during the course of our research: the National Endowment for the Humanities for a two-year Basic Research Grant (1981–1983); the Radcliffe Research Scholars Program for a fellowship for research at the Schlesinger Library (Rupp, 1979–1980); the Graduate School of the Ohio State University for two research grants (Rupp, 1978–1979; Taylor, 1979–1980); the College of Humanities of the Ohio State University for a one-quarter research leave (Rupp, 1979–1980); and the College of Humanities and the College of Social and Behavioral Science of the Ohio State University for a grant-in-aid to support a local interviewing project (1982–1983).

REFERENCES

Banks, Olive (1981). *Faces of Feminism: A Study of Feminism as a Social Movement.* Oxford: Martin Robertson.

Berg, Barbara J. (1978). *The Remembered Gate: Origins of American Feminism.* New York: Oxford University Press.

Bernard, Jessie (1981). *The Female World.* New York: The Free Press/Macmillan.

Bowles, Gloria, and Renate Duelli Klein (1983). *Theories of Women's Studies.* London: Routledge & Kegan Paul.

Bramson, Leon (1961). *The Political Context of Sociology.* Princeton: Princeton University Press.

Cook, Blanche Wiesen (1977). "Female Support Networks and Political Activism: Lillian Wald, Crystal Eastman, Emma Goldman." *Chrysalis,* 3: 43–61.

Cook, Judith A., and Mary Margaret Fonow (1986). "Knowledge and Women's Interests: Feminist Methodology in the Field of Sociology." *Sociological Inquiry,* 56.

Currie, Elliot, and Jerome Skolnick (1972). "A Critical Note on Conceptions of Collective Behavior." In *Collective Violence.* Ed. J. F. Short, Jr. and M. E. Wolfgang. Chicago: Aldine Atherton.

Daniels, Arlene Kaplan (1975). "Feminist Perspectives in Sociological Research." In *Another Voice: Feminist Perspectives on Social Life and Social Science.* Ed. Marcia Millman and Rosabeth Kanter. New York: Anchor Books.

DiIorio, Judith (1980). "Toward a Phenomenological Feminism: A Critique of Gender Role Research." Paper presented at the National Women's Studies Association conference, Bloomington, Indiana.

Eichler, Margrit (1980). *The Double Standard: A Feminist Critique of Feminist Social Science.* New York: St. Martin's Press.

——— (1983). "The Relationship Between Sexist, Non-Sexist, Woman-Centered and Feminist Research." Paper presented at the American Sociological Association conference, Detroit.

Evans, Sara (1979). *Personal Politics: The Roots of Women's Liberation in the Civil Rights Movement and the New Left.* New York: Knopf.

Ferree, Myra Marx, and Beth B. Hess (1985). *Controversy and Coalition: The New Feminist Movement.* Boston: Twayne.

Freedman, Estelle (1979). "Separatism as Strategy: Female Institution Building and American Feminism." *Feminist Studies,* 5: 512–29.

Freeman, Jo (1975). The Politics of Women's Liberation. New York: David McKay.

Gordon, Linda (1978). "What Should Women Historians Do?" *Marxist Perspectives,* 3: 128–36.

Gould, Meredith (1980). "The New Sociology." *Signs*, 5: 459–67.
Graham, Ruth (1977). "Loaves and Liberty: Women in the French Revolution." In *Becoming Visible: Women in European History*. Ed. Renate Bridenthal and Claudia Koonz. Boston: Houghton Mifflin.
Jenkins, J. Craig (1983). "Resource Mobilization Theory and the Study of Social Movements." *Annual Review of Sociology*, 9: 527–53.
Krieger, Susan (1983). *The Mirror Dance: Identity in a Women's Community*. Philadelphia: Temple University Press.
Lerner, Gerda (1979). *The Majority Finds Its Past*. New York: Oxford University Press.
Lowe, Marian, and Ruth Hubbard (1983). *Woman's Nature: Rationalizations of Inequality*. New York: Pergamon Press.
McCarthy, John D., and Mayer N. Zald (1977). "Resource Mobilization and Social Movements: A Partial Theory." *American Journal of Sociology*, 82: 1212–41.
Mies, Maria (1983). "Towards a Methodology for Feminist Research." In *Theories of Women's Studies*. Ed. Gloria Bowles and Renate Duelli Klein. London: Routledge and Kegan Paul.
Miller, David L. (1985). *Introduction to Collective Behavior*. Belmont, Calif.: Wadsworth Publishing Co.
Millman, Marcia, and Rosabeth Kanter (1975). *Another Voice: Feminist Perspectives on Social Life and Social Science*. New York: Anchor Books.
Molotch, Harvey (1979). "Media and Movements." In *The Dynamics of Social Movements*. Ed. Mayer N. Zald and John D. McCarthy. Cambridge, Mass.: Winthrop Publishers.
Oakley, Ann (1981). "Interviewing Women: a Contradiction in Terms." In *Doing Feminist Research*. Ed. Helen Roberts. London: Routledge & Kegan Paul.
Perry, Joseph B., and M. D. Pugh (1978). *Collective Behavior*. St. Paul: West Publishing Co.
Quarantelli, E. L., and Jack M. Weller (1974). "The Structural Problem of a Sociological Specialty: Collective Behavior's Lack of a Critical Mass." *American Sociologist*, 9: 59–68.
Reinharz, Shulamit (1983). "Experiential Analysis: A Contribution to Feminist Research." In *Theories of Women's Studies*. Ed. Gloria Bowles and Renate Duelli-Klein. London: Routledge & Kegan Paul.
Roberts, Helen (1981). *Doing Feminist Research*. London: Routledge & Kegan Paul.
Rubin, Lillian (1976). *Worlds of Pain*. New York: Basic Books.
Simon, Barbara Levy (1987). *Never Married Women*. Philadelphia: Temple University Press.
Smith, Dorothy (1974). "Women's Perspective as a Radical Critique of Sociology." *Sociological Inquiry*, 44: 7–13.
Smith-Rosenberg, Carroll (1971). "Beauty, the Beast and the Militant Woman: A Case Study of Sex Roles and Social Stress in Jacksonian America." *American Quarterly*, 23: 562–84.
Sochen, June (1973). *Movers and Shakers: American Women Thinkers and Activists, 1900–1970*. New York: Quadrangle/The New York Times Book Co.
Spender, Dale (1981). *Men's Studies Modified: The Impact of Feminism on the Academic Disciplines*. New York: Pergamon Press.
Stanley, Liz, and Sue Wise (1983a). " 'Back into the Personal' or: Our Attempt to Construct 'Feminist Research.' " In *Theories of Women's Studies*. Ed. Gloria Bowles and Renate Duelli Klein. London: Routledge & Kegan Paul.
——— (1983b). *Breaking Out: Feminist Consciousness and Feminist Research*. London: Routledge & Kegan Paul.
Tilly, Charles (1978). *From Mobilization to Revolution*. Reading, Mass.: Addison-Wesley.
Wood, James L., and Maurice Jackson (1982). *Social Movements: Development, Participation, and Dynamics*. Belmont, Calif.: Wadsworth Publishing Co.

8. OBJECTIVITY AND TRUTH

Problems in Doing Feminist Research

JOAN ACKER, KATE BARRY, AND
JOHANNA ESSEVELD

This paper examines principles of feminist research and discusses the authors' attempts to use these principles in a systematic way in their own research. Three principles of feminist research are identified: research should contribute to women's liberation through producing knowledge that can be used by women themselves; should use methods of gaining knowledge that are not oppressive; should continually develop a feminist critical perspective that questions dominant intellectual traditions and can reflect on its own development.

Consciously applying these principles in a research study of the relation between changes in consciousness and the changes in the structural situation of individuals raised several methodological issues and dilemmas. These include the impossibility of creating a research process that completely erases the contradictions in the relationship between the researcher and the researched; the difficulties in analyzing change as a process; the tension between the necessity of organizing the data and producing an analysis which reveals the totality of women's lives; and problems of validity, particularly those raised when the research process becomes part of the process of change.

Introduction

What methods should be used in a feminist[1] analysis of society? Are there modes of thinking, data collection and analysis that are more appropriate than others for studying the situation of women from a feminist perspective? These questions were raised early in the contemporary feminist critique of the social sciences (Bart, 1971; Bernard, 1973; McCormack, 1975; Smith, 1974) and are still being explored and developed. Feminist scholars have analyzed the male bias in the social sciences (see, e.g., Sherman and Beck, 1979) and are beginning to make a distinctive contribution to long-standing debates about theory and method (Smith, 1977; 1979; 1980; Westkott, 1979), sharing the concern of others with basic and enduring controversies such as the nature of science, its epistemological foundation, the possibility of a science of society, and the role of science in maintaining or undermining systems of power (see, e.g., Blumer, 1969; Bernstein, 1978; Hughes, 1980). In addition, we are beginning to consider how these debates become translated into problematic methodological issues

Reprinted from *Women's Studies Int. Forum*, Vol. 6, No. 4, (1983), 423–435.

for those doing empirical studies within a feminist perspective (e.g., Roberts, 1981).

The goals of feminist social science have developed in the context of the criticism of the established natural science model of sociology and related disciplines (Bernard, 1973). Extending that critique, some feminist perspectives share the critical view of the Marxist and interpretive traditions within the social sciences, while adding their own emphasis and content (Smith, 1974; 1977). These feminists have argued that the traditional approach to social science is compatible with the aims of those in particular locations or positions of management and control in society (Smith, 1977) whose goals include such things as managing workers more effectively, dealing with civil disorder, and encouraging women to enter or leave the work force in accord with changing economic conditions; thus, what is taken as problematic in much of social science has also been what is problematic for those who control and manage the society. Moreover, in addition to problem definition, the concepts, frames of reference, and perspectives that define traditional sociology express the interests of and arise out of particular social institutions where the governing and organizing of society takes place (Smith, 1979). Almost all those who rule and manage are male; interesting and important phenomena are identified from a male perspective as well as from the perspective of those who manage and control. Women are largely absent from this world; the female domain of production and reproduction that provides the necessary infrastructure for the male world is, despite its importance, invisible, uninteresting to many social scientists, and largely unconceptualized. Thus, in the history of sociology, the development of an approach to knowledge with the goal of control has contributed to the failure to study the situation of women, as well as to a conceptualization of women that is consistent with continuing male dominance (Acker, 1973).

In the last fifteen years, attempts to deal with the exclusion, distortion, and neglect of women have produced many useful theoretical and empirical studies. One significant result of this research has been identification of many regularities and correlations that describe women's situation. However, this has limitations for building a tradition of research *for* women because it leaves largely unexamined the social processes lying behind the correlations. Understanding the processes that result in inequalities is a necessary step toward changing women's position. For us this understanding comes from a theoretical perspective which has its roots in feminism, Marxism, and critical theory. This means a commitment to a social science that can help change the world as well as describe it. "Women's devaluation and the consequences of this devaluation are reinforced by a social science which records these conditions while systematically ignoring alternative possibilities" (Westkott, 1979: 428).

The goals of a sociology *for* women, one that is in the interests of women rather than only about women, must be emancipatory (Esseveld, 1980; Hartsock, 1979; Westkott, 1979). Emancipation, as we use the term, means the eventual end of social and economic conditions that oppress women and the achievement of a free society. The ideal is that women should be self-emancipating and our conviction is that social scientists can contribute to this process (Karabel, 1976) by analyzing how the personal is political and by pushing that analysis beyond individual experience to comprehension of "its determination in the larger socioeconomic structure" (Smith, 1977). An emancipatory social science would provide women with understandings of how their everyday worlds, their trials and troubles, were and are generated by the larger social structure.

The emancipatory aim of a women's sociology derives, from its close connections with the contemporary women's movement as well as from our particular position as women researchers. Women's research is intimately connected with the political aims of the women's movement in a number of ways. The movement provided the necessary social basis for legitimation and political support that allowed women researchers to start publicly asking some of the questions they had long been asking privately. Moreover, the women's movement outside of academia posed new questions and new formulations of women's situation which then could be taken up in the academic setting. Women researchers, in addition, were usually members of the women's movement and had, and still have, a political commitment to ending women's oppression. This commitment supplied a general standard against which to assess the kinds of questions and problems that should be dealt with. At the same time, women researchers were developing analyses of their own locations in the larger socioeconomic structure, for in some fundamental ways their positions were and are similar to those of their subjects. As women, they too may have husbands and children, they too keep house as well as work, they too have to cope with sexism in their daily lives. Thus, a sociology *for* women has emancipatory possibilities for the researchers as well as the researched, for as women researchers we also have been absent and unheard within the main sociological traditions.

Having accepted the above critique of traditional social science, and recognizing that in all social science, women have been peripheral and their lives misrepresented, it is clear that a radical rebeginning is needed in feminist research.

For us, a radical rebeginning has meant understanding gender as central in constructing all social relations and taking individual women's lives as a problematic (Hartsock, 1979; Smith, 1980). What is to be explained is what actually happens in women's everyday world and how these events are experienced. We begin, then, with the ordinary life of women, but neither stop there nor move into a search for individual psychological sources of feelings, actions, and events. Although we view people as active agents in their own lives and as such constructors of their social worlds, we do not see that activity as isolated and subjective. Rather, we locate individual experience in society and history, embedded within a set of social relations[2] which produce both the possibilities and limitations of that experience. What is at issue is not just everyday experience but the relations which underlie it and the connections between the two. In this analysis, we use a dialectical method, in order to arrive . . . "at adequate description and analysis of how it actually works. Our methods cannot rest in procedures for deciding among different formalized 'opinions' about the world"

(Smith, 1977). Rather, this is a method of exploration and discovery, a way to begin to search for understandings that may contribute to the goals of liberation. Exploration, in our usage, means an open and critical process in which all the intellectual tools we have inherited from a male dominated intellectual tradition are brought into question, including ideas about the basic nature of human beings, the nature of social life, the taken-for-granted world-view of traditional science, what concepts and questions might help to illuminate our shared condition, and how we should go about developing such knowledge.

In developing this knowledge we also try to maintain a critical perspective toward some of the assumptions made within the social sciences. For example, the assumption that the researcher must and can strive to be a neutral observer standing outside the social realities being studied is made by many who use quantitative and qualitative methods in a natural science model. This assumption is challenged by the feminist critique of social science that documents the male bias of theory and research which has previously been taken as a neutral account of human society. A feminist methodology must, therefore, deal with the issues of objectivity in social science and, in the process, deal also with the issue of the relationship between the researcher and the researched. As researchers, we must not impose our definitions of reality on those researched, for to do so would undermine our intention to work toward a sociology for women. Our intention is to minimize the tendency in all research to transform those researched into objects of scrutiny and manipulation. In the ideal case, we want to create conditions in which the object of research enters into the process as an active subject.

Recognizing the objects of the research as subjects in their own right suggests that researchers must take care not to make the research relationship an exploitative one. This has been a concern at least since the 1960s when New Left criticism of the subtle and obvious repressions of bureaucratic society included an evaluation of the research process as oppressive. It becomes a critical issue for feminist researchers who themselves might be cast in the role of the research object and who, as women, have experienced the objectification of women in society. Perhaps more important, research that aims to be liberating should not in the process become only another mode of oppression. But this aim poses an ongoing contradiction; ultimately the researcher must objectify the experience of the researched, must translate that experience into more abstract and general terms if an analysis that links the individual to processes outside her immediate social world is to be achieved. Objectification would be minimized and the emancipatory goal furthered if both researcher and researched could participate in the process of analysis. But this is not always possible, because the preconditions of such participation, some similarity of interest, ideology, and language between researcher and researched, are sometimes absent. Even with a similarity of interest, there are still problems of a practical nature. The impossibility of eliminating all objectification exists in all social research, and the problem cannot be solved by creating the illusion that no relationship exists between the researcher and her research object.

In summary, the following are some of the principles of feminist research with which we begin this project:

1. Our goal was to contribute to women's liberation through producing knowledge that can be used by women themselves.
2. The methods of gaining this knowledge should not be oppressive.
3. We should continually develop the feminist critical perspective that questions both the dominant intellectual traditions and reflects on its own development.

In the pages that follow we begin to develop a methodology for doing feminist research based on the view of a social science outlined above.

Women in Transition—An Example of an Attempt to Do Feminist Research

We, the authors of this paper, started a research project in 1976 with the intention of doing a study that might contribute to the liberation of women. We tried to apply the principles of feminist research discussed above and, in the process, learned about some of the difficulties with this approach. The following is an account of our research process and the problems we encountered.

The feminist critique of social science and our own commitment to the women's movement led us to select a particular problem. The choice of the problem, together with the critique, dictated a qualitative method of investigation. We chose repeated, unstructured, individual interviews as well as some group interviews. Although this proved to be difficult and we are critical of our work at many points, the choice of a qualitative approach also produced new insights, new for us at least, about some of the issues raised above. As the project is concluding with the writing of a report, we are still convinced of the value of the method.

The Problem and the Method

The problem we chose was the relation between changes in the structural situation of women and changes in consciousness. We decided to look at the experiences of women who had been primarily mothers and wives and were attempting to move into the labor market. This group has participated in one of the major demographic changes in women's lives, their increasing entry into the paid labor force. We believed that these women, involved in a process of changing life circumstances, would come to see themselves differently as women and would reinterpret their problems, particularly in a social context that includes a widely-discussed feminist movement. The question of consciousness was important to us from a political point of view; consciousness raising is an essential component of the feminist movement, and a necessary part of feminist action (Bartky, 1975; Westkott, 1979). An understanding of how women's consciousness changes or doesn't change might be helpful to other women. Consciousness is important in a framework that views people as actors who intentionally try to affect their own situations. The oppression of women has limited our ability to actively intervene in working out our own destiny, but changing work opportunities and the feminist challenge to a whole range of barriers should have increased the possibilities for purposive action. An examination of whether or not this was occurring was thus relevant to our theories about the relation between individuals and social structure.

We were convinced that middle-aged women who had spent most of their lives as wives and mothers had been ignored by much of the movement, and we hoped that we might give voice to some of their perspectives. We were also interested in this group because their long commitment to being housewives and mothers might make them resistant to change in a feminist direction. We also had a theoretical concern about adult life. At the time of the beginning of the research, very little had been written on middle-aged women; collectively as social scientists, we knew next to nothing about the middle years of adult life. We were critical of what little literature existed and were skeptical of widely held assumptions about women of this age. For example, we questioned the idea that women suffered from having an "empty nest" syndrome, an assumption that has since been discounted by a number of other researchers, e.g., Rubin (1979). This was our general theoretical orientation, but consistent with the feminist critique that we, along with others, were working out, we decided not to structure interviews with predetermined definitions of consciousness. Rather, we entered our interviews in an unstructured way, getting women to talk about the changes occurring in their lives, leaving the definition of consciousness as an emergent knowledge that would come out of the discussions. This would allow us to develop a more thorough understanding of the women's own perspectives as well as get unanticipated information about events and problems.

The women were interviewed in their own homes by one of the three of us as investigators. We had interviews with 65 women and followed a subgroup of 30 women for four to five years. We tried not to impose our ideas about what was important; our intention was to let the concepts, explanations, and interpretations of those participating in the study become the data we would analyze (Glazer and Strauss, 1973). While we tried to avoid determining what was to be considered in the content of consciousness, we were still aware of our own theoretical ideas. In our continual process of analysis we had to confront discrepancies between our ideas and interpretations and those of the women we interviewed. As the interview process proceeded, we decided to bring up certain questions if they did not emerge in the interviews. The areas most likely to be unmentioned were the women's movement, feelings about aging, and sexuality. However, in most of the repeated interviews, the topics that we thought would be important came up spontaneously. Sometimes we did direct the interview. For example, after discussing present life situation and changes, we asked about past history beginning with adolescence unless the interviewee herself initiated the subject of earlier experiences. We got accounts of significant childhood experiences, as the women perceived them in the present. We also gathered information on education and work experience, on relationships with parents, husbands, children, and friends, and on their aspirations and hopes for the future.

In second and subsequent interviews, we filled out areas not touched on before, but particularly focussed on the changes that had taken place since the previous interview, as well as on the issues that seemed to be paramount at the time of the interview. During the whole period of interviewing, which for some of the participants extended over five years, we in the research group had extensive discussions of the interviews and of the interview process. In these discussions we were in an ongoing process of reformulating our ideas, examining the validity of our assumptions about the change process, about how to conceptualize consciousness, the connections between changing life circumstances and changing views of self, others and the larger world, and how to link analytically these individual lives with the structure of industrial capitalism in the U.S.A. in the 1970s. Each of us had both formal training and considerable past experience in interviewing. Consequently, although we discussed the interview process, our main focus was on the analysis and integration of the data.

The initial interviews and many of the second interviews were taped and transcribed. Later interviews were treated differently—we took notes during the interview and then wrote, immediately afterward, to the best of our ability, a process account of the interview. Some of the taped interviews were not transcribed. Instead, we listened to the interviews, perhaps several times, noting down topic areas and their locations on the tapes so that they could be listened to again when we were working on a particular theme. We then made detailed summaries of each woman's situation that included the main facts about her current life (marital status, number of children, work status, class, age), her perception of her problems, her goals, her consciousness of the women's movement, and the dilemmas or contradictions that we saw in her life. We made similar summaries at later interviews. At the same time, we were trying to identify common themes and also differences in experience. This analysis went on during the whole period of interviewing. We will return to the analysis process later, but here we want to discuss some other issues related to the interview process, in particular the influence of our relationship with our study participants.

The Research Relationship

The idea of neutrality and objectivity in the social sciences has been extensively criticized by those working within the interpretive traditions (Blumer, 1969; Hughes, 1980) and by some Marxists and critical theorists of the Frankfurt School (Habermas, 1972; Bernstein, 1978). Taking a women's perspective adds to that critique in some important ways. The ideal of objectivity is to remove the particular point of view of the observer from the research process so that the results will not be biased by the researcher's subjectivity. "Recent versions of this ideal of objectivity have emphasized the importance of the universal application of social science methods as the best guarantee against the bias of subjectivity" (Westkott, 1979). These methods are designed to separate the knower from the object of study. Rejecting the notion that such a separation is possible, Smith (1977) argues that the illusion of this separation can be maintained so long as the knower can be posited as an abstract being and the object can be posited as the "other" who cannot reflect back on and affect the knower. "Once women are inserted into sociological sentences as their subjects, however, the appearance of impersonality goes. The knower turns out not to be the 'abstract knower' after all, but a member of a definite social category occupying definite positions within the society" (Smith, 1974; 16–17). It also turns out that research is embedded in a definite social relationship in which there is a power differential in favor of the knower who assumes the power to define in the process of the research. Research reports reflect only one side of this social relationship—that of the more powerful "knower."

That there is a relationship between the subject and object of study is more easily made visible when women are researching women.

> Women studying women reveals the complex way in which women as objects of knowledge reflect back upon women as subjects of knowledge. Knowledge of the other and knowledge of the self are mutually informing because self and other share a common condition of being women. (Westkott, 1979)

The research process becomes a dialogue between the researcher and researched, an effort to explore and clarify the topic under discussion, to clarify and expand understanding; both are assumed to be individuals who reflect upon their experience and who can communicate those reflections. This is inherent in the situation; neither the subjectivity of the researcher nor the subjectivity of the researched can be eliminated in the process.

Our commitment to reducing so far as we could the unequal power in the research relationship and acknowledging the subjectivity of our study participants took a variety of forms. One strategy was encouraging the interviewee to take the lead in deciding what to talk about. This did not always work; people have ideas about what it is like to be interviewed and they want to be asked questions so that they can give the "right responses." Some women were uneasy with us because we were from the university. Others did not want to set the terms of the discussion because they felt that there couldn't be anything interesting about their lives. However, those with whom we had more than one interview increasingly took the lead in discussions and even took the initiative to get in touch with us to tell us what had been happening to them. Unstructured interviewing and letting the women take an important part in the discussion helped to counter some of the problems other researchers have confronted when using a more standard sociological methodology. Thus we did not have the problems encountered by Woodward and Chisholm (1981: 177), who used more structured interviews and, as a result, enlarged the gap already existing between them and their subjects of study: "The very nature of our questions about employment and the domestic division of labour served to reveal our pre-occupation with work, marital conflict and women's oppression, rather then with the satisfaction of motherhood and housewifery."

Another part of the attempt to deal with the subject-object problem was to try to establish some reciprocity by offering, at the end of the first interview, to tell the women something about ourselves if we had not done so earlier. Often we didn't have to offer—it was a request made to us. We always responded as honestly as we could, talking about aspects of our lives that were similar to the things we had been discussing about the experience of the interviewee—our marriages, our children, our jobs, our parents. Often this meant also that our relationship was defined as something which existed beyond the limits of the interview situation. We formed friendships with many of the women in the study. We were offered hospitality and were asked to meet husbands, friends, and children. Sometimes we would provide help to one or another woman in the study. For example, one woman became very depressed and called the interviewer, who then went to the interviewee's house and spent several hours with her while she talked about her troubles and gradually became less distressed. However, we recognized a usually unarticulated tension between friendships and the goal of research.[3] The researcher's goal is always to gather information; thus the danger always exists of manipulating friendships to that end. Given that the power differences between researcher and researched cannot be completely eliminated, attempting to create a more equal relationship can paradoxically become exploitation and use. We recognized this more as the research progressed and tried to avoid it.

During the interviews we were also often asked for information, which we provided. We viewed this as an additional opportunity to reciprocate for the help they were giving us by participating in the study. Now, at the stage of writing, we continue to have feelings of obligation to the women we interviewed—to finish the writing and find a way to publish our—their—material. If we do not do this, we will have failed on our part of our joint project.

A high degree of participation in the research was not established with all interviewees. As we noted above, repeated interviews resulted in more involvement. However, not only the number of interviews, but also the experiences women were having at the particular time that we first interviewed them influenced our contact. With those women who experienced this period as a critical period in their lives, we seem to have established the best rapport. Although our lives differed from most of the women we interviewed, with many we shared a sense of uneasiness, an experiencing of dilemmas and contradictions as well as a willingness to acknowledge them.

Another way that we tried to overcome the distance between researchers and researched was to show our written material to the women we wrote about. We did not do this with every woman in the study. We shared most of this material with the women with whom we had the most interviews, who were those who identified themselves as consciously trying to change. Since change was the central issue of the study, there was a theoretical rationale for spending more time with them. And, given the focus on change as well as our limited time and other resources, it made more sense to ask these women to reflect on our written material. They were, as we mentioned above, also women who most shared our world view; a common frame of reference provided the grounds from which a dialogue could proceed. We have to admit to some reluctance to share our interpretations with those who, we expected, would be upset by them. There was a potential conflict between our feminist frame of reference and their interpretations of their own lives. Our solution to this conflict was not to include them as active participants in the analysis of our research. Whether or not to confront groups or individuals with interpretations of their lives which are radically different from their own is an ethical question faced by anyone attempting critical social research. This is particularly true when the researcher's interpretation is not only different but potentially threatening and disruptive to the subject's view of the world. For example, many of the women who were housewives defined themselves as very independent whereas our perspective defined the conditions of their lives as creating both a structural and personal dependence. These housewives had a stake in their own definition which was also a source of worth and dignity, while we as feminist researchers interpreted their situations differently. At that moment, we were dealing with a tension between the goal of reducing the power differences between the researcher and the researched and the difficulties of carrying this out when there is a lack of agreement on the meaning of experiences. We have not solved this problem; we believe that the solution lies in accepting the dilemmas and maintaining an awareness of when and why we are not able to make the research process a true dialogue, thus giving full legitimacy to the subjectivity of the other as well as to our own. At least then we can articulate the difficult balance between granting respect to the other's interpretation of her reality, while going beyond that interpretation to comprehend its underlying relations.

Problems of Analysis

As we pointed out, our commitment to minimizing the power differentials of the relationship in the research was further confounded when it came to the analysis. We found that we had to assume the role of the people with the power to define. The act of looking at interviews, summarizing another's life, and placing it within a context is an act of objectification. Indeed, we the researchers took the position that some process of objectification of the self is a necessary part of coming to an awareness of one's own existence; it is not less a part of coming to an understanding of others. Acknowledging that a necessary part of understanding others' experience involves an act or moment of objectification poses further problems and contradictions. The question becomes how to produce an analysis which goes beyond the experience of the researched while still granting them full subjectivity. How do we explain the lives of others without violating their reality? This is part of a larger problem: a critique of objectivity which asserts that there can be no neutral observer who stands outside the social relations she observes can easily become relativism in which all explanations are subjectively grounded and therefore have equal weight. When all accounts are equally valid, the search for "how it actually works" becomes meaningless. Though we don't claim to have resolved this problem, we tried to avoid it by claiming a validity for our analysis (see discussion below) while not in the process forcing that analysis into categories such as worker, housewife and mother, or divorced and married, which fracture women's experience.[4] However, in the actual task of analysis, we initially found ourselves moving back and forth between letting the data "speak for itself" and using abstracted categories.

Our feminist commitment had led us to collect data that were difficult to analyze and had provided us with so much information that it was difficult to choose what was "essential" at the same time that we tried to give a picture that provided a "totality." Our solution to this series of problems was to present a number of life histories, expressed largely in the women's own words, to typify what we thought were particular patterns of change. We based these patterns on apparently discrete categories such as whether change was occuring and how it was initiated.

This attempt to make sense out of our information by placing the women into categories of "changers" and "nonchangers" obscured the complexities of women's lives. Although it was possible to categorize women using simple and rigid criteria, the boundaries between changers and nonchangers were not at all clear. We at first called all women who enrolled in school or were looking for a job "changers." But interviews revealed that some of the nonchangers were going through an active process of rethinking their lives while some of the changers (a small minority, but nevertheless bothersome in terms of a neat analysis) were actively resisting all but very superficial changes.[5]

We were pushed to develop our analysis further by women in the study whom we asked to read the manuscript. They were hesitant about being negative, but were clearly critical. What they wanted, they said, was more of our own sociological analysis. They wanted us, the researchers, to interpret their experience to them. Here, once more, we faced incompatibilities between various components of our feminist approach to social research. If we were to fulfill the emancipatory aim for the people we were studying, we had to go beyond the faithful representation of their experience, beyond "letting them talk for themselves," and put those experiences into the theoretical framework with which we started the study, a framework that links women's oppression to the structure of Western capitalist society.

Both the ways in which we were categorizing experience and the kinds of categories we then developed were still somewhat antithetical to our theoretical position. We experimented with dividing our interviewees into housewives and workers for the purpose of analysis. We had tried to only recruit housewives for the study, but—not surprisingly—found that about half of the women we interviewed had had considerable work experience. Almost all of them had continued to see themselves as housewives. How should we see them? What is the critical cutting point in work experience that can tell us how to differentiate? We came to the obvious conclusion (Acker, 1978) that the stationary concepts of housewife and paid worker are problematic ones. Most women move from unpaid work to paid work during their lifetime, and only a few fit totally within the unpaid work/paid work dichotomy, as quantitative data clearly show (Maret-Havens, 1977). Our concepts do not reflect the reality of women's lives; this was demonstrated to us again in our qualitative data. Our initial use of traditional categories, despite our own feminist critique of them, illustrates the power of conventional ways of thinking about the social world and the difficulty of breaking out of its boundaries.

Another difficulty we faced was the difficulty of conceptualizing process. We first tried to solve this and the categorizing problem together by thinking up categories of change process or categories of ways that women engaged in the change process. Thus, we tried talking about those who initiated change in an active way as contrasted to those who were forced into changes by outside events. We soon found that this categorization fell apart as we looked in depth at the actual processes. We also rejected a life cycle perspective, partly because of its biological determinist implications and partly because we could not find a common pattern among the women we interviewed in the time that change began in either the family or the individual life cycle.

We also attempted to categorize feminist consciousness and, to some extent, were successful.[6] However, again, the boundaries were unclear, and we felt that the strategy of analysis was not productive. We were not gaining any new insights nor deepening our understanding of the relationship between the individual and social structure, and it was in this part of the research process that these connections had to be made explicitly.

At the same time that we were trying to find some fruitful categories in which to group our interviewees, we were analyzing issues or themes in the interviews. The contradictions between our commitment to a dialectical analysis; our aim of reconstructing women's experience in a way which accounts for both their and our explanations of that experience and the relation between the two; and our actual use of rigid categories, sent us back to our theoretical beginnings in Marxism, feminism, and critical theory. We saw that the themes of everyday life we were identifying could be understood as manifestations of contradictions or dilemmas inherent in the underlying social relations. We explore the nature of these relations in our account of the research itself (see, e.g., Acker et al., 1981). As the analysis proceeded we tried to understand what was changing in these women's lives and whether or not the underlying dilemmas we had identified were being resolved or were reappearing in new ways as the specific conditions of their lives were altered in a society that was both changing and remaining static. In the process of analysis we refined and reshaped our initial questions, trying to make the act of objectification analagous to a moment of critical reflection. The concepts and questions that are central in our final report are different from those with which we started. We know that this is the history of many other research projects, although usually an unwritten history. We expected to work in this way, but if we had understood beforehand how long and difficult the process would become, we might have more consciously and more quickly worked out strategies of analysis.[7]

Problems of Validity

The research perspective outlined in the first section of the paper makes problematic the conventional way of evaluating the products of the research. How shall we decide whether what we have done—the knowledge we develop—is worthwhile? How shall we decide if what we say is true? The first question about the development of worthwhile knowledge has to be answered in terms of an emancipatory goal. We might ask whether our findings contribute to the women's movement in some way or whether they make the struggles of individual women more effective or easier by helping to reveal to them the conditions of their lives. We know that this is the case for some of the women in our study. This is also an historical question which can only be resolved in the future. An emancipatory intent is no guarantee of an emancipatory outcome. Perhaps the best we can do is to guard against the use of our research against women, although that also may be difficult.

The second question, how to decide what is true or valid, is one we have in common with all social scientists. We differ with many of them, however, in how we conceive of this truth. We are not interested in prediction, but adequate reconstruction (Schutz, 1963). We conceive of this at two levels. The first has to do with adequacy of interpretation and involves selection, organization, and interpretation of our findings with the help of our social theory. The other level of concern is with the adequacy of our findings. We want to know that our research results fairly and accurately reflect the aspects of social life that we claim they represent.

If validity is to be judged by the adequacy of interpretation, we must return to our theoretical orientation to determine the criteria of adequacy. This, as briefly discussed above, is a position that has its origins in feminism, Marxism, and critical theory. It is a position that is working toward a sociology *for* women. The first criterion of adequacy in this approach is that the active voice of the subject should be heard in the account. Our interpretation should avoid transforming the acting and thinking human being solely into an object of study, while recognizing that some objectification is inherent in the process of interpretation or reconstruction. Moreover, seeing persons as active agents in their own lives, we will not view them as totally determined or lacking in comprehension of the social world. For example, we consider the concept "false consciousness" inadequate as part of a valid interpretation.

A second criterion for adequacy is that the theoretical reconstruction must be able to account for the investigator as well as for those who are investigated. The interpretation must locate the researcher in the social structure and also provide a reconstruction of the social relations that produce the research itself. For example, what are the social relations that produce this research situation and the enterprise of research itself? What makes it possible to raise this research problem at this time, in this place, in this society? What are the processes that have resulted in the researched and the researchers coming together in a particular kind of social relationship? Such a reconstruction should be possible, in principle, although we do not argue that every research report should spell it out in detail.

Our third criterion for adequacy is that the reconstruction should reveal the underlying social relations that eventuate in the daily lives we are studying. This is the heart of the idea of a sociology *for* women; we want to understand how the underlying organization of actions and practices results in the ordinary daily lives of women. This is a complex task, perhaps an impossible task. For example, to trace back from the daily experience of a working class mother, getting three or four children ready for school in the morning, unassisted by another adult, packing lunches, buttoning coats, etc., to the arrangements and relations that put her there, would be to describe much of the organization of the society. Thus, we need to make decisions and choices; this is part of the process of analysis that we have discussed above.

The adequacy of the interpretation fundamentally depends upon the accuracy of our descriptions of the experiences we wish to locate within the social relations of the society. Have we told it the way that it actually happens? This is the question we turn to now.

Our research problem demanded that we try to understand reality from the perspective of the people experiencing it. Since we directly asked them about their experience we did not have the problem of developing indicators of concepts. Rather, we wanted to maximize direct communication in their terms. We assumed that our study participants would have a better chance of telling us about their worlds as they saw them if their active participation in defining the dialogue were encouraged. As we have indicated above, we are confident that in most of our interviews the interviewees felt comfortable about stating their own case.

In qualitative work, the accuracy of listening and hearing may be as important as the openness of telling. The fact that we, the interviewers, were women who have been married, divorced, and had children (one of us had a baby after the study began) increased the validity of our data. We did not have to go through the process of getting to know the special perspectives and nuances of meaning of those we were studying—a process that is often identified as necessary if the qualitative researcher wants to avoid errors that simply come from ignorance (see, e.g., Filstead, 1970). We were studying people who had experiences very similar to ours, although of course there were important differences (the most important one being our status as researchers) and we were thus sensitive to problems and issues that might otherwise have been invisible.[8]

We think that it was also important that we were feminists. Our feminist analysis of women's oppression, which constituted much of the theory informing our work, also increased our sensitivity and awareness in the interview process, and contributed to the emergence of an empathetic atmosphere in the interaction process. A faithful account is best pursued, we are arguing, in research such as ours where changing consciousness is the central question, through the close and sympathetic involvement with the informant rather than through distancing and objectifying. At the same time such closeness may create certain kinds of blindness in the researcher. One protection we developed against this was in the ongoing process of analysis in the research group. Our analytic discussions, of necessity, forced us to distance ourselves from our subjects.

We have confirmation of the accuracy of our findings from those women we interviewed. We received extensive feedback from many of them in both individual and group discussions. Some read their interviews or listened to their tapes. We also discussed our written material with many and in those discussions our findings and our interpretations were confirmed.

Much more difficult problems of validity began to emerge in the interviews that were continued over a period of four years. These problems have to do with how reality is constructed and reconstructed in the process of talking and thinking about it and how the process of research becomes part of the process of change. We will leave the psychological aspects of the reconstruction of reality to the psychotherapeutic professions. Here, we will limit ourselves to specific methodological issues and only discuss the content of the change process in relation to them. Our insights into these issues come from women in our study, and, in particular, from one person whom we asked to participate in a workshop on developing a feminist methodology in social science.[9] Her comments on the experience of being the researched tell us a great deal about the validity of interview or questionnaire data. We will give a brief account of her experience as a background to further comments on validity.

J. began the first interview with a positive attitude toward the research. She knew that the objective was to contribute to the goal of women's liberation; she herself had a feminist orientation, and she was anxious to cooperate. During the interview, she did her best to be honest and open. The interview lasted for three hours, and both the interviewer and J. thought it was a good interview. However, reflecting on what she had said during the next few days, J. realized that she had omitted some very important aspects of her life and had unintentionally misrepresented others. She felt that the account she had given was chaotic, unclear, and disorganized. In the months between the first and second interviews, she thought about her life and tried to clarify events, relationships, and feelings; in the second interview she discussed herself within this altered point of view. Still, reviewing later what she said, she again was dissatisfied with the accuracy of her presentation of her current and past life. Once more, she went through a process of self-examination and rethinking. The third interview was somewhat better, but she was not yet satisfied. Only after the fourth interview did she begin to feel she was portraying her life as she actually lived it. By the fifth interview she had arrived at a coherent explanation of her experiences. J. said that this was the first time in her life that she was able to put together a reasonable account for herself. She believes that her first accounts were chaotic and disorganized because that was the way her life was, filled with multiple and conflicting demands from her husband, her five children, her jobs, her volunteer work in the community, and her friends. In the research process, between interviews, she spent long hours analyzing those relationships; her work on herself was part of the work of the research. She, as the researched, was constantly checking out the validity of the data she was giving to us, the researchers. But in the process, these data changed in some ways. The facts of the past were not altered, but they were elaborated and important omissions were filled in. Her own definition of what was important also changed in the process. Although it seems the best validity check to have the study participant determine accuracy, one could also argue that the first interview might have reflected her conscious assessment of the reality of her life at that time, while the fifth interview reflected an equally valid picture at a later time. Are we thus getting a more and more valid account, or are we getting several accounts that reflect the process of change? Certainly for J., the interviews were part of a change process in which she was trying to deal with fundamental contradictions in her life situation. Her understanding of her present dilemmas became clearer too, clearer in that she was more satisfied with them.

Such problems have been discussed by others many times (see, e.g., Becker and Geer, 1957), arguing that retrospective accounts are suspect in terms of validity. For example, Becker and Geer stated (1957: 141):

> Changes in the social environment and in the self inevitably produce transformations of perspectives, and it is characteristic of such transformations that the person finds it difficult or impossible to remember his [sic] former actions, outlook or feelings. Reinterpreting things from his new perspective, he [sic] cannot give an accurate account of the past, for the concepts in which he [sic] thinks about it have changed and with them his perceptions and memories.

We take a different position, arguing that both the past and present accounts are accurate. The first account was, we think, a true representation of J.'s conscious thoughts about her life at that time, with all the things she forgot, held back, and interpreted in ways she thought would be acceptable. But now that we have her own analysis of the process, we cannot take that interview as anything more than a reflection of her conscious thoughts at the time; we cannot take it as adequate "data" about her life history or her present situation. Her interpretations at the first interview were more narrow than the broader perspectives she had during the fifth interview, which was informed by social theory and by the interactions with the researchers. At this moment we have left our discussion of validity in a narrow sense and returned to our view of science in which an emancipatory goal is an essential part (Touraine, 1980). To return to our discussion: we should not take that first interview as filled with "error," although critical omissions may make our interpretations suspect. Especially painful memories or difficult experiences may be obscured—events such as the birth of an illegitimate child put out for adoption, abortion, rape, an illicit love affair, may be clouded over or simply seen as unimportant, when from the point of view of the outsider, they are critical to understanding a life.

These obscured experiences are central to the systematic devaluation of women in a male dominant world. A feminist perspective redefines these experiences as part of women's oppression, helping women to see their feelings as legitimate and eroding the taboos against discussing such life events. Moreover, distance and some confidence in the interviewer that has been built up over time may make it possible to reveal such events while altering the ways that they are assessed by the person who experienced them.

Unless a relationship of trust is developed, we can have no confidence that our research on women's lives and consciousness accurately represents what is significant to them in their everyday lives, and thus has validity in that sense. This is particularly true if we are trying to understand lives in their totality, as ongoing processes in which the person plays an active part. Certain survey data becomes, then, even more suspect. We have difficulty in assessing the validity of even the most factual data, to say nothing of data about opinions and attitudes. Even "in depth" interviews present problems of interpretation, as the above discussion indicates. We are probably faced with another unresolvable dilemma: working from a perspective in which we are trained to want to give a reasoned and connected account, we face live material that is constantly in the process of transformation, that is not organized in the way of academic theories, Virginia Woolf, among other novelists, may give a better account of the conscious experiencing of life in all its episodic and unorganized ways than we sociologists can achieve. However, as sociologists we can find representations of such experience that allow us to build a sociology for women, a sociology that connects experience at that level to its structural determination in the wider society. What distinguishes us from those who are not social scientists lies in our method of systematically attempting to reconstruct social reality and to put these systematic reconstructions into a social theory which we share with other social scientists. We are part of a group endeavor to understand society, even though the group is scattered and many of its members unknown to us.

Summary

In this paper we have discussed our attempt to use principles of feminist research in a systematic way as we carried out a research project. For us, feminist research should contribute to the liberation of women. We chose our research problem with this goal in mind. The problem was the relation between changes in consciousness and changes in the structural situation of individuals. Women who were at the end of their period of intensive mothering were the ones we chose to study. Our problem dictated qualitative data gathering. This method of data collection forced us to confront issues about the research relationship and influenced our data analysis. It was extremely difficult to analyze process, even though we had at least some relevant data. We still tended to look at our participants at one interview and then at the next, observing the changes but unable to adequately account for the intervening process. Yet, that process may be most important to understand if we are to comprehend the ways the larger structure penetrates the life of individuals, as well as the ways that individuals in their daily lives both reproduce and undermine that structure.

Our commitment to bringing our subjects into the research process as active participants[10] influenced our rethinking of our original categories, strengthened our critique of research methods, and forced us to realize that it is impossible to create a research process that completely erases the contradictions in the relation between researcher and researched.

In the relationship with those women who were actively changing both their life circumstances and their understandings of their lives, we were able to glimpse the research process as consciousness raising or emancipatory. Many of them told us that they experienced the interviews in this way. However, the emancipatory potential could only be partially attained even with those who were most aware of subjective change. The limits were in the restricted possibilities for satisfying work and financial independence facing all the women in our study. The research process was not consciousness raising for those whose life situation had not brought them into contact with the movement nor confronted them with the necessity to reflect upon their experiences. These were the women who were not in the process of trying to establish new forms of daily life and those whose interests seemed to be farthest from ours, the researchers. As we evaluate our experiences in interviewing these women, we are led to another dilemma of feminist research—should we do research that is not consciousness raising for the participants? Is such research an oppressive process that of necessity exploits the subject? If our answer to these questions is yes, we are faced with the possibility of only doing research with people who are very much like us, eliminating most women from our view and limiting the usefulness of our projects. Perhaps this is another necessary tension in the ongoing project of feminist investigation.

We have not solved the problems of doing emancipatory research. By trying to make our hopes and failures explicit, perhaps we have made a contribution toward that end.

NOTES

This is an extensively revised version of "Problemstillinger in Kvinneforskningen" av Joan Acker og Johanna Esseveld in samarbeid med Kate Barry in *Kvalitative metoden i samfunnsforskning*, Redigert au Harriet Holterog Ragnvald Kalleberg. Universitets forlaget, Oslo, 1982.

1. The term feminist refers to diverse groups of people who take varying positions on particular issues and who identify with a range of political positions. In our usage here, feminist refers to a point of view that (1) sees women as exploited, devalued, and often oppressed, (2) is committed to changing the condition of women, and (3) adopts a critical perspective toward dominant intellectual traditions that have ignored and/or justified

women's oppression. Some people who identify themselves as feminists accept the natural science model of sociology.

2. The term social relations here signifies a particular epistemology derived from the Marxist tradition and is not equivalent to the notion of social relationships. We are not referring to interactions between individuals. Rather we see individuals' activities in daily life as producing their social worlds; yet at the same time we recognize that there is an underlying organization of these activities which results in similar outcomes. This organization is what sociologists call social structure, but this is usually conceptualized as a fixed determinate abstract category which is apart from or radically other than individual action. The term social relations is a way of overcoming this dichotomy: to give centrality to the organization of social life without positing either "the individual" or "the social structure" as separate and oppositional. See the work of Dorothy Smith (1977; 1979; 1980) for a feminist interpretation of this concept.

3. Arlene Daniels discusses a similar problem in "The low-caste stranger in social research" (1967).

4. For a perceptive discussion of the need to reconceptualize social structure in ways that do not push women's experience into categories that are no longer reflective of that experience, see Joan Kelly's "The double vision of feminist theory" (1979).

5. This attempt to categorize was related also to our initial statement of our problem, the relationship between certain "exterior" changes—going to school or work—and certain "interior" changes—consciousness of self as woman who exists in a particular world and the interpretations of that world.

6. We used two categories, personal feminism and political feminism. These are explained in Acker et al. (1981).

7. Our commitment to doing feminist research and thus the attempt to do away with the hierarchy so often present in reseach may have prolonged the time the research took us as well. We tried to work in a nonhierarchical way as a research team and also tried to do all the necessary work. This included transcribing interviews ourselves, with some positive and negative results.

We, three researchers with different theoretical traditions and with specializations in different areas of sociology, had the same interests and political goals. By working closely together we developed the central concerns of our research. During our discussions we also developed a common theoretical perspective in which no person attempted to dominate or impose her own views. Differences in interpretation could then be more democratically resolved. This way of working was often a long drawn-out process, but we believe a necessary one for working with the kind of questions in which we were interested. The research process was also prolonged by our decision to do all the work ourselves. This meant that we would do the transcribing, as we believed that to be one of the most oppressive tasks in the research. We did the transcribing during the few extra hours left us after we had taken care of our teaching, work loads, and family responsibilities. It was a tedious process, especially since we were not trained transcribers. Eventually we decided to have some of the interviews transcribed or listened to the tapes, noting down topic areas and their location on the tapes.

Looking back, we may have overemphasized the overcoming of hierarchy and may have lost some of the expert knowledge and differential experience in the group. It might have been better to include in the project the person doing the transcribing instead of trying to deal with the oppressiveness of transcribing by doing the work ourselves.

8. Taking the position that the idea of the neutral observer is a false assumption has implications for validity. The researcher does not stand outside social structure. Her location in society enters into the research relationship. To recognize and take this into account as we did contributes to a better understanding of reality and greater validity.

9. We wish to thank Joanne Ferrero for contributing her perceptive insights to our workshop on feminist methodology and to this paper.

10. The research process affected us as researchers and in our own lives. Our role as

researchers was greatly changed because of the more active involvement of the women in our study, something which became especially clear during the analysis when our interpretations were being questioned. During the interviewing, we faced a tension between being expected to take the initiative and wanting more of a dialogue. Personally, it helped us to reflect on our own situations and influenced future personal choices.

REFERENCES

Acker, Joan. 1973. Women and social stratification: a case of intellectual sexism. *Am. J. Sociology* 78 (4): 936–45.
———. 1978. Issues in the sociological study of women's work. In Ann Stromberg and Shirley Harkess, *Women Working*. Mayfield, Palo Alto.
Acker, Joan, Kate Barry and Johanna Esseveld. 1981. Feminism, female friends, and the reconstruction of intimacy. In Helena Z. Lopata, ed., *The Interweave of Social Roles*, vol. 2, J.A.T. Press, Greenwich, Conn.
Bart, Pauline. 1971. Sexism in social science: from the iron cage to the gilded cage—The perils of Pauline. *J. Marriage Family* 33(2): 741.
Bartky, Sandra Lee. 1975. Toward a phenomenology of feminist consciousness. *Social Theory Practice* 3 (4): 425–39.
Becker, Howard S., and Blanche Geer. 1957. Participant observation and interviewing: a comparison. *Hum. Org.* 16:28–32.
Bernard, Jessie. 1973. My four revolutions: an autobiographical history of the ASA. In Joan Huber, ed., *Changing Women in a Changing Society*. University of Chicago Press, Chicago.
Bernstein, Richard. 1978. *The Restructuring of Social and Political Theory*. University of Pennsylvania Press, Philadelphia.
Blumer, Herbert. 1969. *Symbolic Interactionism. Perspective and Method*. Prentice Hall, Englewood Cliffs, N.J.
Daniels, Arlene Kaplan. 1967. The low-caste stranger in social research. In Gideon Sjoberg, ed., *Ethnics, Politics and Social Research*. Schenkman, Cambridge, Mass.
Esseveld, Johanna. 1980. Critical social research: women's perspective. In Mette Kunøe and Bergitta Possing, eds, *Kvindeforskning 1980: Rapport Fra Hindegavl Seminaret*. Aalborg universitetsforlag, Aalborg, Denmark.
Filstead, William J. 1970. *Qualitative Methodology*. Markham, Chicago.
Glazer, Barney and Anselm Strauss. 1973. *The Discovery of Grounded Theory: Strategies for Qualitative Research*. Aldine, Chicago.
Habermas, Jurgen. 1972. *Knowledge and Human Interest*. Beacon, Boston.
Hartsock, Nancy. 1979. Feminist theory and the development of revolutionary strategy. In Zillar R. Eisenstein, ed., *Capitalist Patriarchy and the Case for Socialist Feminism*. Monthly Review Press, New York.
———. 1981. Fundamental feminism: process and perspective. In *Building Feminist Theory: Essays from Quest*. Longman, New York.
Hughes, John. 1980. *The Philosophy of Social Research*. Longman House, Essex.
Karabel, Jerome. 1976. Revolutionary contradictions: Antonio Gramsci and the problems of intellectuals. *Politics Society* 6(2): 123–72.
Kelly, Joan. 1979. The double vision of feminist theory: a postscript to the 'Women and Power' conference. *Feminist Studies* 1:216–27.

Maret-Havens, Elizabeth. 1977. Developing an index to measure female labor force attachment. *Mon. Labor Rev.* 199(5):35–38.

McCormack, Thelma. 1975. Towards a non-sexist perspective on social and political change. In Marcia Millman and Rosabeth Moss Kanter, eds. *Another Voice: Feminist Perspectives of Social Life and Social Sciences*. Anchor, Garden City, N.Y.

Roberts, Helen, ed. 1981. *Doing Feminist Research*. Routledge and Kegan Paul, London.

Rubin, Lillian. 1979. *Women of a Certain Age*. Morrow, New York.

Schutz, Albert. 1963. Concept and theory formation in the social sciences. In H. Hatanson, ed., *Philosophy of the Social Sciences*, pp. 231–49. Random, New York.

Sherman, Julia A. and Evelyn Torton Beck, eds. 1979. *The Prism of Sex: Essays in the Sociology of Knowledge*. University of Wisconsin Press, Madison, Wisc.

Smith, Dorothy. 1974. Women's perspective as a radical critique of sociology. *Sociological Inquiry* 44:7–13.

———. 1977. Some implications of a sociology for women. In Nona Glazer and Helen Waehrer, eds, *Women in a Man-Made World: A Socioeconomic Handbook*, 2nd ed. Rand McNally, Chicago.

———. 1979. A sociology for women. In Julia A. Sherman and Evelyn Torton, eds, *The Prism of Sex: Essays in the Sociology of Knowledge*. University of Wisconsin Press, Madison, Wisc.

———. 1980. An examination of some sociological methods of thinking from the standpoint of a sociology for women, and an alternative. Unpublished manuscript prepared for the meetings of the American Sociological Assocation, New York.

Touraine, Alaine et al. 1980. *La Prophète Anti-Nucléaire*. DuSueil, Paris.

Westkott, Marcia. 1979. Feminist criticism of the social sciences. *Harv. Educational Rev.* 49(4):422–30.

Woodward, Diana and Lynne Chisholm. 1981. The expert's view? The sociological analysis of graduates' occupational and domestic roles. In Helen Roberts, ed., *Doing Feminist Research*. Routledge and Kegan Paul, London.

9. Separate but Equivalent

Equal Pay for Work of Comparable Worth

RONNIE STEINBERG AND LOIS HAIGNERE

Introduction

In 1870, Miss Virginia Penny advised her readers that "in the different departments of woman's labor, both physical and mental, there exists a want of harmony of labor done and the compensation." Writing on *How Women Make Money: Married or Single*, she offered a comparable worth comparison: "a gilder [typically male] in a book bindery gets $6 a week . . . which is equal to ten cents an hour. A girl, at most mechanical employments, receives for her sixty hours' labor, $3 a week . . . [or] five cents an hour" (Penny, 1870: xiii). The "want of harmony" remains. Over a century later, in 1981, the National Research Council of the National Academy of Sciences (NRC/NAS) concluded: "Not only do women do different work than men, but the work women do is paid less, and the more an occupation is dominated by women the less it pays" (Treiman and Hartmann, 1981: 28).

The policy of equal pay for work of comparable worth has evolved to rectify the wage discrimination that is a by-product of occupational segregation. This policy broadens the earlier policy of equal pay for equal work, which prohibited wage discrimination if women and men were doing the same or essentially similar work. Dubbed "comparable worth" for short, equal pay for comparable worth means that different and dissimilar jobs of equivalent worth to the employer should be paid the same wages.

Conceptually, the goal of equal pay for work of comparable worth, or pay equity, concerns the issue of whether work done primarily by women and minorities is systematically undervalued because the work has been and continues to be done primarily by women and minorities. By systematic undervaluation, we mean that the wages paid to women and men engaged in historically female or minority work are artificially depressed relative to what those wages would be if the jobs had been and were being performed by white males. Operationally, pay equity involves correcting the practice of paying women and minorities less than white men for work that requires equivalent skills, responsibilities, stresses, personal contacts, and working conditions.

Reprinted from *Gender at Work: Perspectives on Occupational Segregation and Comparable Worth*, Women's Research and Educational Institute of the Congressional Caucus for Women's Issues, 1984, 13–26.

Because minorities, as well as women, are disproportionately concentrated in low status, low-paying jobs, it is surprising that this policy goal has been labeled a "middle class white women's" reform. Comparable worth studies examine potential wage discrimination in such predominantly female jobs as garment worker, launderer, food service worker, institutional caretaker, retail salesworker, and entry level clerk typist. Minorities are disproportionately represented in these jobs as well.

Moreover, comparable worth is being extended to encompass jobs disproportionately held by minority males even though, until recently, the question of the fairness of wages under this policy was defined almost exclusively as a woman's issue. In a comparable pay study of New York State government employment, for example, estimates of undervaluation will be made for such job titles as youth division aide, window washer, elevator operator, janitor, cook, barber, and bus driver. The cultural processes perpetuating undervaluation are the same, whether the source of differential treatment is sex or race or ethnicity.

Comparable Worth: Historical Background

The activities surrounding comparable worth are best understood as an outgrowth of equal employment opportunity policy. The wage gap between women and men is one of the oldest and most persistent symptoms of sexual inequality in the United States. As far back as 100 years ago, working women and men were pressuring for the elimination of the wage gap through the demand for equal pay for equal work (Cook, 1975). By World War II, some progress had been made in achieving this policy. Employees, largely through their trade unions, had obtained over 2,000 equal pay adjustments through the National War Labor Board in the one-year period between November 1942 and October 1943 (Milkman, 1981). Several states, including New York and New Jersey, passed equal pay acts or fair employment practices acts prohibiting discrimination in compensation.

Most important, the issue of comparable worth had its origin in a 1945 case brought to the War Labor Board by the Electrical Workers' Union against General Electric and Westinghouse. In this case and a similar one in 1946, the Board decided in favor of the union's position and stated:

> the jobs customarily performed by women are paid less, on a comparative job content basis, than the jobs customarily performed by men, [and] this relative underpayment constitutes a sex discrimination. (as quoted in Steinberg, 1982).

The next significant wave of national government activity involved the enactment of the 1963 Equal Pay Act and of Title VII of the 1964 Civil Rights Act, and the promulgation of Executive Orders 11246 and 11375. These constituted an impressive body of national standards to eliminate all forms of employment discrimination, including discrimination in compensation.

Over the almost two decades since the enactment of these laws, policymakers, activists, and social scientists deepened their understanding of the nature of discrimination in the labor market and of the subtle institutional mechanisms perpetuating it. Court case after court case and research study after research study brought forth compelling evidence that the source of employment discrimination was not the intentionally evil behavior of a marginal group of employers, but was instead embedded in a firm's personnel procedures and policies concerning hiring and initial assignment, promotion, and compensation (Alvarez and Lutterman, 1979). Examination of work organizations uncovered occupational sex and race segregation as a major barrier inhibiting labor market equality along such dimensions as hiring, initial assignment, etc. The systematic approach to discrimination found in Title VII provided the conceptual, if not yet the legal, foundation for efforts to achieve comparable worth policy. In addition, the 1972 amendments extended Title VII rights to the public sector.

In the area of discrimination in compensation, the link between the wage gap and occupational segregation was also being established through a number of separate activities in the early 1970s. Two of these were the Washington State Comparable Pay Study and the Title VII Compliance Program of the Electrical Workers against Westinghouse, which culminated in the *IUE v. Westinghouse Electric Corporation* (CA 3, 1980, 23 FEP cases 588) decision.

Comparable worth policy began to achieve some national visibility in 1977 when Eleanor Holmes Norton, then Chair of the Equal Employment Opportunity Commission (EEOC), identified the issue as a priority of her agency. The EEOC contracted with the National Research Council of the National Academy of Sciences to form a committee to determine the feasibility of implementing a comparable worth policy. Norton selected the NRC/NAS because she wanted, if possible, the opinion of "organized science" to support the contention that wage discrimination was pervasive and that a comparable worth policy was a realistic way to correct it. Also, in April 1980, the EEOC held hearings on the issue of wage discrimination and comparable worth. The published testimony ran to over 1,200 pages (Equal Employment Opportunity Commission, 1980). Perhaps most important, Norton's actions and commitment served as a stimulus for forming a national network of groups and individuals working to attain comparable worth, including the National Committee on Pay Equity and the Comparable Worth Project.[1]

By 1980, comparable worth was a visible national policy goal supported largely by women's rights organizations, commissions on the status of women, and trade unions. But the type of wage discrimination addressed by a comparable worth policy had yet to be institutionally acknowledged and legitimized. Then, in 1981, three very different events contributed to the further development of the policy.

In June, the Supreme Court ruled in *County of Washington v. Gunther* that wage discrimination claims brought under Title VII are not restricted to claims for equal pay for substantially equal work. One month later, the public employees of San Jose, California struck to obtain contract language accepting the principle of comparable worth and providing approximately $1.5 million to begin adjusting wages in underpaid, female-dominated jobs. Finally, the National Research Council of the National Academy of Sciences issued *Women, Work and Wages: Equal Pay for Jobs of Equal Value*, which concluded:

> on the basis of a review of the evidence, our judgment is that there is substantial discrimination in pay, [and] . . . in our judgment job evaluation plans provide measures of job worth that, under certain circumstances, may be used to discover and reduce wage discrimination. (Treiman and Hartmann, 1981: 91, 95)

And further that:

> women are systematically underpaid . . . [and] the strategy of "comparable worth" . . . merits consideration as an alternative policy of intervention in the pay-setting process. (Treiman and Hartmann, 1981: 66–67)

The comparable worth activities of the last half-dozen years represent a new and exciting stage in the long-term efforts to achieve labor market equality for women. In the late 1960s and early 1970s, more and more people came to understand that discrimination is not merely intentional but systematic. It is, in other words, intrinsic to the operation of most work organizations and of the labor market as a whole. Understanding of this fact created an environment conducive to broadening the definition of discrimination through court decisions, strong and detailed administrative guidelines, and, finally, an amended Title VII. Reform of national and state legislation, in turn, provided the impetus to address other and newly identified sources of discrimination.

Indeed, among the major activities of the last half-dozen years have been general information-gathering and the completing of comparable worth studies. Most state and municipal studies have been initiated by local unions, especially in the public sector, or by state commissions on the status of women. Funding for the studies has been provided in a variety of ways—through state funds under the Comprehensive Education and Training Act, legislative appropriations, governor-sponsored appropriations, or funds bargained for in labor-management contracts. All the studies have found substantial undervaluation of women's work. A technical basis for estimating the extent of wage discrimination has been hotly debated by proponents and opponents of comparable worth. It is to this issue that we turn next.

Comparable Worth: Methodological Issues

The concentration of women and minorities in jobs not commonly done by white men can contribute to the wage gap in one of two ways. First, women and minorities may be systematically channeled into jobs that require less skill, effort, and responsibility than jobs filled by white males. One study completed by NRC/NAS staff found that job content differences such as degree of complexity and supervisory duties did explain some small percentage of the difference in earnings (Roos, 1981). Affirmative action policies are in place to eliminate this source of the wage gap through incentives and sanctions that increase the mobility of women and minorities into higher-paying jobs.

Second, women and minorities may be segregated into jobs that require the equivalent amount of skill, effort, and responsibility as white male jobs, but are paid less for that equivalent work. Put somewhat differently, their jobs are systematically undervalued *because* the work is performed predominantly by women and minorities. This type of wage discrimination is the focus of comparable worth. Comparable worth, then, is only concerned with eliminating those differences in wage rates that cannot be accounted for by productivity-related job content characteristics.

In turn, comparable worth studies must first determine whether the salaries associated with female- and minority-dominated job titles accurately reflect an explicit and consistently applied standard of value or whether they are artificially depressed because women and minorities fill the jobs. Second, the studies must pinpoint job titles that are undervalued and then develop estimates of the potential costs of correcting for this wage discrimination. We need a methodology, then, by which different jobs can be assessed to establish equivalent worth.

Evaluating Relative Job Worth

The technique of job evaluation has been used to assess whether or not pay equity exists in a firm. But in order to use this approach for comparable worth, it is necessary to use one relatively bias-free evaluation system to classify all jobs (Remick, 1984). A job evaluation system that is free of bias must:

- *describe job content* (i.e., behaviors, tasks, functions) accurately, comprehensively, and consistently; and
- *assign to each specific content factor a standard of worth* that can be systematically applied without bias across all jobs in the specified work force.

The first of these two processes is called *job content analysis* and the second is called *job evaluation*.

Job Content Analysis

The general purpose of job content analysis is to gather thorough and accurate descriptions of the range of tasks, behaviors, or functions associated with a job (Beatty and Beatty, 1984). Accurate job descriptions are not only a function of asking the "right" questions about job content in a well-designed questionnaire, however. Equally important are (1) selecting a sample of job titles representative of the range of work performed in the work organization, (2) selecting a large enough sample of incumbents within a job title to ensure that the information collected is representative of the range and variety of the work actually performed in the job, and (3) carrying out some procedure for averaging across specific positions within a job title.

In order to obtain job content information, such broad job characteristics as skill, effort, responsibility, and working conditions may be examined. Alternatively, the characteristics of a job may be defined more specifically to include such items as job-related experience, formal training time required, frequency of review of work, total number of personnel an employee is responsible for, impact on and responsibility for budget, physical stress, time spent working under deadlines, time spent in processing information, and so on. Information typically is gathered through questionnaires (completed by job incumbents, supervisors, job analysts, or some combination of these) and/or observation by a job analyst of a group of employees performing their jobs.

Job Evaluation

The purpose of job evaluation is to specify standards of worth by applying a single set of job-content criteria to *all* job titles in a work organization. Typically, jobs are assigned points in terms of the weighting of these criteria. (These weights are derived either from classical job evaluation systems [see Remick, 1984], or through a statistical analysis that is reviewed and can be modified by the parties to a labor contract.) Most important for the discussion here is that, based on the point value, wages are established for a job in relation to the wages paid for all jobs in that organization.

Furthermore, there are two major approaches to job evaluation: an a priori approach, using a predetermined system of factors and factor weights to evaluate jobs within a specific firm, and a *policy-capturing* approach, using a statistical analysis of an individual firm as the basis for creating factors and factor weights to apply to jobs in that firm.

The level of objectivity in measurement by either approach should not be confused with a mistaken vision that there is or can be objectivity in values. Both approaches are ways of systematizing value systems, and both potentially include or remove more or less of the discrimination embedded in an existing classification system. Both are geared to describe *what is* in the firm or in some other labor market. Neither starts from scratch in describing *what should be*.

Readers who are interested in more detail on the a priori and policy-capturing approaches are referred to the Appendix.

The Results of Comparable Worth Studies

Comparable worth studies have been and are being carried out across the country, primarily in the public sector. Close to a dozen studies have been or are being completed. Almost double that number are being proposed through unilateral action of personnel departments. Using at least four varieties of job analysis/job evaluation, completed studies consistently report that female-dominated job titles receive between five and twenty percent lower pay than male jobs with the same number of factor points.

In 1974, Washington State commissioned a comparable worth study, the results of which showed that state employees in traditionally female jobs received about twenty percent less on average than state employees in traditionally male jobs of comparable value. In 1975, an update of this study

Table 1: Illustrations of the Wage Gap

Location	Job Title	No. of Points	Monthly Salary	Differ-ence
Minnesota	Registered Nurse (F)	275	$1,723	$537
	Vocational Ed. Teacher (M)	275	$2,260	
San Jose,	Senior Legal Secretary (F)	226	$ 665	$375
California	Senior Carpenter (M)	226	$1,040	
	Senior Librarian (F)	493	$ 898	$221
	Senior Chemist (M)	493	$1,119	
Washington State	Administrative Services Manager A (F)	506	$1,211	$500
	Systems Analyst III (M)	426	$1,711	
	Dental Assistant I (F)	120	$ 608	$208
	Stockroom Attendant II (M)	120	$ 816	
	Food Service Worker (F)	93	$ 637	$332
	Truck Driver (M)	94	$ 969	

extended it to eighty-five more jobs (additional updates were done in 1979 and 1980).

A Connecticut study completed in February 1980 found that, for jobs of equivalent worth, individuals in "women's" jobs earn from eighty-one to ninety-two percent of the salary of individuals in "men's" jobs. In Idaho, in 1975, the implementation of a revised classification plan, which was formulated without an explicit concern with comparable worth, resulted in larger salary increases for predominantly female classifications than for traditionally male classifications. A Michigan study found that the "actual maximum pay rates for female-dominated jobs were lower than would be predicted" (Michigan Department of Labor, 1981).

The consistent pattern of undervaluation of "women's work" revealed by the studies done to date is illustrated in Table 1. The examples included in the table are drawn from three studies (Steinberg, 1984). Studies such as these provide indisputable evidence that the jobs that are held predominantly by women are underpaid relative to their evaluated worth.

Criticisms of the Use of Job Evaluation to Determine Comparable Worth

Those attempting to discredit comparable worth reforms frequently level two criticisms at job evaluation techniques. The first is that comparing different jobs is like comparing apples and oranges. The second is that job evaluation techniques are inadequate for estimating wages because they seemingly do not take market factors and supply and demand into account.

Apples and Oranges—Poets and Plumbers

In 1976, Governor Dan Evans, as a result of the 1974 comparable worth study, appropriated $7 million to begin implementing comparable worth in Washington State. Evan's successor, Dixie Lee Ray, removed these appropriations, stating that comparing different jobs is like comparing apples and oranges. Seven years later, a Justice Department official seeking to dismiss the U.S. District Court ruling against Washington State (discussed below) said that one can't compare poets and plumbers. Both of these claims are catchy; neither provides sound criticism of job evaluation.

We note that, in fact, apples and oranges can and have been compared by any number of empirical standards. For example, they can be systematically assessed in terms of number of calories, vitamin content, or mineral content. A nutritionist could then establish equivalencies among fruits for a person needing to follow a special diet. Similarly, jobs that are not identical are comprised of tasks and characteristics that can be empirically described. Jobs may then be ranked from high to low based on their characteristics, and equivalencies established according to a consistently applied set of standards. This can be translated into a wage rate. In fact, this is just what employers have been doing for decades in order to justify their existing wage structures. The *Dictionary of Occupational Titles,* published by the U.S. Department of Labor, is a ranking of jobs from most important and valuable to least important and valuable according to three general categories (U.S. Department of Labor, 1977). This ranking has been offered to and used by thousands of firms as an aid to setting salaries.

Some of the same employers who for years have been using classification techniques to compare dissimilar jobs now say that job evaluation systems cannot be used to compare male-dominated and female-dominated jobs (see Livernash, 1980, for example). And yet, as indicated earlier, the National Research Council of the National Academy of Sciences did conclude that such comparisons could be made with caution. One chapter of their report recommends formulas for correction of point factor systems to remove the impact of "femaleness" and "minorityness" (Treiman and Hartmann, 1981). Perhaps even more compelling is that job evaluations are being performed in states and other public jurisdictions. These studies are finding that jobs historically performed by women are undervalued. Pay equity adjustments based on study findings are being made.

Supply/Demand and the Market

The second general criticism of the use of job evaluation for assessment of comparable worth is that it fails to pay attention to the market, that is, to supply and demand as the true basis by which wages are set. This criticism reveals a serious misunderstanding of how job evaluation is done. Both the a priori and policy-capturing techniques mentioned above and reviewed in the Appendix do incorporate market considerations in the weighting of job content factors. Resulting wages are based on the productive contribution of jobs to the firm.

The point factors assigned to jobs in a priori approaches have been developed by management consultants on the basis of what the market pays for a given job content characteristic. These general point values are further grounded in the particular labor market by taking a set of so-called "benchmark" jobs with the same number of points and averaging across the specific wages paid for each job in other geographically proximate firms.

Policy-capturing represents the actual wage policy of a firm. So, to the extent that the firm has been basing its wage structure on the external market, the model of compensation will reflect "market" wages.

However, the proper use of both the a priori and policy-capturing techniques in comparable worth studies requires removing the elements of bias against "women's" and "minorities' " work that may be embedded in wage rates for female- and minority-dominated jobs. Therefore, comparable worth standards must be based only partly on market wages, since, as the NAS/NRC report stated, these market wages reflect many factors other than the "marginal productivity" of a job, including discrimination (Treiman and Hartmann, 1981: 65).

Moreover, while there is considerable overlap in wage rates across firms, the overall wage structure within a firm will differ from that of other firms, depending on such market factors as types of jobs, unionization, and character-istics of the industry (Milkovich, 1980). Comparable worth studies must take these firm-based market differences into account in developing a dis-crimination-free wage structure. For these reasons, the standards used in determining worth must be derived partly from market wages and, perhaps more important, they must be firm-based. Where there is no union representa-tion, the standard has to be determined by the employer. Where unions bargain with employers over wages, it is necessary to take the perspectives of both management and labor into account.

The Destruction of the Free Market

A related concern of comparable worth critics is that a job evaluation-based wage structure will wreak havoc on the economic system. This is surprising, given that well over two-thirds of all employees work in firms where there now exists some form of job evaluation underlying the wage structure (Treiman and Hartmann, 1981: 71). Comparable worth is not the only social reform about which subsequent system destruction has been predicted. For instance, in Massachusetts some time ago, employers testified that a proposed law would lead to chaos in the productive process, that employers would move out of the state, that it would destroy the excellent relationship between employers and employees, and that it would lead the country into socialism. The dangerous reform around which these claims were made was child labor laws. The year was 1880.

Interference with the free market is very common in our society. Sometimes we interfere for economic reasons to protect employers. We bail out Lockheed or protect the auto industry from the import of Japanese cars. Sometimes we interfere to protect employees, as with child labor and other wage and hour

laws. We also have laws that prohibit paying women, blacks, and other protected classes less than white males just because they will accept lower wages.
Finally, employers have been known to manipulate the so-called free market.
The National Association for Working Women, 9 to 5, discovered the existence
of the Boston Survey Group, a group of employers that meets each year to fix
the wages of clerical workers in the Boston area. Similarly, in the *Lemons v.
City of Denver* case (22 FEP cases 959), the defense showed that hospital
administrators meet each year to set the salaries of nurses in the Denver
metropolitan area. It may be that, when it comes to the free market, the
question is not so much *whether* it can be interfered with, but *who* can
interfere with it.

Comparable Worth: Implementation of Equity Adjustments

Once a job evaluation study has been completed, a firm or public jurisdiction
usually develops a plan to implement pay equity adjustments. Washington
State's failure to implement pay adjustments led Judge Jack Tanner of the U.S.
District Court to award back pay to 1979 in *AFSCME v. State of Washington*
(No. C82-465T). Indeed, Tanner's rulings became a media event, and the
reform was catapulted into national attention and criticized as a costly and
irresponsible reform.

Voluntary pay equity adjustments have received less attention in the media
and elsewhere, however. Nevertheless, corrections have been made through
legislation in Minnesota and through collective bargaining in San Jose, California. A number of Connecticut unions have already negotiated an adjustment
and the set-aside of monies for implementation in anticipation of study results.

A comparison of the Washington State and Minnesota experiences can allevi-
ate opponents' concerns that comparable worth implementation is inevitably
enormously costly. *It was the back pay award, and not simply the correction of
the undervaluation of women's jobs, that created the high price of the Washington State ruling.*[2] In 1977, the same year that Governor Dixie Lee Ray removed
the $7 million appropriation to begin implementation of comparable worth, the
Washington State legislature had amended state compensation statutes to
instruct state officials to provide it with separate supplemental comparable
worth salary schedules in addition to recommended salary schedules. The
express purpose was to provide the legislature with specific costs of eliminating
past wage discrimination and on-going disparities in pay. Despite receiving
these estimates, the legislature took no action from 1978 through 1982. Only
after the AFSCME law suit was filed in 1983 did the legislature appropriate
$1.5 million to implement the elimination of pay disparity. It was too late.
Judge Tanner, holding that the state had intentionally violated Title VII of the
1964 Civil Rights Act, awarded back pay to 1979. According to estimates
provided by the Manager of Standards and Surveys in Washington State,
Tanner's order will cost about $325 million in back pay and $75 million per year
in the future. With back pay, this amounts to over twenty-five percent of

payroll but, *without back pay*, it amounts to roughly five percent of annual payroll.

In contrast to Washington State, the Minnesota legislature moved quickly to make comparable worth adjustments. The Council on the Economic Status of Women, a legislative advisory body, established a Task Force on Pay Equity in October 1981. Using the job point evaluation system already in place in Minnesota, this task force put together a pay equity report estimating the undervaluation of traditionally female jobs. By March 1982, a pay equity bill was passed that provided for a phased-in equalization over four years. The cost over this four-year period was:

- Seven million dollars the first year, correcting twenty-five percent of the undervaluation;
- Fourteen million dollars the second year, correcting an additional twenty-five percent of the problem while still covering the first twenty-five percent;
- Twenty-one million dollars the third year, correcting seventy-five percent of the undervaluation;
- Twenty-eight million dollars the fourth year, completing the correction for undervaluation.

The political lessons drawn from the Washington State and Minnesota cases appear to be, first, what can be done in the next legislative session should not be put off for a decade, and, second, voluntary corrections are much cheaper than after-the-fact, litigation-based corrections.

In addition to being cheaper, voluntary corrections allow flexibility in phasing-in implementations of comparable worth. For instance, in New York State, the comparable worth study includes an economic forecasting component that will both assess potential costs of closing any gap in wages and project several options for carrying out phased-in pay equity adjustments in a voluntary and efficient fashion. Estimates will vary according to different assumptions regarding both the amount of time to close any gap that may be found and various orders of priority in closing the wage gap. For instance:

- Should the greatest gap be closed first?
- Should the gap be closed across the board?
- Should the gap in the lowest salary grades be closed first?

The results of this cost estimation exercise should provide labor and management with the information necessary to implement change in a fair and fiscally responsible fashion.

Concluding Remarks: Reflections on Social Reform

Activities involving comparable worth issues have proliferated in the last five years. There have been well over 125 state and municipal government initiatives ranging from information-gathering (including hearings), to job evaluation studies, to the enactment of comparable worth legislation, to the specification of enforcement efforts, and, finally, to comparable pay adjustments (Cook, 1975; Dean et al., 1983). Indeed, the authors learn of new initiatives at the rate of approximately two to three a week.

There is now sufficient experience to permit identification of the conditions necessary to move from information-gathering to pay equity adjustments within a jurisdiction. At the center of the change process is the completion of a job evaluation study—to identify the overall extent of undervaluation as well as to pinpoint disparities on a job-title by job-title basis. A study of this type appears to be a necessary, but not sufficient, condition for change. A notable exception is New Mexico, where in 1983, $3.3 million was appropriated to upgrade the lowest paid job titles, an overwhelming majority of which are female-dominated, without the completion of a study.

In order for a study to have led to changes in the structure of wages, three further political conditions appear to have been necessary. First, in almost all jurisdictions, efforts to undertake a study were initiated by organized groups of women and were spearheaded by the State Commission on the Status of Women and/or unions. Unions and state commissions on the status of women and/or state legislative task forces have combined forces to press for a study in Washington State, Connecticut, Minnesota, and Maine, to cite a few instances. Unions alone have proven instrumental in New York State and in several municipalities.

Second, in every case of pay equity adjustments, the study design included an advisory committee, often a joint labor and management committee, to influence, monitor, and review the study. More recently, legislative forces with representation from labor and management have initiated and monitored the completion of studies. In Washington State and in Connecticut, for example, the committee assisted the consultant in the process of assigning evaluation points to jobs. In San Jose, California, the Women's Committee of Local 101, AFSCME, trained union members in filling out job description questionnaires.

Finally, after the study results were announced, these organized constituent groups had to exert considerable pressure in many institutional arenas to gain salary adjustments for undervalued job titles. In Connecticut, the unions have combined collective bargaining with litigation and legislation. In Washington, a union litigated against the state. In Minnesota, a legislative commission pressured from within. In San Jose, the local union, after attempting negotiations with the city manager as well as filing a complaint with the regional EEOC office, won its demand when workers went out on strike. As comparable worth policy gains legitimacy, it is likely that implementation will immediately follow study completion. In New York State, for example, Governor Cuomo was recently quoted in the major Albany newspaper as saying:

> [Comparable worth] is a problem in this society and a very real one, and we all know it . . . I am committed to doing everything I can reasonably to fight the problem . . . That's why I have the study, which is going to report in the spring of '85 while I still have time in my term to get something done. (*Times Union*, February 12, 1984: A-9)

It appears that the parameters of a comparable worth policy are presently being formulated at the state and municipal levels. Studies are still needed because, while there is growing awareness of wage discrimination in general, there is no political consensus about which jobs are undervalued and by how much. Interest groups must combine strategies to bring about equity adjustments because the affected employees are relatively powerless, and the nature of comparable worth goes against the grain of the theoretical operating principles of the U.S. political economy. Despite this, there have been notable successes and these successes have generalized consequences. For example, collectively bargained agreements implementing pay equity adjustments have not only been significant to the employees they cover, they have also been powerful models for other employees seeking to eliminate wage discrimination in their employment contracts. Firm-level studies of the parameters of wage discrimination not only provide information to correct a specific wage structure, but also provide important material for educating women workers and the general public about the contours of wage discrimination.

Similarly, court cases established precedents for eliminating the most flagrant instances of intentional sex discrimination in compensation.[3] Once these precedents were in place, they served as a resource for employee groups to pressure for change in their workplaces. In addition, they provided a foundation for further legal precedents making more subtle forms of wage discrimination illegal.

As proponents of comparable worth build up a body of scientific evidence, establish legal precedents, and introduce pay equity adjustments into contracts, they negate the arguments of critics of comparable worth. Criticisms are best addressed when the policy is effectively implemented and without deleterious consequences. Moreover, as more firms adopt comparable worth, the resultant salary adjustments will permeate the wage structure of local markets. Through the process of pressure, innovation, education, imitation, and adjustment, the wages paid for work done primarily by women will catch up with the other profound changes in women's place in the labor market. These concrete actions transform a highly charged and controversial political demand into what no doubt eventually will become a routine and institutionalized feature of equal employment.

While this paper has focused largely on technical considerations in assessing wage discrimination and in correcting it through an evolving policy of comparable worth, comparable worth is less a technical than a political issue. The very emergence of the issue of comparable worth can be regarded as both a cause and a consequence of the change in the power position of women in the labor market. The considerable progress that has been made on comparable worth since 1977 demonstrates the power women and minorities are able to command when they organize and press for legal and political change.

Moreover, what most women and minorities might have considered a "fair" relative wage even twenty years ago is now proving unacceptable to them. Fundamentally, comparable worth is an issue of fairness. And, as Eleanor Holmes Norton said, it is the equal employment issue of the decade.

NOTES

1. The National Committee on Pay Equity is a membership organization of over 100 organizations and individuals, including labor unions, professional associations, women's and civil rights groups, and state and local government agencies. The three goals of the Committee are to support ongoing pay equity initiatives, encourage new ones, and assist in strategy development among the diverse constituencies. These efforts spilled over into the development of comparable worth networks on the West Coast. The Comparable Worth Project emerged as a California-based clearinghouse on comparable worth activities.

2. Ironically, the case Tanner ruled on might not have been before the court had Governor Dixie Lee Ray not removed the appropriated monies.

3. After the Washington State decision, it was widely implied that the way to avoid doing comparable worth adjustments was not to do a study—that the mistake was doing a study, rather than failing to implement adjustments based on study findings. Such implications are shortsighted. As more than 20 studies are either being undertaken or completed, the lack of a study may be taken as a demonstration of bad faith.

REFERENCES

Alvarez, Rodolfo, and Kenneth G. Lutterman and Associates. *Discrimination in Organizations*. San Francisco: Jossey-Bass, 1979.

Beatty, Richard W., and James R. Beatty. "Problems with Contemporary Job Evaluation Systems." In Helen Remick (ed.), *Comparable Worth and Wage Discrimination*. Philadelphia: Temple University Press, 1984.

Bellak, Alvin. "The Hay Guide Chart—Profile Method of Job Evaluation." In *Handbook of Wage and Administration*, second edition. New York: McGraw-Hill, 1982.

Cook, Alice. *Pay Equity: A Multi-National History and Comparison*. Honolulu: University of Hawaii Industrial Relations Center, 1975.

Dean, Virginia, Margaret Klaw, Joy Anne Grune, and Susan Bluer. *State and Local Government Action on Pay Equity: New Initiatives*. Paper commissioned by the National Committee on Pay Equity, Washington, D.C., 1983.

Equal Employment Opportunity Commission. *Hearings on Job Segregation and Wage Discrimination*. Washington, D.C.: U.S. Government Printing Office, 1980.

Livernash, E. Robert (ed.). *Comparable Worth: Issues and Alternatives*. Washington, D.C.: Equal Employment Advisory Council, 1980.

McAdams, Kenneth G. "Job Evaluation and Classification." *Journal American Water Works Association* 66: 7, 1974, pp. 405–409.

Michigan Department of Labor, Office of Women and Work. *A Comparable Worth Study of the State of Michigan Job Classifications: Technical Report*. Lansing: Michigan Department of Labor, 1981.

Milkman, Ruth. *The Reproduction of Job Segregation by Sex: A Study of the Sexual Division in the Auto and Electrical Manufacturing Industries in the 1960's*. Doctoral dissertation, Department of Sociology, University of California at Berkeley, 1981.

Milkovich, George T. "The Emerging Debate." In E. Robert Livernash (ed.), *Comparable Worth: Issues and Alternatives*. Washington, D.C.: Equal Employment Advisory Council, 1980.

Penny, Virginia. *How Women Can Make Money: Married or Single*. Springfield, Mass.: D. E. Fisk, 1870.

Pierson, David A., and Karen S. Koziara. *Study of Equal Wages for Jobs of Comparable Worth: Final Report*. Philadelphia: Temple University Center for Labor and Human Resource Studies, 1981.

Remick, Helen. "Dilemmas of Implementation: The Case of Nursing." In Helen Remick (ed.), *Comparable Worth and Wage Discrimination*. Philadelphia: Temple University Press, 1984.

Remick, Helen, and Ronnie J. Steinberg. "Technical Possibilities and Political Realities: Concluding Remarks." In Helen Remick (ed.), *Comparable Worth and Wage Discrimination*. Philadelphia: Temple University Press, 1984.

Roos, Patricia A. "Sex Stratification in the Workforce: Male-Female Differences in Economic Returns to Occupation." *Social Science Research* 10, September 1981, pp. 195–224.

Steinberg, Ronnie J. *Wages and Hours: Labor and Reform in Twentieth Century America*. New Brunswick: Rutgers University Press, 1982.

———. " 'A Want of Harmony': Perspectives on Wage Discrimination and Comparable Worth." In Helen Remick (ed.), *Comparable Worth and Wage Discrimination*. Philadelphia: Temple University Press, 1984.

Steinberg, Ronnie, and Lois Haignere. *Barriers to Advancement: Promotion of Women and Minorities into Managerial Positions in New York State Government*. Center for Women in Government Working Paper No. 10. Albany: Center for Women in Government, 1984.

Treiman, Donald J. *Job Evaluation: An Analytic Review*. Washington, D.C.: National Academy of Sciences, 1979.

Treiman, Donald J., and Heidi I. Hartmann (eds.). *Women, Work and Wages: Equal Pay for Jobs of Equal Value*. Committee on Occupational Classification and Analysis, National Research Council. Washington, D.C.: National Academy Press, 1981.

U.S. Department of Labor. *Dictionary of Occupational Titles*, fourth edition. Washington, D.C.: U.S. Government Printing Office, 1977.

Appendix
Job Evaluation:
The A Priori and Policy-Capturing Approaches

Typical a priori systems define work content in terms of broad categories such as skill, effort, responsibility, and working conditions. Hay Associates, perhaps the foremost management consulting firm on classification issues, offers four analogous groupings: know-how, problem-solving, accountability, and, when appropriate, working conditions (McAdams, 1974; Bellak, 1982). Hay Associates also offers two reasons for its groupings: (1) the most significant elements of work are "the knowledge required to do a job, the kind of thinking needed to solve the problems commonly faced, and the responsibilities assigned"; and (2) "factors appear in certain kinds of patterns that seemed to be inherent in certain kinds of jobs" (Bellak, 1982: 1). Each factor is broken down into subcomponents and, within each subcomponent, levels are created with points assigned to each level. These are provided graphically by the consultant in so-called Guide Charts for use by committees of employees or by the consultant in assigning points to a job. The assignment of points is based on the description provided for that job. Descriptions are gained either through what are called "desk audits" by consultants (which are reviewed by a job incumbent and a supervisor for that job) or derived from responses to what is generally an employee questionnaire asking such broad questions as: "Describe the most significant tasks associated with your job."

The points for each category are tallied to obtain a total score for the job. For example, in a sample job evaluation reported in an article describing the Hay System, a supervisor of keypunch operators received a total of 268 points: 152 for know-how, 50 for problem-solving, and 66 for accountability. The job receives 152 points for know-how because:

> 1) the job classification requires advanced vocational training (slotted in the D column); 2) the job is first-line supervision of a single-function (slotted in column I for managerial know-how); 3) the job involves proficiency in human relations, since such skills are critical in motivating people at this level (McAdams, 1974).

This score becomes the basis for assigning a wage rate to the job. All other things being equal, jobs with the same number of points receive the same wages.

By contrast, typical policy-capturing approaches develop a compensation model that statistically indicates the relationship between the current wages paid for a job in a firm and the content of a job. In this approach, specific job content features such as the number of persons supervised, type of training needed to work with machines, and extent of traveling overnight on the job become the basis for describing job content. Then, through statistical analysis, characteristics important in predicting wages and the weighting of these characteristics can be determined. These may vary from firm to firm. For example, a public sector jurisdiction may value supervision, responsibility for budgetary decisions, and writing skills. By contrast, a manufacturing firm may value supervision, cost effective production monitoring, and manual dexterity. In other words, the presence or absence of these job dimensions in a specific job and the value of a job dimension to a particular firm predicts the wages assigned to that job in that firm.

Once these relationships have been established for a firm, the model can be adjusted statistically to remove the impact of what is called "femaleness" or "minorityness." This correction procedure will provide a compensation model that can then be applied to each female- and minority-dominated job title to obtain a prediction of what the wage would be if wage discrimination were removed. A policy-capturing study conducted by two industrial psychologists at the Center for Labor and Human Resources Studies at Temple University under the auspices of Council 13 of AFSCME found, for instance, that "the average difference between existing wages for female jobs and predicted wages for female jobs based on wages for male jobs was $1.10 per hour. This represents an annual amount of about $2,228" (Pierson and Koziara, 1981).

Each of the two systems of job evaluation—a priori and policy-capturing—has technical strengths and limitations, and both must be tempered by political realities (see Remick and Steinberg, 1984, for a fuller discussion). For example, a priori systems have the advantage of making explicit the values used in evaluating jobs. The systems thus allow employer and employee alike the opportunity to study the underlying value system of the evaluation instrument in an accessible, nonmathematical framework. The major limitations of these systems are their resistance to modification, general lack of flexibility or responsiveness to firm-specific factors, and probable bias. On the other hand, procedures labeled as policy-capturing make fewer assumptions than a priori systems about what the firm should value because they build an evaluation system that is firm-specific. The procedure involves using multiple regression techniques to determine which elements of jobs are correlated to pay practices for that firm. However, if the statistical analysis is not carried out with care and sensitivity, the compensation model could be used incorrectly, and inaccurately capture the firm's values. As a result, it could lead to the incorrect setting of the relative wages of jobs in that firm.

We prefer the policy-capturing approach, although we recognize that the choice between the two approaches to evaluation most likely will be made for political reasons. In some settings, certain systems will be preferred because of previous working relationships with consulting firms. A priori systems will be preferred where they are seen as more understandable and explainable. On the other hand, regression models as used in policy-capturing systems are more likely to be preferred in settings with strong tastes for sophisticated math models and computers (regression virtually cannot be done without reliance on computers) and for firm-specificity.

10. THE DIFFERENT WORLDS OF WOMEN AND MEN

Attitudes toward Pornography and Responses to *Not a Love Story*— A Film about Pornography

PAULINE B. BART, LINDA N. FREEMAN, AND PETER KIMBALL

Men and women viewing the antipornography documentary Not a Love Story *were surveyed about their opinions and attitudes toward pornography and toward the film. Women were found to be significantly more negative toward pornography than men and experienced greater attitude and belief changes from the film. In addition, men's and women's attitudes toward pornography were found to differ in their factor structure; the authors infer that acceptance or rejection of pornography has different significance for men and women. Background variables such as current marriage, sex of children, and amount of pornography previously seen affected men's attitudes more than women's. The authors conclude that gender-free, "humanist" standards according to which pornography could be evaluated do not exist, and that approaches to pornography control based on its role in the particular oppression of women are valid.*

"You and all fem libbers have created the monster of fantasy. You *idiots*. First, men had to resort to porno movies, *making* them and *watching them*, to show women *enjoying* sex, *enjoying* blow jobs, and *enjoying* orgasm—because in real life it's headache time . . ."—anonymous letter to Bart.

A. Background

Pornography is a controversial issue that only recently has begun to be adequately studied. Although the President's Commission on Obscenity and Pornography purported to prove definitely that pornography was not only harmless but under certain circumstances could indeed be beneficial (Report of the Commission on Obscenity and Pornography, 1970), more recent research has shown the methodological inadequacy of the Commission's reports (Diamond, 1980; Bart and Jozsa, 1980).

Reprinted from *Women's Studies Int. Forum*, Vol. 8, No. 4 (1985), 307–322.

Irene Diamond has pointed out that the President's Commission used a catharsis model which stated that exposure to pornography would enable individuals to drain off harmful sexual needs. The Commission "contends that at worst pornography is merely harmless and at best it provides for 'more agreeable and more openness in marital communication' " (Diamond, 1980: 193). Bart and Jozsa (1980) noted that, while the President's Commission on Violence concluded with a learning theory model which essentially stated "the more you see the more you do," the commission on Obscenity, with its cartharsis model, implied "the more you see the *less* you do."

Bart and Jozsa (1980) point out the following methodological flaws in the Commission's report as well as the spin-off papers in a special issue of *The Journals of Social Issues*. After noting McCormack's (1978) critique of the sexist premises of the model, they go on to remark that in the Report and in the *Journal of Social Issues* the terms "erotica," "pornography," and "explicit sexual material" are used interchangeably, that most research was done before explicit violence pervaded pornography, that the researchers and subjects were overwhelmingly male, and that the effect on women was inferred from married women's responses in their husbands' presence. They further point out that if the catharsis model were correct, then since the amount, visibility and legitimacy of pornography has been increasing, rape and other sexual violence against women should be withering away, like the state after the revolution. This does not appear to be the case.

More recently the psychological experiments of Malamuth and Donnerstein (1984) show the links between viewing pornography and violence in an "erotic" context. Donnerstein *et al*. (1984) demonstrate a causal relationship between viewing "R"-rated films which depict violence in an "erotic" context, e.g., *The Tool Box Murders,* and *Halloween,* and male subjects' desensitization to rape. As they view more of these films they laugh more at the violence, see less violence, and identify more with the assailant. When these subjects assumed the role of jurors in a simulated rape case, they judged less harm done to the rape victim. This finding is particularly disturbing in light of studies showing that about a third of men would rape if they were sure they would not be caught (Malamuth, 1981).

Additionally, Zillmann and Bryant (1982) found that viewing sexually explicit but not "violent" pornography, showing sexual activity between "consenting" adults, results in college students becoming less sensitive to the harm of rape and more hostile to the Women's Movement. Thus, while 71 per cent of men who were not exposed to pornography supported the Movement, only 49 per cent of the men with intermediate exposure and 25 per cent of men massively exposed supported the Movement. A "massive" exposure meant that the student subjects saw a *total* of 4 hrs. and 48 min. of "erotic" films over a six-week period. Those with medium exposure saw 2 hrs. and 24 min. of erotic films and a similar quantity of non-erotic films. A third group saw only non-erotic films, and a fourth group no films at all. What is most striking about this research is that these films were about sexual acts between "consenting" adults without any overt violence. But the women in these films played one of the standard female roles in pornography—they were sexually insatiable and more eager for the various acts than the men.

Furthermore, the autobiography of Linda Marciano (formerly known as Linda Lovelace) (1982), describes how she was manipulated into going off with and then forced to marry Chuck Trainer, who then forced her physically and psychologically to participate in prostitution and the making of pornographic films, raises the issue of the legitimacy of the assumption that women in pornography are "consenting." Clearly Marciano did not consent. Thus, in addition to the desensitizing effects of pornography on the viewer, women (and children) in pornography performances may be coerced, and thus victims of this "victimless" crime.

As the sociology of knowledge points out (MacKinnon, 1983), our perspective is shaped by our location in the social structure. Thus rich people view the world differently from poor people, white people view the world differently from people of color, old people view the world differently from young people, and men view the world differently from women. We maintain that pornography presents a male ideology of sexuality which depicts women behaving in ways that are most pleasing to men. (See quote at beginning of paper.)[1] The view of rape presented in pornography, in which there is no injury and indeed the woman enjoys the sexual experience as she never has before (Smith, 1976; Stock, 1983), leads us to conceptualize pornography as pro-rape propaganda. To use Marxist terminology, pornography is sexual imagery, purveyed as a commodity in a society characterized by male domination.

The proposed Minneapolis ordinance defines pornography as:

> the sexually explicit subordination of women, graphically depicted, whether in pictures or in words, that also includes one or more of the following: women presented as sexual objects, things or commodities; or as sexual objects who experience sexual pleasure in being raped; or as sexual objects tied up or cut up or mutilated or bruised or physically hurt; or in postures of sexual submission; or as whores by nature; or being penetrated by objects or animals; or in scenarios of degradation, injury, abasement, torture, shown as filthy or inferior, bleeding, bruised, or hurt in a context that makes these conditions sexual; or women's body parts are exhibited in such a way that women are reduced to those parts.

In light of the above statements our major hypothesis is as follows:

I. There will be gender differences in attitudes toward pornography: males will be more favorable to pornography than females and these differences will be affected by (a) being a parent of female children (child), and (b) self-definition as feminist or profeminist.

II. Viewing the antipornography documentary *Not a Love Story* will result in self-reported attitude changes and information acquisition.[2]

B. Conduct of the Study

We first handed out stamped, addressed, prefolded questionnaires to patrons exiting a theater showing the film. This questionnaire asked only for the gender of the respondent. After telling them the importance of the issue, they were asked to cooperate by writing their reactions to the film including any changes it had made in their attitudes about pornography, what they liked and didn't like about the film, what they learned, if anything, and anything else they wanted to tell us. (See appendix for copy of this form.) The return rate was between 15 and 20 per cent. We also interviewed people who had seen the film.

We then produced a questionnaire grounded in the statements made in response to the first questionnaire and the interviews (Glazer and Strauss, 1967). Each of the 42 items on the questionnaire was taken directly from the answers.[3] The statements were about equally divided between pro- and anti-pornography attitudes. The subjects were asked to indicate degree of agreement with each statement, ranging from "strongly agree" to "strongly disagree." There was no zero point.

Standard demographic questions were included, as well as a question asking respondents if they were feminist or profeminist. If they said they were, they were asked to classify themselves as to type of feminism (radical, Marxist/ Socialist, or moderate). We also included a blank space on the questionnaire, which they were told they could use to say anything they wanted.

Of the 668 respondents whose questionnaires were analyzed quantitatively, 608 viewed the film at an art film house during a five-week period. The film was shown three times per day. While we did not study each audience, each viewing time and each day of the week is represented in the sample. The remaining 60 respondents were students who saw the film at Northwestern University.

The audience was given the questionnaire before they viewed the film, and the lights were left on after the film so they could fill out the instrument. Either Bart, Freeman, or a worker in the theater distributed and collected the questionnaires. In each case, about 90 per cent of the audience cooperated. Because this was a "natural" audience, rather than one assembled for experimental purposes, and the theater's schedule did not allow extra time for the study, Bart thought dealing with some logistical problems before the film would result in a higher response rate, since people's interest might be aroused and their departure would not be unduly delayed. This may have affected the results in some unknown way.

The audience was told we were from the University of Illinois, that pornography was an important issue that was not studied enough, and we asked for their cooperation.

The answers to these 42 precoded questions were cross-tabulated by gender and by type of feminism or profeminism with gender controlled. Chi-squares and measures of association were obtained. Responses were then divided by gender and entered into an oblique factor rotation. Five factors were extracted from the female responses and four from the male responses.

The written comments were analyzed in two ways. First, Freeman examined all the comments and constructed a typology. In order to have a more rigorous qualitative analysis, a second classification was then constructed, independently of the Freeman classification, which could account for each response. This latter scheme, which included 24 categories, was developed on the basis of an expanded sample including responses from students who saw the film at Stanford, the University of Toronto, and the University of Illinois at Chicago. The answers were then coded using these categories.

C. Initial Quantitative Findings

Responses from 332 males and 318 females were used for the quantitative analysis using cross-tabulations. (For gender, as for every question, there were an appreciable number of no-responses.) Twenty per cent (133) of the respondents had arrived by themselves, 42 per cent (288) had come with a member of the opposite sex, 25 per cent (168) with a person of the same sex and 8 per cent (57) with a mixed gender group. The sample was overwhelming between 20 and 39 years of age; almost half were between 20 and 39. Seventeen per cent (114) were 40 and over.

The general hypothesis (Hypothesis I), that there would be gender differences in response, women being more opposed to pornography than men, was overwhelmingly supported by the responses to the survey. We found highly significant differences between the sexes in the predicted direction on every item. The following items called forth particularly large differences between women and men: "Pornography has its place" and "Some of the increase in the rate of rape can be attributed to pornography" (see Table 1). Most of the differences between women and men on other items were not about whether or not they agreed or disagreed with the statement, but whether they agreed or disagreed moderately or strongly.

Hypothesis II, that the film would result in self-reported attitude changes

Table 1. Most salient gender differences in response

	Female agree			Male agree		
	strongly (%)	mod-erately (%)	Total 100% N	strongly (%)	mod-erately (%)	Total 100% N
Pornography has its place	5	24	100% (297)	23	38	100% (313)
Some of the increase in the rate of rape can be attributed to pornography*	35	46	100% (80)	16	35	100% (58)

*The smaller N can be accounted for by this item being added later in the survey.

Table 2. Women's and men's attitude changes associated with viewing *Not a Love Story*

	Female agree			Male agree		
	strongly (%)	mod-erately (%)	Total 100% N	strongly (%)	mod-erately (%)	Total 100% N
I didn't know pornography was that violent	21	27	100% (305)	12	28	100% (308)
The film made me angrier about pornography	53	26	100% (310)	27	36	100% (315)
The film taught me the fear men have of women and their needs	19	37	100% (303)	10	45	100% (307)
The film made me aware of how pornography does not show either male or female feelings	63	30	100% (298)	46	41	100% (303)
Before I saw the film I didn't know how much money was involved . . . that pornography was big business	35	20	100% (193)	27	18	100% (175)

and information acquisition, also was supported. The following items reflected these changes: "I didn't know pornography was that violent," "The film made me angrier about porn," "The film taught me the fear men have of women and their needs," "The film made me aware of how pornography does not show either male or female feelings, their humanity," and "Before I saw the film I didn't know how much money was involved—that pornography is big business" (see Table 2).

It should be pointed out that those knowledgeable antipornography people, e.g., radical feminists, might have disagreed with these statements, the first and last especially, because they already knew these facts. Indeed, these factors constituted part of their analysis of pornography. But for the majority of the respondents these items correlated with other questions reflecting an antipornography attitude.

On the five items measuring attitude change and information acquisition, that is, greater awareness of the effects of pornography and of their feelings toward it, we see substantial self-reported attitude change for both men and women. Women's attitudes changed somewhat more then men's attitudes. This difference was most prominent on the item referring to the film making them angrier about porn.

D. Factor Analysis and Findings on Attitude Structure

A factor analysis attempts to determine which items tend to have similar responses, or to "cluster together," with an end to determining underlying, more fundamental dimensions which affect behavior. The sociology-of-knowledge viewpoint which informed this study led us to reject the assumption that women's and men's attitudes and responses must be organized along the same dimensions.

As Table 3 shows, the factors which were produced are composed of quite different combinations of items for male and female respondents. The names attached to the factors are of course the products of our own intuitive analysis.

In what ways are these clusterings really different? All nine factors are highly correlated with each other for both male and female respondents. The differences in the composition of the two sets of the factors can be traced to significant differences between males and females in the correlations among smaller groups of two or three items which compose the factors.

For example, in the female-derived factor *F2* (resistance to "liberal humanism") are Q18 (Nobody is hurt by pornography), Q39 (The woman in the movie [an actress in some peep-show footage] wanted to suck the pistol), Q1 (Pornography has its place), and Q25 (I am concerned about the effect the antiporn groups have on the First Amendment). The first two express opinions on whether pornography is actually harming people (women); in the second case it taps the perception of the actress in a degrading scene as a victim of porn. The last pair represent a commitment to a generally pluralist society, in which pornographers are one of many groups whose interests are protected by the First Amendment.

The male-derived factor analysis puts Q18 and Q39 in a different cluster from Q1 and Q25. On inspection, we find that the two pairs of questions are much more strongly associated for women than for men (see Table 4). One way of interpreting this is to say that women are more inclined than men to make their affirmation of pluralistic society dependent on whether or not they believe harm is being done to women or vice versa.[4] To put it another way, men (more than woman) may favor a pluralist society tolerant of pornography *regardless* of what is happening to women.

As another illustration, the Spearman correlation between Q5 (My gut anti-porn feelings were validated) and Q6 (The movie's attitude toward men was off-base) –0.19 for women ($N = 278$) and –0.37 for men ($N = 291$). The male factor analysis places these in the same factor, M1 (Sympathy for Feminism);

Table 3. Factors extracted from oblique factor rotations performed for females and for males separately

FACTORS DERIVED FROM RESPONSES OF FEMALES

Factor F1: "Involvement with film"

Q2	I liked the feminist writers.	(Agree)
Q3	The film is important.	(Agree)
Q4	The movie was boring.	(Disagree)
Q7	It touched me deeply.	(Agree)
Q8	I was moved by the growth and unfolding of the stripper.	(Agree)
Q9	The film shows how pornography is an expression of anger and hate against women.	(Agree)
Q13	The film was understated.	(Disagree)
Q14	The stripper was not genuine.	(Disagree)
Q15	There were too many artists, writers, poets, etc.	(Disagree)
Q17	The film made me angrier about porn.	(Agree)
Q20	I would like to learn more about pornography.	(Agree)
Q22	It was an interesting personal approach to a serious issue.	(Agree)
Q23	The film taught me the fear men have of women and their needs.	(Agree)
Q24	The film was an experiential learning process.	(Agree)
Q26	The audience was seriously absorbed and interested.	(Agree)
Q31	I didn't understand why Robin Morgan was there with her family.	(Disagree)
Q32	I liked the Robin Morgan and her family scene.	(Agree)

Factor F2: "Rejection of liberal humanism"

Q1	Pornography has its place.	(Disagree)
Q6	The attitude toward men was off-base.	(Disagree)
Q10	A problem with the film is that it was not objective.	(Disagree)
Q11	The film would have been better if it also showed the violence of women against men.	(Disagree)
Q16	There was too much pornography in the film.	(Disagree)
Q18	Nobody's hurt by pornography.	(Disagree)
Q25	I am concerned about the effect the anti-porn groups have on the First Amendment.	(Agree)
Q33	There was an overemphasis on equating porn and sex.	(Disagree)
Q38	An idea can't be called bad if everyone involved wants it.	(Disagree)
Q39	The woman sucking the barrel of the pistol wanted to be doing that.	(Disagree)

Factor F3: "Anger/commitment"

Q5	My gut anti-porn feelings were validated.	(Agree)
Q21	I didn't like it when people in the audience laughed.	(Agree)
Q27	Sadism is not erotic.	(Agree)
Q29	The film gave me more ammunition for my anti-porn point of view.	(Agree)
Q42	Some of the increase in the rate of rape can be attributed to pornography.	(Agree)

Factor F4: "Rejection of (pro-male) sexual 'deregulation'"

Q12	Pornography is made by men for men.	(Agree)
Q34	The film made me aware of how pornography does not show either male or female real feelings, their humanity.	(Agree)
Q35	Most pornography shows good sex, with love.	(Disagree)
Q36	The film showed pornography as a symptom of a larger social problem—making objects out of women and sometimes men	(Agree)
Q37	I found a few of the pictures erotically appealing.	(Disagree)

Factor F5: "Learned from film"

Q19	I didn't know pornography was that violent.	(Agree)
Q30	The film made porn more real.	(Agree)
Q41	Before I saw the film I didn't know how much money was involved—that pornography was big business.	(Agree)

FACTORS DERIVED FROM RESPONSES OF MALES:

Factor M1: "Sympathy for feminism"

Q2	I liked the feminist writers.	(Agree)
Q5	My gut anti-porn feelings were off-base.	(Agree)
Q6	The attitude toward men was off-base.	(Disagree)
Q9	The film shows how pornography is an expression of anger and hate against women.	(Agree)
Q15	There were too many artists, writers, poets, etc.	(Disagree)
Q17	The film made me angrier about porn.	(Agree)
Q18	Nobody's hurt by pornography.	(Disagree)
Q23	The film taught me the fear men have of women and their needs.	(Agree)
Q29	The film gave me more ammunition for my anti-porn view.	(Agree)
Q32	I liked the Robin Morgan and her family scene.	(Agree)
Q36	The film showed pornography as a symptom of a larger social problem—making objects out of women and sometimes men.	(Agree)
Q39	The woman sucking the barrel of the pistol wanted to be doing that.	(Disagree)

Factor M2: "Good movie"

Q3   The film is important. (Agree)
Q4   The movie was boring. (Disagree)
Q7   It touched me deeply. (Agree)
Q8   I was moved by the growth and unfolding of the stripper. (Agree)
Q14   The stripper was not genuine. (Disagree)
Q16   There was too much pornography in this film. (Disagree)
Q19   I didn't know pornography was that violent. (Agree)
Q22   It was an interesting personal approach to a serious issue. (Agree)
Q24   The film was an experiential learning process. (Agree)
Q26   The audience was seriously absorbed and interested. (Agree)
Q30   The film made porn more real. (Agree)
Q34   The film made me aware of how pornography does not show either male or female real feelings, their humanity. (Agree)

Factor M3: "Rejection of 'Liberal concerns'"

Q1   Pornography has its place. (Disagree)
Q10   A problem with the film is that it was not objective. (Disagree)
Q11   The film would have been better if it also showed the violence of women against men. (Disagree)
Q25   I am concerned about the effect the anti-porn groups have on the First Amendment. (Disagree)
Q37   I found a few of the pictures erotically appealing. (Disagree)
Q41   Before I saw the film I didn't know how much money was involved—that pornography was big business. (Agree)
Q42   Some of the increase in the rate of rape can be attributed to pornography. (Agree)

Factor M4: "Lack of phallic defensiveness"

Q12   Pornography is made by men for men. (Agree)
Q27   Sadism is not erotic. (Agree)
Q28   Some people went to the film to get turned on. (Disagree)
Q31   I didn't understand why Robin Morgan was there with her family. (Disagree)
Q33   There was an overemphasis on equating porn to sex. (Disagree)
Q35   Most pornography portrays good sex, with love. (Disagree)
Q38   An idea can't be called bad if everyone involved wants it. (Disagree)

Notes on methods: For each gender group of respondents, the factors were extracted from an oblique factor rotation performed using the matrix of Spearman rank-order correlations among items as input. In each of the analyses, factor scores were computed (for each respondent) as the sum of response values in agreement with the factor, *minus* the sum of the response values for items in disagreement with the factor, plus a constant of such size that the potential is centered at zero.

Table 4. Spearman rank-order correlations: Q1, Q25 By Q18, Q39

Two "harm to women" items	Two "liberal pluralism" items	
	Q1 (Pornography has its place)	Q25 (I am concerned about the effect the anti-porn groups have on the First Amendment)
Q18 (Nobody's hurt by pornography)	0.4368 (N = 294)	0.2448 (N = 295)
	(0.3830) (N = 304)	(0.1668)* (N = 306)
Q39 (The woman sucking the barrel of the pistol wanted to be doing that)	0.3260 (N = 275) (0.1870) (N = 285)	0.1378† (N = 273) (0.0801)‡ (N = 285)

0.4368 = correlation among female respondents
(0.3830) = correlation among male respondents

All corrections are significant at 0.001 level except:
*$p = 0.002$;
†$p = 0.011$;
‡$p > 0.05$ (not significant).

the female analysis divides them into two factors, with Q6 associated with the four items discussed above (Q1, Q18, Q25, Q39). Some insight is gained by looking at the cross-tabulation of Q5 and Q6. As Table 5 shows, no more than 30 per cent of women in any category of Q5—even those who gave the most pro-pornography answer—agreed that the film's attitude to men was off base. With some license, these women may be interpreted as saying to the filmmakers, "I cannot be against pornography, since that would not be liberal; but I sympathize with your concerns and I know that what you describe is not simply a reflection of your hatred of men." Pro-pornography men, on the other hand, said, "I reject your concerns and scorn your description." The majority of men giving the pro-porn answers to Q5—and nearly half of those moderately anti-porn—saw the film's attitude to men as off base.

These examples, and many others like them, suggest that it is not only the case that women are more antipornography than men. It is also true that "for" and "against" pornography are not the same thing for women as for men. The choices are made along different dimensions within a different frame of reference.

What, for example, does it mean for a man, or a woman, to say that "Pornography has its place" (Q1)? We can examine the differences by looking at

Table 5. Cross-tabulation: Q6 by Q5 by gender

Females

Q6 (The attitude toward men was off-base)	Q5 (My gut anti-porn feelings were validated)			
	Strongly agree (per cent)	Moderately agree (per cent)	Moderately disagree (per cent)	Strongly disagree (per cent)
Strongly agree	2.3 (3)	2.8 (2)	6.7 (2)	7.7 (1)
Moderately agree	15.2 (20)	18.1 (13)	23.3 (7)	15.4 (2)
Moderately disagree	25.8 (34)	34.7 (25)	50.0 (15)	46.0 (6)
Strongly disagree	56.8 (75)	44.4 (32)	20.0 (6)	30.8 (4)
Total (247)	100 (132)	100 (72)	100 (30)	100 (13)

Males

Q6 (The attitude toward men was off-base)	Q5 (My gut anti-porn feelings were validated)			
	Strongly agree (per cent)	Moderately agree (per cent)	Moderately disagree (per cent)	Strongly disagree (per cent)
Strongly agree	6.2 (4)	9.5 (8)	23.5 (10)	37.8 (14)
Moderately agree	20.0 (13)	38.1 (32)	39.7 (27)	37.8 (14)
Moderately disagree	41.6 (27)	35.7 (30)	25.0 (17)	16.2 (6)
Strongly disagree	32.3 (21)	16.7 (14)	11.8 (8)	8.1 (6)
Total (254)	100 (65)	100 (84)	100 (68)	100 (37)

the results of a regression analysis in which the response to Q1 was explained on the basis of male and female derived factors, for men and women separately (see Table 6).

When the male-derived factors M1-M4 are used to explain the item, male responses are much more closely related to M1 (Sympathy for feminism) than female responses. For females the effect of M3 (rejection of liberal concerns) is more significant. (Note that since response values for disagreement are higher than those for agreement, a positive effect by a factor on Q1 implies a negative effect on belief that porn has its place, and vice versa.)

In addition, M2 (Good movie) has a significant *negative* effect for males alone. One is tempted to conclude that males' agreement to statements about the importance or touching qualities of the film had no real content and served only as impression-management preparatory to taking a pro-porn position.

The differences on the female factor structure are even more striking. For females, F2 (rejection of liberal humanism) weighs heaviest, with F4 (rejection of sexual deregulation) second and F3 (anger/commitment) barely significant. This is true even though F3 is composed in part of two items directly concerned with anti-porn attitudes, Q5 (My gut antiporn feelings were validated) and Q29 (The film gave me more ammunition for my anti-porn view). For males F3 is the most powerful influence, with F2 second, a negative effect of F1 third (doubtless this is impression-management on the movie items again) and F4 having no effect whatever.

The statement "porn has its place" has different "meanings" for men and women. For men, it is most closely linked with their general attitude toward feminism (M1); as far as they are concerned, it is a feminist issue (or an antifeminist one)! But for women, the factor which explains the most variation is F2 (rejection of liberal humanism). How can it be that F3 (commitment) is unimportant? We believe it is because there is so little variation among women in their gut feelings about pornography (see Table 5). Variation among women is not mostly about whether they like pornography; they do not. They dislike it. But some feel ideologically called upon to tolerate what they can never like in order not to feel marked as an enemy of liberty, or perhaps to gain approval from men. On the other hand, men who say that porn has its place are more likely actually to approve it.

There were eight items on the questionnaire which called for direct expressions of attitude or opinion on pornography. We combined these items into a summary measure of antipornography attitude and tested the effect on it of several background variables (items are listed in the notes to Table 7). As Table 7 shows, the most pronounced effects on antiporn attitude were those of gender and of self-described feminism. Gender alone accounts for 22 per cent of the variation of this index among 447 respondents; the male and female means are separated by nearly a full standard deviation.

The effects of feminism and type were nearly as strong: the classification of respondents as not feminist, moderate feminist or profeminist, and radical (including socialist) feminist or profeminist, accounted for 18.5 per cent of the

Table 6. Regression of Q1 (Pornography has its place) on male- and female-derived factors for males and females

	Male respondents (N = 218)			Female respondents (N = 242)		
Independent variables	Beta	F	Significance	Beta	F	Significance
(Model 1—Factors F1–F4, derived from responses by females)						
F1	−0.21	6.627	<0.05	−0.03	0.249	n.s.
F2*	0.36	22.321	<<0.01	0.40	42.048	<<0.01
F3	0.45	31.545	<<0.01	0.15	4.566	<0.05
F4	0.09	1.453	n.s.	0.23	13.994	<0.01
	(R-square = 0.37)			(R-square = 0.39)		
(Model 2—Factors M1–M4, derived from responses by males)						
M1	0.48	29.181	<<0.01	0.38	21.414	<<0.01
M2	−0.26	11.785	<0.01	−0.08	1.206	n.s.
M3*	0.32	24.276	<<0.01	0.35	37.816	<<0.01
M4	0.09	1.644	n.s.	0.06	0.895	n.s.
	(R-square = 0.40)			(R-square = 0.37)		

Standardized regression coefficients (Beta)

See Table 3 for computation of factor scores.
*For this analysis only, Q1 was omitted from the computation of M3 and F2.

Table 7. Regression coefficients for the prediction of antipornography attitude on the basis of background variables

Independent variables	Unstandardized coefficient	Standardized coefficient	F	Significance level
(Model 1: Gender alone. N = 447, R-square = 0.22)				
Gender	-4.19	-0.47	126.7	<<0.001
Constant	6.72			
(Model 2: Feminism alone. N = 456, R-square = 0.19)				
Feminist	3.17	0.29	42.10	<<0.001
Radical/Socialist	2.47	0.24	30.17	<<0.01
Constant	1.58			
(Model 3: Gender and Feminism interacting. N = 447, R-square = 0.33)				
Gender	-2.90	-0.33	10.99	<0.01
Feminism (F's)	2.65	+0.30	10.67	<0.01
Radical/Socialist (F's)	2.01	+0.17	14.31	<0.01
Profeminist (M's)	1.76	+0.18	9.20	<0.01
Radical/Socialist (M's)	2.51	+0.17	14.18	<0.01
Constant	3.72			
(Model 4: Gender interacting with background variables. N = 447, R-square = 0.23)				
Gender	-2.94	0.33	5.88	<0.05
Male Children (M's)	-1.92	-0.11	4.93	<0.05
Female Children (M's)	1.40	0.08	2.51	n.s.
Married (M's)	1.62	0.12	5.994	<0.05
College Graduate (M's)	-0.38	-0.04	0.392	n.s.
Age Group (M's)	-0.28	-0.10	0.696	n.s.
Male Children (F's)	-0.36	-0.02	0.152	n.s.
Female Children (F's)	-0.05	0.00	0.00	n.s.
Married (F's)	-0.73	-0.05	1.176	n.s.
College Graduate (F's)	-0.03	0.00	0.00	n.s.
Age Group (F's)	0.29	0.09	0.70	n.s.
Constant	6.17			

(Model 5: Gender interacting with background variables and feminism, $N = 447$, R-square $= 0.35$)

Gender	-1.87	-0.21	1.84	n.s.
Feminist (F's)	2.63	0.30	10.283	<0.01
Radical Socialist (F's)	2.24	0.17	14.77	<0.01
Profeminist (M's)	1.80	0.19	9.39	<0.01
Radical Socialist (M's)	2.50	0.17	13.94	<0.01
Male Children (M's)	-1.97	-0.11	5.89	<0.05
Female Children (M's)	1.62	0.09	3.80	~<0.05
Married (M's)	1.16	0.09	3.46	n.s.
College Graduate (M's)	-0.83	-0.09	2.05	n.s.
Age Group (M's)	-0.15	-0.05	0.24	n.s.
Male Children (F's)	-0.26	-0.01	0.09	n.s.
Female Children (F's)	0.52	0.03	0.36	n.s.
Married (F's)	-0.49	-0.04	0.61	n.s.
College Graduate (F's)	-0.20	-0.02	0.15	n.s.
Age Groups (F's)	0.20	0.07	0.33	n.s.
Constant	3.40			

Explanation of variables:

GENDER—Coded = 0 for females, 1 for males.

FEMINIST (Dummy variable)—Answered "yes" to "Are you a feminist or pro-feminist?"

RADICAL/SOCIALIST (Dummy variable)—Identified self as either "radical" or "Marxist/Socialist" feminist.

MARRIED (Dummy variable)—married at time of survey.

AGE GROUP—(1) <20, (2) 20–29, (3) 30–39, (4) 40–49, (5) >50.

All other background variables are dummy variables and self-explanatory. In models 3–5, all variables except gender are gender-specific, e.g. "Married (F's)" is coded (1) for currently married women and (0) for other women and for all men.

ANTIPORN ATTITUDE—A scale constructed from the following eight questionnaire items:

Q1	Pornography has its place	(Disagree)
Q18	Nobody's hurt by pornography	(Disagree)
Q25	I am concerned about the effect the anti-porn groups have on the First Amendment	(Disageee)
Q35	Most pornography shows good sex, with love	(Disagree)
Q5	My gut anti-porn feelings were validated	(Agree)
Q9	The film shows how pornography is an expression of anger and hate against women	(Agree)
Q29	The film gave me more ammunition for my anti-porn view	(Agree)
Q42	Some of the increase in the rate of rape can be attributed to pornography	(Agree)

(Scores had a possible range of +12 to –12)

variance.[5] Gender and feminism together accounted for 32.5 per cent of the variance.

No significant effect of marriage or of sex of children was observed for female respondents. For male respondents, there are effects of both female and male children which are significant at the 0.05 level. When profeminism is controlled for, fathers of boys are significantly more pro-pornography and fathers of girls were significantly more antipornography than nonfathers. We found this despite the small number of parents in the sample—about 20 per cent of respondents.

When feminism is not controlled for, it is found that married men are significantly ($p < 0.05$) more antipornography than single and divorced men considered as a group. This effect loses significance when feminism is controlled for, mainly because married men were more likely to describe themselves as profeminist.

Hypothesis I is thus further supported and extended in the case of male respondents. There is a statistical tendency for men to take the interests of members of their family members into account. Married men and fathers of girls are more opposed to pornography; fathers of boys favor it more. (Sexual solidarity begins at home.) The fact that this effect is not exhibited by female respondents does not imply that women do not take into account the interests of their female children; women know its effects as women without having to imagine its effects on their children.

Finally, another variable which has a strong influence on attitude toward pornography is the amount of pornography to which the respondent has been previously exposed. One of the items on the questionnaire asked if respondents had previously seen "a lot" of pornography, "some," or "none." Men had seen more than women—16 per cent of women, but only 4 per cent of men, had seen "none," while 17 per cent of men, compared with 8 per cent of women, had seen "lots."

Whether or not other demographic variables were controlled for, women who had seen more pornography were significantly less antipornography. Women who had seen the most pornography scored 2.6 points lower on the scale of antiporn attitude than women who had seen none.

But the effect on men was more than twice as great. The amount of pornography men had seen explained nearly as much of the variation in their attitude as their self description as profeminist. While feminism and other background variables accounted for 15 per cent of the variation in attitude among men, the addition of the two dummy variables representing having seen "some" and/or "lots" of pornography accounted for another 10 per cent of the variance.

Table 8 tells the story, even though the numbers are not large. Note that self-described "proradical" or "socialist feminists" who had seen lots of pornography scored almost as low on the attitude scale as nonfeminist men who had only seen *some* pornography.

A plausible explanation of this strong relationship might be that the level of exposure to pornography is the effect, not the cause, and that the men with antiporn attitudes avoid it as a consequence while men with pro-porn attitudes

Table 8. Cell means: Antiporn attitude of male respondents by amount of pornography seen and self-description as feminist

Amount of pornography seen	Not profeminist	Self-description: moderate profeminist	Radical/socialist profeminist
None	5.9445	5.8200	4.8889
	(N = 3)	(N = 2)	(N = 3)
Some	1.3757	2.9219	5.9913
	(N = 52)	(N = 87)	(N = 32)
Lots	−2.6101	−0.1800	1.5972
	(N = 13)	(N = 14)	(N = 8)

Sample mean = 2.5137(N = 214).

consume it. But this explanation has to be rejected on statistical grounds. If level of exposure were a consequence of attitude, it would display an association with the background variables which are most closely linked with attitude. For example, if antiporn attitudes caused low levels of exposure, then, since profeminism is linked with antiporn attitudes, profeminism would be related to low levels of exposure.

As the table suggests, and further analysis demonstrates, level of exposure is totally unrelated to profeminism of either type. It is also unrelated to the other variables which are causally linked to attitude. The causes of low or high levels of exposure are therefore independent of attitude. This being so, the hypothesis suggests itself that repeated exposure to pornography brings about a pro-porn attitude. This hypothesis should be studied further.

Some men involved may say that their experience with pornography has imparted to them the knowledge that pornography is innocuous. An equally plausible viewpoint in our opinion is that pornography desensitizes men not only to rape and violence but to itself. Like other commercially successful commodities such as heroin, pornography creates and nurtures its own market.

E. Qualitative Data Analysis I

About 40 per cent of the sample made comments in the space provided. Freeman's reading of the responses resulted in sixteen categories, of which ten had more than one respondent. Her analysis was based only on the Chicago art film house and Northwestern samples.

One of the most interesting categories, which also was present in the second qualitative analysis discussed below, is the subject's use of intellectual defenses as a way to avoid dealing with the emotional impact of the film. Examples of such defenses were methodological criticism, e.g. "there should have been a zero point among the answers," or "the questionnaire was biased." (Another way of diluting the emotional impact of the film was "film criticism," discussed in the next section.)

Another major category consisted of responses to the effect that the film was antimale and antisex, e.g., "I objected to women defining male sexuality and then putting it down." "Pornography is institutional in male sexuality. It must have a reason. Don't tell me its bad. Tell me what is better. What is erotic???" Freeman has another category reserved for angry men (including men who express sexual aggression), epitomized by the comment "Fuck you, Pauline B. Bart."

A third category consisted of people who objected to the amount of violence shown, e.g., "I feel the film was rather manipulative and misleading by concentrating on violent pornography which I feel is only a segment of the whole." A fourth category is composed of women who found the violence terrifying, shocking, and/or debilitating, e.g., "I'm very tired of being on guard against men who are potential harmers. My feelings range from just tiredness and exhaustion to rage and absolute terror. I felt terror during the pistol scene, the meat grinder scene and the hoisting-by-the-heels scene. These feeling are much stronger than rage."

Additionally, people commented on the educational value of the film, while still another group of people denied gender differences, claiming that everyone likes pornography including women:

> The film was far too biased and emotionally charged. What about *Playgirl*, Chippendale and Sugar Shacks? [The latter two are clubs where men strip for women.] What about freedom of choice? I consider the policy implications of the view presented frightening.

Others erased gender by noting *all* human exploitation, and the equally important degradation of men. (The erasure of gender differences, as in the term "family violence" rather than "woman abuse" and in maintaining that men are as oppressed as women, is a hallmark of antifeminist thinking in the guise of humanism.)

A common response was a critique of the film's not distinguishing pornography from erotica. A less common but interesting response came from subjects Freeman calls "Guilty Women." One such woman said:

> The film showed me many things about myself. I found some of the scenes erotic. They turned me on. At the same time it was wrong. Pornography represents not only men's fear of equality but the socialization of women to hate and degrade themselves by a patriarchal culture *and I am one of them* (emphasis added). Perhaps a stronger connection should be made between soft core porn, objectification, and violence.

Other categories are the civil libertarians concerned with the danger of "Puritanism," the "bizarre" responses, and a few "Moral Majority" people, although only one made a comment. One could identify these latter people since they disagreed that pornography had its place but also disliked the feminist writers. There was also a touching liberal faith in free will and choice as meaningful options. As one respondent said, while he felt sorry for the girls [sic], "if they don't really like it then they should find another or better jobs." (Such as Chief Executive Officer of a Fortune 500 corporation, for example?)

F. Qualitative Analysis II

This analysis includes comments made by students at the University of Toronto, the University of Illinois at Chicago, Stanford University, and viewers at the Meetings of the Society for the Scientific Study of Sex, as well as the other two groups studied. For this analysis categories were constructed from the comments people made in the space provided on the questionnaire. Of the twenty-four categories which were derived, the following were used most frequently:

(1) The film failed to distinguish between erotica and pornography, or the film was antisex. Seventeen men and 12 women made such comments.

(2) Film criticism. Thirty-five men and 28 women fell into this category. As we stated above, methodological criticisms and film criticism may function as intellectual defenses or as ways of blunting the emotional impact of the film.

(3) General positive attitude. This category reflected the gender differences we hypothesized. Thirty-four women but only 24 men responded in this manner.

(4) "Film not objective." Nine men and five women criticized the film for not being "objective," a response which assumes objectivity on pornography is either possible or desirable. (See MacKinnon, 1983, for a discussion of this issue.)

(5) Autobiography. Equal numbers of men and women (11 and 12) gave comments about their lives in relation to the film.

(6) Humanism—denial of gender differences. Five men and two women explicitly criticized the film for this reason, e.g. "Men are victims too."

(7) General hostility toward film and/or researchers. Five men and one woman exhibited such hostility, which included pornographic pictures drawn on the questionnaire as "jokes."

(8) Emotional response. Four men and 20 women responded emotionally, e.g. "deeply moved . . . that's it," "made me sick and mad."

(9)"Use film as an educational tool for men and women." Thirteen women but only one man gave this response.

(Appendix C gives the complete categorial scheme.)

Only one of the five men who gave hostile responses said he was not a feminist. With the exception of the classification "film not objective," the majority of men who made comments, including hostile comments, defined themselves as feminist or profeminist. (We use the term "profeminist" when speaking of men since we believe that one must inhabit a female body to have the experiences that make one a feminist. This position is consistent with the sociology-of-knowledge analysis informing this paper.)

In no category were there more women who defined themselves as nonfeminists than as feminists. It appears as if the term "feminist," at least for this qualitative analysis, is relatively meaningless.

G. Conclusion and Policy Implications

This paper has studied pornography and has demonstrated that the test used in U.S. obscenity law, that the work violates community standards,[6] is based on a false assumption. In fact, there are no "community standards"—there are male standards and female standards.

We have examined the responses of women and men to an antipornography documentary, *Not a Love Story*. As the sociology of knowledge shows us, the intellectual productions of a society are related to the interests of the dominant class. In our society, particularly with respect to violence against women, it is useful to conceptualize men and women as different classes with different interests. Pornography represents male interests. Women in pornography are required to behave as male fantasies would have them behave. Thus it is no accident that men are more pro-pornography than women.

But why has there been such an explosion of pornography, at least in North America? First, one might suggest that pornography in general, and in particular the use of younger and younger women, even children, and the increasing depiction of violence to women's bodies, can be a reaction to the growing influence of feminism. Adult women may be seen by many men as threatening.

Secondly, it can be looked on as part of a wider process in which male dominance of women has adapted to the forms of the capitalist marketplace. Pornography is a commodity which is produced for the sake of private profit, not in the name of abstract artistic value. In the struggle to maintain or increase their markets, producers of pornography must provide not only more porn but ever more "novel," ever more extreme stimuli to overcome the effects of desensitizing which the research has demonstrated to occur as a result of watching it.

It is clear that the catharsis model promulgated by prefeminist research is unsatisfactorily. If pornography indeed resulted in carthasis, then we would have less sexual violence against women because there is more pornography available. Clearly this is not the case.

The newer research, discussed above, demonstrates that pornography desensitizes men to violence against women and in fact can be considered prorape propaganda. The merger of sex and violence is exemplified by the fact that men who are "successful" with women are called "lady-killers."

The implications of the current research and analyses such as this one are that pornography is not a "victimless crime." It ought not to be viewed as a set of isolated magazine purchases by men, or a developmental stage through which individual adolescent males pass. It is a social phenomenon in which men are socialized into an insensitivity to female needs and are reinforced in their inaccurate fantasies about women. Myra Marx Ferree, when trying to eliminate the showing of pornographic films in the dormitories at the University of Connecticut, was told by the upperclassmen that it was necessary for the new male students to see the films so they would know how to act on dates.[7] When women outside of pornography are expected to behave as women in pornography do—particularly those women in pornography who "enjoy" pain and brutalization or are sexually "insatiable"—the stage is set for physical and mental abuse of women. The advent of pornographic home video, both on television and privately purchased, exacerbates this problem.

The issue is not primarily the effect of a single film or magazine, but the cumulative effect on women and men of life in a society pervaded by pornography. Women who oppose this state of affairs by various means, including those provided under the Dworkin and MacKinnon statute, should be viewed as defending the freedom of the oppressed and ending the silence of those who have been silenced by pornography.

NOTES

The authors would like to express gratitude to Catharine A. MacKinnon for her prompt reading of the manuscript and for her valuable critique. We take responsibility for its final form. We also thank Facets Multimedia Theater for their cooperation.

Qualitative Analysis II was conducted by Ms. Pam Sawyer and Ms. Janice Schreckengost.

1. In this light it is not surprising that Sophie Laws has pointed out that there are no menstruating women in Western pornography. (Unpublished paper, Warwick University, England.)

2. Bart believes that *Not a Love Story* is to the antipornography movement what the novel *Uncle Tom's Cabin* was to the antislavery movement. The merits of the former as a film *per se* have as little relevance as the literary merits of the latter. Furthermore, the case can be made that it is precisely *because* the film is liberal rather than radical that it is so effective. It may well be that the same analysis holds for the latter. The term "Uncle Tom" is now used derisively to refer to Blacks who have been co-opted by whites. But this sympathetic, accommodating, faithful servant was a character for whom whites could feel sympathy, thereby being motivated to work for the abolition of slavery.

3. Question 42, on the relationship between pornography and rape, was only added after someone in the audience brought the subject up and asked us why we hadn't included such a question. Thus the number of responses to that question is less than to the others.

4. A strong ideological commitment to pluralism might lead women to deny that harm is done to women. In the movie *Gone with the Wind*, Rhett Butler carries a struggling Scarlett O'Hara up the stairs, clearly stating his intention to have intercourse with her. Elizabeth Pleck referred to this scene in a paper on violence against women in American films of the 1930s, presented at the Berkshire Conference on Women's History, Smith College, 1984. Ruby Rich, a film critic who had criticized *Not a Love Story* and chaired

the session, remarked to her afterwards that some feminists do not consider this scene to depict rape. Rich apparently agrees with that position (Personal communication from Pleck to Bart.)

5. We combined self-identified radical feminists with self-identified socialist feminists because the layout of the questionnaire allowed ambiguous answers. We recognize that their analyses of pornography are not identical; indeed, a substantial number of self-identified socialist feminists are not antipornography.

6. "Whether the average person, applying contemporary community standards, would find that the work taken as a whole appeals to the prurient interest . . . whether the work depicts or describes in a clearly offensive way sexual conduct." Miller v. California, 413 U.S. 15 (1973).

7. Personal communication to Pauline Bart, December 1983.

REFERENCES

Bart, P., and M. Jozsa. 1980. Dirty books, dirty films and dirty data. In L. Lederer, ed., *Take Back the Night: Women on Pornography,* pp. 204–217, Morrow, New York.

Diamond, Irene. 1980. Pornography and repression: A reconsideration of 'Who' and 'What'. In L. Lederer, ed., *Take Back the Night,* pp. 187–203. Morrow, New York.

Donnerstein, Edward, and Daniel Linz. 1984. Sexual violence in the media: A warning. *Psychology Today* 18(1), 14–15.

Glazer, Barney, and Anselm Strauss. 1967. *The Discovery of Grounded Theory.* Aldine, Chicago.

MacKinnon, Catherine. 1983. Feminism, Marxism, method and the State: Toward feminist jurisprudence. *Signs* 8(4), 635–58.

Malamuth, Neil. 1981. Male proclivity to rape. *J. Social Issues* 37(4), 138–57.

Malamuth, Neil, and Edward Donnerstein. 1984. *Pornography and Social Agression.* Academic Press, New York.

Marciano (Lovelace), Linda. 1982. *Ordeal.* Berkeley, New York.

McCormack, T. 1978. Machismo in media research: A critical review of research on violence and pornography. *Social Problems* xxv(5), 552–54.

Report of the Commission on Obscenity and Pornography. 1970. U.S. Govt Printing Office, Washington.

Smith, Don. 1976. Sexual aggression in American pornography: The stereotypes of rape: Paper presented at the annual meeting of the American Sociological Association, New York City.

Stock, Wendy,. 1983. Effects of exposure to violent pornography. Paper presented at the meeting of the Society for the Scientific Study of Sex, Chicago, November.

Zillmann, Dorf, and Jennings Bryant. 1982. Pornography, sexual callousness, and the trivialization of rape. *Journal of Communication* 32(4), 10–21.

Appendix A
The First Amendment to the Constitution of the United States

Congress shall make no law respecting an establishment of religion, or prohibiting the free exercise thereof; or abridging the freedom of speech, or of the press; or the right of the people peaceably to assemble, and to petition the Government for a redress of grievance.

Appendix B

Andrea Dworkin and Catharine A. MacKinnon wrote a statute expressing their analysis and remedy for the problem of pornography. This statute was prepared at the request of the Minneapolis (Minnesota, U.S.A.) City Council. The statute is noteworthy for, among other things, making available civil rather than criminal remedies and thus not employing the police power of the state. Obscenity law, in contrast to the Dworkin/MacKinnon statute, is based on the assumption that sex in general, and women's bodies in particular, are "dirty." Selected sections of the ordinance follow.

The City Council of the City of Minneapolis do ordain as follows:

SECTION 1(A). THAT SECTION 139.10(A) OF THE ABOVE ENTITLED ORDINANCE BE AMENDED BY ADDING THERETO A NEW SUBSECTION (A) (1) TO READ AS FOLLOWS:
(A) (1) *SPECIAL FINDINGS ON PORNOGRAPHY:* THE COUNCIL FINDS THAT PORNOGRAPHY IS CENTRAL IN CREATING AND MAINTAINING THE CIVIL INEQUALITY OF THE SEXES. PORNOGRAPHY IS A SYSTEMATIC PRACTICE OF EXPLOITATION AND SUBORDINATION BASED ON SEX WHICH DIFFERENTIALLY HARMS WOMEN. THE BIGOTRY AND CONTEMPT IT PROMOTES, WITH THE ACTS OF AGGRESSION IT FOSTERS, HARM WOMEN'S OPPORTUNITIES FOR EQUALITY OF RIGHTS IN EMPLOYMENT, EDUCATION, PROPERTY RIGHTS, PUBLIC ACCOMMODATIONS AND PUBLIC SERVICES: CREATE PUBLIC HARASSMENT AND PRIVATE DENIGRATION; PROMOTE INJURY AND DEGRADATION SUCH AS RAPE, BATTERY AND PROSTITITION AND INHIBIT JUST ENFORCEMENT OF LAWS AGAINST THESE ACTS: CONTRIBUTE SIGNIFICANTLY TO RESTRICTING WOMEN FROM FULL EXERCISE OF CITIZENSHIP AND PARTICIPATION IN PUBLIC LIFE, INCLUDING IN NEIGHBORHOODS; DAMAGE RELATIONS BETWEEN THE SEXES; AND UNDERMINE WOMEN'S EQUAL EXERCISE OF RIGHTS TO SPEECH AND ACTION GUARANTEED TO ALL CITIZENS UNDER THE CONSTITUTIONS AND LAWS OF THE UNITED STATES AND THE STATE OF MINNESOTA.

Sections of THE MINNEAPOLIS ANTI-PORNOGRAPHY ORDINANCE, passed by the City Council and vetoed by the Mayor
An amendment to the Minneapolis Civil Rights Ordinance would establish pornography as a form of discrimination on the basis of sex.
Because pornography is a systematic practice of exploitation that sexually subordinates women, it violates the Fourteenth Amendment, which guarantees civil equality to all citizens. Under the Fourteenth Amendment, human rights are violated when people are abused, exploited, or held in an inferior status because of a condition of birth.
Proposed by City Council members Charlee Hoyt and Van White, and written by feminist author Andrea Dworkin and University of Minnesota Law professor Catharine MacKinnon, the amendment is the first of its kind in the country.

(1) Pornography is the sexually explicit subordination of women, graphically depicted, whether in pictures or in words, that also includes one or more of the following:

   (A) women are presented *DEHUMANIZED* as sexual objects, things, or commodities; or

(B) women are presented as sexual objects who enjoy pain or humiliation; or

(C) women are presented as sexual objects who experience sexual pleasure in being raped; or

(D) women are presented as sexual objects tied up or cut up or multilated or bruised or physically hurt; or

(E) women are presented in postures of sexual submission; or

(F) women's body parts—including but not limited to vaginas, breasts, and buttocks—are exhibited, such that women are reduced to those parts; or

(G) women are presented as whores by nature; or

(H) women are presented being penetrated by objects or animals; or

(I) women are presented in scenarios of degradation, injury, abasement, torture, shown as filthy, bleeding, bruised, or hurt in a context that makes these conditions sexual.

(2) The use of men, children, or transsexuals in the place of women in (1) (A–I) above is pornography for purposes of sections (1)–(p) of this statute.

Section 4. That Section 139.40 of the above entitled ordinance be amended by adding thereto a new subdivision (1) to read as follows:

(ff)   that the person has previously posed for sexually explicit pictures for or with anyone, including anyone involved in or related to the making of the pornography at issue; or

(gg)   that anyone else, including a spouse or other relative, has given permission on the person's behalf; or

(hh)   that the person actually consented to a use of the performance that is changed into pornography; or

(ii)   that the person knew that the purpose of the acts or events in question was to make pornography; or

(jj)   that the person showed no resistance or appeared to cooperate actively in the photographic sessions or in the sexual events that produced the pornography; or

(kk)   that the person signed a contract, or made statements affirming a willingness to cooperate in the production of pornography; or

(ll)   that no physical force, threats, or weapons were used in the making of the pornography; or

(mm) that the person was paid or otherwise compensated.

Section 6. That Section 139.40 of the above entitled ordinance be amended by adding thereto a new subsection (n) to read as follows:

(n) *Forcing pornography on a person.* Any woman, man, child, or transsexual who has pornography forced on them in any place of employment, in education, in a home, or in any public place has a cause of action against the perpetrator and/or institution.

Section 7. That Section 139.40 of the above entitled ordinance be amended by adding thereto a new subsection (o) to read as follows:

(o) *Assault or PHYSICAL ATTACK due to pornography.* Any woman, man, child, or transsexual who is assaulted, PHYSICALLY ATTACKED OR INJURED in a way that is directly caused by specific pornography has a claim for damages against the perpetrator, the maker(s), distributor(s), sellers(s), and/or exhibitor(s), and for an injunction against the specific pornography's further exhibition, distribution, or sale. NO DAMAGES SHALL BE ASSESSED (A) AGAINST MAKER(S) FOR PORNOGRAPHY MADE, (B) AGAINST DISTRIBUTOR(S) FOR PORNOGRAPHY DISTRIBUTED, (C) AGAINST SELLER(S) FOR PORNOGRAPHY SOLD, OR (D) AGAINST EXHIBITORS OR PORNOGRAPHY EXHIBITED PRIOR TO THE EFFECTIVE DATE OF THIS ACT.

Section 8. That Section 139.40 of the above entitled ordinance be amended by adding thereto a new subsection (p) to read as follows:

(p) *Defenses*. Where the materials which are the subject matter of a cause of action under subsections (l), (m), (n), or (o) of this section are pornography, it shall not be a defense that the defendant did not know or intend that the materials are pornography or sex discrimination.

SECTION 9. THAT SECTION 139.40 OF THE ABOVE ENTITLED ORDINANCE BE AMENDED BY ADDING THERETO NEW SUBSECTION(S) (Q) AND (R) TO READ AS FOLLOWS:

(q) *Severability*. Should any PART(S) of this ordinance be found legally invalid, the remaining PART(S) remain valid.

Appendix C
Categorical Scheme for Qualitative Analysis II

1. Failure to distinguish between "erotica" and pornography/violent pornography.
2. The film is antisex.
3. The film is antimale.
4. The money to be made in pornography makes it difficult to stop it.
5. The women are not attractive enough.
6. More input needed from and about men.
7. Methodological criticism, e.g., questions biased.
8. Film criticism.
9. Shocked by what learned about men.
10. Moralistic.
11. Feminist antifilm criticism.
12. Concern with Puritanism.
13. Men see pornography because of their own problems.
14. Denial of injury for "normal" people.
15. Want help in understanding men.
16. Offended by explicit sexuality.
17. Homophobic response (to lesbians).
18. General positive response.
19. Fatalism regarding porn—can't do anything about it.
20. Feels sad, unhappy.
21. Feels anger or disgust.
22. Ambivalence.
23. Concern with First Amendment.
24. Not objective.

11. HOUSEHOLD RESOURCES AND U.S. WOMEN'S WORK

Factors Affecting Gainful Employment at the Turn of the Century

CHRISTINE E. BOSE

Using the Census Public Use Sample, we focus on household composition and resources which influenced the distribution of paid work to female adult and younger members of households in 1900. Controls for individual and geographic variables are included. Two different household-level processes lowered women's rate of gainful employment, although their usage varied by race and ethnicity. First, home-based alternatives inhibited seeking jobs for which women might have been recorded as gainfully employed. Second, alternatives were structured by household composition. Families with older daughters or related single adults might urge these members to work, engendering a trade-off between the labor of wives and their older children or relatives. The presence of men or nonfamily also plays an important role. Advantages of our model include the study of work and family life as a single set of relations; the integration of the detail of historical studies in single cities with the measurement of national patterns through aggregate Census materials; and a focus on factors reducing the reporting, as well as actual rates, of women's gainful employment.

With the rising importance of sociohistoric studies there has been a concomitant increase in research on women's employment and family roles between the Census years of 1880 and 1920. This time span is usually chosen to represent the period of rapid industrialization beginning with the mixed commercial, early industrial, and agricultural-based economy found at the time of the 1880 Census and culminating in the impact of World War I on industry's technological development as measured in 1920.

Unfortunately, few of these studies are national in scope and the exceptions (Abbott, 1910; MacLean, 1900), published early in the century, are hampered by lack of access to sophisticated techniques of data analysis. Further, most studies limit their investigations to particular occupations, cities, or ethnic groups. Detailed occupational studies focus on factory work (Tentler, 1979), domestic service (Katzman, 1978; Glenn, 1980), or clerical employment (Davies, 1974). Local studies done within a single city such as Pittsburgh (Butler, 1909), Philadelphia (Hershberg, 1981), Detroit (Zunz, 1982), Boston (Bosworth, 1911; Modell and Hareven, 1973), or Buffalo (McLaughlin, 1973) are

Reprinted from *American Sociological Review*, Vol. 49 (August 1984), 474–90.

usually limited to the industrialized East Coast or the Midwest (for an East-West Coast comparison see Mason and Laslett, 1983). Because immigrants were likely to engage in urban factory employment, many of these studies examine the numerous turn-of-the-century ethnic households (Zunz, 1982; Ehrlich, 1977). There are also studies of specific groups, such as Italian (McLaughlin, 1973; Pleck, 1978) or Irish women (Turbin, 1979). While data on occupations, cities, or immigrants are able to give detailed pictures of the lives of their subjects and to illustrate the range of individual variation in patterns of employment, such research is limited in its generalizability. This is particularly true for a time when different regional rates of urbanization meant that opportunities for women's factory, clerical, or service employment would vary around the country. On the other hand, while aggregate national studies often mask variation by region or by demographic group, they do indicate the frequency of each identified pattern and offer the possibility of subunit comparisons.

Our study of the factors affecting female employment at the turn of the century uses 1900 national Census data, controlling for geographic variation and performing separate analyses for various subgroups of women. The detailed information in our data allows us to build a household-focused model which maintains many of the advantages of in-depth historical studies, while testing the generalizability of prior findings based on single cities.

The full model we posit divides the determinants of women's entry into gainful employment into three categories: individual, household, and structural opportunity (geographic or regional economy) variables. While all three levels are included in our analysis, we particularly seek to understand how households allocated women's labor in response to this industrializing era. We begin here because households are the structures within which people live and organize their resources. For example, in examining the rise of the family-wage[1] economy in England and France from the eighteenth through the twentieth centuries, Tilly and Scott (1978) find that family prosperity and women's employment are dependent upon family composition, and in a contemporary study of the U.S., Oppenheimer (1982) concurs on the importance of the family as an income-earning group. Thus, despite the dominance of individual status attainment models, there is support for the assumption that American households at the turn of the century attempted to survive the lack of labor protections by developing strategies based on household resources at a given point in time. Households had a number of different possible income strategies, only one of which included adult women's employment alone or in combination with other options. These options included surviving on the adult male family wage, engaging many members of a household in a family farm or business, sending adolescents out to work, incorporating other family members into the household to help in support, taking in boarders, or engaging in cottage industry.[2]

We test the hypothesis that the utilized strategy varied with household composition, even when controlling for individual or geographic influences. Thus a woman's employment should depend, in part, on who else resided in her household. This contention is confirmed for several large northeastern cities by Tentler's study (1979) of industrially employed women in the period between 1900 and 1930. She indicates an apparent trade-off in working-class families between married women's employment and that of adolescents: most women worked outside the home as adolescents, but once married and with children they did not seek employment unless necessary. Unfortunately, such research ignores the reciprocal effects of married women's or brothers' presence on daughters and the role of other women such as female household heads or the existence of an extended family. Ethnic-group research (McLaughlin, 1973; Pleck, 1978) also indicates that household composition was a major factor affecting turn-of-the-century employment rates for both black and Italian wives.

While early theoretical models of people's responses to industrialization stressed the removal of the workplace from the home site and the development of "two separate spheres" (Cott, 1977), it is now generally accepted that these two spheres of work and home actually interact continuously (Sokoloff, 1980). The household resources model is one way to reconceptualize this integration of work and family life. It concretely illustrates the variety of connections integrating household family life with individual employment. What are these household resources? They include some of the variables important to an individual lifecycle approach, but go beyond this framework in several ways. First, the model does not assume that the household will be characterized by the life stage of a particular individual such as the wife. Rather it is characterized by all its members. For example, the individual variables of age or gender are aggregated into measures of household age and gender structure such as the number of single adult women ages 15–64 (excluding the respondent), the number of single adult men, or the number of resident children under ten years old. Other variables such as literacy (reads a language, writes a language) remain individual ones. Second, in our model, household composition is a function not only of the demography of its members but of its economic situation as well. Some nonfamily household members, such as servants, reflect a more secure economic position, independent of any one individual's life stage, while boarders or related family members reflect both a need for further income and an additional resource to the household.

Finally, the household allocation approach is useful in uncovering alternative income sources which reduce the *reporting* of women's gainful employment. Beyond those household labor sources which suppress the likelihood of women's actual paid employment, the availability of unpaid family farm and small-business work or of home-based sources of income (e.g., boarders) allows women to engage in forms of self-employment and not report it (Bose, 1980; Ciancanelli, 1981). In a certain sense, men's self-employment in family farms or businesses "hid" women's employment. McLaughlin (1973) suggests that work in family enterprises and taking in boarders were common, particularly among some ethnic groups, such as southern Italians, who valued women staying at home. In fact, Jensen (1980) estimates that in several states large portions of household income were provided through women's unreported work with boarders and the sale of cloth or dairy products during the 1890 to 1905 period, while Smuts (1959) suggests urban women frequently kept chickens or had vegetable gardens.

Aside from the reticence of married women to report employment, the Census definition of "gainful employment" used from the beginning of our period through 1930 did not encourage recording women's work. The term "gainful worker" defined as employed those persons ten and over who reported an occupation, whether or not they were working or seeking work at the time of the Census. Since it included those who were not seeking work at the time, this concept is not comparable to "labor force participation" and may even over-count male employment. At the same time, it encouraged women to report their prime role as housewife, even if they actually worked fifteen hours or more in a family business or were employed "temporarily."[3]

There are certainly contemporary parallels to this situation wherein women's home labor in cooking, gardening, making clothes, or doing childcare "takes up the slack" at times of low family income (Weinbaum and Bridges, 1976; Soko-loff, 1982; Milkman, 1976). This unreported work also points to the lifetime nature of women's role in bringing money into the household. Unpaid family work was rarely counted as gainful employment at the turn of the century, but persons who work fifteen hours or more as unpaid workers in a family business are now included among the "civilian employed" by the Bureau of Labor Statistics. In 1900, when 37% of the population lived on farms and 53% lived in rural areas (under 1000 people), women had more opportunity than now (with 3% of the population on farms in 1978) for unpaid family work, and thus less structural incentive to enter gainful employment. In fact, it is only with the more recent increase in the size of the industrial sector that (white) female work rates have increased (Haber, 1973). Although one cannot reinterview turn-of-the-century women to learn their employment status using current definitions, one can look at the degree to which the presence of boarders, a family enterprise, or farm residence suppresses the probability that women report themselves as gainfully employed.

With the opening of the 1900 manuscript Census and the development of a 1900 Public Use Sample by the University of Washington, national turn-of-the-century data incorporating individual, household, and geographic variables are now available with which to study the determinants of women's gainful employ-ment. The later 1910 Public Use Sample and the 1920 Census itself are not yet available for access to household-level data. On the other hand, the earlier 1890 Census shows only the very beginning of the changes caused by urbanization: the increase in married women's paid employment from 3% to 9% only starts in 1890; declining family size does not show its full effects until after 1900; the decrease in household boarders and servants, caused by immigration limita-tions and changing work opportunities, begins around 1900; and child labor laws are not enacted until after 1900. Thus our use of the 1900 Census data is not only pragmatic. The data provide an opportunity to look at processes in transition rather than before (1880) or after (1920) industrialization has had its major impact. It is a time when new demographic and employment patterns have emerged and the technological developments of World War I have not yet arrived. We use the 1900 Census data to characterize these patterns at a national level and to test the generalizability of prior findings drawn from local studies of women's turn-of-the-century work. We also develop and assess the effectiveness of a household resource model in predicting women's reported employment.

Hypothesis: The Household, the Individual, and the Region

Household Composition: The Family

In 1900 most households relied upon a married male as the prime wage earner. However, Census data indicate that a second person was employed in a substantial number of households, either to help support the family or to send money to European relatives. This section develops hypotheses about the impact of male and female household composition (exclusive of respondents) on daughters, wives, heads, and other female relatives separately.

We expect the presence of young children (under 10) in a household to decrease married women's employment, as it does in more recent times, but to correlate positively with an increase in home-based work (taking in boarders) for wives. Children may also necessitate paid employment for older daughters (ages 15 and above) or the presence of an additional single, related adult (brothers, sisters, cousins) helping in household support or aiding in childcare. It is in this sense that research by Tilly and Scott (1978) or Tentler (1979) leads one to expect a substitution of adolescent paid labor for that of wives. However, our analysis will separate out the substitution effects of younger adolescents (ages 10–14), who might be expected to remain in school, from those of children fifteen and older. There is no prior basis on which to predict whether the presence of young children under ten, employed adolescent and older children, or an extended family will more greatly suppress wives' reported gainful employment.

Female employment is a function not only of women's or children's presence in the household. Since males generally earn more than females, the presence of employable married and single men and of adolescent boys is expected to reduce the likelihood of employment for wives, daughters or extended family women. Female household heads represent a different situation. Due both to the lack of sanctions against supporting their families and to their obvious income needs, female heads are expected to be the most likely women to report an occupation. Presence of other women in the household will not reduce that need greatly; married men are unlikely to be in residence; and only the presence of single young men, perhaps sons, might be predicted to provide an income large enough to suppress female heads' employment.

Household Composition: Nonfamily Members

There are three types of nonfamily household members: servants, employees, and boarders.

The presence of resident servants probably indicates sufficient household income to render unnecessary the gainful employment of family women. The few exceptional women might have been those who used a high-income background to enter the professions or upper-white-collar jobs. Thus, on the whole we expect servants in the home to depress the likelihood of daughters' or other female relatives' employment.

Resident employees were most frequently found in rural areas, on farms. We view presence of employees as indicative of the type of self-employment which should depress the reporting of female unpaid family work. Although women may have served as de facto boardinghousekeepers for the employees, both Census interviewer instructions and cultural expectations would have encouraged them to see such work as part of their usual home role. We predict that only for a woman who is the employer and household head will these circumstances increase the likelihood of reporting work.

One might similarly expect the presence of boarders to depress women's employment because it is female homemaking labor which supports the lodgers. However, since it is primarily wives who "take in" boarders, we expect this household alternative to depress only their employment and not that of other women. Boarders indicate one income source for a household, but their presence also reflects a household need for further money (Modell and Hareven, 1973; Mason and Laslett, 1983). Thus, if boarders indicate a last economic resort, it is possible that their presence will also be associated with the use of other family resources: i.e., employing daughters and other relatives. Researchers agree that taking in boarders was primarily an urban alternative income source, but they disagree as to whether lodgers were more common among immigrant or native-born families.

Household Composition: Economic Position

Although it would be ideal to measure household economic position in wages, income data are not available from the 1900 national Census. Thus, to investigate the effect of household income need on female employment, we must rely on occupational coding as a surrogate for class. The PUS codes jobs using the 1900 Census scheme. It also indicates how jobs would be recoded using the 1950 classification system and what prestige would be assigned. Since contemporary occupational prestige ratings do not accurately reflect women's income or the ranking of turn-of-the-century jobs, and since existing ranking systems for nineteenth-century occupations do not systematically include women (Katz, 1975; Armstrong, 1972; Conk, 1981), we recode occupations into eight major groupings similar to those used in other socio-historical studies of the period (except that all managers are coded within the professions as upper-white-collar jobs). The categories are: professionals and managers; craft; clerical and sales; operative and laborer; service; agriculture; employed-unclassifiable; and unemployed.

We predict that in households where the male head engages in professional or craft employment, with a potentially high income, there will be no second person in the labor force and neither wives nor daughters will work. On the other hand, in households with an unemployed head bringing in no income, we expect both wives and daughters to increase their work rates. In other intermediate cases, where a head is in clerical, operative, labor, or service employ, a daughter would be the most likely female to seek a job if needed. Of course, as indicated earlier, self-employment on a family farm or as a merchant is predicted to lower reported work for all women.

Using contemporary data, one would predict female-headed households to be in a dire economic position and to have all possible labor sources employed. We temper this expectation with a note of caution. Since female household heads were frequently widows who ran family farms, their own employment may be recorded, but unpaid family work by other members may be suppressed.

Household Composition: Race and Ethnicity

Ethnicity reflects a wide variety of cultural attitudes toward the acceptability of women's employment in general, and of the type of work (factory, domestic, or home-based) sought in particular. Literature on individual cities predicts Irish and French Canadian women to have the highest rates of employment, with German, Eastern European and Russian women close behind them (Kessler-Harris, 1982). Italian women are usually described as having among the lowest rates (McLaughlin, 1973), while there is disagreement about the work of Latin American women. Employment rates of some groups, such as Italians, actually varied with the regional economy. We investigate the extent to which urban-based predictions are supported at that national level.

The relative importance of ethnicity and class in predicting employment strategies has been debated, with Zunz (1982) maintaining that ethnicity was primary in the 1880 to 1900 period, but claiming class became more important from 1900 to 1920 as ethnic groups diffused geographically. Others (McLaughlin, 1973) feel that class and ethnic variation, as well as regional differences, continued to be important determinants of women's employment. Although we measure occupation, rather than class, we predict that both ethnicity and head's occupation will have a significant impact on women's employment at the turn of the century.

We also predict household strategy differences among the families of native born, first- and second-generation immigrant women. First-generation immigrants frequently needed a second income, but are predicted to rely on daughters' rather than wives' paid labor. Second-generation immigrants may be more accepting of wives' employment, but may not need it. However, boarders are predicted to be more common among immigrant generations than among native-born Americans.

The role of race is more complicated than that of ethnicity. Race may represent cultural attitudes (Pleck, 1978), but it also represents a structural position in a segregated economy. By 1880, with continued post–Civil War poverty, married black women began to enter the labor force at rates exceeding other groups. Although often segregated into domestic or agricultural pursuits, black and other minority women are predicted to be more likely than white women to report employment, independent of their relationship (wife, daughter) to the household head.

Individual Variables

Age and marital status are often cited in urban historical studies as predictors of women's employment, with single women under twenty-five depicted as the major component of the female work force. However, this is a misleading image of 1900. It is probable that *older* single daughters obtained a job before younger sisters, while young single relatives would be asked to help in household support before married or older widowed ones. Therefore we predict that single women will be more likely to enter gainful employment than married women and, controlling for relationship to head, older daughters and younger relatives will be significantly likely to hold a job.

The role of education is also complex. Contemporary studies indicate women's education is positively correlated with employment; yet in 1900 educated upper-class women might be discouraged from work. Unfortunately, only literacy, and not years of education, was recorded in 1900: 88 percent of all women were able to read and 86 percent were able to write a language. This lack of recorded differentiation among women leads to a prediction that literacy will have no significant effect. However, if illiteracy is an indication that women left school prematurely to take jobs, it may have a positive effect on gainful employment.

Regional and Economic Structure

Most research on turn-of-the-century female employment draws on data limited to urban areas in the most industrialized sections of the country where opportunities for factory work were relatively high and those for unpaid family-farm work may have been lower than elsewhere. Accordingly, we expect urban and North Atlantic residence to increase female employment significantly over rural areas and other regions. Since boarding was a largely urban phenomenon, controlling for urban residence may reduce the importance of lodgers in predicting women's work. However, geography should have no other influence on the role of household composition variables. Within a region, specific local industries might attract (textiles) or suppress (iron molding) female employment (Tilly and Scott, 1978), but this should not affect our test of the generalizability of Northeastern patterns to other regions.

Data and Methods

The 1900 Census Public Use Sample, made available by the Center for Studies in Demography and Ecology at the University of Washington, is a nationally representative 1-in-760 sample of individuals (N = 100,438), recorded in household units (N = 27,069). All the individual and household data available in the original 1900 Census enumerator sheets are included.

In this study, individual adult women between fifteen and sixty-five[4] drawn from the PUS will be the unit of analysis and their gainful employment (GE) is the dependent variable. (Women who performed unpaid family-farm work or took in boarders, but did not report themselves as working, are not considered as gainfully employed.) Independent variables fall into the three identified groups of household, individual, and geographic measures.

Three different approaches were considered for measuring family household composition. The first utilized the total number of persons in the eight various age, gender, and marital status categories suggested by our hypotheses: children (0–9); seniors (65 and over); male and female adolescents (10–14), counted separately; and married men, single men, married women, and single women (15–64). The second measure, intended as an indicator of income need, was a dependency ratio calculated as the total number of children (under 10) and seniors (over 64) divided by total household size. A third measure was based on the proportion of persons employed within each status category. The first method, based on the total number in each grouping, combined with presence or absence of relatives, boarders, employees, or servants, proved most useful. In fact, the second measure is essentially embedded in the first, while the third measure was later incorporated as "proportion employed of all combined male and female relatives (over age 10 and excluding the respondent)."

Other household-related variables fall within two groups: family economic position and race or ethnicity. Minority race is measured by a dummy variable indicating nonwhites. Ethnicity is assigned for immigrant women (first generation) or those with at least one foreign-born parent (second generation), creating two dummy variables for each of eleven groups: English (English, Scotch, Welsh, and Australian); Irish; Scandinavian; German; East European; Italian; other European (Belgian, Swiss, French, Greek, Spanish, and Portuguese); Russian; Latin American; and French and English Canadian. The excluded group are women born in the U.S. of American-born parents. The categories represent cohesive groups which were in the U.S. in large numbers.

Family economic position is measured both by the proportion employed in the household and by the occupation of the head. Occupation is measured in two ways: first, as a dummy variable indicating self-employment in agriculture or as a merchant; and second, as a series of seven occupational categories, described above, where employment in agriculture is the excluded category.

A note of caution must be interjected about the household resources model: it is applicable only to women living in their own family homes and not women living elsewhere. All respondents are associated by the Census with the household data of their residence and not with that of their nativity. Thus servants, employees and boarders, whose other individual-level information is maintained, are recorded with the household data of their employer or boarding-house. Since it is not appropriate to predict these women's employment based on household resources they are excluded in this analysis. One effect of such exclusion is that working-class households whose daughters are employed elsewhere as servants or boarding out will appear to have fewer family members earning income than is actually the case. Therefore the impact of our measures "proportion employed" and "numbers of female adolescents" may be underestimated.

Beyond the household variables, which are our major focus, geographic and individual-level variables are included. Geographic variables indicate both urbanization and region. The former is measured by a dummy variable for towns with a population of over 1,000 people. The latter is a series of five dummy variables based on the 1900 Census definition of regions: South Atlantic; North Central; South Central; the West; and military reservations (including territories, Alaska, and Hawaii). North Atlantic is the excluded category, since the northeast region is the most frequently studied. Individual variables include indicators of marital status (1 = married, spouse present), ability to read a language (1 = reads), and the continuous variable of age.

We turn now to our method of analysis. Because our dependent variable, GE, is dichotomous, its aggregate interpretation is as the probability that an individual woman was gainfully employed. While OLS and logistic regression provide similar results when the mean of a dependent variable ranges from 25 to 75 percent (Goodman, 1976), outside of this range OLS can underestimate the effects of continuous independent variables relative to those of dummy variables (Vanneman and Pampel, 1977). As indicated in Table 1, 22 percent of the total sample are gainfully employed. It is the wives, comprising 57 percent

Table 1. Women's Gainful Employment by Marital Status and Relation to Head (Women 15 and Older)

Group of Women	% Gainfully Employed
Marital Status Groups:	
(N = 31,755)	21.6
Married, Spouse Present	4.3
Single, Never Married	45.3
Widowed	34.8
Divorced	59.8
Married, Spouse Absent	38.6
Relation to Household Head:	
(N = 31,835)	21.7
Head	47.3
Wife	4.0
Daughter	33.1
Other Female Relative	24.6
Servant	99.0
Employee	98.6
Boarder	56.7
Other Nonrelative	7.9

of adult women, whose dramatically low rate of employment (4%) brings down the average for the whole group. Therefore in the next section the results of OLS and logistic regression are compared.

We further contend that household composition effects on gainful employment (GE) should be separately examined for women with different relationships, as recorded by the Census, to the household and its head: wives; daughters; other relatives; and female household heads. In order to study effects of household composition on family members, it is important to know their own location in that family. Further, Table 1 indicates that gainful employment rates vary with position in the family. Given the possible different processes occurring for each group, we use separate equations for women with different relationships to the household.

Household Composition: Comparing OLS and Logistic Regression

Table 2 presents all OLS b-values (A columns) and logit coefficients for significant variables (B columns) in the regressions of GE on the household composition measures. Unfortunately, logit analysis cannot handle many independent variables; ethnicity and detailed occupational variables had to be eliminated from the logit regressions because they created too many distinct covariate patterns to perform the analysis. Thus, for comparative purposes, these variables were also eliminated in the OLS regressions.

The household composition variables account for 23.0 percent of the variance in GE for all women, with a range of 9.1 percent for wives up to 17.1 percent for daughters. In spite of the skewed nature of GE, we find the same variables significant in each pair of OLS and logit equations, usually at the same level of probability, for female heads, wives, daughters, and other relatives (columns 2 through 5). Since logit coefficients are difficult to interpret, we provide t-values beneath them and for all significant OLS b-values. The t-values for these variables are also very similar. There are only two differences between the OLS and logit findings. The OLS regression underestimated the impact of the number of resident married men on female household head's GE (column 2). The logit analysis indicates that the effect is significant, even if there are few married men residing with female household heads. Second, the OLS regression for wives (column 3) overestimated the impact of the dummy variable, presence of extended family, which logit indicates is significant only at $p = .10$. Apparently the presence of extended family does not significantly depress wives' employment. Given the very skewed nature of GE for wives (96:4) and the large number of variables involved, these two differences are minor. Therefore, although we must be cautious in interpreting the significance of these two variables, we continue the discussion of household composition using the more easily interpreted OLS regression results. Because logistic regression cannot handle the additional ethnic, individual, or geographic variables necessary to our model, and because of the similar results found using the two methods, our further analyses will also be carried out using OLS regression.

Table 2. Comparison of OLS (Col. A) and Logistic (Col. B) Regressions of Gainful Employment on Household Composition Characteristics for Women 15 to 64 by Relationship to Head[a]

Variables	All Women (1)		Household Heads (2)		Wives (3)		Daughters (4)		Other Female Relatives (5)	
	(1A) b/(t)	(1B) Coef/(t)[b]	(2A) b/(t)	(2B) Coef/(t)	(3A) b/(t)	(3B) Coef/(t)	(4A) b/(t)	(4B) Coef/(t)	(5A) b/(t)	(5B) Coef/(t)
FAMILY										
Number Children 0–9	.007*** (3.86)		.004		−.007*** (6.13)	.185*** (5.87)	.024*** (4.79)	−.135*** (4.80)	.026** (3.07)	−.137** (3.04)
Number Seniors 65+	−.069*** (11.35)		−.038		.011		.078*** (5.92)	−.391*** (5.30)	.032	
Male Adolescents 10–14	.015*** (4.16)		.042* (1.95)	−.195* (1.99)	−.002		.030*** (3.47)	−.156** (3.25)	.035	
Female Adolescents 10–14	.021*** (5.55)		.066** (3.03)	−.312** (3.13)	.002		.029** (3.24)	−.164*** (3.30)	.035	
Married Men 15–64	−.363*** (63.85)		−.191 (1.71)	.657** (2.76)	.010		−.159*** (8.74)	.931*** (8.41)	−.272*** (10.42)	1.64*** (9.43)
Single Men 15–64	−.048*** (17.63)		−.068*** (4.79)	.259*** (4.83)	−.004		−.077*** (13.4)	.429*** (12.7)	−.106*** (8.34)	.559*** (7.47)
Married Women 15–64	.264*** (51.51)		.034		−.009		.081*** (4.33)	−.497*** (4.67)	.222*** (7.20)	−1.36*** (7.16)
Single Women 15–64	.016*** (6.04)		−.041** (3.08)	.157** (2.71)	.005* (2.33)	−.129* (2.28)	.027*** (4.94)	−.110*** (3.72)	.030** (2.59)	−.133* (2.17)
Extended Family Present	.028*** (5.49)		.079** (2.86)	−.341** (2.92)	−.010* (1.97)		−.054*** (3.93)	.270*** (3.48)	not included[c]	

NONFAMILY

Boarders Present	.038*** (5.71)	.058* (2.17)	-.274* (-2.20)	.012* (2.44)	-.307* (-2.35)	.024		.069* (2.41)	-.328* (-2.25)
Servants Present	-.052*** (5.56)	-.102* (1.97)	.517* (2.12)	-.003		-.151*** (6.06)	.916*** (5.67)	-.085* (2.42)	.427* (2.07)
Employees Present	.011 (.84)	.468*** (5.79)	-2.68*** (-4.35)	.001		-.073* (2.09)	.523* (2.25)	.054	
RACE, NO ETHNICITY									
Racial Minority	.205*** (31.10)	.340*** (12.86)	-1.66*** (-11.6)	.196*** (39.5)	-2.65*** (-30.8)	.140*** (7.66)	-.688*** (-7.11)	.129*** (4.45)	-.615*** (-4.22)
ECONOMIC POSITION									
Proportion Employed	.356*** (12.23)	.064 (1.19)		omitted[b]		.933*** (26.3)	-4.87*** (-23.4)	.758*** (11.69)	-3.69***
Head Is Farmer or Merchant (male)	-.054*** (24.58)	not included[c]		-.010** (3.11)	.278** (3.08)	-.191*** (17.0)	1.07*** (16.4)	-.140*** (7.06)	.705*** (6.51)
Constant	.287***	.469***	.104	.022*	3.64	.153***	1.66	.167***	1.46
Adjusted R^2	23.0%	12.3%		9.1%		17.1%		13.2%	
N	27,121	2,114		15,936		6,818		2,253	

[a](1) Using stepwise logistic regression, coefficients are not available for nonsignificant variables and significance level is not available for constants; (2) logit coefficient signs are opposite b's, as the former predict nonwork and the latter predict gainful employment; (3) A columns give OLS b-values and B columns give logit coefficients. Since the latter are not easily interpretable, t-values for both methods are given in parentheses under each significant variable.

[b]Omitted. Variables in column 3 created too many covariate patterns to perform a logit analysis; logit for column 1A could not be run without dropping so many variables as to effectively change the model being tested. The problem does not occur for OLS regression.

[c]Excluded on theoretical grounds. In Col. 2, respondents are household heads and there is no male head. In Col. 5, other women relatives are themselves extended family.

*p ≤ .05.
**p ≤ .01.
***p ≤ .001.

Household Composition: The Family

The column one results in the top panel of Table 2 indicate that all nine family composition variables significantly influence women's gainful employment. Yet, this overview obscures the differential impact which composition has on women in different household positions. The much-discussed role of children is a good example.

On the whole, children (0–9) tend to increase the employment of women, probably because a larger family needs more income. However, as predicted, children significantly decrease the employment of wives (column 3), who then have less time available, while daughters over 14 (column 4) and other resident female relatives (column 5) are indeed likely to enter gainful employment. The preferred strategy of wives with young children was to have other relatives helping out and not to bring in boarders: of women living with five or fewer children under ten years old, 21 to 33 percent also lived with extended family, while only 5 to 10 percent lived with boarders. The first child increased the number of extended family, however residence of both extended family and boarders declined with each additional child (up to five youths). It is likely that household space limitations prevented escalating the number of "outsiders" with the number of children. Thus, it is no surprise that the number of young children is negatively correlated (– .048) with presence of boarders and only slightly positively related (.007) to presence of extended family (see Table 3). Our prediction that children would increase homebased work might hold for unrecorded cottage industry or family-farm employment, but young children definitely did not increase boarding as a household income strategy.

The role of adolescent children (age 10–14) is more complicated than that of younger ones. Adolescent labor does not appear to substitute for the GE of older women, as others have suggested. To the extent that such substitution can be measured by a significant coefficient for male or female adolescents in any column of Table 2, we instead find significantly positive impact upon the GE of daughters, household heads, and women as a whole. Presumably, older daughters or heads would rather go to work themselves than pull these adolescents out of school. At the same time, adolescents are old enough not to need a parent's full-time attention nor to depress wives' employment. However, in regressions (not shown) using adolescent employment, instead of presence, we find a significant positive effect of employed adolescent girls on wives', daughters', and other family women's work, and a similar effect of boys on female heads' GE. While the preference may have been not to have female adolescents seek employment, once they are employed most other household female labor resources were also called upon. Rather than substituting for adult labor, adolescent female paid employment may have been a last resort of many families. This interpretation is consistent with the significant influence of the variable, proportion of the household employed (fourth panel, Table 2): the greater the percentage of persons employed, the more likely a woman will be employed.

Table 3. Correlation Coefficients for Household Composition Variables, Excluding Ethnicity, for All Women Ages 15 to 64

	Gainful Employment	Children	Seniors	Male Adolescents	Female Adolescents	Married Men	Married Women[a]	Single Men	Single Women[a]	Extended Family	Boarders	Servants	Employees	Racial Minority	Head is Farmer or Merchant	Proportion Employed
Children	-.114	1.00														
Seniors	.031	-.125	1.00													
Male Adolescents	.005	.218	-.068	1.00												
Female Adolescents	.009	.218	-.063	.091	1.00											
Married Men	-.294	.254	-.327	.084	.073	1.00										
Married Women[a]	.164	-.001	.013	.109	.094	.291	1.00									
Single Men	.058	-.123	.046	.128	.099	-.160	.128	1.00								
Single Women[a]	.152	-.120	.029	.093	.081	-.216	.085	.228	1.00							
Extended Family	.071	.007	.304	-.028	-.034	-.011	.181	.097	.144	1.00						
Boarders	.047	-.048	-.024	-.048	-.031	-.031	-.013	-.034	-.003	.018	1.00					
Servants	-.042	-.051	.039	-.036	-.028	-.008	.002	.004	.012	.053	.035	1.00				
Employees	-.019	.000	.025	-.014	-.010	.010	.013	-.018	-.006	.014	-.016	.064	1.00			
Racial Minority	.200	.090	-.025	.030	.055	-.051	-.018	-.031	-.004	.043	-.003	-.071	-.044	1.00		
Head is Farmer/ Merchant	-.086	.124	.045	.108	.084	.092	.059	.083	-.015	.010	-.071	-.043	.153	.045	1.00	
Proportion Employed	.070	-.383	-.200	-.080	-.148	.139	-.023	.360	.108	.008	.006	-.028	-.016	.024	.005	1.00
N = 27,121																

[a]Married and single women refer to women other than the respondent.

It is not only children who influence women's employment. As predicted, the presence of single or married men between 15 and 64 does significantly decrease the probability of employment for daughters, other female relatives and household heads. The ability to draw on the income of several male householders reduces the need for women's usually low wages. Interestingly, male presence has no impact on wives' employment, probably because male presence is usually correlated with that of wives.

Adult women in the home have a less uniform effect on employment than do men. Understandably, married women increase the employment probability of daughters and of other relatives, who are often single. Yet single women (older than 14), whose presence may require more family income, also have a surprisingly positive effect on GE for wives, daughters (other than themselves), and female relatives (Table 2, columns 3 to 5).

Extended family also have a mixed impact. They significantly affect female household heads, whose GE they increase. However, extended family reduce the likelihood that daughters will need to work (Table 2, column 4), perhaps entering the labor force in the daughters' stead.

In sum, the European findings of Tilly and Scott (1978) and the urban U.S. ones of Tentler (1979) are only weakly supported for turn-of-the-century America. Adolescents do not substitute for or depress mothers' paid labor; and when younger female adolescents (10–14) are employed, so are older daughters (over 14) and other relatives. In only one sense do older daughters and other family members substitute for wives: when there are young children (0–9) at home, necessitating more income, it is the daughters or other relatives who usually seek work. Wives may do unrecorded factory outwork or family-farm labor at home in such circumstances, but they do not hold GE or bring in additional boarders.

While family composition other than number of children has relatively little impact on wives, it does have the predicted significant influence on other women. Only adult men and extended family can depress daughter's GE, while increased numbers of any other household group raise daughter's employment probability. Other relatives behave in a similar manner, except that they are unaffected by adolescents or seniors. Female household heads behave somewhat differently. They will increase their GE probability with the presence of adolescents or extended family to support, but will decrease their rates with adult males or single females present who can substitute for them.

Nonfamily Household Composition

The second panel of Table 2 contains the nonfamily variables. As hypothesized, servants suppress women's gainful employment and appear to reflect a high household income. The effect is strongest for daughters, but is significant for all women other than wives.

Self-employment of the household head, as indicated by resident employees, has a mixed impact on women, decreasing the probability of daughters' paid work (column 4) but simultaneously increasing that of female heads (column 2); thus they balance each other out in aggregated form. Employee residence was most common on farms or in small businesses. In such situations, we argue that daughters' negative coefficient indicates unreported and unpaid family work, while female heads' positive coefficient indicates that women who hired hands were more willing to indicate their own farm or business employment. This is one indicator that self-employment did suppress the GE of family dependents.

Boarders, in contrast to employees, were an urban phenomenon, found more frequently in towns over 1,000 than in rural areas. In general, taking in boarders was not regarded by the Census as gainful employment unless it was the main source of family income (Ciancanelli, 1981), even though it was a key form of income earning for married women. As a consequence, 28 percent of all women and only 5 percent of wives living with boarders reported themselves as employed in 1900 (Bose, 1980). Because of this undercounted work we predicted that the presence of boarders would depress wives' GE. However, we find that boarders significantly increase wives', heads', and relatives' gainful employment. Since these women predominantly report nonboardinghouse jobs, the family requires both boarders and women's gainful employment for support. Therefore we confirm research suggesting that families took in lodgers when financial needs were severe and all available income sources needed to be utilized (Modell and Hareven, 1973; Mason and Laslett, 1983). Boarders were a supplement, rather than an alternative, to female paid labor. It is unusual that daughters appear unaffected by boarders, but in such needy households they may have left for domestic or factory work elsewhere.

Racial and Ethnic Composition

Racial minority women represent 11 percent of the sample and black women are 96 percent of minorities; first- and second-generation ethnic women constitute a full 37 percent of the sample.

The third panel of Table 2 supports our earlier prediction that minority race is a strong positive factor in facilitating women's employment. Regardless of relationship to household head, and controlling for other composition features, minority women are more likely to work than white women. In fact, standardized coefficients indicate that race is the predominant household factor influencing wives' gainful employment.

The impact of ethnicity is not nearly as strong as that of race although, as predicted, ethnic women's absolute aggregate rates of gainful employment vary widely by cultural group. Irish and French Canadians had the highest GE at 24 and 27 percent respectively; they were followed by Russians and English Canadians at 18 percent. No other group had a higher rate than the 17 percent of third-generation American women. German and English women had a GE rate of 15 percent, Eastern Europeans of 14 percent, and Italians of 13 percent, followed by Scandinavians, Latin Americans, and other European groups at 12 percent. Thus GE rates are not the lowest for Italians and, contrary to the historical literature, Eastern European rates are not among the highest.

In order to investigate the net effects of ethnic background on women in various household positions we return to OLS regression. Since logistic regressions in Table 2 (and thus the OLS comparative ones) could not include all variables in the full model, a second OLS regression of GE on all household composition, geographic, and individual-level variables was performed. The results for ethnicity are presented in the third panel of Table 4. Examining the regression coefficients for all women (column 1), we find as predicted that the employment rates of first- and second-generation Irish and French Canadian, first-generation Russian and Latin American, and second-generation German women were significantly different from third-generation Americans. Standardized coefficients indicate that the impact is greatest by far for the second-generation Irish (.046). It is next largest for second-generation Germans (.020) and all French Canadians (.022 and .024). It is least for first-generation Irish (–.018), Russian (.010) and Latin American (–.011) women, the latter of whom are significantly unlikely to record employment.

On the whole, ethnic household strategies relied considerably on the employment of both first- and second-generation immigrant daughters (column 4) and, in a very limited way, on other relatives of the second generation. In fact, ethnic daughters were significantly more likely to be employed than third-generation American ones, while their mothers' low rates of gainful employment were not different from those of nonethnic wives. Therefore, literature indicating a unique propensity of Italian, Latin American, or other ethnic wives to stay at home is not supported.

Generation effects are also important. Other regressions (not shown), which include generation and exclude country of origin, indicate that second-generation immigrants were significantly more likely than third-generation Americans to record employment, while first-generation immigrants were not significantly divergent from third. In fact, immigrant women had an average GE rate of 13 percent, second-generation women of 22 percent, and third-generation American women of 17 percent. Perhaps the households of second-generation women retained the strong income needs of immigrants while having increased the cultural legitimacy for female employment. However, first-generation immigrants were more likely to do home-based work: 13 percent of first-generation immigrant women lived with boarders, while 10 percent of second-generation ethnic and 10 percent of third-generation American women lived with boarders. Thus it is not all ethnic women, as often predicted, who have greater numbers of boarders, it is only first-generation immigrant women. Of course, the rates of boarder residence also varied with ethnic group: Italian (25%) and Russian women (21%) were most likely to reside with boarders, followed by French Canadian (17%), Eastern European (16%), and Scandinavian (14%) women. The German, Irish, and English were no more likely than third-generation American women to have boarders (10%).

Because of the range of cultures involved, it is difficult to summarize suc-

Table 4. Regression of Gainful Employment on Household Composition, Individual, and Geographic Characteristics. Women 15 to 64, by Relationship to Head

	All Women (1)	Household Heads (2)	Wives (3)	Daughters (4)	Other Female Relatives (5)
FAMILY					
Children (0–9)	.005**	−.029*	$.006^{-1}$	.026***	.030***
Seniors 65+	.008	−.047	.021**	.042**	.046*
Male Adolescents	.006	.019	.001	.040***	.034
Female Adolescents	.010**	.037	.008**	.043***	.024
Married Men	−.061***	−.185	−.012	−.080***	−.080
Single Men	−.041***	−.063***	−.014***	−.082***	−.104***
Married Women	−.069***	.061	.005	.057*	.041
Single Women	.015***	−.017	.006*	.019***	.022
Extended Family Present	$−.005^{-1}$	.071**	−.011*	−.027*	omitted[a]
NONFAMILY					
Boarders Present	.024***	.068*	.011*	.018	.068*
Servants Present	−.044***	−.108*	.004	−.130***	−.062
Employees Present	.014	.420***	.002	−.051	.035
RACE ETHNICITY					
Racial Minority	.194***	.199***	.167***	.216***	.173***
English (1)	−.010	−.070	−.006	.023	.044
English (2)	.015	.034	$−.003^{-1}$	.004	.042
Irish (1)	−.042***	−.071	−.007	.088	.048
Irish (2)	.078***	.011	−.009	.109***	.105**
Scandinavian (1)	.027	−.053	−.003	.111	.097

Table 4. (Continued)

Scandinavian (2)	-.004	-.049	.002	.047	.018
Other European (1)	-.016	-.094	-.011	.017	.075
Other European (2)	.026	-.088	-.014	.069	.102
German (1)	.001	-.059	-.002	.158***	.034
German (2)	.029***	-.033	-.008	.056**	.098*
East European (1)	.009	.003	-.007	.167*	.085
East European (2)	.045	-.468	.018	.112*	-.220
Italian (1)	-.008	.075	.009	.061	-.118
Italian (2)	-.053	no cases	-.038	-.054	.061
Russian (1)	.042*	.069	-.021	.386***	.062
Russian (2)	.033	no cases	-.014	.015	no cases
French Canadian (1)	.105***	-.116	.036*	.334***	.043
French Canadian (2)	.133***	.180	-.019	.230***	.110
English Canadian (1)	.028	.031	-.017	.110*	.100
English Canadian (2)	.026	.143	-.015	.039	.078
Latin American (1)	-.088*	-.361*	-.044	-.005	-.106
Latin American (2)	-.067	.402	-.070	-.143	-.072
ECONOMIC POSITION					
Proportion Employed	.261***	.108*	.136***	.890***	.660***
Professional or MOP	-.018*	omitted[a]	-.004	-.026	-.031
Clerical & Sales	-.007	omitted[a]	-.010	.032	-.009[-1]
Craft	.014	omitted[a]	.006	.048*	.017
Operative & Laborer	.035***	omitted[a]	.009*	.041*	.025
Service	.173***	omitted[a]	-.006	.050	.086
Unclassified	.030	omitted[a]	.009	-.068	.096
Unemployed	-.159***	omitted[a]	.039***	.126***	.003

GEOGRAPHIC

Urban	.045***	-.136***	.010*	.130***	.097***
South Atlantic	-.001	.099**	.024***	-.063***	-.059
North Central	-.023***	-.016	.002	-.058***	-.056*
South Central	-.024***	.062	.014**	-.122***	-.111***
West	-.028**	.023	.003	-.092***	-.088
Military, Territories, Alaska, and Hawaii	.008	-.141	.041	.436	-.121
INDIVIDUAL					
Age	$.008^{-1}$***	-.008***	$-.009^{-2}$	.008***	-.004***
Reads	-.036***	-.003	-.021***	-.076**	-.021
Married	-.381***	omitted[a]	omitted[a]	-.309***	-.256***
Constant	.360***	.946***	$.003^{-1}$	-.105*	.270***
Adjusted R^2	29.0%	17.0%	10.0%	22.8%	16.8%
N	27,121	2,114	15,936	6,818	2,253

[a]Omitted variables were eliminated on theoretical grounds. e.g.: female heads' occupations cannot be predicted by their own occupations: other female relatives are extended family: wives are always and heads are rarely married, spouse present.

*p ≤ .05.
**p ≤ .01.
***p ≤ .001.

cinctly the role of race and ethnicity. Controlling for all variables, standardized coefficients indicate that race is the major determinant of wives' employment, while it is one of several important factors for daughters, other relatives, and female household heads.

Ethnicity, on the other hand, has its greatest significant impact on daughters, separating them out from their third-generation peers. Like race, ethnicity generally facilitates rather than suppresses female employment, especially as predicted for Irish, German, Russian, Eastern European and French Canadian women. In fact, ethnicity only depresses gainful employment for first-generation Latin American household heads. Other ethnic groups, including the often-discussed Italians, are not actually very different from nonethnics.

Economic Position of the Household

The fourth panel in both Tables 2 and 4 reports the regression results for variables of economic position.

In general, when greater proportions of household members over age 14 are employed, all women (column 1) are more likely to enter GE. The effect is strongest for daughters and other relatives, but it significantly impacts even wives as more income is needed. Female household heads are only influenced by it once region and individual characteristics are controlled (Table 4).

Turning to specific occupations, we see that the self-employment of a household head in farming or as a merchant does significantly reduce the probability of GE for all women (columns 3 to 5, Table 2) who do not themselves head a family. If the male head is self-employed in agriculture, 16% of all household women report an occupation; when he is a merchant, 22% do so; and when the head is otherwise employed, 26% of sampled women are working. Typically, the effect is strongest on daughters and relatives: the respective rates of gainful employment for daughters under the three conditions are 22, 25, and 40 percent and for relatives they are 24, 28, and 36 percent. Thus, the hypothesis that male self-employment suppresses female employment is again supported by these straight percentages.

Not all women had the opportunity to do (unrecorded) work in a family farm or business. In order to examine the effects of household heads' nonagricultural employment we must turn to the fourth panel of Table 4, which compares seven occupational groupings to the excluded one of work in agriculture. As predicted, heads' high-status professional or managerial employment significantly reduces the probability of women's GE (column 1). In fact, only 12 percent of such women work. In contrast, the poverty reflected by heads' unemployment significantly increases both wives' and daughters' work (columns 3 and 4). In the status range between these two groups, heads' operative or laborer work also increases wives' and daughters' work, and service employment increases all women's GE. Apparently these households shared in the low income of the unemployed and frequently needed wives' GE to supplement sons' or daughters' income. Employment of other household heads in clerical, craft or unclassified occupations did not affect women very differently from their employment in general agricultural work, where 14 percent of all women sought gainful employment.

We turn now to the relative role of class and ethnicity in developing family employment strategies. The question is raised by Zunz (1982), who argues that after 1900 class became the predominant influence. Of course, the issue has little import for the eight percent of all women who head their own households and whose work defines their own status. However, using the above results for male heads we might define professional or managerial employment as a measure of upper-middle-class membership, clerical, craft or unclassified work as indicative of a lower-middle-class position, and operative, laborer, service work or unemployment as indicative of working-class or poor households. Examining panels three and four in Table 4, we find the greatest number of significant ethnic and occupational variables for daughters (column 4), whose standardized coefficients are largest for head's unemployment, followed by a mixture of ethnicity and other occupational measures. Few ethnicity or occupational measures are significant for all other women, although standardized coefficients indicate occupation is slightly more important for wives and only ethnicity is important for other relatives. Therefore we conclude that class, as loosely measured by household head's occupation, did not completely predominate over ethnicity in determining family deployment of female labor; and the relative impact of class and ethnicity varied with women's position in the household.

In summary, household economic standing does significantly influence the probability of women's gainful employment, but it is not the sole nor always the prime determinant. Historical literature referring to working-class women's needs to find jobs is correct to the extent that it alludes to the wives and daughters of operatives, laborers, service workers, or the unemployed. Alternatively stated, the greater the household need, as measured by proportion employed, the more likely any woman will work.

On the other hand, well-off households with a professional or managerial head suppress women's employment. Head's self-employment in agriculture or business also depresses women's employment below the level found in households headed by clerical workers, crafts persons, or average agricultural workers.

Regional and Economic Structure

Much research on turn-of-the-century women's work draws on data from urban areas in the northeast. The fifth panel of Table 4 addresses differences which could occur in other regions of the country or away from towns.

As hypothesized, urban residence increases the probability of women's reported employment over that in rural areas (column 1). Controlling for urbanization does not change the impact of boarders' presence; they are associated with increased women's GE in all parts of the country. However, female household heads, often widows running farms, are more likely to report work in rural areas than in urban ones (column 2).

Regional economic variation also plays an important role. As predicted, residence away from the North Atlantic region, especially in the North and South Central or Western states, significantly reduces employment for all women (column 1). However, this masks variation occurring for different groups of women. Wives (column 3) are significantly more likely to report work in the South (Atlantic and Central regions) than in the North Atlantic; female household heads (column 2) also increase their probability of work in the South Atlantic; daughters (column 4) are significantly more likely to enter employment in North Atlantic industries than anywhere else; and other relatives (column 5) have difficulty obtaining employment in the North and South Central portions of the United States.

These differences clearly indicate that the industrial composition of various regions favored the employment of different demographic groups of women. The many studies which only examine northeastern employment patterns must certainly overlook the higher rates of wives' and female heads' employment in southern states and the latter's employment in rural areas.

Individual Variables

The sixth and final panel of Table 4 shows the regression results for individual-level variables.

Married daughters and other relatives are significantly less likely to work than are singles. Thus, the historical archetype is largely supported.

Age, while significant for all women (column 1), shows the predicted range of impacts. Younger female heads and relatives are more likely to record employment than older ones. On the other hand, older daughters' GE rate is significantly higher than that of their younger sisters. Interestingly, age is unimportant for wives.

Even though the majority of women were literate in 1900, reading ability significantly suppresses gainful employment for wives (column 3) and daughters (column 4). Yet, it is not literacy per se which removes women from the labor market. The causality is probably in the other direction: the need to work pulled women from school before they could perfect their reading skills. This interpretation is supported by the significant negative correlations between reading ability and family heads' employment in operative and laborer jobs (−.043), in service work (−.025), and with proportion employed (−.019). Thus households that need income utilize women's employment, and in turn women's employment lowers educational opportunity. Since correlations are not necessarily indicative of causation, we can minimally assert that households that need women's employment also cannot prioritize women's education.

In comparing Tables 2 and 4, we see that ethnicity, individual-level variables, and the rarely considered geographic controls of our full model increase the explained variation in gainful employment by three to six percent for daughters, female relatives, and heads. However, standardized coefficients indicate that wives are most influenced by the two household variables of race (.257) and the proportion employed (.116). Other significant variables have betas below an absolute value of .1. Daughters are influenced by many more variables than wives, but the composition measures of proportion employed (.349), number of single men (–.178), and minority race (.136), as well as urban residence (.138) and being married (–.110), have standardized regression coefficients above .1.

In contrast to wives and daughters, individual and regional variables are more likely to reduce the previously described effects of composition on female household heads' and relatives' GE. Age (–.183), urban residence (–.134), and the three household composition variables of race (.158), number of single men (–.115), and presence of employees (.107) retain betas of greater than .1 for female heads. Female relatives' probability of gainful employment, though modified by the controls, is determined by factors similar to those of daughters: proportion employed (.261), number of single men (–.190), and minority race (.122), along with being married (–.184), age (–.134), and urban residence (.104), have the greatest standardized coefficients (over .1).

In summary, all three individual-level variables are significant in the directions hypothesized. However, individual characteristics do not dominate household or regional variables in their ability to predict women's gainful employment; and all three levels of explanation are significant.

Conclusions

This paper uses data from the national 1900 Census to analyze the effects of individual, household, and geographic variables on the probability of women's gainful employment (GE) at the turn of the century. Household resource factors are the main focus of our model. These are further subdivided into family composition measures of the number of youngsters, adolescents, adult married and single men and women, senior citizens, and extended family; nonfamily resources such as presence of boarders, servants or employees; cultural influences of various ethnic generations and groups, as well as racial minority status; and economic position measures. Individual factors include age, marital status, and reading ability; while urban residence and region are the geographic indicators. The impacts of these variables on wives', daughters', female heads', and other relatives' GE are separately investigated and compared.

A major purpose of this analysis it to test the support given by national data for the generalizability of results drawn from local studies. Many regional findings are corroborated. For example: age is significant, with younger female relatives and household heads more likely to hold GE; married daughters or relatives are less likely to work than single ones; New England provides the best employment opportunities for daughters and relatives; and urban areas indeed show more recorded employment for wives and daughters than do rural areas. Turning to the household level, national data substantiates findings that race is a major determinant of employment for all women; that Irish, German, East European, Russian, and French Canadian daughters have significantly higher GE rates than nonethnic daughters; that working-class families headed by an operative, laborer, or unemployed person increase the GE of both wives and daughters; that single men in a household will depress women's work; and that older daughters will enter GE before their mothers do so.

On the other hand, national-level conclusions do run counter to some local findings. For example: age has a positive, rather than a negative, impact on daughters; illiteracy increases women's gainful employment; rural residence increases female household heads' GE; while wives record more employment in southern regions than in the northern ones useful to their daughters. At the household level, we do not verify the stereotyped differences between ethnic household heads or wives and third-generation American women; we find, counter-intuitively, that boarders are associated with increased women's employment; young children do not depress wives' employment and actually increase daughters' and relatives' paid work; while adolescents (age 10 to 14) do not substitute for wives and are a last resort, employed only after older siblings are also employed or extended family sought out. Many of these differences can be attributed to the narrower geographic or ethnic focus of prior studies. Further, such studies did not usually examine the reciprocal effects of male and female household members on each other, or on subgroups of women.

This is one of the reasons our second goal of building a household resource model is important. Our findings illustrate that household-level variables are among the most significant for all groups of women, and that regional and individual controls do not reduce the impact of household composition on wives or daughters. Two different household-level processes affect women's gainful employment in 1900. First, alternatives are structured by household composition: female household heads are the women most likely to work; while in other households single men are the family's first choice, depressing employment of all women; their next option is daughters (age 15 or over) or other relatives, especially if there are younger children at home; the presence of boarders or employed adolescent women is associated with using all other household resources, including wives' employment. Second, home-based alternatives can reduce the reporting of women's work, particularly with farm self-employment in rural areas, but also in the urban family small businesses, which were less common. Thus, urbanization may have decreased the amount of accessible uncounted work for women. On the whole, the household resources model, controlling for frequently used individual and geographic variables, is a useful one with which to illustrate concretely the integration of work and family life for women at the turn of the century.

Our findings suggest directions for future research. First, differences in household resources used by black, ethnic and third-generation white American households can be explored using separate equations for each group. The importance of race for all women and the significant differences among ethnic daughters indicate the importance of this analysis.

Second, the structural and economic factors which delimit occupations available in a region need to be investigated. We have shown that the rates of boarders' presence vary by degree of urbanization, and that different subgroups of women increased their gainful employment in various regions of the country. We seek to understand whether household strategies also vary when there are more occupations available for wives or household heads, and which industries favor their employment.

Finally, we hope to contrast the predictors of turn-of-the-century women's work with those of 1950 or 1960, when about 60 percent of the population was urban, or with a later period when rates of male self-employment were lower than that reflected by a 1900 farm population. Part of the difference, of course, will be in what is being predicted, since in 1900 gainful employment was defined somewhat differently than is the post-1940 concept of labor force participation. However, if some of this definitional gap can be surmounted, such a contrast could uncover any changed dynamic in the allocation of women's labor over time.

NOTES

The research reported herein was partially supported by grant number 320-7519A. SUNY Research Foundation. The opinions in this paper are the author's and do not necessarily represent those of the Research Foundation. I am grateful to Glenna Spitze, the Women and Work Research Group (especially Roslyn Feldberg, Myra Ferree, Natalie Sokoloff, and Carole Turbin), and anonymous reviewers for their helpful comments.

1. The family wage is one wage (usually that of a married male) which will support a whole family.

2. In some cases a second income may be needed, but not apparent, because of women's unrecorded labor in "cottage" industry. This type of work will be difficult to detect, but may be imputed in research at a later date by incorporating knowledge of specific regional industries.

3. Ironically, when the Census used a better definition in 1910 and encouraged enumerators to "never (take for) granted, without inquiry, that a woman, or child, has no occupation," it later bemoaned the "overcount" for women's work that was produced. This occurred particularly because women who worked regularly at outdoor farm work on family farms for no wages were to be recorded as farm laborers.

4. Although the Census records occupations for those ten and over, this age was chosen in order to make comparisons with Census materials from 1940 to 1960, when the age of recording employment was fourteen. For comparisons with 1980 and a sixteen-year-old cut-off, fifteen- and fourteen-year-old respondents can be dropped from the sample.

REFERENCES

Abbott, Edith
　1910　Women in Industry. Arno Press.
Armstrong, W. A.
　1972　"The use of information about occupation." Pp. 191–310 in E. A. Wrigley (ed.),
　　　　Nineteenth Century Society, London: Cambridge University Press.
Bose, Christine E.
　1980　"Women and productive labor: the U.S. in 1900." Paper presented at the
　　　　Annual Meeting of the National Women's Studies Association, Bloomington,
　　　　Indiana.
Bosworth, Louise Marion
　1911　The Living Wage of Women Workers. New York: Arno Press.
Butler, Elizabeth Beardsley
　1909　Women and the Trades: Pittsburgh, 1907–1908. New York: Charities Publica-
　　　　tion Committee.
Ciancanelli, Penelope
　1981　"Women, commodity production and the census." Paper delivered at the
　　　　Allied Social Science Association Conference, Washington, D. C.
Conk, Margo Anderson
　1981　"Accuracy, efficiency and bias: interpretation of women's work in the U.S.
　　　　Census of Occupations, 1870–1940." Historical Methods 14:65–72.
Cott, Nancy F.
　1977　The Bonds of Womanhood: "Women's Sphere" in New England, 1780–1835.
　　　　New Haven: Yale University Press.
Davies, Margery
　1974　"Women's place is at the typewriter: the feminization of the clerical labor
　　　　force." Radical America 8:1–28.
Ehrlich, Richard L. (ed.)
　1977　Immigrants in Industrial America, 1850–1920. Charlottesville: University
　　　　Press of Virginia.
Glenn, Evelyn Nakano
　1980　"Japanese-American domestic workers." Paper presented an Annual Meeting
　　　　of the American Sociological Association, New York.
Goodman, Leo A.
　1976　"The relationship between modified and usual multiple-regression approaches
　　　　to the analysis of dichotomous variables." In David Heise (ed.), Sociological
　　　　Methodology. San Francisco: Jossey-Bass.
Haber, Sheldon
　1973　"Trends in work rates of white females, 1890 to 1950." Industrial and Labor
　　　　Relations Review 26:1122–34.
Hershberg, Theodore
　1981　Philadelphia: Work Space, Family and Group Experience in the Nineteenth
　　　　Century. New York: Oxford University Press.
Jensen, Joan M.
　1980　"Cloth, butter and boarders: women's household production for the market."
　　　　The Review of Political Economics 12(2):14–24.
Katz, Michael
　1975　The People of Hamilton, Canada West. Cambridge: Harvard University Press.
Katzman, David M.
　1978　Seven Days a Week: Women and Domestic Service. New York: Oxford
　　　　University Press.

Kessler-Harris, Alice
  1982 Out to Work: A History of Wage-Earning Women in the United States. New York: Oxford University Press.
MacLean, Annie Maria
  1900 Wage-Earning Women. New York: Arno Press.
Mason, Karen Oppenheim, and Barbara Laslett
  1983 "Women's work in the American West: Los Angeles, 1880–1900, and its contrast with Essex County, Massachusetts, in 1880." Population Studies Center: University of Michigan.
McLaughlin, Virginia Yans
  1973 "Patterns of work and family organization: Buffalo's Italians." Pp. 136–51 in Michael Gordon (ed.), The American Family in Social Historical Perspective. New York: St. Martin's Press.
Milkman, Ruth
  1976 "Women's work and the economic crisis: some lessons from the Great Depression." The Review of Radical Political Economics 8:73–97.
Modell, John, and Tamara K. Hareven
  1973 "Urbanization and the malleable household: an examination of boarding and lodging in American families." Journal of Marriage and the Family 35: 467–79.
Oppenheimer, Valerie K.
  1982 Work and Family: A Study in Social Demography. New York: Academic Press.
Pleck, Elizabeth H.
  1978 "A mother's wages: income earning among married Italian and black women, 1896–1911." Pp. 490–510 in Michael Gordon (ed.), The American Family in Social-Historical Perspective. Second Edition. New York: St. Martin's Press.
Smuts, Robert W.
  1959 Women and Work in America. New York: Schocken Books.
Sokoloff, Natalie J.
  1980 Between Money and Love: The Dialectics of Women's Home and Market Work. New York: Praeger.
  1982 "The changing nature of women's work, 1940–1980." Paper presented at Annual Meetings of American Sociological Association, San Francisco.
Tentler, Leslie Woodcock
  1979 Wage-Earning Women: Industrial Work and Family Life in the U.S., 1900–1930. New York: Oxford University Press.
Tilly, Louise A., and Joan W. Scott
  1978 Women, Work, and Family. New York: Holt, Rinehart & Winston.
Turbin, Carole
  1979 " 'And we are nothing but women': Irish working women in Troy." Pp. 202–22 in Carol R. Berkin and Mary Beth Norton (eds.), Women of America: A History. Boston: Houghton-Mifflin.
Vanneman, Reeve, and Fred Pampel
  1977 "The American perception of class and status." American Sociological Review 42:422–37.
Weinbaum, Batya and Amy Bridges
  1976 "The other side of the paycheck: monopoly capital and the structure of consumption." Monthly Review 28(3):88–103.
Zunz, Olivier
  1982 The Changing Face of Inequality: Urbanization, Industrial Development, and Immigrants in Detroit, 1880–1920. Chicago: University of Chicago Press.

12. WOMEN IN AGRICULTURE

Counting the Labor Force in Developing Countries

RUTH DIXON-MUELLER

The theme of woman as invisible worker has captured the imagination of a number of critics of standard labor force statistics (e.g., Boserup, 1970, 1975; Youssef, 1977; Perez-Ramirez, 1978; Blumberg, 1979; Fong, 1980a; Palmer and von Buchwald, 1980; UN Secretariat, 1980; Wainerman and Recchini de Lattes, 1981). Not only has domestic labor—a predominantly female activity in all societies—been excluded from censuses and national accounts such as the gross national product (Jain et al., 1979; International Center for Research on Women, 1980; Rogers, 1980), but even women's work in the fields has eluded the collectors of rural labor force statistics. In some countries, female unpaid family helpers in agriculture are systematically excluded, resulting in a consistent undercount of the agricultural labor force and an underestimate of the female proportion. In other countries, women appear and disappear in large numbers from one survey to the next. In 1954, the Algerian census counted 981,000 women agricultural laborers (37 percent of the farm labor force), but in 1966 only 23,000 (2 percent of the total). The census of India counted 49 million women in agriculture in 1961 but only 26 million in 1971, a drop from 36 to 20 percent of the total. And Brazil's 761,000 women in the agricultural labor force in the 1950 census grew to 3 million in a 1976 household survey, up from 7 to 21 percent of the total agricultural labor force.

Problems of definition and procedure plague the collection of labor force statistics in almost all situations, in industrialized and developing countries alike, for young and old, male and female (see, for example, the discussion of the complexities of measuring economic activity and under- and unemployment in UN Department of Economic and Social Affairs, 1967:339–96). Yet women (and children) in farm work are disproportionately undercounted in most population censuses for a number of reasons, some relating to the strict definitions of economic activity proposed in international guidelines (ILO 1976) and some relating to the selective application of these guidelines, as when farm wives and children (especially students) are simply assumed not to be economically active. Since the extent of undercounting is not consistent across countries or even within countries over time, census-based labor force statistics form a

Reprinted from *Population and Development Review* 8, No. 3 (September 1982).

shaky basis for analyzing international trends and variations. The examples just cited suggest that the observed differences are often statistical artifacts rather than real behavioral patterns.

A quite different picture of female labor force participation emerges from rural time-use studies that count the labor contributions of all household members, male and female, adult and child. By measuring the duration, regularity, and intensity of work throughout the year, these surveys describe the flow of productive labor (apart from domestic work) through the days and seasons rather than the stock of workers at one point in time (Fong, 1980b; FAO, 1978). As a consequence, they generally reveal a far higher rate of participation by women and children. In Egypt, for example, where the 1960 census counted women as only 4 percent of the total agricultural labor force, a detailed rural labor record survey indicated that about one-quarter of all nondomestic productive work in farm households was done by women (ILO, 1969:27). An in a sample of eight villages in Sharquiyya Governate considered representative of the diverse cropping regions of the Nile Delta, women performed 44 percent of adult family farm labor and 27 percent of the work of hired hands (calculated from Richards and Martin, 1981: Tables 2, 17).

Although the growing number of time-use surveys offers a wealth of information on household patterns of labor allocation within particular communities and farming systems, most cannot be generalized to larger populations. At the aggregate level, then, we are left with large-scale national censuses or surveys of often dubious repute. Even here, however, it is possible to compare the results of different approaches to counting the stock of workers. For example, the effects of changes in definition or practice from one census or survey to the next can be assessed quite readily for some countries. Counts from national population censuses and labor force surveys can also be compared with estimates from the International Labour Office that attempt to standardize labor force series in each country for changes in data collection methods over time. And, in turn, estimates from the ILO can be compared with counts obtained for a number of countries from a quite different source—the censuses of agricultural holdings coordinated by the Food and Agriculture Organization of the United Nations. Finally, the ILO-FAO comparisons form a basis for deriving new estimates of the sex composition of the farm labor force for all countries, reflecting the contrast between the generally more restrictive ILO approach and the more inclusive approach of the FAO.

Conceptual Problems in Counting Agricultural Workers

Concepts and methods of reckoning labor force participation based on contemporary Western experience have proven inadequate when applied to developing countries, where workers are more likely than their Western counterparts to be self-employed rather than wage earners, to work seasonally rather than year-round, to be underemployed rather than formally unemployed, and to engage in a fluid or sporadic pattern of diverse and shifting economic activities (Durand, 1975; Standing, 1977; Mueller, 1978; Blacker, 1978, 1980). Moreover, the boundary between domestic production for the household's own consumption and economic activity for sale or exchange is less clearly drawn in developing countries, especially in rural areas, and especially among women (Boserup, 1975; Boulding, 1976; Fong, 1980a).

These difficulties are compounded in the agricultural sector, where subsistence farmers may sell very little of their produce, where unpaid labor on their own land alternates with wage or exchange labor on another's, where children may regularly tend animals and women grow foodstuffs in their kitchen gardens or process crops in their compounds but not work in the fields, and where trade or small crafts are added to agricultural work in a seasonal mix of household activities. Indeed, the conceptual distinctions between persons who are economically active and inactive, and between agricultural and non-agricultural occupations, can become hopelessly blurred, particularly in the case of women (and children). Efforts to sharpen the distinctions by enforcing a strict (i.e., more Western) definition of labor force participation inevitably result in a poor description of economic activity in the agricultural sector.

Consider, for example, this day in the life of Soherey Devi, a Bihari woman of northern India:

> First . . . I must wash the pots and sweep. Then I go to collect word and cow dung for fuel and grass for the bullock. If there is food I cook a mid-day meal. . . . In the afternoon I must go again to collect grass for the bullocks, and then if there is food I prepare the evening meal. If I am needed I work in the fields too. I must plant the paddy, spread the fertilizer, turn over the earth around the maize, and help in the harvest. (Stokes, 1975:219)

Would Soherey Devi be counted as a member of the agricultural labor force? This depends, among other considerations, on the particular definition of economic activity used, on whether she is asked about her secondary as well as primary occupation, on the timing of the survey during the agricultural cycle and the length of the reference period, and on whether the interviewer actually asks her about what she does rather than assuming that she is "just a housewife."

What Is Economic Activity?

According to the United Nations, economically active persons are "all the persons of either sex who furnish the supply of labor for the production of goods and services during the time-reference period chosen for the investigation" (Blacker, 1978:47).[1] Planting, cultivation, and harvesting in anticipation of profit, preparation of products for sale, care of livestock, and repair of farm equipment are included; excluded are "household duties such as the preparation of food and the care of chickens and other livestock which are used for consumption instead of for exchange" (Boulding, 1976:318).

Despite UN recommendations, the definition of economic activity varies greatly from country to country; and it is in the classification of female work that the application of various standards seems most capricious. Countries such as Turkey and Thailand count almost all farm women as unpaid family helpers, resulting in an enumerated agricultural labor force that is half female. But if unpaid workers are excluded, women are reported as only 5 percent of Turkish farm labor and about 20 percent in Thailand. Other countries apply the definition of economic activity selectively so that female (but not male) unpaid family helpers are excluded. This practice explains the wide fluctuations in the reported female labor force in three North African countries. The 1966 census of Tunisia, specifically excluding 250,000 female family helpers, reported a farm labor force that was only 2 percent female. Added back in, women become 38 percent of the total in 1966, the same proportion as was reported in the 1956 census. Similar observations can be made for Algeria and Morocco.

Between these two extremes, whether women in farm families are defined as economically active or inactive depends in part on a necessarily arbitrary decision as to where the household ends and the farm begins, in spatial terms, or where housework ends and production begins, in economic terms. How, for example, does one classify such borderline activities as collecting water and fuel, tending kitchen gardens, processing and storing crops, or feeding chickens? (In one effort at clarification, a Fiji survey specified that tending more than ten chickens was an economic activity, but fewer was housework [see Blacker, 1978:48].) Why, critics ask, should the production of raw foodstuffs be regarded as economic activity while their preparation and cooking, which is necessary for their consumption, is not?

> Let us take, for example, the chain of processes leading to the production of a loaf of bread: the harvesting of the wheat, the threshing and winnowing of the grain, the milling or pounding of the grain into flour, the kneading of the flour into dough, and the baking of the dough into bread. Where, it may be asked, in this series of action does economic activity begin and end? I suggest that in practice the answer is determined not by the intrinsic nature of the operation but by the point at which it is performed by "housewives"—i.e., by female unpaid family workers. (Blacker 1980:72)

One solution to the dilemma created by the artificial statistical dichotomy imposed upon a natural continuum would be to classify as economic production all household work such as cooking, sewing, and child care, recognizing its function of reproducing the labor force and of substituting for goods and services that might otherwise be purchased (e.g., prepared foods, ready-made clothing, hiring housekeepers). Although this solution would satisfy those who wish to see the value of women's domestic production recognized in national accounts statistics, recourse to it would guarantee that virtually all able-bodied women (and men and most children above a certain age) would be economically active, with little if any variation over time and space. Important information would be lost about the responsiveness of female economic activity patterns in agriculture to economic and social change in each society. At the other extreme, one could include in the economically active population only those who actually earn money on a daily, weekly, monthly, or lump sum basis (Blacker, 1978) or even only those who are full-time wage and salary earners in "modern type occupations" (Boserup, 1975:87–88). Census practices fall between these two poles, however, continuing to rely on arbitrary distinctions between activities in the middle range. Where the line is drawn in each case is a crucial determinant of the statistical outcome.

Minimum Hours of Work

A second key distinction in the definition of economic activity is the number of hours a person must work. The ILO recommends that unpaid family workers assisting in the operation of a business or farm be considered as employed only if they worked at least one-third of the normal working time during the specified reference period. No minimum is set for those who generate cash earnings, however: "As long as money is involved, the person is always classified as employed" (UN, 1958:25).

If women are excluded in the first round on the grounds that their work does not constitute economic activity, then it may be irrelevant how many hours they actually put in. According to the 1960 census of Egypt, for example, 31 percent of the total rural population was in the labor force. When a more detailed ILO study added those wives and children whom the census had classified as inactive but who had worked at least one-third of normal working hours, the overall economic activity rate rose to 42 percent—a substantial alteration (ILO, 1969:32–33).

Primary and Secondary Occupations

Of 145 censuses conducted between 1955 and 1964 that collected occupational information, only 27 asked for the respondent's secondary occupation (UN, 1974:80).[2] Yet if such a question is asked, the results can be greatly affected. In Sudan, for example, the age-standardized labor force participation rate for women in 1956 was less than 10 percent when only primary occupations were included, but 40 percent with secondary occupations (Durand, 1975:53). And in India the female labor force in agriculture was cut in half—from 49 to 26 million—between the 1961 census, which defined as economically active anyone who engaged in nondomestic work for even one hour a day, and the 1971 census, which excluded all those for whom work was not the *main* activity (Jain et al., 1979:142).

What do respondents choose to report as their main occupation? This depends on a number of factors such as season and time-reference period, the order in which questions are asked, and the perceptions of enumerators and respondents regarding appropriate roles for women and men. The essence of the problem is that census takers, male respondents, and even women themselves often view a wide range of activities other than domestic labor as housework. In Chile, Garrett (1976:35) noted that "even if the wife herself works on the lands to which the family has access, she may or may not regard this as agricultural work. We were struck in interviewing women on large estates by the number of women who defined even planting and harvesting as homemaking rather than agricultural work."

Women's self-perceptions are not the only obstacle, however; Youssef believes that underenumeration of women in agriculture—at least in Muslim countries—is due largely to the reluctance of male farmers to report that their wives and daughters work outside the home (Youssef, 1977; see also ILO, 1969:27). This would probably be true of higher caste groups in South Asia as well, and perhaps in many Latin American settings, where social status considerations discourage the involvement of women in work outside the home.

Census interviewers may also choose to ignore women's work, or may be instructed to do so for some age categories. Standing (1977:29) reports that in some labor force surveys and censuses, women living on farms are classified as economically inactive merely on the basis of their sex and relationship to other household members, without regard to their actual activities. Instructions can be quite specific: enumerators in the 1966 Algerian census were apparently told to disregard field work or cottage industry in recording women's economic activities if they were secondary to their role as housewife (Blacker, 1978:49). "Unless enumerators are explicitly instructed to ask about the possible economic activity of women in the household in the same way as about that of men, they may tend automatically to enter women as homemakers, particularly if the women are married . . ." (Blacker, 1980:71–72). Similar problems occur in the enumeration of young persons of both sexes who attend school and thus may be assumed to do little if any agricultural work.

More revealing responses are elicited if interviewers begin the questioning about main occupations with a list of possible activities rather than probing after the initial response, or not probing at all (Wainerman and Recchini de Lattes, 1981).[3] Deere (1982) points out that "if the first question asked in a census questionnaire is that of the person's principal occupation, Latin American peasant women uniformly reply 'their home.' . . . In contrast, if a questionnaire begins with a description of the activities in which the person engages for remuneration or which contribute to family income, the response is quite different."[4]

Clearly, accuracy is not enhanced by highlighting truly marginal activities, but a statement to the respondent that clarifies the types of work included in a definition of economic activity—such as planting or harvesting the crops— would help to produce more reliable results.

Time Reference Periods and Seasonal Fluctuations

Whereas the gainful worker approach to economic activity inquires about a person's normal occupation, with a reference period extending up to one year, the more common labor force approach stresses current activity in a specified brief period such as the day or week preceding the interview (ILO 1976; Standing, 1978; FAO, 1978).[5] The ILO (1976) recommends that the time-reference period not be longer than one week except "where it is considered that classification on the basis of current activity over this brief time period does not reflect year-round activities, particularly where there is a highly seasonal pattern of employment . . ." Freedman and Mueller (1977:27) recommend a one-year reference period for the rural labor force because agricultural incomes and expenditures are usually reckoned on this basis. Fong (1980a:30) recommends both approaches: "the gainful worker approach to 'catch' regular, including seasonal activities, and the labor force approach to record the entire span of activities, regardless of their frequency, of the preceding week" (see also FAO, 1978). Again, the differences can be significant: in Peru the 1940 census counted women as 31 percent of the agricultural labor force when the question was based on "usual" occupation, but as only 14 percent of the total when the question was based on "present" occupation in a specified week, which probably excluded a large number of seasonal workers (Durand, 1975:241).

In many countries up to twice as many persons may work during planting or harvesting as in the slack season (FAO, 1971:208). If a long reference period is specified, then this seasonal work—for which women and children form a reserve labor pool—is likely to be reported. If a short reference period is specified, their contributions will count only if the census is taken during the busy season.

Child Labor

International guidelines set the age of eligibility for the economically active population at 15 years, although countries may set lower limits where children are commonly employed. In 25 of 40 countries for which comparisons of the sex composition of the agricultural labor force are possible by age, females form a significantly higher proportion of child labor than of adult labor. In 14 countries the sex ratios are similar for both age groups, and in only one is the child labor force disproportionately male. The comparative femaleness of child labor is especially marked in North Africa and the Middle East. In Algeria in 1966, females were only 1 percent of the adult agricultural labor force but 19 percent of child labor; in Syria in 1960 the corresponding figures were 8 and 28 percent; in Morocco in 1960, 8 and 23 percent; in Libya in 1964, 1 and 12 percent. In Egypt, where the proportion of boys under 15 who were economically active declined slightly between 1937 and 1960 from 12 to 10 percent, the proportion of girls who were counted as economically active increased from 12 to 36 percent (Nagi, 1972:624). Nagi observes that ". . . it is a common practice among rural families to put girls to work on their farms or as paid seasonal workers to substitute for boys who go to school" (1972:623).

The extent to which reducing the age limit to include children not only enlarges the total labor force but also alters its sex ratio depends in part on the differential sex ratios reported above and in part on the relative numerical importance of child labor per se (see Rodgers and Standing, 1981). Again, young girls apparently perform a remarkably high share of all female farm labor in North Africa and the Middle East: 30 percent on the average for eight countries, but as high as 52 percent in Egypt and 58 percent in Algeria (Youssef, 1977; El Shafei, 1960:348). In sub-Saharan Africa, Asia, and Latin

America, however, boys under 14 or 15 form about 7 to 8 percent of the total male agricultural labor force on the average; for girls the corresponding figure is about 10 to 12 percent. In these cases, the proportions of child workers are too small to alter the overall sex composition of the labor force, even when the children are disproportionately female.

It is clear that differences of concept and method—some of which are outlined above—can play havoc with the comparability of agricultural labor force statistics across countries and over time. In the next section we compare data derived from population censuses and labor force surveys with estimates, prepared by the ILO, that attempt to minimize inter- and intracountry discrepancies. We will argue that in its efforts to put forth a standardized model, the ILO has incorporated and perpetuated one of the major biases responsible for the undercounting of women in the agricultural labor force in a number of countries of the developing world—namely, the exclusion of most unpaid female family workers from that category.

Estimates by the International Labour Office

In 1977 the ILO published a second edition of *Labour Force Estimates and Projections, 1950–2000* with revised figures for 1950, 1960, and 1970, bringing national labor force statistics into conformity with standard concepts of economic activity and adjusting for changes in definition over time. The size and occupational structure of the labor force, as well as economic activity rates by age and sex, are estimated for over 100 developing countries, including many with inadequate census data (e.g., in sub-Saharan Africa).[6] Time series within countries were standardized, where necessary, in the following ways:

1. "Where countries shifted from the 'usual activity' approach to the 'current activity' approach, from one census or survey to the next, the statistics corresponding to the 'current activity' approach were generally used" (ILO, 1977, vol. 6:6). No countries shifted in the other direction.
2. Discrepancies in counts of unpaid family workers, generally affecting only women, were adjusted "by analogy with the predominant pattern in other countries of the region that had similar levels of development" (1977, vol. 6:7). In the Muslim societies of North Africa and the Middle East, where unpaid female family helpers were most likely to be underrecorded in censuses, the ILO did not alter the original figures because "good statistical information on which to build a reasonable model to produce estimates . . . was lacking" (1977, vol. 6:11)
3. Changes over time in the reference period or in the season of the year were adjusted to obtain a comprehensive estimate of labor force participation throughout the year that takes into account seasonal fluctuations.
4. The lower age limit was standardized at ten years for those developing countries in which a sizable proportion of youth under 15 years work in agriculture.

For 66 countries in which direct comparisons are possible, we find, first, that the ILO estimates of the total agricultural labor force are almost always higher than the population censuses or surveys—substantially so in eight of every ten countries, about the same in one of ten, and somewhat lower in the rest.[7]

Second, the discrepancies in the totals are larger for the male than the female labor force. The summary in Table 1 reveals that labor force participation rates for men based on the ILO estimates average 42.1 percent across 66 countries (unweighted), compared with 37.2 percent based on censuses. For women, the corresponding figures are 15.4 and 14.1 percent. Averages of ILO rates for men are substantially higher than census rates in all five regions, whereas ILO rates for women are substantially higher only in Asia. The coefficient of relative variation (CRV) within and across regions is generally lower for the ILO figures, as one would expect if the standardization procedure is ironing out unusual fluctuations due to definitional changes, although the female rates in North Africa and the Middle East and in the Caribbean are an exception.

Third, ILO estimates show a slightly lower percentage of females within the agricultural labor force than do censuses or surveys—an average of 20.6 percent compared with 21.3 percent for the 66 countries.[8] Among regions, only in Asia is the ILO average estimate higher than the corresponding figure based on censuses and surveys.

The ILO estimates are helpful in providing time series data for countries where censuses and surveys are unreliable or lacking, and in eliminating some of the more unpredictable fluctuations due primarily to differences of definition or practice between one survey and the next. But standardization techniques emphasizing the "current" over "usual" activity approach where practices changed, in some cases drastically minimizing the numbers of unpaid family helpers reported, leave significant biases in the reported sex composition of the agricultural labor force. The figures are marred by the arbitrary exclusion of women who labor without pay on their family holdings. New estimates produced by the ILO in 1986 have attempted to correct some of these biases for certain African countries (ILO, 1986), but they have by no means been eliminated.

Fortunately, we can turn to other sources of evidence for some idea of the possible extent of this undercounting. Although detailed rural household surveys are usually limited to relatively small geographical areas, agricultural censuses conducted under the auspices of the Food and Agriculture Organization of the UN generally claim to be nationally representative. Available for a smaller number of countries and frequently limited to a single agricultural census, these enumerations differ from population censuses and labor force surveys both in their coverage and in their approach to defining labor force participation. As the comparisons will make clear, agricultural surveys typically classify a far larger number of women as part of the labor force than do the more conventional sources.

Table 1 Comparison of population censuses and ILO estimates of the sex composition of the agricultural labor force, and of male and female activity rates, 66 countries, most recent dates

Region	Number of countries		Females as percent of agricultural labor force		Activity rates age 10+			
					Males		Females	
			Census	ILO	Census	ILO	Census	ILO
Sub-Saharan Africa	17	Mean	34.5	33.5	50.2	56.7	29.9	30.8
		CRV	.49	.44	.31	.29	.73	.65
North Africa, Middle East	12	Mean	17.7	13.2	26.5	33.9	7.3	7.8
		CRV	.93	1.27	.39	.34	1.70	1.90
South, Southeast Asia	11	Mean	28.6	32.6	46.7	49.7	21.2	27.2
		CRV	.53	.37	.36	.29	.79	.63
Central, South America	19	Mean	5.6	4.5	31.7	36.8	2.0	1.8
		CRV	.71	.55	.34	.37	.82	.65
Caribbean	7	Mean	27.0	26.3	23.6	25.9	9.3	10.0
		CRV	.33	.43	.73	.73	1.18	1.34
Total	66	Mean	21.3	20.6	37.2	42.1	14.1	15.4
		CRV	.81	.84	.46	.43	1.28	1.22

NOTE: The coefficient of relative variation, CRV, is the size of the standard deviation expressed as a proportion of the mean, for all countries within the region.

Censuses of Agricultural Holdings

Ninety-three industrialized and developing countries participated in FAO's 1970 round of decennial agricultural censuses,[9] although not all of them included (or tabulated) questions on the labor force. Intended primarily for the collection of data on crop and livestock production, the census has as its unit of analysis the *agricultural holding*, not the household or the individual worker. "A holding, for census purposes, is all land which is used wholly or partly for agricultural production and is operated by one person (the holder), alone or with the assistance of others, without regard to title, size, or location" (FAO, 1971:13). Livestock kept for agricultural purposes without land is considered as a holding, but establishments engaged in the production of only forest products, fish, or wild game are not (FAO, 1977:19).[10]

Usually a minimum land area is specified for a holding, although the criterion varies considerably between countries. For livestock holdings without land, minimum requirements can include some rather colorful specifications, as in Chile: "10 beehives, [or] 1 adult animal (horse, cattle, mule), 2 young animals (horses or cattle), 5 sheep, goats, pigs, or auchenia; 25 geese, turkeys or rabbits; 100 cocks, hens or pullets" (FAO, 1971:20).

Interviewers inquire about the number of persons engaged in agricultural activities on the holding during a specified period preceding the interview, preferably one week.[11] Agricultural work includes "feeding and caring for livestock and poultry; working in the field; working in the market or kitchen gardens; planning farm work; supervising other agricultural workers, keeping farm records, taking farm products to market; bringing feed, fertilizer or other supplies from town to the holding; repairing fences, farm equipment, machinery, etc." (FAO, 1977:45). It excludes construction work by hired contractors, home repairs, handicraft production, and domestic household work.

A person who performed any agricultural work during the specified period, regardless of the time involved, is usually counted as a worker in the holding.[12] The holder is always counted, whether or not he or she actually performed any work. Male and female workers are then classified into three groups: holders and members of their household not paid full cash wages; permanent hired workers receiving pay for their services and employed regularly on the holding (usually a minimum of half of the regular agricultural season); and temporary and occasional hired workers employed less than half the working year for wages or a share of the crop (or in some cases as exchange workers or receiving meals only).[13]

Clearly, the FAO procedures are also problematic in ways that threaten the accuracy and comparability of their findings. Since the unit of analysis is the agricultural holding, landless households from which a substantial portion of the farm labor force is recruited are excluded from direct enumeration. If the survey is conducted during the peak planting or harvest season, however, then landless workers who are laboring on enumerated holdings during the one-week reference period will be counted, as will household members whose major labor contributions occur during this period (e.g., women, children, the aged). There is some possibility of doublecounting of temporary or occasional workers who move from one holding to another during the time-reference period, or of holders or members of their households who work on someone else's land as well as their own, especially if the reference period extends beyond one week (FAO, 1971:208; Pollitt, 1977).

An additional problem of comparability arises from the incompleteness of some of the agricultural censuses. In some countries the labor force is not counted at all, or the census is restricted to certain categories of workers (e.g., members of the holder's household only in Senegal, 1960, and Turkey, 1962–63). In others, some categories of workers are not classified by sex (e.g., permanent hired workers in the Republic of Korea, 1960, Pakistan, 1971–73) or are reported only as total "man-days" of labor in the past week. Finally, although limiting the agricultural census to the traditional sector in the Congo, Central African Republic, and Cameroon in the 1972–73 rounds may not substantially affect the resulting female proportions in the labor force, there is likely to be significant bias in the restriction of the census to European holdings in Namibia, South Africa, and Kenya in the 1960 rounds.

In general, however, the labor force concept used in the agricultural census is more inclusive than that used in population censuses in at least six important respects: subsistence production is counted as economic activity; unpaid family helpers are routinely included; minimum hours of work are not specified; all agricultural work (whether primary or secondary to some other activity) is recorded; the survey is usually taken in the peak season; and the definition of agricultural work includes kitchen gardening, raising poultry, and transporting crops to market. These differences would certainly lead us to expect higher numbers, especially of women, in the agricultural surveys.

Indeed, comparisons drawn from 32 countries with both ILO population estimates and FAO censuses of agriculture for comparable dates reveal, first, that agricultural censuses identify a larger agricultural labor force than the ILO estimates in two-thirds of the countries.[14] This is so in some cases even where the FAO census was restricted to certain subsectors of agriculture—for example, European holdings only in Namibia, traditional farms only in the Congo and Cameroon. The major exceptions are Kenya, where European holdings constitute only a small fraction of all farms; Malaysia; and Turkey, where the population censuses have traditionally included most farm women and the FAO has excluded hired laborers. Overall, the ratio of the agricultural labor force as reckoned by the FAO and by ILO averages 1.27 to 1 across 35 possible comparisons (excluding Kenya, and including two observations each for four countries).

Second, the additional workers are disproportionately female.[15] The agricultural surveys counted more women workers than the ILO estimates in 26 of the 32 countries listed, even in some cases in which the total counts are lower—for example, in the Central African Republic, South Africa, Saudi Arabia, Argentina, and El Salvador. Again, Kenya and Turkey are important exceptions. Although the ratio of FAO to ILO counts of men in the agricultural labor force across countries is 1.01 to 1, suggesting that the two approaches make little difference on the average, the corresponding ratio for females is a remarkable 5.46 to 1.[16] That is, the agricultural censuses on the average include in the labor force the same number of men as do the ILO estimates, but more than five times as many women. The ratios for females are much higher than the average in some countries: nine to one in Jordan, 25 to one in the Dominican Republic, and 45 to one in Iraq.

The ILO-FAO differences are reflected in the agricultural activity rates for the total population of men and women aged 10 and over (Table 2).[17] The average FAO rate for men is slightly lower than the ILO rate—42.9 versus 45.1 percent across 32 countries—although the FAO estimates are higher in Asia, Latin America, and the Caribbean. By contrast, the higher average FAO rate for women—27.6 versus 19.7 percent overall—characterizes all regions, most notably Asia and the Caribbean.

It follows that the FAO agricultural censuses almost all report higher female shares of the agricultural labor force—35.6 versus 21.8 percent for the 32 countries. The shift is characteristic of all regions but is most pronounced in those areas where the ILO estimates are most conservative, that is, in North Africa and the Middle East (where the FAO's female share is twice as high as those given by the ILO) and in Latin American (where the share is three times as high).

Although not shown in Table 2, contrasts between the two data sources for individual countries illuminate the artificial nature of the low reported levels of female participation in farm work in some countries. According to FAO's figures, in Iraq, for example, women become 41 rather than 2 percent of the labor force; in Jordan 36 versus 4 percent; in Saudi Arabia 26 versus 6 percent; in Egypt 20 versus 6 percent. Similarly in Brazil, women make up 32 instead of 9 percent of the agricultural labor force, in Paraguay 25 versus 9 percent, and so on throughout Latin America. (El Salvador appears to be an exception.) If the FAO figures are adopted, not only do the average female proportions in the agricultural labor force increase from 22 to 36 percent in the 32 comparison countries, but the coefficient of variation declines from .82 to .44. With a more inclusive definition of labor force participation, differences within and between regions in the sex composition of the agricultural labor force become less pronounced.

New Estimates of the Female Share in the Agricultural Labor Force

The comparison of FAO and ILO results for individual countries offers a basis for making new estimates of the female proportions in the agricultural labor force for countries that did not conduct FAO-type farm surveys or tabulate data on farm employment in their agricultural censuses. New estimates of agricultural activity rates could also be devised, although these are not proposed here. The statistical regression techniques for making the new estimates, along with

Table 2 Comparison of FAO censuses of agriculture and ILO estimates of the sex composition of the agricultural labor force, and of male and female activity rates, 32 countries, most recent dates

Region		Number of countries	Females as percent of agricultural labor force		Activity rates age 10+			
					Males		Females	
			ILO	FAO	ILO	FAO	ILO	FAO
Sub-Saharan Africa	Mean	11	38.8	47.2	59.1	48.6	41.4	49.0
	CRV		.32	.25	.30	.48	.52	.56
North Africa, Middle East	Mean	6	12.2	25.2	42.7	38.0	11.0	11.5
	CRV		1.48	.50	.27	.45	2.01	.73
South, Southeast Asia	Mean	5	26.4	40.2	39.6	42.8	15.4	28.6
	CRV		.40	.20	.14	.34	.42	.22
Central, South America	Mean	8	5.6	19.0	37.5	39.8	2.1	9.9
	CRV		.55	.42	.44	.62	.76	.88
Caribbean	Mean	2	31.5	54.0	20.0	28.0	7.5	27.0
	CRV		.47	.03	.07	.40	.47	.21
Total	Mean	32	21.8	35.6	45.1	42.9	19.7	27.6
	CRV		.82	.44	.39	.48	1.15	.86

the results for individual countries, are described in an earlier paper (Dixon, 1982:556–59). The ILO estimates for 101 developing countries were adjusted according to a formula developed on the basis of the ILO-FAO comparisons for a smaller number of countries included in Table 2. Most relevant here are the overall results by world region as summarized in Table 3.

For all 101 countries combined, the proportion of women in the agricultural labor force increases from 26 to 37 percent, and the variation around the mean is substantially reduced. As expected, the discrepancy between the two sets of figures is least where the ILO estimates are originally the highest: in sub-Saharan Africa (35.8 versus 45.6 percent) and in Asia (35.5 versus 45.3 percent). The gap is widest in North Africa and the Middle East (11.5 percent female versus 28.8 percent).

Although the new estimates are only approximate, many fall quite close to figures obtained from population censuses that the ILO ignored because they were unusually high in comparison with other sources in the same country or in "culturally equivalent" neighboring countries. (On the other hand, several of the revised figures may overestimate female labor force participation in those countries where the ILO chose the more liberal "deviant year" as a basis for its estimates, as in India, Bangladesh, Pakistan, and Nepal.) In Sudan, where the ILO estimated only 9 percent female in the agricultural labor force, the revised estimate of 30 percent tallies with the 1956 census figure of 27 percent that was presumably obtained with a more inclusive definition of economic activity. (Recall that the ILO chose a conservative standard for including female family helpers in North Africa.) Similarly, there is evidence that women have been counted as at least one-third of the agricultural labor force in at least one population or farm census in much of North Africa and the Middle East (Morocco, Algeria, Tunisia, Turkey, Cyprus, Syria, Jordan, Iraq) and in Pakistan, and as at least two-fifths in Egypt and Saudi Arabia—figures quite unlike those in the generally low estimates of the ILO. For example, whereas the ILO estimated only 2 percent female in the agricultural labor force in Iraq in 1970, the 1977 population census reports 37 percent female and the FAO agricultural census of 1971 reports 41 percent. The new estimates alter substantially our image of the sexual division of labor in agriculture in these Muslim countries.

Conclusions

Probing and correcting for the selective undercounting of women's (and children's) participation in agricultural activities are of obvious statistical interest. Understanding the extent of such undercounting also has implications for development planning and theory. Sex-related biases in labor force statistics may lead planners wrongly to assume that women's economic contributions to subsistence or cash crop production, processing, and marketing are negligible, resulting in the exclusion of women from access to crucial production inputs such as technical assistance in crop raising or animal husbandry, agricultural credit, training in farm equipment operation, and other resources—with oft-

Table 3 Females as percent of the agricultural labor force according to ILO estimates, FAO censuses of agriculture, and revised estimates, by region, 1970

Region	Comparison countries							All countries					
	Number of countries	ILO est.		FAO census		Revised est.		Number of countries	ILO est.		Revised est.	
		Mean	CRV	Mean	CRV	Mean	CRV		Mean	CRV	Mean	CRV
Sub-Saharan Africa	11	38.8	.32	47.2	.25	47.3	.16	41	35.8	.39	45.6	.21
North Africa, Middle East	5	4.5	.37	27.0	.43	26.7	.04	15	11.5	1.31	28.8	.36
South, Southeast Asia	5	26.4	.40	40.2	.20	39.9	.16	19	35.5	.33	45.3	.18
Central, South America	8	5.6	.55	19.0	.42	18.6	.17	19	4.6	.56	17.8	.14
Caribbean	2	—	—	—	—	—	—	7	26.0	.44	38.8	.21
Total	31	22.6	.80	36.5	.43	35.8	.40	101	25.6	.70	37.3	.37 + 11.7

cited negative effects on women and on overall productivity (Palmer, 1979; Dixon, 1980; Rogers, 1980). Similarly, distorted statistics can impede efforts to analyze the theoretical bases of the sexual division of labor at the household, community, and national level, and to understand the structural and cultural determinants of trends and variations in patterns of labor allocation.

Of the three major sources of agricultural labor force data reviewed in this paper, the population censuses (including labor force surveys and official estimates) generally yield the lowest female proportions in the agricultural labor force, whereas the censuses of agriculture conducted under the sponsorship of FAO yield the highest proportions. As unpaid family helpers and seasonal workers become progressively incorporated into definitions of the labor force, the sex composition changes. More specifically, contrasts between sources confirm that the total farm labor force is generally larger, and women (and children) form a higher proportion of the total, when the definition of economic activity includes:

— farm production for subsistence only, as well as production intended in whole or in part for sale or exchange;
— unpaid work by family helpers;
— homestead-based crop processing, preparation of crops for storage, transport to markets, raising small animals and poultry, and cultivating kitchen gardens, in addition to field-based production and processing activities.

The female proportion is also generally higher when:

— a low minimum number of days or hours of work is specified as a criterion for inclusion in the labor force;
— a longer reference period is defined during which economic activity is to be assessed, for example, during the preceding cropping season or year rather than the preceding day or week;
— the survey is conducted during the peak season of agricultural activity, especially if the reference period is brief;
— respondents are asked for a secondary activity or occupation as well as a main activity, and a usual activity as well as a current one;
— the interviewer probes the specific activities, based on knowledge of the crops and animals raised, rather than accepting without question the woman's definition of herself as housewife, or her possible assumption that farm work refers only to wage-earning employment;
— the interviewer questions women in the household directly rather than asking male household members to report on women's activities; and
— the work of children between the ages of 10 and 15 is routinely included.

The new estimates of the female proportions within the agricultural labor force proposed in this paper, while raising the overall levels of women's participation and reducing considerably the variation across and within regions, reveal that important differences remain even when the general and country-specific undercounting of women has been taken into account. In regions characterized by high female proportions in the agricultural labor force, revised estimates for sub-Saharan Africa range widely from 26 percent in Guinea-Bissau to 58 percent in Botswana, around a regional average of 46 percent, and in Asia from 31 percent in Pakistan to 57 percent in North Korea, around a regional average of 45 percent. Moving into the more male-dominated systems, North Africa and the Middle East averages 31 percent female in the agricultural labor force, ranging from 25 percent in Iraq to 52 percent in Cyprus and Turkey. Important variations occur within each country, too, although that situation is not considered here.

What remains for future research is to analyze the major determinants of these inter- and intraregional differences. Can they be explained by purely structural factors such as variations in the average size or distribution of landholdings, the level of agricultural technology, or the availability of urban jobs? Or must one also turn to cultural factors such as attitudes toward women's roles or norms of female seclusion to explain such differences? The conventional sources discussed in this paper provide only initial help in answering such questions. More complete analysis will require the combination of these aggregate data with more detailed rural time-use surveys and intensive ethnographic studies of the sexual division of labor in agriculture in a variety of settings.

NOTES

This research was supported by grants from the Ford Foundation and the Social Science Research Council as part of a larger investigation of the role of women in Third World agriculture. I am indebted in Marco Orru for his assistance in compiling the labor force data, and to Marco Orru and Christine Fry for their helpful comments on an earlier draft.

1. Recchini de Lattes and Wainerman (1981:4) propose a modification of this definition to read "all persons of either sex who furnish or want to furnish the supply of labor for the production of goods and services during a specified minimal proportion of the time-reference period. . . ." In this paper the special problems of counting the unemployed are not considered, however.

2. Seventy-seven asked "principal or main occupation," 57 asked "present occupation," and 12 asked "usual or normal occupation."

3. This is rarely done in censuses, however. In Latin America, for example, most ask only one question, usually of the form, "What did you do during the previous week?" followed by the choices "at work," "unemployed," and "inactive." Only those who answered affirmatively to the first option are then asked about specific occupations (Recchini de Lattes and Wainerman, 1981:7–8).

4. Fong (1980b) has designed a questionnaire module for the agricultural labor force that begins, "In the past seven days, did you spend any time doing work that produced an income for yourself or for the household in the form of money, food, or other benefits?" It then goes on to ask about work with specific crops and animals. However,

this suggestion is unrealistic for standard census formats not only because of the obvious cost constraints but also because it requires detailed knowledge of local cropping patterns. For other questionnaire modules see Freedman and Mueller (1977); FAO (1978, 1981); and Anker (1980).

5. Of 147 censuses conducted from 1955 to 1964 with information on economic activity, only 102 specified a time reference: the census date in 36 cases, the week prior to the census in 23; the preceding month in 4; the preceding year in 31; and other periods in 8 (UN, 1974:70). The short periods were more typical of Europe, the longer periods of the developing countries.

6. For an analysis of the statistical problems related to women's economic activity in the earlier ILO estimates for 1950 and 1960, see Boserup (1975).

7. Comparisons are limited to developing countries with a labor force of over 100,000 persons and at least 10 percent of the total labor force in agriculture. Population census and survey figures are drawn from ILO, *Yearbook of Labour Statistics, 1960*, Table 4: *1965*, Tables 2A, 2B; and *1970 to 1980*, Tables 2A, 2B. ILO estimates of the number of men and women in the agricultural labor force are drawn from ILO (1977), vols. 1–6, Table 3. Activity rates of males and females ages 10 years and over were calculated with numerators from the above sources, and denominators interpolated or extrapolated to the relevent year from ILO (1977), vols. 1–6, Table 2. A table including these figures, and the FAO figures discussed in the next section, is available on request from the author, Department of Sociology, University of California, Davis, CA 95616.

8. The same observation can be made when all 146 possible comparisons between ILO estimates and population censuses are drawn, that is, using all corresponding dates for each country rather than the most recent date only.

9. Including 21 in Europe, 25 in Latin America and the Caribbean, 7 in the Near East, 10 in the Far East, 22 in Africa, 6 in Oceania, plus the United States and Canada.

10. Argentina, Brazil, Costa Rica, Mexico, and South Africa included forestry operations in their 1970 rounds.

11. Some countries in both the 1960 and 1970 rounds established a time reference of one day, one month, an agricultural season, or even one full year (FAO, 1971:207).

12. Some countries did set a minimum number of hours, however. Argentina's 1969 census of agriculture included all holders regardless of the time worked daily on the holding, but counted unpaid members of the holder's family only if they worked at least one-third of the normal time.

13. Temporary workers work less than half but at least one-third of the normal time; occasional workers work less than one-third. Reported separately in the 1960 and 1970 rounds of farm censuses, these categories are combined in the 1980 rounds.

14. Labor force figures for the censuses of agriculture are drawn from FAO (1971:210–11) and FAO, *Report on the 1970 World Census of Agriculture*, with activity rates calculated as described in note 7.

15. These additional women workers are found primarily among unpaid family helpers, those who worked on their holding fewer than one-third of the normal working hours, or who worked longer hours but were not considered eligible for gainful worker status by census interviewers. Some may also have been recorded in the census with nonagricultural occupations. In the few countries for which comparisons of the employment status of workers are possible (the data are not shown here), the FAO surveys report higher proportions of those women who are in the agricultural labor force as unpaid family members in eight of nine cases, and higher proportions of all unpaid household farm workers as female in 12 of 13 cases. This is not surprising in view of the tendency of most agricultural surveys to count those who did "any" work on the holding during the reference period, regardless of its duration or intensity. The two sources differ less notably in their treatment of wage workers, as we would expect, although even here the FAO finds more women workers. In Egypt, for example, the 1966 population census reported that 4 percent of all farm wage laborers were women, whereas the 1960–61 FAO census reported 31 percent.

16. For 35 comparisons, the mean FAO/ILO ratio of total numbers of agricultural workers is 1.27, with a standard deviation of .42 and a coefficient of relative variation of .33. For males, $\bar{X}$ = 1.01., S = .26, CRV = .26; for females, $\bar{X}$ = 5.46, S = 9.42, CRV = 1.72.

17. Activity rates were calculated with numerators drawn from FAO reports of the total numbers if males and females economically active in agriculture, and denominators drawn from ILO estimates of the total male and female population aged 10 and over, interpolated or extrapolated to the appropriate FAO census year.

REFERENCES

Anker, Richard. 1980. *Research on Women's Roles and Demographic Change: Survey Questionnaires for Households, Women, Men and Communities with Background Explanations*. Geneva: International Labour Office.

Blacker, J. G. C. 1978. "A critique of international definitions of economic activity." *Population Bulletin of ECWA*, no. 14 (June): 47–54.

———. 1980. "Further thoughts on the definitions of economic activity and employment status." *Population Bulletin of ECWA*, no. 19 (December): 69–80.

Blumberg, Rae Lesser. 1979. "Rural women in development: Veil of invisibility, world of work." *International Journal of Intercultural Relations* 3, no. 4: 447–71.

Boserup, Ester. 1970. *Woman's Role in Economic Development*. New York: St. Martin's Press.

———. 1975. "Employment of women in developing countries," in *Population Growth and Economic Development in the Third World*, ed. Léon Tabah, vol. 1, pp. 79–107. International Union for the Scientific Study of Population. Dolhain, Belgium: Ordina.

Boulding, Elise, Shirley A. Nuss, Dorothy Lee Carson, and Michael A. Greenstein. 1976. *Handbook of International Data on Women*. New York: Halsted.

Deere, Carmen Diana. 1982. "The division of labor by sex in agriculture: A Peruvian case study." *Economic Development and Cultural Change* (Chicago: University of Chicago Press).

Dixon, Ruth B. 1980. "Assessing the impact of development projects on women." AID Program Evaluation Discussion Paper no. 8. Washington, D.C.: Bureau for Program and Policy Coordination, US Agency for International Development, May.

———. 1982. "Women in agriculture: Counting the labor force in developing countries," *Population and Development Review* 8, no. 3 (September): 539–66.

Durand, John D. 1975. *The Labor Force in Economic Development: An International Comparison of Census Statistics*. Princeton, N.J.: Princeton University Press.

El Shafei, Abdel Moneim N. 1960. "The current labor force survey in Egypt." *International Labour Review* 82, no. 5 (November): 432–49.

Fong, Monica. 1980a. "Victims of old-fashioned statistics." *Ceres: FAO Review on Agriculture and Development* 13, no. 3 (May–June): 29–32.

———. 1980b. "Statistics on women's participation in agricultural production." Rome: Food and Agriculture Organization of the United Nations.

Food and Agriculture Organization of the UN. 1971. *Report on the 1960 World Census of Agriculture*, vol. 5. Rome: FAO.

———. *Report on the 1970 Census of Agriculture*, Bulletin no. 8 (Dec. 1974), 9 (March 1975), 10 (May 1975), 17 (May 1977), 18 (Sept. 1977), 19 (Dec. 1977), 20 (Feb. 1978), 21 (Mar. 1978), 23 (Sept. 1978), 25 (Feb. 1979). Rome: FAO.

————. 1977. *Report on the 1970 World Census of Agriculture*. FAO Statistics Series no. 10. Rome: FAO.

————. 1978. *Collecting Statistics on Agricultural Population and Employment*. FAO Economic and Social Development Paper no. 7. Rome: FAO.

————. 1981. "Preparation of baseline studies on women in rural households." Home Economics and Social Programmes Service, W/P2333. Rome: FAO.

Freedom, Deborah, and Eva Mueller. 1977. *A Multi-Purpose Household Question-naire: Basic Economic and Demographic Modules*. Washington, D.C.: International Bank for Reconstruction and Development.

Garrett, Patricia M. 1976. "Some structural constraints on the agricultural activities of women: The Chilean hacienda." Research Paper no. 70. Madison, Wisconsin: Land Tenure Center, University of Wisconsin.

International Center for Research on Women. 1980. "The productivity of women in developing countries: Measurement issues and recommendations." Washington, D.C.: Office of Women in Development, US Agency for International Development, April.

International Labour Office. 1969. *Rural Employment Problems in the United Arab Republic*. Geneva: ILO.

————. 1976. *International Recommendations on Labour Statistics*. Geneva: ILO.

————. 1977. *Labour Force Estimates and Projections, 1950–2000*, 2nd ed., vols. 1–6. Geneva: ILO.

————. 1986. Economically Active Population 1950–2025: Estimates and Projections, 3rd ed., vols. 1–6. Geneva: ILO.

Jain, Devaki, Nalini Singh, and Malini Chand. 1979. "Women's work: Methodological issues," in *Women and Development: Perspectives from South and Southeast Asia*, ed. Rounaq Jahan and Hanna Papanek. Dacca: The Bangladesh Institute of Law and International Affairs.

Moir, Hazel. 1980. "Economic activities of women in rural Java: Are the data adequate?" Occasional Paper no. 20. Canberra: Development Studies Centre, The Australian National University.

Mueller, Eva. 1978. *The Design of Employment Surveys for Developing Countries*. Ann Arbor: Population Studies Center, University of Michigan, September.

Nagi, Mostafa H. 1972. "Child labor in rural Egypt." *Rural Sociology* 37, no. 4 (December): 623–27.

Palmer, Ingrid. 1979. "The Nemow case. Case studies of the impact of large scale development projects on women: A series of planners." New York: The Population Council.

Palmer, Ingrid, and Ulrike von Buchwald. 1980. "Monitoring changes in the conditions of women: A critical review of possible approaches." Geneva: United Nations Research Institute for Social Development.

Perez-Ramirez, Gustavo. 1978. "Unveiling women in statistics." *Populi* 5, no. 1: 17–22.

Pollitt, Brian. 1977. "Some problems in enumerating the 'peasantry' in Cuba." *The Journal of Peasant Studies* 4, no. 2 (January): 162–80.

Recchini de Lattes, Zulma, and Catalina H. Wainerman. 1981. "La medición censal de la actividad economica femenina América Latina." Unpublished paper.

Richards, Alan, and Philip L. Martin. 1981. "Rural social structure and the agricultural labor market: Sharqiyya evidence and policy implications." Agricultural Development Systems Project Working Paper, University of California, Davis, May.

Rodgers, Gerry, and Guy Standing. 1981. "The economic roles of children in low-income countries." *International Labour Review* 120, no. 1 (January–February): 31–48.

Rogers, Barbara. 1980. *The Domestication of Women*. New York: St. Martin's Press.

Standing, Guy. 1977. *Studies of Labour Force Participation in Low-Income Areas:*

Methodological Issues and Data Requirements. Geneva: International Labour Office, May.

————. 1978. *Labor Force Participation and Development*. Geneva: International Labour Office.

Stokes, Olivia. 1975. "Women of rural Bihar," in *Indian Women*, ed. Devaki Jain, pp. 217–28. New Delhi: Publications Division, Ministry of Information and Broadcasting, Government of India.

United Nations. 1958. *Handbook of Population Census Methods*, vol. 2. New York: United Nations.

United Nations, Department of Economic and Social Affairs. 1967. *Proceedings of the World Population Conference, Belgrade, 1965*, vol. 4. New York: United Nations.

United Nations, Department of Economic and Social Affairs, Statistical Office. 1974. *Handbook of Population and Housing Census Methods*, Part IV, Sect. 2. Studies in Methods, Series F., No. 16/Add. 4. New York: United Nations.

United Nations Secretariat. 1980. "Sex-based stereotypes, sex biases and national data systems." ST/ESA/STAT/99. New York: United Nations, 11 June.

Wainerman, Catalina H., Zulma Recchini de Lattes. 1981. *El Trabajo Femenino en el Banquillo de los Acusados: La Medición Censal en América Latina*. Mexico: Editorial Terra Nova and the Population Council.

Youssef, Nadia. 1977. "Women and agricultural production in Muslim societies." *Studies in Comparative International Development* 12, no. 1 (Spring): 41–58.

13. Coauthorship, Gender, and Publication among Sociologists

KATHRYN B. WARD AND LINDA GRANT

Collaboration is a work style thought to be more common among women than men academics, yet collaboration conflicts with normative views of science as an individualistic, autonomous enterprise. In this study we examine one form of collaboration among women and men sociologists: coauthorship of published articles. We find that being female and writing about gender increase the propensity to produce joint-authored rather than solo-authored works. Coauthorship is least common in mainstream national sociology journals, the outlets which perhaps most strongly embody norms that science is an autonomous enterprise. We suggest a clash between women's preferred modes and methods of production of scholarly research and publication patterns of major journals that may disadvantage women scholars and women and men carrying out research on gender issues.

Collaboration is a work style more characteristic of women than of men academics (see, e.g., DuBois et al., 1985; Keller, 1985; Ferber, 1988; Simeone, 1987; Stanley and Wise, 1983). These authors suggest several reasons why women are more likely than men to collaborate in the production of scholarship: (1) female preference for a group work environment; (2) women's higher evaluation of collaborative efforts; and (3) collaboration as a survival strategy.

In this paper we discuss theoretical and practical reasons for women's propensity to coauthor. Then, examining the population of 3,686 articles published in ten sociology journals in ten years, we explore three empirical questions related to one form of collaboration: coauthorship of published papers. These questions are: (a) are women more likely than men to coauthor? (b) are articles on gender more likely to be coauthored than articles on other topics? and (c) is coauthorship related to publication of research in regional or specialty journals versus national mainstream journals? We also consider how women scholars' methods, topic choices, and styles of authorship are incompatible with prevailing norms used in evaluation of scholarly works and how these incompatibilities might constitute significant barriers to career advancement of women scholars.

Reasons for Collaboration

Group Context

Developmental and feminist theorists argue that women derive greater satisfaction from social relationships and may even become anxious about individualistic achievement (Bakan, 1972; Bernard, 1973; Carlson, 1972; Gilligan, 1982; and Mackie, 1985). Research conducted by women is characterized by a communal approach, emphasizing collaboration with other scholars and sometimes with research subjects (Duelli-Klein, 1983; Mies, 1983; Reinharz, 1979). The lines between expert and subjects of research are blurred, and status distinctions among those on the research team are minimized. The process is compatible with the relational skills that Gilligan and these authors see as more characteristic of women than of men. Male scholars, in contrast, prefer agentic approaches which emphasize individually-produced work and separation of researcher and subject. Such approaches are compatible, these authors believe, with separation and abstraction, qualities valued more by males than by females.

Studies of small groups—the types in which scholarly collaborations usually are carried out—show that women more than men are likely to form cooperative groups without a clearly definable leader, where members share responsibility for tasks (see, e.g., Aries, 1976). Fuehrer and Schilling (1985: pp. 35–36) write that "women may experience a sense of personal failure in the autonomy lauded by the academic establishment, and their male colleagues may view them as less able because of their desire for connection." Other writers also have suggested that women researchers are less comfortable than men in hierarchically-organized research teams and prefer to work in egalitarian groups (Hood, 1985; Oakley, 1981; Roberts, 1981; Stanley and Wise, 1983; Woodward and Chisolm, 1981). Yet products of collaborative ventures are evaluated according to norms that attribute greater credit and rewards to the first and/or most senior author. Some papers carry notes attributing equal credit to coauthors, but it is unclear whether this information is seriously considered in evaluating scholars' productivity within their disciplines or institutions.

Value of Collaboration

Women more than men may value the products of collaborative efforts. Bernard (1973) has argued that because women's lives are more involved than men's in status-nexus exchanges (where relationships, rather than objective achievements, are central), women are less likely to believe that a single, objective social reality exists. Rather, many subscribe to the view that individuals of varying backgrounds and experience will hold divergent perspectives on social life. Enlarging the range of perspectives on social reality through collaboration may improve the quality of research by making it more inclusive, more complete (see also Cook and Fonow, 1986; DuBois et al., 1985; Roberts, 1981; Smith, 1974, 1977).

This position is related to what Cook and Fonow (1986) identify as a central tenet of feminist methodology: that self-reflection is an appropriate, indeed valuable, source of knowledge. (For statements of this philosophy, see the introductory sections to such diverse works as DuBois et al., 1985; The Boston Women's Health Collective, 1984; Frieze et al., 1978; Haraway, 1988.) Guided by this viewpoint, women and feminist scholars seek collaboration within their disciplines and also with scholars in other disciplines and persons outside the academy, including research subjects (Duelli-Klein, 1983; Oakley, 1981). Collaboration is thus a valuable means to acquire feedback on content, scope, methods, and interpretation.

Survival Strategy

Collaboration is a survival strategy for many women scholars, especially those doing research and writing that is controversial and not wholly acceptable as "real" scholarship by gatekeepers in their disciplines and institutions (DuBois et al., 1985; Fox and Faver, 1985; Hood, 1985; Nebraska Sociological Feminist Collective, 1984; Simeone, 1987; Stanley and Wise, 1983). For example, in our prior work we have found it valuable to have at hand a colleague enthusiastic about research in environments otherwise non-supportive to feminist research. Off-campus colleagues often can serve the same purpose, giving "pep talks" to encourage pursuit of research that local colleagues do not find valuable.

Collaborative work groups can provide both instrumental and social support for pursuing alternative modes of research and teaching (Fuehrer and Schilling, 1985). In our past work dividing the labor of what seemed at first a mammoth task (e.g., examining more than 3,600 published articles) was helpful, as was pooling knowledge and expertise. Bringing to the task our diverse backgrounds (e.g., concentration in micro versus macro sociology, expertise in quantitative versus qualitative approaches) not only enriched the work at hand but also enlarged our store of knowledge and expertise that could be carried into other ventures. Some examples of using collaboration as a survival strategy are efforts by groups such as Sociologists for Women in Society, which has attempted to form networks of women scholars who can provide instrumental and emotional support for women academics and scholars carrying out research on gender. At the University of California, Santa Cruz, the Women's Studies program established collaborative research groups involving faculty and students. Duelli-Klein (1983) and others argue that in the future methods courses in women's studies departments increasingly will emphasize collaboration with women inside and outside academia as a basic research process.

Coauthorship and Evaluation

Collaborative work, however, is often devalued within academia. Keller (1985) argues that norms of science value individual accomplishments and ownership of ideas. This perspective, she believes, is a corollary of the belief in objectivity. If scientists recognize that subjectivity always enters the research process, that one's angle of vision always influences what is seen and unseen, then concern about ownership of ideas will diminish.

Simon (1974) found that sociologists identified as eminent by others in their discipline most typically worked alone. Those who collaborated worked with junior colleagues or graduate students, but usually only after the senior scholar had first established his reputation. (All the eminent scholars identified by the panel of judges used in Simon's study were male.) The patterns were similar for natural scientists studied by Roe (1952).

Reskin (1978) has argued that coauthoring works with a senior male author may be problematic for women junior faculty or graduate students. Even if women are first authors, their works may be credited to the more-established male (Oramer, 1977). Also, women may be presumed to be incapable of producing high-quality research without guidance from their mentors.

The preference for individual work is apparent in evaluation systems of some academic departments, which grant proportionally much greater credit for the production of individually authored rather than joint-authored works. Although criteria vary, in many departments coauthored work receives less credit than solo-authored articles or books (Simeone, 1987).

We distinguish conceptually between collaboration and joint authorship. Although the two often go hand in hand, they are not the same. Coauthorship has been the usual means of operationalizing collaboration in research studies (see Mackie, 1985). As Hood (1985) has noted, little if any sociological work is produced by a single, isolated scholar. Sociologists are dependent upon colleagues, students, research assistants, peers, anonymous reviewers, editors, and the past works of social scientists in the production of research. Few clear standards exist about when such intellectual debts are and are not acknowledged at the level of coauthorship or a lesser form of recognition, such as a printed note of thanks. Also, systematic gender differences may exist in judgments about when a contribution has been substantial enough to warrant coauthorship or other acknowledgment.

The increasingly common pattern of multiple publication and extensive secondary analysis of a single dataset creates new forms of collaboration that might or might not result in coauthorship. Data collection carried out by several persons might result in single-authored works. Conversely, data collected by a single scholar might become the basis for subsequent coauthored works. Nearly all empirical examinations of scholarly collaboration have used coauthorship as the measure of collaboration, although researchers have recognized that coauthorship represents only one form of collaboration (Mackie, 1977).

Double-blind review, used by major sociological journals, also creates questions about whether evaluators are aware of whether papers are solo or joint-authored.[1] Although there is ambiguity with some papers, descriptions of methods generally make it clear whether work is individually or collaboratively produced. Identifying solo and joint-authored work is more difficult for theoretical or other nonempirical work, but such papers constituted less than 12 percent of papers published in major sociological journals in 1974–83 (Grant, Ward, and Rong, 1987).

Research on Coauthorship

Despite persistent speculation about links between gender and authorship patterns and collaborative versus individualistic work, little empirical research has appeared on the frequency of coauthorship by women and men scholars. Past research on coauthorship in scholarly publication is not wholly consistent.

A recent study by Ferber (1988), examining works in economics and sociology published in a single year, suggested that women are more likely than men to collaborate. An earlier study of publication patterns of women and men in a single journal, *The Sociological Quarterly,* from the period 1960 to 1979 also revealed that women coauthored more frequently than men did (Thompson et al., 1980). Although both studies suggest a relationship between gender and propensity to solo-author or coauthor published work, each is limited by a narrow sample and therefore does not provide a firm basis for generalization about women and men scholars' collaborative patterns.

Two papers by Mackie (1977, 1985) suggest changes over time in women's and men's propensities to coauthor in five general sociological journals in 1967, 1973, and 1981. In the earliest years covered by Mackie's research, women constituted only 12 percent of published authors in the five journals she surveyed. By 1981 they constituted 24 percent (Mackie, 1985), a figure consistent with our previous findings (Ward and Grant, 1985). Over time coauthorship had increased significantly for women and men, which Mackie takes as evidence that collaboration now is the normative pattern of production of published sociological research. Mackie interprets greater coauthorship by women as evidence of women's increased incorporation into research-producing teams within sociology. Her interpretation differs from our argument that coauthorship might be disadvantageous in the evaluation process for women. Perhaps women who published earlier, as tokens in their disciplines, had atypical experiences. As women's publication became more common, publication patterns might have reflected work patterns preferred by women.

Goals of This Study

Inconsistent findings of previous studies and limited samples suggest a need for further research. The studies cited above have analyzed research appearing in single or noncontinuous years and/or have been limited to a small number of journals. Findings might have been skewed by idiosyncrasies of particular editors and/or editorial boards or by publication of special issues that constituted large proportions of articles in certain years of journals. (See Mackie, 1985, for a discussion of this effect.) In addition, previous studies have concentrated on the effects of gender of author and have not addressed the speculation of feminist scholars that works focused on gender issues might be coauthored more often than works on other topics. Finally, no empirical work has examined whether or not collaborative versus individual authorship is related in a systematic way to the outlet in which research is published. If valuation of individually-produced scholarship exists in sociology, we would anticipate that the most prestigious journals would publish relatively fewer coauthored works. We anticipate that these journals more than the less-frequently-read specialty or regional journals would reflect norms supportive of individually-produced scholarship. Regional journals or specialty journals, in contrast, might be more likely to accept joint-authored papers. Alternatively, writers of coauthored papers might elect to publish them in specialty or regional journals more frequently than in national mainstream journals.

Specifically, we examine the following hypotheses:

1. Women scholars more often than men scholars have been involved in coauthored publication in sociology journals.

2. Works focused on issues of gender, sex roles, or sexuality have been coauthored more frequently than works focused on other topics.

3. Joint authorship has been more common for papers appearing in regional or specialty journals than for papers appearing in mainstream sociological journals.

Data and Methods

Data were collected from a review of all issues of ten sociology journals from 1974 to 1983. We reviewed all journals published by the American Sociological Association, except *The American Sociologist*, which was not published in all years covered by our review, and *Contemporary Sociology*, a book-review journal. We also examined several reputable regional and specialty publications. The selected journals were the *American Journal of Sociology* (AJS); *American Sociological Review* (ASR); *Journal of Health and Social Behavior* (JHSB); the *Pacific Sociological Review* (PSR), now titled *Sociological Perspectives; Social Forces* (SF); *Social Problems* (SP); *Social Psychology Quarterly* (SPQ) (formerly *Sociometry*); *The Sociological Quarterly* (SQ); *Sociology of Education* (SOE); and *Work and Occupations* (WORK), formerly *Sociology of Work and Occupations*.

We examined all full-length articles in the journals during this period (N = 3,686), but omitted research notes, commentaries, letters, and book reviews. Articles whose titles and/or abstracts used terms such as women, men's roles, sex, gender, male, female, or sexuality were identified as gender articles. The articles were credited to a total of 6,010 authors, or an average of 1.6 per published article. Of all articles, 53% were solo authored. Women's share of solo authorships (relative to men's) was 20%. Women made up 21% of first authorships and 25% of subsidiary authors of coauthored work. For all published papers we recorded gender of each solo, first, and subsidiary author. A subsidiary author was one whose name appeared in any position other than first. Coauthored articles were classified as male- or female-authored on the basis of the gender of first author. Previous studies have found that most coauthored works are produced by scholars of the same gender, the major exception being works produced by husband-and-wife teams (Mackie, 1985).

Results

Author Gender and Coauthoring

We turn first to the question of whether women coauthored more frequently than did men. Table 1 presents data aggregated for all journals over ten years. Since we present population data, we have not computed tests of statistical

Table 1 Percentage of Women and Men Solo, First, and Subsidiary Authors of Articles Published in Ten Sociology Journals, 1974–1983[a]

		Authorship Position			
		Solo Authors	First Authors	Subsidiary[b] Authors	Total
Women	%	29	27	44	100
Authors	(N)	(389)	(372)	(592)	(1353)
Men	%	34	29	37	100
Authors	(N)	(1562)	(1363)	(1732)	(4657)
All	%	32	29	39	100
Authors	(N)	(1951)	(1735)	(2324)	(6010)

[a]Journals were *American Journal of Sociology* (AJS); *American Sociological Journal* (ASR); *Journal of Health and Social Behavior* (JHSB); *Pacific Sociological Review* (PSR), now *Sociological Perspectives; Social Forces* (SF); *Social Problems* (SP); *Social Psychology Quarterly* (SPQ), formerly *Sociometry; The Sociological Quarterly* (SQ); *Sociology of Education* (SOE); *Work and Occupations* (WORK) formerly *Sociology of Work and Occupations*.
[b]A subsidiary author is one whose name appears in any position other than first.

significance. The table shows first that coauthorship was more common than solo-authorship for both women and men. Nevertheless, men were more likely than women to have been solo authors of published articles (34 percent in comparison to 9 percent). Women and men held near-equal shares of first authorships (27 and 29 percent, respectively). Women were represented more heavily than were men in the subsidiary author category (44 as compared to 37 percent).

Article Topic Effects

Table 2 shows authorship breakdowns for the 693 gender articles and 2,993 nongender articles covered by our review. This table also shows that women and men who write any type of article (gender or nongender) are more likely to coauthor than to be solo authors. The highest proportion of solo authorship occurs for men writing nongender articles (36 percent). Thus, both male and female sociologists, and writers of both gender and nongender articles, coauthor more often than they publish single-authored papers.

The table reveals an interesting gender-of-author by article-type effect. Women's solo author rates and first author rates are lowest, and their representation in the subsidiary-author category highest, for nongender articles. Conversely, men's solo authorship rates are lowest, and their representation in the subsidiary-author category highest, for gender articles. The one exception to this pattern is men's somewhat higher first-authorship rates for gender as compared to nongender articles (35 percent versus 28 percent). With fewer male-authored nongender articles written collaboratively, men had fewer opportunities to be first authors. Gender is a sociological subarea where women

Table 2 Authorship Order (By Percentages) by Author Gender and Article Type (Gender or Nongender)[a] in Ten Sociology Journals, 1974–1983.

	Solo Authors (%)	First Authors (%)	Subsid-iary Authors (%)	Coauthor %	Total N
			Total		
Women authors, gender articles	28% (129)	34% (153)	39% (177)	72%	(459)
Women authors, nongender articles	30% (260)	24% (219)	46% (415)	70%	(894)
Men authors, gender articles	21% (156)	35% (255)	44% (322)	79%	(733)
Men authors, nongender articles	36% (1406)	28% (1108)	36% (1410)	64%	(3924)
			N = 3686 articles		

[a]Analysis is based on 3,686 full-length articles. Because of joint authorship, number of authors exceeds number of articles.

are more heavily represented than in other specialties (Skipper, DeWolf, and Dudley, 1987).

The table also shows that article type (gender versus nongender) had a stronger impact on men's propensity to coauthor than it did on women's. Women solo authors were nearly as common for gender as nongender articles (28 versus 30 percent). In contrast, there were 15 percent fewer male solo authors of gender articles than male solo authors of articles on other topics (21 versus 36 percent). Stated another way, 79 percent of men's, but only 72 percent of women's, gender publications were coauthored. This is a reversal of patterns for nongender articles, where 70 percent of women's but only 64 percent of men's articles were joint-authored. Writing on gender reduced men's propensity to write alone, but topic had a less dramatic effect for women authors.

The patterns suggest a "domain" effect, with gender articles stereotyped as female turf. Men publishing gender articles usually did so with a woman coauthor. Men also were more heavily represented for gender than for nongender articles as subsidiary authors (44 percent as compared to 35 percent). An alternative, but plausible, interpretation is that men writing about gender were more sensitive to equity issues and/or more sympathetic to women colleagues and women's work styles than were other men.

The domain effect is less strongly supported by the data for women and nongender articles. Women were less common as first authors for nongender than gender articles (24 versus 34 percent) and more heavily represented as subsidiary authors (46 versus 38 percent), but their solo authorship rates for nongender articles were only fractionally higher than solo authorship rates for gender articles. Nevertheless, women's relatively heavy representation in the subsidiary author category for nongender articles suggests that many might have needed sponsorship of male or more-established female scholars to publish on these topics.

Type of Journal Effects

There were variations across journals in women's and men's share of authorship categories for gender and nongender articles. We previously reported that certain journals were much more likely than others to have published gender articles. Highest ratios of gender articles were in JHSB (31%), WORK (28%), and SPQ (23%), while lowest ratios of gender articles were found in SF (13%), AJS (13%), PSR (15%), and SQ (18%). ASR (19%), SP (20%), and SOE (21%) fell between these groups (see Ward and Grant, 1985).

Because of variations in proportions of gender articles appearing in the journals in the ten years, we examined distributions of women and men across authorship categories for each journal first for gender articles and then for nongender articles.

The journals surveyed can be divided into three categories: national general, or mainstream, sociology journals (AJS, ASR); national specialty journals (JHSB, SP, SPQ, SOE, WORK); and regional general sociology journals (PSR, SF, SQ). Table 3 shows distributions of women and men across authorship categories for gender articles appearing in 1974–83.

Women authors were fairly evenly distributed across authorship categories for all journals. A specialty journal, SP, stood out as having had a large proportion of women solo authors of gender articles (49 percent). SQ, a regional journal, also had a high percentage (44) of women solo authors of gender articles. The two most prestigious journals, AJS and ASR, had higher proportions of women in the subsidiary rather than solo or senior author status for gender articles. AJS and ASR are read more often, and by a more diverse range of sociologists, than other journals. Articles published in these sources are cited more frequently than those published in other journals. Yet these journals give a distorted image of women's participation in more-senior authorship positions within sociological publishing generally. Also, names of subsidiary authors customarily are dropped in citations and indices, contributing to an invisibility for female subsidiary authors. When women's work is placed in sources where it is apt to attract the most attention, women are in authorship positions that limit their visibility and the growth of their reputations within academia.

The bottom panel of Table 3 shows distributions of men across authorship categories for gender articles. Men were most heavily represented in the subsidiary-author category. Their representation as solo and as first coauthors in the mainstream journals AJS and ASR exceeded slightly their overall proportions as solo and first authors. Men's representation as solo authors also was

Table 3 Authorship Order for Women and Men Authors of Gender Articles Published 1974–83, by Journal

| | Women Authors | | | | | | |
| | Solo Authors | | First Authors | | Subsidiary Authors | | |
	N	(%)	N	(%)	N	(%)	Total N
AJS	5	(19)	8	(30)	14	(52)	27
ASR	13	(25)	18	(34)	22	(42)	53
JHSB	15	(19)	24	(30)	40	(51)	79
PSR	6	(25)	10	(42)	8	(33)	24
SF	4	(12)	17	(50)	13	(38)	34
SP	39	(49)	23	(29)	18	(23)	80
SPQ	7	(16)	18	(40)	20	(44)	45
SQ	17	(44)	11	(28)	11	(28)	39
SOE	5	(24)	4	(19)	12	(57)	21
WORK	18	(32)	20	(35)	19	(33)	57
Total	129	(28%)	153	(33%)	177	(39%)	459 (100%)

| | Men Authors | | | | | | |
| | Solo Authors | | First Authors | | Subsidiary Authors | | |
	N	(%)	N	(%)	N	(%)	Total N
AJS	13	(28)	18	(38)	16	(34)	47
ASR	24	(22)	41	(38)	43	(40)	108
JHSB	22	(17)	40	(31)	65	(51)	127
PSR	13	(41)	9	(28)	10	(31)	32
SF	21	(23)	34	(37)	37	(40)	92
SP	17	(27)	18	(29)	27	(44)	62
SPQ	16	(14)	43	(37)	58	(50)	117
SQ	12	(24)	18	(35)	21	(41)	51
SOE	15	(25)	22	(36)	24	(39)	61
WORK	3	(8)	12	(35)	21	(58)	36
Total	156	(21%)	255	(35%)	322	(44%)	733 (100%)

relatively higher for gender articles in regional journals. Patterns for specialty journals were less consistent. Men were relatively high in solo authorships in SP and SOE, but low in JHSB, SPQ, and WORK. The patterns suggest underrepresentation of male scholars as solo or senior authors of gender articles in three specialty areas where women sociologists have been especially active: medical, social psychology, and work and professions (see Ward and Grant, 1985).

Table 4 provides for nongender articles the same data presented for gender articles in Table 3. The top panel of Table 4, reporting data for women authors of nongender articles, shows that women were less well represented in all categories of authorship for nongender in comparison with gender articles with the exception of the category of solo author. Twenty-nine percent of solo

Table 4 Authorship Order for Women and Men Authors of Nongender Articles Published 1974–83, by Journal

	Women Authors						N of Women Authors of Nongender Articles
	Solo Authors		First Authors		Subsidiary Authors		
	N	(%)	N	(%)	N	(%)	
AJS	15	(25)	12	(20)	33	(55)	60
ASR	27	(30)	14	(15)	50	(55)	91
JHSB	28	(19)	36	(25)	80	(55)	144
PSR	16	(53)	7	(23)	7	(23)	30
SF	21	(26)	34	(43)	25	(31)	80
SP	55	(41)	29	(21)	51	(38)	135
SPQ	29	(19)	38	(25)	83	(55)	150
SQ	32	(35)	19	(21)	41	(45)	92
SOE	13	(22)	16	(28)	29	(50)	58
WORK	24	(44)	14	(26)	16	(30)	54
Total	260	(29%)	219	(24%)	415	(46%)	894 (100%)

Men Authors

	Solo Authors		First Authors		Subsidiary Authors		Total N
	N	(%)	N	(%)	N	(%)	
AJS	179	(42)	115	(27)	137	(32)	431
ASR	206	(35)	165	(28)	217	(37)	588
JHSB	62	(19)	104	(33)	154	(48)	320
PSR	127	(49)	65	(25)	66	(26)	258
SF	251	(40)	182	(29)	194	(31)	627
SP	189	(42)	103	(23)	153	(34)	445
SPQ	91	(20)	150	(33)	208	(46)	449
SQ	168	(41)	111	(27)	131	(32)	410
SOE	75	(32)	71	(30)	91	(38)	237
WORK	58	(36)	42	(26)	59	(37)	159
Total	1406	(36%)	1108	(28%)	1410	(36%)	3924 (100%)

authors of nongender articles were women, compared to 28 percent of gender articles. One regional journal (PSR, 53 percent) and two specialty journals (WORK, 44 percent and SP, 41 percent) stand out as having higher proportions of women solo authors. Another regional journal, SF, had an unusually high proportion of women first authors for joint-authored works (43 percent). Otherwise, there were no consistent patterns for regional and specialty journals.

The bottom panel of Table 4, reporting data for men authors, reveals that men were much more heavily represented as solo authors in most journals than were women authors of nongender articles or women or men authors of gender articles. The pattern appeared in all the regional journals. It also was found in one mainstream journal, AJS, where 42 percent of men were solo authors. In the other mainstream journal, ASR, men's proportion of solo authorships was approximately equal to their representation in this category across all the journals (35 percent as compared to 36 percent). Men's lowest shares of solo authorship and highest shares of subsidiary authorship occurred in specialty journals in fields where women are particularly active. There was little variation for men authors of nongender articles in the proportions of first authorships across journals.

The data provide weak and not wholly consistent evidence for patterns of association between author gender, article topic, type of journal in which a work is published, and rate and form of coauthorship. Coauthorship was rarer in mainstream journals than in others, and women occupied fewer dominant authorship positions (solo or first author) in these journals in comparison with others for both gender and nongender articles. Specialty journals had higher proportions of women as solo or first authors than did mainstream or regional general sociology journals. These journals published higher ratios of coauthored works than others.

Methods and Mainstream Visibility

We did not examine methods use for the entire population of 3,686 published articles. However, our prior work based on a sample of 856 articles drawn from this population discovered a significant association between author gender, article topic (gender or nongender), and methods use (Grant, Ward, and Rong, 1987). Quantitative articles were the most common for women and for men, and for coauthored as well as solo-authored work, in the sociological literature in 1974–83. Overall, men's articles were slightly more likely to be quantitative than were women's articles. Contrary to our expectations, however, published articles focusing on gender were more likely than all other articles to be quantitative. This was especially true for gender articles written by men.

We speculated that nonquantitative gender articles represented double nonconformity to norms of sociological research on grounds of both topic and method. To get published in mainstream journals, authors of gender articles might have turned to normative methods to maximize chances of success. Our data for the 856 articles also show that quantitative articles were more likely to have been coauthored than other-method articles. This is not surprising given that the quantitative articles involved large datasets and separable tasks, a situation amenable to collaboration.

In our earlier work we raised the question, posed earlier by Mackie (1985), whether women researchers and gender scholars might be more likely to use qualitative methods when publishing in feminist or gender-oriented journals. Examination of the first volume of a new journal, *Gender & Society*, provides some insight into this question. This journal is published by the Sociologists for Women in Society. The first volume (1987) contained 14 articles. Of these, eight had female solo authors, and one had a male first author. There were one female and three male subsidiary authors. Only three articles used quantitative methods. Of the others, eight were qualitative and three were theoretical and nonempirical. The patterns suggest that women might use qualitative methods more often when they perceive publication outlets to be receptive to such approaches. These journals also provide women with more senior authorship visibility. More sustained analysis of publication patterns in feminist or gender versus mainstream journals in sociology and other disciplines is needed to see if this is a common pattern. It also is important to explore the consequences for career advancement and for personal satisfaction of various choices of publication outlets.

Discussion

The results reveal five important findings. First, women coauthor more frequently than do men, although joint-authorship is the modal form of production of scholarly work for sociologists of both genders publishing in the journals we studied. Second, scholars writing on gender coauthor more frequently than scholars writing on other topics. Third, a gender-of-author by topic-of-article interaction reverses the usual patterns of association, with men who write on gender coauthoring more frequently than women who write on these topics. Fourth, rates of coauthorship are lower in national mainstream journals than in other sources. Fifth, women are less likely to occupy dominant-author positions in papers published in these mainstream journals than elsewhere. Finally, there appear to be systematic, but complex, links between gender, methods, collaboration, and publication outlets that are worthy of further analysis by feminist researchers.

For nongender articles, our findings that women coauthor more than men is consistent with past research on women's authorship and collaboration styles. Women also have high coauthorship rates for gender articles, although not quite so high as men's. However, women's authorship patterns are not consistent with those observed for mainstream journals, where solo authorship is more common than in other types of publications. We suggest that the model of the individual, autonomous scholar continues to be more highly valued by social scientists who control publication in national mainstream journals. Because these journals are so widely read, publication in them tends to be highly rewarded. Yet the coauthorship mode of production that characterizes larger shares of women's work and larger shares of research about gender topics is less well represented in the national general sociology journals.

Writing on gender increases the likelihood that works will be joint-authored, especially for male scholars. Since gender articles make up only 20 percent of published articles during the period we studied, males' atypical collaborative patterns within this category are not strong enough to alter the more general pattern of less coauthorship by men sociologists. The individualistic/ autonomous style discussed above might result in a subtle evaluative bias that regards solo-authored research as better science. This bias can disadvantage women scholars and women and men social scientists who write about gender. Gender research might be less highly evaluated on two counts: topic and coauthorship. If, as many feminist critics argue, collaboration produces better scholarship on gender, then scholars who share this outlook might want to coauthor, but nevertheless will experience pressure to work in styles that are less comprehensive. Avoidance of coauthorship in response to perceived biases of leading journals thus might negatively affect the quality of scholarship on gender. Nonetheless, we propose that collaboration provides an important model for research on gender and nongender topics. Collaboration can involve greater reflexivity, differing perspectives, and practical and emotional support for innovative work—rewards that far outweigh institutional resistance.

If sociological research on gender is stereotyped as a female domain (albeit a discredited one within the larger discipline), men may need female sponsorship to participate in scholarship in this domain and/or might have to adopt work modes characteristic of women. The precursors of men's participation in research on gender, and the influence which it has on their work styles and careers, merits further research.

Institutional and departmental preferences also condition researchers' choices of solo or coauthorship and discourage formal collaboration when coauthored research is discounted in promotion and tenure decisions. Choices made at earlier career points also influence collaboration patterns later on. Doing quantitative research using large datasets might predispose researchers toward later coauthorship more than doing qualitative, participant observation studies. Unanticipated problems might arise when scholars move from one departmental or institutional context where collaboration is valued into another where it is not, or the reverse.

Given the lower rates of coauthoring in national mainstream journals and the limited number of female solo or first authors, what are the implications for distribution and evaluation of women's work and work about gender? We have identified patterns affecting the visibility of women authors and evaluations of their work. First, the first-author syndrome hierarchically ranks authors and downplays contributions of subsidiary authors, even for works which are explicitly labeled as equal contributions by all authors. Second, many departments and institutions discount subsidiary authorships and place heavy emphasis on solo and first authorships in allocating institutional rewards (tenure, promotion, salary increases, travel money, reduced teaching loads as rewards for research productivity, etc.) Finally, publication in national mainstream journals frequently brings comparatively greater rewards than does publication in regional or specialty journals. Yet our research suggests that the mainstream journals are least hospitable to products of collaborative work styles that characterize scholarship produced by women and scholarship focused on gender issues more than other work. When women do coauthor articles published in mainstream journals, they more often are subsidiary rather than senior authors in comparison with their works placed in other sources.

The underrepresentation in mainstream journals of qualitative studies, especially qualitative studies focused on gender, represents a similar type of clash. This clash might be the basis of women's underrepresentation in senior authorship positions in the most prestigious journals, a pattern which in turn perpetuates their subordinate status in male-dominated social science.

This study encourages continued attention to workstyles and authorship patterns of women and men and the ways in which these patterns can affect the placement and evaluation of their work. Women's success as scholars, and the integration of research on gender into sociological thinking generally, is very much dependent upon the receptivity of those who control journal publication. Our research provides evidence of an association between scholarship-production patterns and placement of published articles. The coauthorship style which apparently characterizes women's work and research on gender topics is more strongly associated with publication in specialty or regional than in mainstream sociology journals. But work placed in specialty journals is seen by smaller proportions of sociologists, and hence might be limited in its impact. Specialty-journal papers also can be evaluated less favorably in reviews in scholars' works. Feminist journals might be more hospitable outlets for women's scholarship and gender research but might be devalued in reviews by nonfeminist and antifeminist colleagues. Nevertheless, many women scholars have chosen to place their work primarily in these sources or to divide published papers between feminist and mainstream journals. The consequences of these strategies in sociology and in other disciplines should be explored more thoroughly.

Our study cannot address why coauthored papers are more common in some journals than in others, but this topic needs more research. Scholars might elect to send more of their single-authored papers to mainstream than to other journals. Women or men scholars might have more successful outcomes of reviews of single-written or joint-authored papers at various journals. But it might be the case that the mainstream sociology journals, which have strong influence because of their high readership and prestige, have been influenced more than other publications by the view that science is or should be an individualistic, autonomous enterprise. Feminist journals provide alternative visions of science but face the challenge of gaining respect throughout academic disciplines so that alternative views will be aired.

NOTES

An earlier draft of this paper was presented at the 1987 American Sociological Association meetings, Chicago. We appreciate comments on earlier drafts from Judith A. Cook, Mary Margaret Fonow, Beth Hartung, Rachel A. Rosenfeld, and Davita Silfen Glasberg. We acknowledge aid in data collection from James Coverdill, Mary Jane Hamilton, Seanza Prasai, and John Vinyard.

1. Double-blind review is rarer in other disciplines, especially the natural sciences. It also is not used in some forms of review, such as evaluation of grant proposals.

REFERENCES

Aries, Elizabeth. 1976. "Interaction Patterns and Themes of Male, Female, and Mixed Groups." *Small Group Behavior* 7: 8–18.

Bakan, David. 1972. "Psychology Can Now Kick the Science Habit" *Psychology Today* 5: 26–28, 86–88.

Bernard, Jessie. 1973. "My Four Revolutions: An Autobiographical History of the ASA." Pp. 11–29 in *Changing Women in a Changing Society*, ed. Joan Huber. Chicago: The University of Chicago Press.

Boston Women's Health Collective. 1984. *Our Bodies, Ourselves*. 4th ed. New York: Simon and Schuster.

Carlson, R. 1972. "Understanding Women: Implications for Personality Theory and Research." *Journal of Social Issues* 28: 17–32.

Cook, Judith, and Mary Margaret Fonow. 1986. "Knowledge and Women's Interests: Issues of Epistemology and Methodology in Feminist Sociological Research." *Sociological Inquiry* 56: 2–27.

Duelli-Klein, R. 1983. "How to Do What We Want to Do: Thoughts about Feminist Methodology." In *Theories of Women's Studies*, ed. G. Bowles and R. Duelli-Klein. London: Routledge and Kegan Paul.

DuBois, Ellen Carol, Gail Paradise Kelly, Elizabeth Laprovsky Kennedy, Carolyn W. Korsmeyer, and Lillian S. Robinson. 1985. *Feminist Scholarship: Kindling in the Groves of Academe*. Urbana: University of Illinois Press.

Ferber, Marianne. 1986. "Citations: Are They an Objective Measure of Scholarly Merit?" *Signs* 11: 381–89.

———. 1988. "Citations and Networking." *Gender & Society* 11: 381–89.

Fox, Mary Frank, and Catherine A. Faver. 1985. "The Process of Collaboration in Scholarly Research," Pp. 126–39 in *Scholarly Writing and Publishing: Issues, Problems, and Solutions*. Boulder: Westview Press.

Frieze, Irene, Jacquelyne E. Parsons, Paula B. Johnson, Diane N. Ruble, and Gail L. Zellman. 1978. *Women and Sex Roles: A Social Psychological Perspective*. New York: Norton.

Fuehrer, Ann, and Karen Maitland Schilling. 1985. "The Values of Academe: Sexism as a Natural Consequence." *Journal of Social Issues* 41: 29–42.

Gilligan, Carol. 1982. *In a Different Voice: Psychological Theory and Women's Development*. Cambridge, Mass.: Harvard University Press.

Grant, Linda, Kathryn B. Ward, and Xue Lan Rong. 1987. "Is There an Association between Gender and Method in Sociological Research?" *American Sociological Review* 52: 856–62.

Haraway, Donna. 1988. "Situated Knowledges: The Science Question in Feminism and the Privilege of Partial Perspective." *Feminist Studies* 14: 575–99.

Hood, Jane C. 1985. "The Lone Scholar Myth." Pp. 111–25 in *Scholarly Writing and Publishing: Issues, Problems, and Solutions,* ed. Mary Frank Fox. Boulder: Westview Press.

Keller, Evelyn Fox. 1985. *Reflections on Gender and Science.* New Haven: Yale University Press.

Mackie, Marlene. 1977. "Professional Women's Collegial Relations and Productivity: Female Sociologists' Journal Publication." *Sociology and Social Research* 61: 277–93.

———. 1985. "Female Sociologists' Productivity, Collegial Relations, and Research Style Examined through Journal Publications." *Sociology and Social Research* 69: 189–209.

Mies, Maria. 1983. "Towards a Methodology for Feminist Research." In *Theories of Women's Studies,* ed. G. Bowles and R. Duelli-Klein. London: Routledge and Kegan Paul.

Nebraska Sociological Feminist Collective. 1984. Special Issue on Feminist Ethics. *Humanity and Society* 8: (4).

Oakley, Ann. 1981. "Interviewing Women: A Contradiction in Terms," Pp. 30–61 in *Doing Feminist Research,* ed. Helen Roberts. London: Routledge and Kegan Paul.

Oramer, Mark. 1977. "Professional Age and the Reception of Sociological Publications." *Social Studies of Science* 7: 381–87.

Reinharz, Shulamit. 1979. *On Becoming a Social Scientist.* San Francisco: Jossey Bass.

Reskin, Barbara. 1978. "Sex Differentiation and the Social Organization of Science." Pp. 6–37 in *The Sociology of Science.* San Francisco: Jossey-Bass.

Roberts, Helen. 1981. "Women and Their Doctors." Pp. 7–29 in *Doing Feminist Research,* ed. Helen Roberts. London: Routledge and Kegan Paul.

Roe, Ann. 1952. *The Making of a Scientist.* New York: Dodd, Mead.

Simeone, Angela. 1987. *Academic Women: Working toward Equality.* South Hadley, Mass.: Bergin and Garvey.

Simon, Rita James. 1974. "The Work Habits of Eminent Scholars." *Sociology of Work and Occupations* 1: 327–35.

Skipper, James, P. L. DeWolf, and C. J. Dudley. 1987. "Sex Differences in Sociology Specializations, 1975–85: Women's Liberation to Ghetto Specialization." *Sociological Focus* 20: 185–94.

Smith, Dorothy. 1974. "Women's Perspective as a Radical Critique of Sociology," *Sociological Inquiry* 44: 7–13.

———. 1977. "A Sociology for Women." Pp. 135–87 in *The Prism of Sex,* ed. Julia A. Sherman and Evelyn Torton Beck. Madison: The University of Wisconsin Press.

Stanley, Liz, and Sue Wise. 1983. *Breaking Out: Feminist Consciousness and Feminist Research.* London: Routledge and Kegan Paul.

Thompson, Martha, Susan E. Wright, Judith Wittner, and Virginia Kemp Fish. 1980. "Women Sociologists in the Midwest: A Status Report." *The Sociological Quarterly* 21: 623–33.

Ward, Kathryn B., and Linda Grant. 1985. "The Feminist Critique and a Decade of Published Research in Sociology Journals." *The Sociological Quarterly* 26: 139–57.

Woodward, Diana, and Lynne Chisolm. 1981. "The Expert's View? The Sociological Analysis of Graduates' Occupational and Domestic Roles." Pp. 159–84 in *Doing Feminist Research,* ed. Helen Roberts. London: Routledge and Kegan Paul.

14. FEMINIST RESEARCH, FEMINIST CONSCIOUSNESS, AND EXPERIENCES OF SEXISM

LIZ STANLEY AND SUE WISE

Models of the "research process" frequently represent this as involving a linear movement from theory to research ("positivist") or from research to theory ("naturalist"), although the actual experience of research may not fit into either. Our own research experience suggests that, for feminist researchers, there may be a more complex interaction between the "research phenomenon," "feminist theory," and "feminist consciousness," as well as more directly personal influences and effects.

The particular research we discuss entailed a direct daily personal involvement with statements about women-as-sexual-objects. This involvement affected our theories about the research phenomenon, our perception of this, and our understanding of the nature of women's oppression. More succinctly, the research and the researched changed the researchers.

Our particular experience suggests that "feminist consciousness" of sexism and the nature of women's oppression, as an ongoing process of examination and reinterpretation of feminist experience, is itself a crucial variable in the research process.

Introduction

Descriptions of the research process in the social sciences often suggest that the motivation for carrying out substantive work lies in theoretical concerns: recognition of a problem or interest leads to research being conducted, based on a series of hypotheses expressing the problem or interest to be investigated (Galtung, 1967; Blalock, 1971; Ferman and Levin, 1975). An alternative mode of research to the positivist or "scientific model" just outlined is that described as "grounded theory," "emergent theory," or as "naturalistic sociology" (Glaser and Strauss, 1968; Blumer, 1969; Matza, 1971; Manis and Meltzer, 1972; Mehan and Wood, 1975). In this alternative approach theory is said to be derived from material collected during the research process, rather than a specific problem or series of hypotheses directing the focus of the research. Within this "naturalistic" approach the "theory" so derived may be that of the investigator, or attempts may be made to present the theories of the research population themselves (Pollner, 1974; Garfinkel, 1967).

Many research reports are presented in terms suggested by these simple linear models. That is, data and discussion are organized around a schema implicit within the model chosen; and this organization is not "realistic," in the sense that it does not seek to describe what happened and when and how it happened. Such reports present an abstraction from events within a prechosen framework. Further, this organization of events presents material in a "logico-temporal" manner: events are unfolded in a way based on logic and argument, not as they occurred in temporal reality. Obviously not all research is always so presented—certainly many naturalistic methods center on the attempt to present material in terms of what happened and when and how it happened. However, we suggest that, firstly, a large body of research material makes no such attempt, whether "positivistic" or "naturalistic" in emphasis. Secondly, more abstract accounts of the research process do present such simple linear models as descriptions of what "doing research" is like (Duverger, 1964; Simon, 1969; Nachmias and Nachmias, 1976).

One effect of such presentations is that the research process appears a very orderly and coherent process indeed—what we would term "hygienic research." And the point at which realization occurs that this is "research as it is described" and not "research as experienced" tends to be the point at which one is seeking to present research to academic colleagues. Pressures to present research material as though order, neatness, and so on had prevailed are very strong, partly because of the increasing use of publications as a criterion of academic standing and achievement (Berger, 1966), and partly because comparatively few examples of other approaches exist. That is, there is always the possibility that lack of neatness, order, and so on is the result of one's failure to do research "properly."

Although many people working in the social sciences privately discuss the idiosyncracies, quirks, and problems of doing research, public discussions and written accounts remain rare. The personal tends to be carefully removed from public statements: these are full of rational argument and careful discussion of academic points of dispute and are frequently empty of any feeling of what the research process was actually like. As we have already suggested, more realistic accounts do exist (Morgan, 1972; Fletcher, 1974; Platt, 1976; Bell and Newby, 1977), particularly in relation to naturalistic approaches. However, these are exceptional even in relation to naturalism, and are even more rare elsewhere in the social sciences.

We argue that feminist research, coming from within a tradition which expressly supports self-examination and sharing, should reflect these two qualities. But apart from this rather abstract and moral reasoning, we also suggest that a recognition of the importance of the personal is fundamental to feminist philosophy. That is, accounts of the personal constitute not only a realm for examination and discussion, but also the subject-matter of feminist theory and thus the basis of feminist political activity. "The personal," for feminist researchers, therefore includes research experiences as well as other experiences. In addition to this, as Mills has emphasized (Mills, 1963), the personal is not only the political, it is also the frequently invisible yet crucial variable present in any attempt to "do research." We emphasize that it should not be absent from "doing feminist research."

However, much present feminist thinking and research appears to reject all things sociological or else to concentrate on structural approaches to the analysis of women's oppression. While having considerable sympathy for many of the criticisms of sociology's unnecessary use of jargon, its pseudo-scientific stance, and its sexist biases, we also feel that a blanket reaction of it is mistaken, as is this emphasis on social structural approaches. By "mistaken" we mean that approaches other than the structural are important and therefore should be accepted as a valid contribution to this analysis, rather than dismissed as the study of false consciousness. Sociology is not a monolithic discipline and contains much that accords with feminist thinking, especially in relation to its emphasis on personal experience. We feel that the phenomenological approach and its many variations, such as phenomenology, interactionism, ethnomethodology, conversational analysis, constitute that part of sociology most in accord with this emphasis. It is therefore unfortunate that phenomenological research and analysis are largely absent from feminist research.

The research experience which forms the starting point for our discussion of feminist consciousness demonstrates very clearly the importance of the personal in carrying out research. This research experience involved a complex interaction between the "research phenomenon," "feminist theory," and "feminist consciousness" and demonstrated to us that "Idiosyncracies of person and circumstance are at the heart not the periphery of the scientific enterprise" (Johnson, 1975; quoted in Bell and Newby, 1977; p. 9). There are a number of important points involved in this complex interaction, and we now briefly outline these.

Inevitably, "theory" precedes research, if we interpret and use the notion of theory as in ethnomethodological discussion (Pollner, 1974; Zimmerman and Pollner, 1970). That is, all people derive "theory" or "second order constructs" from "experience" or "first order constructs" (Ryan, 1970; p. 4). We reject the idea that only social scientists, and not "people" produce general accounts of social reality in this way (Denzin, 1972; p. 80). In this sense, it is possible to argue that all research is "grounded," because no researcher can separate herself from personhood and thus from deriving second order constructs from experience. Following on from this, we also argue that the research experience itself will be subject to ongoing "theorizings." In relation to our own research on obscene phone calls, which we discuss in more detail later, we found that our experience of this research phenomenon affected the basis of our relationships with men other than the "researched" and with other feminists and also involved the development of our increasingly negative feelings about and toward the obscene phone callers themselves. In addition, we found that this experience became both a part of and an outcome of a major shift in our perception of women's oppression. This, in its turn, influenced perception of both current and previous events connected either directly or indirectly with the research phenomenon. And eventually, our experience of the research led to a range of responses to the obscene phone callers—both expressed and constrained—which led to the end of the research period proper.

Frequently researchers are counselled not to allow the occurrence of the kind of involvement we have just outlined (Whyte, 1960; Miller, 1969; Dean and Whyte, 1969). That is, emotional involvement is seen to detract from a professionally-correct detachment for sociologists as it is for prostitutes and for social workers. In contrast, we argue that such involvements cannot be "controlled" by mere effort of will; and, if they could, the effects of such control would themselves constitute an important factor in the research process. More importantly, perhaps, we also suggest that such involvements and consequent possible changes in consciousness must be welcomed for the insights that they may bring—for the "transformation of reality" (Bartky, 1977) that can occur.

Also, of course, emotional involvement is not exclusive to the researchers. Nevertheless, much research literature tends to treat the researched simply as repositories of information waiting to be emptied into questionnaires, tapes of interviews, and so on (Illersic, 1964; Moser and Kalton, 1971; Galtung, 1967). More plausibly, the researched too are actively involved in the research in hand. They may like, dislike, sexually desire, or despise the researcher (Wise, 1978). They will almost certainly construct their own theory about both the research topic and the theory held by the researcher and supply information accordingly (Bruch, 1974). They may seek to preserve face or to present themselves differently to the researcher than to others (Plant, 1975). All these and other activities by the researched will affect not only the presentation of self to the researcher, but also how the researcher feels about given events, situations, and personalities, interprets what has occurred and is occurring, and views the general social context in which the interaction between researched and researcher occurs.

The feelings of the researched to the researchers form the basis of our research, although these feelings were expressed toward us as "women-who-had-a-phone-who-were-lesbians-whose-number-was-known" and not as social scientists. It was also apparent to us that these feelings and the events of the research produced specific responses and more generally contributed to our changing consciousness as feminists. Also, of course, our feelings about and our actual reactions to the callers have affected the form and content of the "research process" as we experienced it. And so what we now do is to discuss why and how the obscene phone calls occurred, briefly outline the content of the calls, and discuss the effects that the calls had on us.

Experiences of Sexism

The focus of this paper is the nature of the relationship between researcher and researched, and feminist consciousness and changes in consciousness. The basis of this discussion is our experience of obscene phone calls. Although analyses of this have been presented elsewhere (Stanley, 1976a,b; Wise, 1978; Wise and Stanley, 1979), we nevertheless feel it necessary here to outline what occurred during this research. This is because our past experience of presenting reports of it suggest that its effects on us are incomprehensible to others without doing so. In addition to this, we have found that the content of these phone calls is outside most people's experiences of, or theorizings about, obscene phone calls. To us the quality of the call content and the effects the calls had on us are rationally and understandably linked. But as we report later, most other people, whether feminsts or not, see our reactions as essentially irrational.

The obscene phones calls did not occur, and were not produced, as part of any academic enterprise. Their occurrence was linked to our involvement in the gay movement in England. Between 1971 and about 1976 our home telephone number was a contact number for several local gay groups. For most of this time the contact number was specifically for a lesbian group. The function of a contact number is to provide information and advice and to refer isolated gay people to gay groups and organizations. It was advertised explicitly in these terms. However, we received obscene phone calls from the time the number was originally advertised in 1971, but increasingly so when our fore- names were advertised with the telephone number in an attempt to encourage more gay women to call. For a period of time in 1975 and 1976 our number was widely advertised on posters and also in newspaper small ads throughout the area. The research occurred during a 7-week period in 1976 in which all obscene calls were recorded verbatim and all other calls connected with the public use of our private number were logged. Before going on to discuss the content of the obscene calls, we think it useful to outline a number of important points about our involvement in "doing research" on the calls.

Most research is voluntary, in the sense that both the research and the experiences which constitute it are synonymous and voluntarily engaged in. For us, to be involved in this research was voluntary, but our experience of it was not. That is, our intent in advertising the number was not to receive obscene phone calls, and we had much rather that they had not occurred. In addition, there was no way that we could prevent obscene phone callers from calling us short of changing the telephone number. Most research also occurs in specific places and at specific times: the researcher can choose to become involved in these events or not. We could not: the specific place this phenom- enon occurred was in our home; the specific time was that chosen by the callers as and when they, individually, decided to call the number. In a sense, our decision to "do research" was one means of coping with what proved to be a constant and massive assault on us.

During the research period, a total of 286 calls were received which derived from the "public use" of our number; private calls from family, friends and so on were not logged. Out of this total of 286 calls, 105 were defined by us as obscene. Here we make no attempt to define or justify our idea of what constitutes an obscene call: this and other matters specific to the research are discussed elsewhere.

In describing the content of some of the obscene calls we do not wish to give the impression that we thereby feel that it is possible to classify calls under any series of discrete headings. Many, or at least a number of the "themes" or preoccupations or concerns can be discerned in each of the calls that we present. That is, most of the calls were multi-dimensional and offered complex mixtures of these "themes" and also of obscenity and ordinariness. The calls that are included here are sequences extracted from total calls—each sequence complete in itself, but either the beginning or the end of the call may be omitted. C signifies the caller and R the recipient.

1. *Violence*
Violent utterances usually consist of threats or descriptions of violence often, but not invariably, expressed toward us personally. Although sexual imagery and behaviors may be used in such utterances, we feel that their intent is not particularly sexual—their sexual content is a vehicle for the expression of violence.

R: Hullo, it's Liz.

C: It won't be for long cos I'm going to get you, tonight or tomorrow night . . . I know where you live, I work in the Post Office and I've found out . . . You'll come out the door and I'll be there. I'll drag you back inside and I'll fuck you like the lesy whore you are . . .

R: Were you ringing about anything in particular?

C: I'm ringing about your wet cunt and me fucking you til you're fucked rigid . . . I'll do you with a bottle then anything else that's around but not my cock even when you beg for it . . . Then it'll be the turn of a nice sharp knife and my initials in your tits you whore . . . (Transcript 15)

2. *Anti-lesbian violence*
These utterances consist of threats or descriptions of violence made toward either us as lesbians or lesbians as a group. Sometimes "final solutions" are offered to the "problem" of lesbianism; sometimes more personal "revenges" are outlined.

R: Hullo, it's Liz.

C: Liz the les is it?

R: I beg your pardon?

C: So you should . . . you need whipping and then stringing up in public as an example.

R: An example of what?

C: Of what happens to degenerates in a decent society.

R: Do decent societies publicly hang people then?

C: They do where there are people like you . . . you're too sick to know what decent means . . . you need making an example of, flaunting yourself and perverting normal women with your sexual practices . . . (Transcript 27)

3. *Sexual violence*
Such utterances concern the infliction of violence on us personally; these descriptions are not directed at us as lesbians nor do they appear to be using sexual description to convey violent intent. Rather, their intent appears to concern the caller's masturbatory activity while making the call. That is, the caller uses descriptions of sexual violence as a means of arousal and of achieving orgasm/ejaculation.

R: Hello, it's Sue.

C: Talk to me while I jerk off, Sue.

R: No, thank you.

C: . . . you're still there I know you've not put the phone down . . . I'll talk to you anyway . . . I've got a big dick and it's getting bigger right now . . . is that turning you on? I'd like to come into your room and shove it up from behind, right up your arse . . . I'd bite you too, you'd scream and you'd love it too . . . you're all fucking mattresses you are, just lie there and take it don't you and love every minute . . . I'll be coming in a bit, it's really big and it's oozing spunk . . .

R: I'm putting the phone down now.

C: Ohhh . . . it's too late I've come now . . . that was good, thanks. (Transcript 44)

4. *Lesbianism as a turn-on*

Utterances of this kind focus on lesbian sexual conduct or, rather, what the caller perceives this to be. The caller either talks about sexual acts involving lesbians or else requests that we should do so. Frequently the caller masturbates while this occurs. Typically, these utterances are directed at us personally; but an alternative approach is one in which the caller presents a series of requests for information, and these are used as sexual stimulation.

C: You're a lesbian, aren't you?

R: That's right.

C: Do you like men, I mean sexually?

R: I don't want to talk to you about that.

C: That's because you're frightened of men, of cocks, but it can be cured . . . I could help you. I'm good with women, they like me to use my prick on them.

R: You think you're a good lover do you?

C: They all come off with me, you would too with a real cock up you and not one of those rubber things . . . Oh Jesus you'd feel come bounce off your vagina . . . I've come off now, have you come off? (Transcript 16)

5. *Sex-service requests*

Sex-service requests are made during calls and appear to be based on the assumption that the number was advertised in order to provide a free sex service for males. However, some callers assume that we are prostitutes providing a sex service, although how payment can be made is never discussed by them. All such utterances ignore, or appear to think irrelevant, the purpose for which the number was advertised—this is seen as a "front" for its real purpose.

R: Hello, it . . .

C: Hello, it's Steve, when can I come round?

R: I think you must have the wrong number.

C: You Sue or Liz?

R: Yes.

C: Which one?

R: None of your business. Why are you ringing?

C: I want to come round and see you give an exhibition and wank in your panties.

R: We're not prostitutes.

C: Why else would you advertise the number, if you didn't want men ringing up for sexy talk? (Transcript 47)

6. Address attempts

These consist of attempts to discover our address by attempting to pass as insurance salesmen, friends of parents, priests, delivery services, and so on. Refusal to give the requested information and statements about our perception of the caller's intent frequently leads them to make other forms of utterance.

R: Hullo, it's Liz.

C: Good afternoon. This is ——— Insurance here. I wonder if you'd be interested in our endowment insurance policies?

R: Oh well, I've just got the details from the ——— Society about theirs.

C: Just give me your address and I'll send you the information so you can compare them.

R: OK . . . Oh no, you don't.

C: Pardon, what's that?

R: I'll tell you what, you give me your name and work address and I'll contact you shall I?

C: I think it would be better if you were to let me send you the information right away.

R: I think you're a dirty phone caller.

C: You're wrong.

R: No, I'm not, I recognize your voice now.

C: You think you're bloody clever, don't you? I'll get to fuck you yet you fucking les. One day I'll get my prick up you . . . (Transcript 30)

7. Heavy breathing

Obviously, heavy breathing calls tend to contain few verbalizations by the callers. Totally silent calls are not included under this heading; heavy breathing calls are only those which terminate in noises associated with ejaculation. Some of these calls are, in addition, terminated by utterances which confirm the nature of the call.

R: . . . I think you may be a dirty phone caller, so if you're not, if you don't say who you are, I shall have to put the phone down.

C: I've come now, thanks. (Transcript 54)

As we have already suggested, most of the calls were multi-dimensional, and what we have outlined above are not categories of calls but a number of the themes present in them. In this sense, it is not possible to give any information about the distribution of the calls among these categories. We can merely say that most of the calls contain a number of these themes and demonstrate this by reference to the following call. In this, call content shifts from one theme to another.

C: Liz?

R: No, it's Sue.

C: Hello, sexy.

R: Can I help you?

C: Yes, you can give me a good fuck, I get turned on by lesies.

R: No, thank you, I'm not interested.

C: That's what you need, a good fuck.

R: Why do you think that?

C: Well, it's the real thing, isn't it? It's better than going with a girl.

R: I don't agree.

C: . . . I'd like to splash spunk in your face, I'd like to fuck you til the come runs down you fucking queer, you fucking cunt you.

R: Have you finished?

C: Er, well, have you anything to add then?

R: What should I want to say to you?

C: . . . talk while I jerk myself off, come on sexy, do us a favour.

R: Do you think I'd do that after you've been so abusive?

C: What do you mean? . . . Come on now, Sue, be nice to me, come on talk to me . . . (Transcript 78)

All the calls, with the exception of two that were unclassifiable, were made by males. Sex of caller was assigned on interpretation of voice sound based on our experience of staffing a contact telephone number over the four- or five-year period leading up to the research period proper. Many of the callers continued to call long after the research period ended; at least one of them is still calling intermittently at the time of writing this paper, but many more continued for over a year. For a period of over two years we were receiving at least one and sometimes a number of such calls each and every day.

Many people have said that they find it difficult to see why the calls should have the negative effects on us that we discuss later. Some have suggested that our responses during the calls demonstrate that we were perfectly able to cope with them. Therefore we would like to emphasize that we had received such calls long before the 7-week research period began, and consequently had worked out verbal and other strategies for dealing with them. In particular, we took great care not to give the callers any suggestion that we felt powerless or vulnerable in the face of their obscene calls. We had learned that this was almost a guarantee that they would ejaculate quickly and effortlessly; and this, in turn, made us feel even more powerless and vulnerable.

We believe that there are three elements of the effects of the phone calls as we experienced them. These elements are concerned with our reactions to the calls, other people's reactions to the calls, and other people's reactons to our reactions. We examine these elements in relation to the short term, medium term and long term.

Short Term

The most immediate impact the calls had on us was to dominate our lives. The calls could and did occur at any time of the day or night and thus, in a physical sense, intruded in our lives to a very marked degree. We have already pointed out that we usually received at least one such call a day. But during the period of time before, during, and immediately after the "research period" we were receiving many of them each day. The calls dominated our lives in another sense: to be subject to a constant barrage of obscenity and sexually-objectifying threats is to experience oppression in a very direct way; and we therefore experienced a need to make some kind of sense of what was occurring in terms of feminist theory and analysis. And so, like any other researchers, we spent a great deal of our lives thinking about our research, the obscene phone calls. In particular, we were concerned with what the calls suggested to us about the nature of the oppression of lesbians, as distinct from gay men, and also what they suggested to us about the oppression of women generally.

Most people appear to view obscene phone callers as sad rather than bad or responsible for their actions, to see them as victims. We came to feel that this was inadequate when applied to the callers who called us. For us, to be confronted with them as voices mouthing the utmost contempt for women—and us in particular—as nothing but holes between legs, as cunts, was to experience them as oppressors and nothing but oppressors. That is, our interpretation of them as such was embedded in the context of the specific series of interactions that took place between us and them and between the two of us (Watson, 1976). And so we are not suggesting that the callers are "nothing but oppressors" generally, merely that toward us they appeared, and presented themselves as "oppressors only."

This categorization of callers as "oppressors only" was further aided by the anonymity of phone calls *per se*. There was no way we could tell who was an obscene phone caller and who was not, in relation to male friends, acquaintances, colleagues, relatives, and so on. For all we knew, any of these could be an obscene caller; and this was a supposition which became more plausible in the light of subsequent male reactions to our research.

The anonymity afforded by the telephone had another dimension. There was no real way of knowing if the threats made in the calls would remain threats should the opportunity for action occur or be created. Certainly some of the callers made attempts to discover our address during the calls, and it appeared probable that at least some of them might have access to other means of discovering it. Also the telephone number was in the directory: if a caller were to find out our surnames, then it would be simple enough to trace the address. The consequence of this was that the calls were frightening not only because they constituted an assault on us at a psychological level, but also because we feared for our safety from sexual or other violent attacks on a physical level.

Medium Term

Our initial theorizing about the calls saw them as an expression of the threat that many heterosexual men appear to experience about lesbianism. Later we also felt that the oppression of gay men was in many important respects quite different from that of lesbians. In addition to this, many gay men experienced the content of the calls as sexually arousing, and some felt that the occurrence of the calls was our responsiblity, in fact our fault. Later still, during a period of time in which initial reports of the research were being made to gay groups and conferences and to academic colleagues, another series of reactions to the calls occurred. In confidence, and in less immediately objectionable terms, other heterosexual and bisexual males told us how they found the content of the calls sexually exciting, how they too were turned on by lesbianism. It began to appear as though every male we spoke to about the calls shared the callers' feelings about lesbianism and about the relationship between sex and violence.

However, no women have ever talked about becoming sexually aroused by the calls. From women we experienced two main forms of reaction, with sexual orientation generally forming the dividing line. Most heterosexual women, whether feminists or not, have said that they agree that the calls may have been annoying or intrusive, but feel that they have no importance other than as a nuisance and that therefore they should have no greater effect on us. For these women, to ignore the calls, to "disassociate" from them or to laugh them off was seen as an appropriate response; our actual responses and interpretations of their meaning were often seen as "extreme" or even as "paranoia." We experienced such responses from other feminists as disturbing and upsetting: they seemed very similar to the responses that most people make to feminist interpretations of all social reality. These women not only rejected our reactions and interpretations as invalid for *them*, they also rejected them as invalid for *us*. However, most lesbians, whether bisexual or homosexual, feminist or not, saw elements of their own experiences reflected in the calls. Specifically, most had experienced threat/titillation responses from males uninterested in them as potential sexual partners until their sexual orientation became known.

During the same period of time in which other people made various interpretations of the calls, we also came to feel such antipathy toward the callers and such outrage and anger about the calls as an extreme manifestation of sexism, that we decided that the research in its existing form could no longer continue. This was not because either of us felt that emotional involvement was in some sense "unprofessional," but because in personal/political terms we could no longer cope with responding to the calls and recording them as we had been. Instead of appearing unemotional and cool, we found ourselves expressing anger and outrage and bandying insults; and so we decided that we would respond to the calls in such a way as to minimize their negative effects on us. In effect, this meant putting the phone down as quickly as possible each time an obscene call was made. This response to the calls appears to us to be closely linked to our altering/altered consciousness of women's oppression and this we discuss later as "consciousness 2" and compare with our "consciousness 1."

Long Term

The feelings about men-as-oppressors that we have already outlined were also extended to our feelings about gay-men-as-men. That is, our experience of their reactions to the calls, and other experiences within the gay movement, led us to believe that the vast majority of gay men remained "Men" and would choose to maintain male privilege wherever possible (Shiers, 1978). We also felt that their reactions to the calls confirmed that many, perhaps most gay men experienced their sexuality in totally phallocentric ways. Such feelings finally resulted in both of us withdrawing from active involvement in the gay movement and deciding that in future neither of us would work with men over any political issue. We became in some sense separatists.

Finally, we later became aware that our responses to all of these things led us often to present our experiences of the obscene calls in a joking way—for people's amusement. We feel that on most occasions this appeared—and appears—the only tolerable way of coping both with our feelings about this "research experience" and also other people's reactions to those feelings.

The changing consciousness of women's oppression that we have referred to briefly has certain facets; and we have borrowed from Bartky's discussion of the phenomenology of feminist consciousness her four themes or types of consciousness within the whole (Bartky, 1977). Before going on to discuss this, we would like to emphasize a number of things. First, that when we speak of "consciousness 1" and "consciousness 2," we are referring to *our* consciousness and not that of feminists in general. We are outlining our own personal, situated interpretations of why and how women are oppressed, not other people's. Second, neither are we implying that "consciousness 2" is in any way better, higher, or more advanced than "consciousness 1," only that it is different. And, third, we make no claims that the content of other feminists' consciousness will be the same as ours. Indeed we suggest precisely the opposite— that the consciousness is grounded in situated, contextual understandings and interpretations. To the extent that feminists share situations and experiences, our consciousness will be similar; but where experiences differ, so will consciousness.

Experience and Consciousness

The concept of a "feminist consciousness" has been discussed by Bartky in terms which describe our own experiences of the processes involved in becoming and being feminist. She suggests that "becoming feminist" is a "profound personal transformation" (Bartky, 1977; p. 23), involving both changes in behavior and changes in consciousness, and goes on to describe the phenomenology of feminist consciousness in terms of four key facets.

She describes these four facets of the whole consciousness as consciousness of "anguish," of "victimization," of "constant exposure" and of "the double ontological shock." Finally, she suggests that "Feminism is something like paranoia" (Bartky, 1977; p. 29), because the consciousness which underlies it enables feminists to interpret social reality in ways which may be radically different from other interpretations. The same events and states are seen through, and become a part of, this transformed consciousness. The same events, behaviors, states, beliefs, and so on come to *mean* something different from what they previously meant.

The process of "becoming feminist," the development of feminist consciousness, we argue is not an "end state." That is, consciousness can best be construed both as a "state" in that we think and talk of "a" consciousness or "the" consciousness as though it had objective reality (Coulter, 1977), and also as a "process" in the sense that different situated and changing understandings underpin any "state" of consciousness. Therefore we maintain that there is not just one feminist consciousness but a multiplicity; and these are derived from differing involvement in, and interpretation of, different situated experiences. But, in addition to this, many feminists may experience subtle or dramatic changes after "becoming feminist." Again, we emphasize that we do not see such changes as a movement from higher to lower or from less advanced to more advanced, but merely as a change, a difference.

Before "doing research" on the obscene phone calls and experiencing other people's reactions to them and to our reactions, our consciousness of women's oppression—"consciousness 1"—might be described as a thoroughgoing "idealism." That is, it involved an understanding and interpretation of "patriarchy" as an *ideology* reflected in institutions and negotiated through interaction. A search for a theory to explain the "origins" of women's oppression we saw as temporal chauvinism: whatever its origins, women's oppression is now infinitely more complex and multi-dimensional. While not opposed to structural analyses, whether of a conventional or phenomenological kind, we felt that women's oppression was essentially ideologically rather than materially based.

In "consciousness 2," however, we adoped a "materialist" theory as used by the callers themselves. This involves an analysis of women's oppression in terms of "phallocentrism." That is, the callers identified power and the penis as in some sense synonymous. Those without penes, those who are pentrated by penes, are without power and therefore are the legitimate objects of contempt. Such a theory therefore identifies phallocentrism as the basis for male ideas about power. These ideas thus also formed the legitimation of the callers' interactions with us. We have "adopted" this theory in the sense that it appears to us reasonable to assume that people's stated understandings and interpretations often are the basis for their actions. In this sense we feel that sexist males are a useful source of information about their sexism and their oppression of women.

The change from "consciousness 1" to "consciousness 2" is now outlined around Bartky's four facets of feminist consciousness.

"Anguish" is described by Bartky as the realization of the intolerableness of women's oppression, both personally and for all women. For us, "anguish" was experienced in this sense in both consciousnesses but in "consciousness 2" it acquired an additional dimension. Here it was experienced as an intolerable but essentially *unchanging* interaction with sexist males who continually expressed phallocentric views, opinions, and interpretations. However we presented ourselves, our presentations were interpreted in sexually-objectified ways: we were seen only as sexual objects there for the callers' sexual use and objectification, and our statements were interpreted in the light of this view of us. We experienced this as a complete powerlessness to affect their one-dimensional interpretation: *their* reactions and interactions with us appeared to occur almost independently of *our* reactions and what took place was governed largely by the callers' intentions.

Bartky describes "victimization" as an awareness of sexism both as a hostile force and also as an offence. Thus it entails a rejection of the "naturalness" of the sexual political system as its legitimation. She further develops this idea by suggesting that two dichotomies are experienced as an integral part of it: victimization as both a diminishment of being and also as an awareness of strength within this new consciousness; and victimization as a double awareness of victimization as women and of privilege as white, middle class and so on. For us it was experienced rather differently.

Both consciousnesses entailed a rejection of any moral or natural legitimation for patriarchy; but in "consciousness 2" we were faced with the dilemma faced by Firestone and others who argue that a physiological basis for women's oppression exists (Firestone, 1970; Koedt *et al.*, 1973). Firestone advocates reproduction outside the female body as her "answer"; are we then compelled to advocate men without penes as ours? The difference between the positon adopted by Firestone and our own is that she seems to argue that physiological structures have inherent meaning; we argue that physiological experience is itself a social product. In interactionist terms, that the world—and penis—is without inherent meaning (Blumer, 1969; Gagnon and Simon, 1973), that meanings are derived from interaction.

We certainly experienced a diminishment of being in the way described by Bartky in both consciousnesses; but in "consciousness 2" this appeared more total and the energy released more destructive than was at all comfortable. Once alive to expressions of phallocentrism, we came across them everywhere, from chance remarks heard on buses to conversations with other feminists. The energy released seemed composed mainly of extreme anger and despair of change, but verbal expressions of these feelings were both too self-destructive and too insufficient. And so such feelings had to be first constrained and then channelled in new directions. This act of constraint was in itself a destructive process, partly because it produced the constant wariness Bartky discusses, but also because the feelings remained.

The dichotomy between victimization and privilege Bartky outlines was something we failed to experience in "consciousness 2." Our exposure to the callers and to phallocentrism appeared and was experienced as so total that it left little of our lives as workers, shoppers, bus users, users of streets, inhabitors of a flat with a phone, that was not open to sexual objectification and degradation by phallocentric males. That those males might have been work-ing-class, black, or under-privileged was irrelevant to the interaction between us.

Bartky describes "vulnerability" as the constant exposure to oppression that most feminists experience. As we have already described, in "consciousness 2" our exposure appeared not only constant but also as total: there was nowhere we could go that was not vulnerable to expressions of phallocentrism.

Bartky uses the term "complexity of reality" to describe the "double ontologi-cal shock." She suggests that this involves both an awareness that events may be different from their appearance and presentation by others (i.e. feminists seeing differently from others) and also not knowing when they are "actually" different and when such difference is "merely imagined." More succinctly, this is the problem of distinguishing between "valid paranoia" and "invalid para-noia." That is, she suggests that the feminist view of social reality involves a valid paranoia but also suggests that there are views of social reality which are invalid. The notion that experience and consciousness can in some sense be "invalid" contradicts much of phenomenological thinking. For us, if something is experienced, then it is validly experienced; if a thing is real in its con-sequences then it is real to the person experiencing those consequences. Obviously we recognize that everyday life occurs around the assumption that an objective reality exists and because of this it is possible to make assessments of the validity and invalidity of experience. It has certainly been our experience that most of the reactions to our interpretation of the calls have been based on the belief that we were out of touch with the "real reality" that the reactor perceived.

The problem of facing attempts to invalidate our experience of reality was compounded by lack of a "support group" of others within easy reach who shared our view of sexual political reality as expressed within the obscene calls. Our previous support groups of other feminists became part of these attempts to invalidate our experience.

"Being feminist" is phenomenologically interesting, not least because it involves what are often seen as contradictory, mutually-exclusive feelings and emotions. Joy, awareness of strength, coexist with anguish and anger. "Con-sciousness 2," as we have described it around Bartky's outline, is less di-chotomous because it appears to involve so few positive aspects. Both of us now feel more profoundly pessimistic about the possibility of sexual political change, about the willingness of males of any sexual orientation to change where this means confronting sexism in their ideas about "doing sex." We also feel pessimistic about the willingness of many, perhaps most, heterosexual femi-nists to accept the validity of views of sexual political reality different from their own. We are not suggesting that they *share* our view, merely recognize the validity of our experiences and any action derived from these. Against this must be set what we feel is a more "realistic," for us, understanding of women's oppression and the part played in this by phallocentric ideas held by both women and men.

Our involvement in the research concerned with the obscene phone calls has had a major impact on our lives, leaving little of it unchanged. Not only has "reality" been in some sense transformed, but our behavioral and emotional involvement in it has also changed and become more constrained. We feel that this impact derives directly from "being feminist." Without any initial feminist understanding, the interaction between consciousness and this understanding and the research phenomenon would have been quite different. Certainly for us the crucial element in all this was the dialectical relationship between consciousness and experiences of sexism in the form of the obscene phone calls.

Discussion

Our research on obscene phone calls was, inevitably, focused on the interaction between us and the obscene callers. Both the content of the calls, as an extreme manifestation of sexism, and the form in which the remarks were made, had great effects on us. These effects included our attitudes to each of the callers and to other males, our theories about the oppression of lesbians and women in general, and our feelings about other women's interpretations of the calls and our reactions to them. These effects were involved in a change in our consciousness of women's oppression and thus of a new transformation in our interpretation of reality.

Research experience, we have suggested, is almost invariably different from most descriptions of social science research. The mythology of "hygienic research" not only presents an over-simplistic picture; it is frequently misleading in that it emphasizes the "objective," "value free" involvement of the researcher and suggests that she can be "there" without having any greater involvement than simple presence. We emphasize that all research involves, as its basis, a relationship, an interaction, between researcher and researched. Such a relationship, we believe, exists even where the "researched" are secondary sources or other objects, because even here the researcher inevitably relates in terms of preferences, likes, dislikes, even if of a theoretical nature. Such a suggestion, of course, is by no means novel and is indeed the basis of the critique of positivism in the social sciences. Essentially, this critique maintains that distinctions between aspects of research which can, and which cannot, be conducted in a value free manner (Weber, 1949) are unrealistic.

Rather than seeing feminist research as particular techniques—"soft" as opposed to "hard" (Bernard, 1973, Oakley, 1974)—as a particular focus—on women (Daniels, 1975)—or as a particular theory, we see it as involving a more general "orientation." That is, simply "seeing reality differently." How this seeing differently occurs, how it is maintained, is of obvious interest not only to the phenomenologically inclined but also to feminism as a practical issue.

Our own "seeing differently" was involved in a symbiotic relationship with our "experiences," both first order in the phone calls and second order in analytic attempts. We too found that this experience was at the center and not the periphery of the research process. "Being feminist" involves, as a phenomenon, experience as a view of reality—a feminist view of all reality, whether obscene phone calls, government statistics, gender stereotyping, economic theory, or religious belief.

However, we feel that there there is a danger that feminist research will be concentrated exclusively on women's experience (Daniels, 1975). Essential though such work is, we feel that feminist research should be concerned with all aspects of social reality and all participants in it. It seems obvious to us that any analysis of women's oppression must involve research on the part played by men, and by interaction between women and men, in this. It is this that is the concern of our work on obscene phone calls: the essence of these was men oppressing us as women and as lesbians and, in doing so, presenting their analysis of the sexual political system. Central to this was that the callers were threatened by the alternative interpretation of sexual reality embodied in lesbianism, and their attempts to re-impose a phallocentric, male, interpretation of sexual reality on us as lesbians.

Feminism directly confronts the idea that one person or set of people have the right to impose definitions of reality on others. Feminist research and researchers should attempt to avoid doing the same thing in research situations. One of the ways of doing this—and also of presenting a less monolithic view of doing research—is through more personalized discussion of the research process. The researcher is a part of the research, and therefore is that part of it most accessible to phenomenological discussion and analysis (Smith, 1974).

We have argued that "consciousness" is based on situated interpretations and is thus personal and in some sense unique. And so if anything general can be made of our experiences, it is that the relationship between feminist consciousness, experiences of sexism and feminist research/theory—or, indeed, consciousness, experiences, and research/theory generally—is inseparable and fundamental to any feminist intellectual work.

NOTES

Some of the material in this paper has also appeared in : L. Stanley (1976). On the receiving end, *OUT* 1, 6–7; L. Stanley, Obscene phone calls, BSA Sexuality Study Group 1976; S. Wise, Labelling theory and societal reactions to lesbianism, unpub. diss. Manchester Polytechnic 1978; and S. Wise and L. Stanley, Societal reactions literature and lesbianism, unpub., 1979.

We would like to express our gratitude to Rod Watson and Alison Kelly, both of the Sociology department, University of Manchester, for reading and commenting on an earlier draft of this paper.

REFERENCES

Bartky, S. 1977. Towards a phenomenology of feminist consciousness. In M. Vetetrling-Braggin *et al.*, eds. *Feminism and Philosophy*. Littlefield, Adams; Totowa, N.J. pp. 22–34.

Bell, C., and H. Newby, eds. 1977. *Doing Sociological Research*. Allen & Unwin, London.

Berger, P. 1966. *Invitation to Sociology*. Penguin, Harmondsworth.

Bernard, J. 1973. My four revolutions: an autobiographical history of the ASA. *Am. J. Sociol.* 78, 773–91.

Blalock, H., ed. 1971. *Causal Models in the Social Sciences*. Aldine, Chicago.

Blumer, H. 1969. *Symbolic Interactionism: Perspective and Method*. Prentice Hall, Englewood Cliffs, N.J.

Bruch, H. 1974. *Eating Disorders*. Routledge & Kegan Paul, London.

Coulter, J. 1977. Transparencies of mind. *Phil. Social Sci.* 7, 321–50.

Daniels, A. 1975. Feminist perspectives in sociological research. In M. Millman and R. Kanter, eds. *Another Voice*, pp. 340–80.

Dean, J., and W. Whyte 1969. How do you know if the informant is telling the truth? In G. McCall and J. Simmons, eds. *Issues in Participant Observation*, pp. 105–115.

Denzin, N. 1972. The research act. In J. Manis and B. Meltzer, eds. *Symbolic Interaction*, pp. 76–91.

Douglas, J., ed. 1970. *Understanding Everyday Life*. Routledge & Kegan Paul, London.

Duverger, M. 1964. *Introduction to the Social Sciences*. Allen & Unwin, London.

Ferman, G., and J. Levin, *Social Science Research*. Schenkman Publishing, New York.

Firestone, S. 1970. *The Dialectic of Sex*. Paladin, St. Albans.

Fletcher, C. 1974. *Beneath the Surface*. Routledge & Kegan Paul, London.

Gagnon, J., and W. Simon. 1973. *Sexual Conduct*. Hutchinson, London.

Galtung, J. 1967. *Theory and Methods of Social Research*. Allen & Unwin, London.

Garfinkel, H. 1967. *Studies in Ethnomethodology*. Prentice Hall, Englewood Cliffs, N.J.

Glaser, B., and A. Strauss. 1968. *The Discovery of Grounded Theory*. Weidenfeld & Nicholson, London.

Illersic, A. 1964. *Statistics*. HFL Ltd., London.

Johnson, V. 1975. Violence in marriage, unpublished thesis, University of New South Wales.

Koedt, A., E. Levine, and A. Rapone, eds. 1973. *Radical Feminism*. Quadrangle Books, New York.

Manis, J., and B. Meltzer, eds. 1972. *Symbolic Interaction*. Allyn & Bacon, Boston.

Matza, D. 1971. *Becoming Deviant*. Prentice Hall, Englewood Cliffs, N.J.

McCall, G., and J. Simmons, eds. 1969. *Issues in Participant Observation*. Addison, Wesley, Mass.

Mehan, H., and H. Wood, 1975. *The Reality of Ethnomethodology*. John Wiley, New York.

Miller, S. 1969. The participant observer and 'over-rapport.' In G. McCall and J. Simmons, eds. *Issues in Participant Observation*, pp. 87–89.

Millett, K. 1969. *Sexual Politics*. Abacus, London.

Millman, M., and R. Kanter, eds. 1975. *Another Voice*. Anchor Books, New York.

Mills, C. W. 1963. *Power, Politics and People*. Oxford University Press, Oxford.

Morgan, D. 1972. The British Association scandal: the effect of publicity on a sociological investigation. *Sociol. Rev.* 20, 185–206.

Moser, C., and G. Kalton 1971. *Survey Methods in Social Investigation*. Heinemann, London.

Nachmias, D., and C. Nachmias 1976. *Research Methods in the Social Sciences*. Edward Arnold, London.

Oakley, A. 1974. *The Sociology of Housework*. Martin Robertson, London.

Plant, M. 1975. *Drugtakers in an English Town*. Tavistock, London.

Platt, J., 1976. *Realities of Social Research*. Sussex University Press.

Pollner, M. 1974. Sociological and common-sense models of the labelling process. In R. Turner, ed. *Ethnomethodology*, pp. 27–40.

Ryan, A. 1970. *The Philosophy of the Social Sciences*. Macmillan, London.

Shiers, J. 1978. Two steps forward, one step back: coming out six years on. *Gay Left* 6, 10–13.

Simon, J. 1969. *Basic Research Methods in Social Science*. Random House, New York.

Smith, D. 1974. Women's perspective as a radical critique of sociology. *Sociological Inquiry* 44, 7–13.

Stanley, L. 1976a. Obscene telephone calls, BSA Sexuality Study Group paper.

———1976b. On the receiving end. *OUT* 1, 6–7.

Turner, R., ed. 1974. *Ethnomethodology*. Penguin, Harmondsworth.

Vetterling-Braggin, M., F. Elliston, and J. English, eds. 1977. *Feminism and Philosophy*. Littlefield, Adams & Co., New Jersey.

Viano, E., ed. 1976. *Victims and Society*. Visage Press, Washington.

Watson, D. 1976. Some conceptual issues in the social identification of victims and offenders. In E. Viano, ed. *Victims and Society*, pp. 60–71.

Weber, M. 1949. *The Methodology of the Social Sciences*. Edited and translated by E. Shils and H. Finch. Free Press, Chicago.

Whyte, W. 1960. *Street Corner Society*. Chicago University Press, Chicago.

Wise, S. 1978. Labelling theory and societal reactions to lesbians, unpublished diss., Manchester Polytechnic.

Wise, S., and Stanley, L. 1979. Societal reactions literature and lesbianism, unpublished.

Zimmerman, D., and M. Pollner 1970. The everday world as a phenomenon. In J. Douglas, ed. *Understanding Everyday Life*, pp. 80–103.

15. SHARING FEMINIST RESEARCH WITH POPULAR AUDIENCES

The Book Tour

LAUREL RICHARDSON

My decision to write a trade book evolved over a period of years. The more I pondered the question, "Sociology for whom?" the more certain was my answer: Sociology for the people. I did not think of my decade of research on single women involved with married men as research *on* women but *for* women (Cook and Fonow, 1986). My findings and analysis, I felt, would help men and women make more informed choices about their intimate lives. For example, I was finding that although a single woman might enter a liaison with a married man believing it would be a short-lived, offhand affair, she often ended up in a long term, emotionally costly relationship due, in part, to the relationship's secrecy in conjunction with overarching gender inequalities. "Other Woman-hood" as an institution, I concluded, continued to profit men as a *class* more than it did women. My research, I believed, could empower women and could help unify single women and wives. I wanted the knowledge disseminated widely, and a trade book seemed the most viable channel.

Fifty thousand books are published each year. Twenty thousand of them are trade books published during a short fall and spring season. The trade books compete, along with cards, sweatshirts, calendars, and the best-selling mass market books, for extremely limited bookstore space. Each book, moreover, demands individual recognition by the potential buyer. There is no other consumer industry like it—so many new products (books) from such a large number of producers (publishers) with so few distributors (bookstores) Consequently, the battle to get books into stores and then purchased is fierce. Most books succumb quickly; the average book is dead in weeks; 90% are dead within the year (Shatzkin, 1982:2–3).

I did not know any of this when I decided to write a trade book. I naively assumed that the book would, like a charismatic idea, naturally reach women. What I found, however, was that to increase the book's chance of reaching its intended audience, considerable work, beyond the completion of a manuscript, is required from the author. Books get to audiences because of publicity about

An earlier version of this article appeared under the title, "Disseminating Research to Popular Audiences: The Book Tour," in *Qualitative Sociology*, 10(2), Summer 1987.

them; publicity is accomplished through the media. My role as a trade book author was to meet the media, over and over again.

In this article, I reflect upon the work I did to help my book, *The New Other Woman: Contemporary Women in Affairs with Married Men* (1985), reach its intended audience. I discuss the publicity campaign, the book tour, including preparing for it and doing it, and the impact of the structure of the media on me. Although little research has focused on these issues (but see Richardson [Walum], 1975; Adler, 1984; Best, 1986), given the current pro-media policy of the profession, the social consciousness of many sociological practitioners, and the voracious appetite of the media (Tuchman, 1974; Tuchman, 1978; Wells, 1979), disseminating research to lay audiences may become a routine extension of the research role for many sociologists.

The Campaign

When the accepted manuscript left the editor's desk, a corps of professional specialists were called upon to design, publicize, and market the book. Seeing the book as a potential winner in the book-wars, the staff planned a major publicity campaign: Without such a campaign, the book, like most books, probably would have been an early casualty. Ironically, however, the campaign which captured the attention of lay audiences sometimes undermined my purposes in writing the book—to empower and unite women.

As the book neared production without a title acceptable to the staff, the publicity director and art director, together, presented a jacket design for the book and a title, *The New Other Woman*. I welcomed the art work, a highly graphic portrait of a woman with a man's profile embedded in her hairline—an almost subliminal projection of the book's conclusions. But I strongly resisted, to no avail, the title, which shunted aside any enduring sociological value the book might have. Not only did it ignore what was *old* about these relationships; it implied a six-month shelf life. (My son proposed a sequel, "The New and Improved Other Woman.") But my concerns for sociological immortality were overridden by *marketing* concerns: New is what attracts the media interest, not Old, and not the sociologically enduring. "What's new?" became the heart of the campaign.

The New Other Woman—as a book and as a social category—was launched, then, through a major publicity campaign. Posters of the book cover were displayed in a light show at the American Bookseller's Convention; subsequently they were sent to magazines and newspapers along with bound galleys. And I was scheduled for a two-week book tour of fourteen major cities. A press release from the publisher described the book as "An intimate look at the *new* phenomenon—and the *new* rules of the other woman in *The New Other Woman*." Publisher's advertising copy emphasized both the book's newsworthiness ("demographic statistics," "contemporary trend") and its entertainment value ("their fascinating compelling tales told in their own words"). After the initial shock of seeing my work described in journalistic jargon, I was thankful that the book was not being advertised as a "peep into the sordid lives of 12 million American women" or as "a manual for successful Otherwoman-hood," possibilities that occurred to me as followups to the book's title.

Publicity packets were sent to radio and television stations, and to print journalists with the copy and "sample questions," including "How does a wife know when her husband is having an affair?" and "What should a wife do when she finds out?"—questions I had not researched and that were divisive, preying on wives' fears. The sample questions were sent to me before they were sent to the media, and although I told the publicist to scratch a number of them, she did not. Her reasoning was that these questions generated controversy, controversy generated media attention, and the media attention fueled sales. Sample questions pertaining to the sex lives of the couple were ones I had, fortunately, researched, since predictably those questions interested the media. Also fortunately, however, the campaign presented a "New Other Woman" for whom sexuality was part of a larger context. The staff and I were in accord: We did not want to reduce the woman's experience to her sex life; indeed, to have done so, would have falsified the book's content and undermined the heart of the campaign.

The Tour

The campaign was successful in attracting the media's attention: the official two-week tour stretched into six months of sporadic travel, approximately 200 radio interviews, forty print interviews, and over a dozen television shows.

During the intensive part of the tour, I was in a different city every day. A typical "city saturation" day consisted of an early morning television show, a radio interview, a newspaper interview, a noon television show, another radio show or two, and another print interview. In the interstices, I went to bookstores, talked to my publicist, took "phoner" interviews, and dealt with the invariable schedule changes. In the evening, I flew into the next city, invariably arriving late.

One of the things that happens to an author during a successful tour is *infantilization*. Like an infant, on the one hand, the author is the center of attention, admired and touted, and, on the other, wholly dependent upon others. Control over the basic biological necessities of life—food and sleep—is lost, and personal ways of satisfying those needs are disrupted. Although one might lead a healthy life at home, tour food is often fast-food and airport snacks, and sleep is severely foreshortened due to schedule changes, overscheduling, and late planes.

On tour, the author is also removed from a support network. There is rarely time to talk to family and friends. Being in different cities, different hotels, meeting different people, being on-stage, on-call, is unmooring. The usual routines, the familiar objects are absent. Dependence on the disembodied voice of the publicist intensifies.

But most infantilizing is that in each city the author has an *escort*. The escort meets the author at the plane, takes the author to the hotel, makes sure the author is up in the morning, drives the author to appointments, introduces the author to the interviewers, makes phone calls for the author, takes the author to bookstores, gets the author's food, answers questions, does necessary errands, and, most importantly, is the only stable element of the day. In brief, the escort is a parent-surrogate.

Between being the center of the universe, no longer responsible for cooking one's meals, cleaning up after oneself, making decisions, making plans, and getting from one place to another to being isolated from one's usual routines, friends, family, objects, unable to depend upon guaranteed sleep, food, exercise, infantilizing happens, even during a short tour.

Release from tending to one's own needs and the needs of others—family, students, pets, plants—frees the energy that is needed to do the tour. An exhilaration occurs as one's normal life is left behind: Giving in to the infantilization helps one to accomplish the work.

Preparation for the Tour

Before the tour began, I prepared myself for what I thought the work would entail. Having had an earlier negative experience with the media over my research on the changing door opening ceremony (1974; 1975), I was especially concerned that the feminist content of the current research reach lay audiences and that I not be attacked, personally or morally, by the media. Knowing that people are judged more on how they look and talk than on what they say, (Henley, et al., 1985) and knowing that I would be meeting people, signing books, and appearing on local and national television focused my energy, during the pre-tour period, on my presentation of self. Much as I had prepared myself for other professional ventures, such as teaching and research, I would need mentors and resource persons to teach me what I needed to know about dealing with the media. These media experts, however, were likely to hold values that were inconsistent with or opposed to mine.

Fears about being "made-over" for public consumption appeared first in my dream life. In a typical dream, I am at a cosmetics counter. The women behind the counter, grotesquely over-laden with heavy creams and colors, are insisting that I accept their help; and I let them "make me up." Looking at the dream-message, I recognized that my fears were more than skin deep: I was afraid that persons I did not respect would reconstruct my persona and my research into their own image. My anxieties were that if I learned how to present myself for the media, I would lose the integrity of *self*; and that, no matter how I tried to control the outcome, the media would "make-up" whatever it chose about me and the content of my research.

Clarifying the anxieties helped me decide what kinds of mentors I needed. To do the best possible job disseminating my research, I needed to know how to present myself and the content of my research. I needed help from the image and communication industries. For the image "making," I called my city's best known modeling studio; for the presentation of content, I turned to communications specialists and colleagues with previous media experience.

I negotiated with the local modeling school a series of lessons on television presentation of self: cosmetics, clothes, body language, and two "live" taping sessions with a "talk show host." Every part of my physical appearance came under the scrutiny of my teacher. My fears about being "made-up" were fulfilled when, during a two hour session on cosmetics, 42 different products were put on my face. Clothing issues, fortunately, were less complicated and more familiar. I was to wear straight lined dresses or blouses and pants in clear, bright colors, with the exception of red or hot pink, both being "too suggestive" given the topic of my book. Patterned, stiff, and heavy-looking fabrics were excluded, as were patterned hose, glittery jewelry, frills, man tailored suits, black, white, flat shoes and very high heels. My gamin haircut, though, was considered "classic" and appropriate. Body presentation meant learning how to stand, walk, and sit, where to look, how to place one's hands, and what to do with them while talking. I was put on the runway, asked to lift my skirt to my mid-thighs, to walk, pivot. I practiced sitting-down using my leg as a feeler for the chair, and getting up in carefully programmed stages. While sitting, I learned where to cross my legs and at what angle and at what distance from the chair my feet should be held. I was video-taped in my make-up and tour clothes going through my paces and my mock interviews.

The modeling school experiences muted my concerns with the presentation of self because I found a label for the media image I was to project in my clothing, bearing, voice, and deportment: the "warm authority." I was already familiar with this image because a research project I had done with colleagues on women professors (Richardson, et al., 1983), had come to a similar conclusion. The women professors who were judged most likeable and competent by their students were those who used teaching strategies which simultaneously projected authority *and* nurturing/caring. Similarly, a women professor on tour, to be listened to and liked, I surmised, was to temper her expertness with "feminine virtues." What was different was how each detail of my *particular* self was scrutinized, evaluated, and integrated with other details so that, in the end, a *consistent* set of messages regarding the self as a *warm authority* was presented. Distracting or double messages, such that underneath one is a prim professor or a struggling writer or a radical feminist, were obliterated through the overpowering effect of numerous, congruent details.

Going on tour, though, meant more than acquiring an image, it meant learning how to deal with the media—print, radio, and television. Because the topic was a juicy one, I thought I might be subjected to impertinent, personal, questions (e.g., Which are you—the Other Woman or the Wife? Have you stopped sleeping with married men yet?). The probability of an interviewer labeling me deviant seemed high. I needed to know how to handle innuendos and broadsides in such a way as to keep the research the topic of discussion, not the researcher, and at the same time to communicate my empathy with the women I had interviewed.

To learn techniques for handling interviewers, I turned to my sociology and feminist networks. Colleagues sent me articles and references and talked about their media experiences. A friend, a communications expert I knew through a woman's organization, put me through mock-television interviews. A colleague-friend told the president of my University about my forthcoming tour, and he asked his press aide to put me through mock-press interviews. She coached me on the "prepared response," and put me in touch with a television interviewer for more practice sessions. Consequently, by the time I was ready to begin the publicity tour, I felt secure, focused, and confident. Because of the preparation, the media had been de-mystified.

An unexpected consequence of the preparation was that, although I was invested in doing well on the tour, my own *ego* involvement had lessened. Hearing from others about the capriciousness of the media, their purely instrumental interest in you ("Their job is to churn out the new everyday"), the lack of control one has over how one's research is used by the media, released me from over investing in any *particular* media event, or nonevent. The more I thought about it, the more I realized that my identity as a feminist-sociologist was intact; I was not interested in being a celebrity, and the good opinion of the talk-show host was not the source of my ego-strength. This meant that a third kind of preparation for the tour was going on—a preparation that I was not fully cognizant of until I began writing this article: What I was doing, in addition to learning how to present myself and manage interviewers' questions, was strengthening my support system. By talking about the issues and problems as they arose, I was letting others into the process.

I turned to family and close friends. But I also enlarged my circle of trusted intimates. Some of the people I talked to lived in the tour cities; I saw them as important supports when actually on tour. Others were sociologists who had had tour experiences; and talking with them had some of the characteristics of "peer counselling," therapeutic for both counselor and counselee. Talking to family, friends, and colleagues kept me aware of my self, goals, and needs. By creating a strong support network when embarking on the new, I was reaffirming the old: friendship, loyalty, trust. In the process of the construction of self or media presentation, the core-self was nurtured; sustained.

Effectiveness of Preparation

During the pre-tour preparation, then, I purposefully focused on the presentation of self and the presentation of content. That preparation worked to a degree. I knew how to present myself as a "warm expert," what to wear, how to answer personal and divisive questions, and how to apply my own television make-up. I was armed, for example, for Mr. Radio's devastating clever repartee: "Well, Laurel, (ha ha) are you (ha-ha) happily (ha-ha) married?" "Yes," I said. I was prepared for the insistence of call-in show hosts that I take a moral stand. "I have," I said. "Male privilege is the problem." And I could handle callers. Even the one who said "men need many women" because "their sperms are too big for one woman."

On television, for the most part, I felt the host and I had the same goals, to present the material and the "expert"—me—in a positive and entertaining way. My credibility was often enhanced by women in the studio audience spontaneously declaring on live television "I am a New Other Woman," or by celebrities talking about their liaisons with married men. But, sometimes in the interest of entertainment, the producer created a three ring circus that concealed the feminist message. On one show, for example, I appeared along with a clinical psychologist and an editor of a soap opera magazine, as well as one "out" other woman, and three in the shadows, including one who was having affairs with six married men, including her ex-husband.

I was only semi-prepared for the Sally Jessy Raphael show, a program I did early in the tour. She began the program by saying, "Yesterday we talked about the wronged wife. Today, we're going to give the Other Woman her day in court." Almost immediately, though, she attacked the Other Woman who was sitting, camera front, on the stage. She riled up her Missouri studio audience. One woman, whose husband had had six affairs that she knew of, said, "I fight for what is mine. I kick. I scratch. I bite." The audience cheered. Another said the Other Woman was mentally ill and needed to find God. Sally Jessy Raphael finally implied I was spearheading a movement of Other Women, or even creating the phenomenon. Although I thought the show was dreadful, disempowering, and divisive, my publicist thought it was great—and that I was great—because I handled the conflict in a way which would generate interest in the book.

By the time I was on the Today Show, five months into the tour, I had no qualms about asking Jane Pauley to culminate the interview with feminist content. She threw away the script that had been written for her and promised time for the feminist analysis. She kept her word.

Dealing with the print media was the easiest of all. For the most part, print journalists are looking for "good quotes" that can be attributed to an expert, and so I had some hard statistics and pithy statements ready. Frequently, a woman journalist began the interview with, "I want you to know, I've read your book and I love it. You've told my story." Others would tell me they were feminists, or were writing books about relationships. Although these interviews were often very penetrating and long, I did not feel attacked or vulnerable; rather I was feeling supported by the feminist network.

At the level of the interviews, then, for the most part, I felt the preparation paid off. The message of my book was reaching large numbers of women and men, and its content had not been reduced to a study of trivial trysts. Sociological-feminist analysis was being disseminated to mass audiences.

Unanticipated Effects

The success of the tour, however, had some unanticipated consequences for me. I had not anticipated the effects of the structure and norms of the media.

The media's attachment to the *novelty principle,* for example, meant that I was "news" for a relatively short period of time. During that time, the media stampedes for coverage, and the author's labor becomes very intensive. Thus, following the official tour, my publicist scheduled me for about six "phoner" interviews a day, many of them hour-long call-in radio shows. I found this use of my time particularly interruptive and tiring; often it was like dealing with recalcitrant, slow-witted, and sexist students. I often doubted whether any of the listeners read books, and I felt angry and irritated with myself and my publicist. I had my regular university teaching and duties, and the publicity process began to feel like a relentless time and energy drain.

Further, because the media operates on the *unpredictability principle,* frequently interview appointments were changed or canceled if something more newsworthy came along. Often, I was not told about the change. When I complained to one radio host who called me two hours later than scheduled, he said, *"This* is radio," as though that explained his behavior. One of the worst examples of the media's "fickleness" was when I flew to Boston to tape a television talk show. After waiting for four hours in a room befouled with smoke, I learned I had been displaced by a new and preferred guest, the son of Bob Guccione, the publisher of Penthouse. I began to feel like an old Other Woman. Entrapped. Waiting for phone calls that did not come, or came when I was not expecting them and had other things to do. My own moral commitments to being on time, following through, and doing what I agreed to do were not reciprocated. I felt expendable, misused, tricked, and angry.

But most emotionally impactful on me were the norms and expectations of the glamour, talk-show television shows. The publicist, of course, recognizes the importance of these shows and encourages—arm twists—the author to meet their demands.

The first demand is for the author to submit to an hour-long, intensive, and often impertinent "pre-interview" with the show's producer. If the author passes the audition by being an "enthusiastic and articulate expert," she may be asked to perform other services for the program. I was frequently asked to procure New Other Women for the show. The Oprah Winfrey Show in Chicago wanted no less than nine Other Women.

Although the television network, not to mention the publisher, had many more structural resources and a much larger social network than I will ever have, procuring women was defined as my problem. If I did not find suitable women for a show, then I would be canceled.

Dealing with the issues around producing Other Women for television caused me more consternation than any other part of the publicity process. I wanted to reach mass audiences, which television certainly made possible. And I felt a loyalty to my editor and publicist, both of whom I felt had worked hard for the book. Would my recalcitrance affect my publicist's willingness to continue to "work hard" for the book, thereby rendering useless all the work I had already done to reach lay audiences? But procurement was a real moral dilemma for me. I was a researcher, not a pimp for the broadcasting industry. Could I ask women whom I had interviewed to appear on television? Was not that stretching the boundaries of my research role and the trust I had established with my interviewees?

I finally called an interviewee, an ex-theater major, who had, during the interview, jokingly proposed going on television as the "quintessential Other Woman." She was pre-interviewed for the Hour Magazine television show and passed gloriously as what they called the "expert victim." She planned her vacation around the appearance. Two weeks later, though, the Hour Magazine changed the "story line." They wanted me to find a different "expert victim": to tell the other one she had been jilted. I refused both tasks.

The media treats such women as objects, props. The producers act as if they are doing the "expert victim" a favor by giving her an opportunity to be on the show and by paying her expenses. As it turned out, moreover, expenses were not always paid, or paid egregiously late. One Boston program refused to pay the extra night expenses incurred because the weather closed the airport; at least two other programs have still not reimbursed their "expert victims." Moreover, reimbursement never includes the loss of salary or professional time.

Worse, the producers often ridiculed and cajoled the Other Woman who asked to be filmed in shadows or to have her voice distorted. A part of the typical talk-show "story line" was that the stigma of being an Other Woman had abated; to prove it, they wanted women who were currently involved with married men to talk "openly" about the relationships. As one attorney who is involved with a married client said about the request she appear camera front, "The networks must be crazy."

In the end, only one woman I personally knew, a colleague who volunteered, and one woman I had interviewed for the book appeared on television with me. I could no longer feel responsible for getting other women. I could not stomach feeling guilty-by-association for their treatment *before* they appeared on the show, not to mention what was happening to them once they were on the program.

I refused to do it any longer, and gave the problem to my publicist. She found women to appear who anticipated secondary gains, such as an unemployed equity actress, who expected to be paid, but was not. By the time the Donahue show suggested that I appear on a program about men who had left their wives for the other woman, a topic that had nothing to do with my book, and that I procure those men (and if possible their previous and current wives), I had little trouble demurring.

Expected to labor intensively, to put my regular life on hold, having my time interrupted, being displaced by the newer and better, being asked to do things that were genuine moral dilemmas for me—all requests that stemmed directly from the structure and norms of the media—then, had major emotional impacts on me. Over the months I felt anger, confusion, frustration, rage, and despair.

The same support network I had nonconsciously been building during the preparation process was what I consciously turned to. Because I had enlarged the network, I was not overly dependent on a few people. I could ask for concrete help—such as teaching one of my classes or talking to a prospective major—from a large number of colleagues. I could be selective about whom I talked to about my feelings. By discussing the dilemmas the tour was creating and the problems of balancing my personal needs and my political goals, I was able to ground myself in my familial, feminist, and sociological networks. Through the network, the felt contradiction between a successful tour and personal distress was explored, validated, and accepted.

Disseminating sociological research to a lay audience through a book tour, then, requires management of some complex and often contradictory feelings. The demands on the author's time and energy are often intense, and the emotional fallout often unexpected. Yet, without the campaign, the book's message would not reach mass audiences. Because of the tour, the ideas of the book reached many feminist journalists who, in turn, carried the message into print, radio, and television. And because of the preparation for the tour, even nonfeminist channels transmitted the book's content.

My purposes in writing a trade book—to empower and unify women—are apparently being met. When an Other Woman writes to me, "Reading your book was a consciousness raising experience. I'll never date married men again," or "Your book goes next to a close friend who is in her 4th year as the 'other woman.' I hope it helps her as much as it has me. Thanks for publishing your results in such an easy-to-read manner," or "At last! You've done what the doctors haven't been able to do. You've cured me of my migraines. Yeah, I *was* the 'other women,' "—when I read these kinds of testimonies, I know the work is empowering women. And when a wife writes, "I read your book to gain insight into my husband's relationship with another woman. Your book has eased my pain and I am giving it to the other woman hoping it will benefit her, too," or, "What a joy to read your beautifully written book on a topic that has been very personally difficult for me. I don't feel so angry anymore at the other woman,"—when I read these kinds of letters, I know the work is uniting women. And when a woman who has been both the wife and the "Other Woman" writes, "You have touched my soul with your book," I know women are being moved.

But further, my experiences with the media point to some larger sociological issues. Linguistic convention has settled during the past decade on a grammatically improper, but sociologically revealing, usage: the *media* has become a singular noun. It is not a question of the "good" print media versus the "bad" television or of the elite organ versus the mass market one: the differences are muted by their sameness. Linguistically, and sociologically, the media is a monolith. Whether one considers print, radio, or television, one finds essential similarities in their standards, goals, and means, and one finds them inexorably linked to each other, feeding off the same fodder.

Sociological research can become that fodder, masticated and remasticated by the media, and intrepid sociologists who journey into the media's field may find themselves engaged in an unanticipated struggle for dominance. The media expects conformance to their standards, even if those are in direct opposition to research canons or personal morality. The assumption is that one will willingly suspend one's life and values because one is flattered by the media attention, on the one hand, and, on the other, awed by its power. Even the puniest of news stations and the feeblest of magazines, for example, act as if they are justified in demanding acquiescence to their standards because they identify themselves as *the media*. For sociologists, then, the naive notion that the media is simply a tool for them to pick up at will, hone, use, and put down should be abandoned. The media and sociology are competing institutions: The task of the sociologist is the discovery and implementation of ways to *use* the media, rather than being used by it.

NOTE

Ernest Lockridge has been very supportive throughout the book tour, has offered technical advice about it, and has critically read multiple drafts of this manuscript. My editor, Joyce Seltzer, and my publicist, Louise Hochberg, have also been wonderful. Many other friends and colleagues are referred to anonymously in the pages of this article—persons who have provided me with support, technical knowledge, and/or critical readings of various versions of this manuscript. These include Fred Anderle, Lynn Atwater, Judith Cook, Arlene Kaplan Daniels, Mary Margaret Fonow, Harriet Ganson, Lisa Holstein, Joan Huber, Edward Jennings, Betty Kirschner, Jerry Lewis, Patricia Lynch, Shulamit Reinharz, and Verta Taylor. I thank each of these people very much.

REFERENCES

Adler, Peter
    1984   "The sociologist as celebrity: the role of the media in field research." Quali-
           tative Sociology 7:310–26.
Best, Joel
    1986   "Famous for fifteen minutes: notes on the researcher as newsmaker." Quali-
           tative Sociology 9(4):372–82.
Cook, Judith A., and Mary Margaret Fonow
    1986   "Knowledge and women's interests: issues of epistemology and methodology
           in feminist sociological research." Sociological Inquiry 56:2–29.
Henley, Nancy, Mykol Hamilton, and Barrie Thorne
    1985   "Womanspeak and manspeak: sex differences and sexism in communication,
           verbal and nonverbal." Pp. 168–87 in Alice G. Sargent (ed), Beyond Sex Roles.
           St. Paul, Minn.: West.
Richardson, Laurel
    1974   "The changing door ceremony: some notes on the operation of sex-roles in
           everyday life." Urban Life, 2:506–15.
    1985   The New Other Woman: Contemporary Women in Affairs with Married Men.
           New York: The Free Press.

Richardson [Walum], Laurel
  1975 "Sociology and the mass media." The American Sociologist 819:28–32.
Richardson, Laurel, Judith A. Cook, and Anne Statham
  1983 "Down the up staircase: male and female university professors' classroom
        management strategies." Pp. 280–87 in Laurel Richardson and Verta Taylor
        (eds), Feminist Frontiers. New York: Random House.
Shatzkin, Leonard
  1982 In Cold Type: Overcoming the Book Crisis. Boston: Houghton Mifflin.
Tuchman, Gaye
  1978 Making News. New York: The Free Press.
———. (ed.)
  1974 The T.V. Establishment: Programming for Power and Profit. Englewood
        Cliffs, N.J.: Prentice-Hall.
Wells, Alan (ed.)
  1979 Mass Media and Society. Palo Alto, Calif.: Mayfield.

CONTRIBUTORS

Joan Acker is the leader of the research group on women and work at Sweden's Center for Working Life and was formerly the director of the Center for the Study of Women in Society at the University of Oregon. She has published on gender and class, women and work, gender and organizational theory, and comparable worth. Her most recent book, published by Temple University Press, is *Doing Comparable Worth: Gender, Class, and Pay Equity*. She is the 1989 recipient of the Jessie Bernard Award of the American Sociological Association.

Kathryn Pyne Addelson is a professor of philosophy and Director of the Program in the History of the Sciences, Smith College. She is the author of numerous articles on feminist ethics and feminist philosophy of science.

Kate R. Barry coordinates Women's Programs and teaches Women's Studies at Lane Community College, Eugene, Oregon. She is also chair of the Women's Education and Employment Network (WEEN), an Oregon statewide women's organization.

Pauline B. Bart has focused on studying violence against women, notably rape avoidance, described in Bart and O'Brien, *Stopping Rape: Successful Survival Strategies,* and is currently interested in how rape reform laws actually reform, particularly from the perspective of the victim. She returned to school after being a trapped housewife in the fifties, studied depression in middle-aged women, and worked on issues in women's health. She is a radical feminist.

Christine E. Bose is an associate professor of sociology at SUNY Albany, where she holds a joint appointment in women's studies and as the director of the Institute for Research on Women. Her academic interests lie in the areas of stratification, labor market studies, gender studies, and methodology. She has co-edited *Ingredients for Women's Employment Policy* (SUNY Press, 1987) with Glenna Spitze and *Hidden Aspects of Women's Work* (Praeger, 1987) with Roslyn Feldberg and Natalie Sokoloff.

Lynn Weber Cannon is professor of sociology at Memphis State University and director of the Center for Research on Women. She is coauthor of *The American Perception of Class* and many journal articles on social class, gender, and race, including publications in *Gender & Society* and *Signs: Journal of Women and Culture in Society.*

Patricia Hill Collins is an associate professor of Afro-American studies and sociology at the University of Cincinnati. She is currently finishing a book on Black feminist thought, forthcoming in 1990.

Judith A. Cook is a sociologist and the director of the Thresholds National Research and Training Center on Long-Term Mental Illness in Chicago, Illinois. She is also a field associate professor in the School of Social Service Administration at the University of Chicago. She has published in the areas of feminist pedagogy, familial bereavement, and mental illness. Her most recent book (with L. Richardson and A. Statham) is *Gender and University Teaching: A Negotiated Difference* (1991).

Ruth Dixon-Mueller is a senior research associate in the Graduate Group in Demography and Program in Population Research at the University of California, Berkeley. Her current research is on the changing role of women in the agricultural labor force in developing countries. She has written on a number of topics relating to women, population, and development. She has served as a consultant on women's issues for the United Nations Secretariat, the World Food Programme, the International Labour Office, USAID, The Ford Foundation, and the International Women's Health Coalition, and as a member of the Committee on Population of the National Research Council

Johanna Esseveld teaches at the Department of Sociology and the Center for Women's Studies at Lund University. During the early 1980s she carried out a research project on women and unemployment in Sweden, and a more recent project on the women's movement in the labor market is nearly completed. So far the project has resulted in a number of articles and a book written with Karen Davies, *Playing Hop-Scotch in the Swedish Labour Market: A Study of Unemployed Factory Women* (Stockholm, 1988).

Mary Margaret Fonow is a sociologist and assistant director of the Center for Women's Studies at The Ohio State University. She has published in the area of women and labor unions, feminist epistemology and methodology, feminist pedagogy, school desegregation, and rape prevention. She serves as special advisor to the Governor of Ohio's Interagency Council on Women and Policy.

Linda N. Freeman is an assistant professor of psychiatry at Rush University Medical School and director of the Child Psychiatric Inpatient Unit. Her research interests include the clinical study of child and adolescent depression and adolescent suicide.

Linda Grant is an associate professor of sociology and faculty associate of the Institute for Behavioral Research at the University of Georgia. Her research has focused on gender relationships, medical sociology, and sociology of education. Recent works have appeared in *American Sociological Review*, *The American Sociologist*, *Sociology of Education*, and *Anthropology and Education Quarterly*.

Lois Haignere is the director of the Department of Research at the United University Professions, the country's largest higher education union. She designs and conducts research concerning labor-management and membership issues, including salaries, benefits, equity, part time workers, and industry standards for shift workers. Her publications include articles concerning pay equity for women and minorities.

Elizabeth Higginbotham is associate professor of sociology at Memphis State University and a research faculty member at the Center for Research on Women. She is the author of many articles on gender and race and women of color, including publications in *Gender & Society, Women's Studies Quarterly,* and *Signs: Journal of Women and Culture in Society*.

Toby Epstein Jayaratne is currently a senior research associate on a study exploring the effects of unemployment on single African American mothers and their children. She is also a lecturer in the Residential College at the University of Michigan. She received her Ph.D. in developmental psychology at the University of Michigan and has published and presented several papers on the topic of feminist methodology. Her research interests include childhood and sex-role socialization and parental belief systems.

Marianne L. A. Leung is a graduate assistant in history at Memphis State University. Her current research interests include issues of birth control pertaining to race, class, and gender. Marianne is a native of Sweden.

Maria Mies is a professor of sociology at the Fachhochschule, Koln, West Germany. She lived in India for many years and has been active in the women's movement since 1969. In 1979 she established the program "Women and Development" at the Institute of Social Studies, The Hague. She is the author of several books, including *Indian Women in Subsistence and Agricultural Labour* (1986), *Patriarchy and Accumulation on a World Scale* (1986), and *Women: The Last Colony* (1988) with S. V. Werlhof and V. Bennholdt-Thomsen.

Laurel Richardson is a professor of sociology at The Ohio State University. She is the author of *The Dynamics of Sex and Gender, The New Other Woman,* numerous scholarly articles, and coeditor of *Feminist Frontiers: Rethinking Sex, Gender and Society* with Verta Taylor.

Leila J. Rupp is a professor of history at The Ohio State University. She is the author of *Mobilizing Women for War: German and American Propaganda, 1939–1945* (1978) and coauthor, with Verta Taylor, of *Survival in the Doldrums: The American Women's Rights Movement, 1945 to the 1960s* (1987). She is currently engaged in research on the international women's movement.

Liz Stanley is a senior lecturer in sociology at Manchester University. She is the author of several books, including *Breaking Out: Feminist Consciousness and Feminist Research* (1983) and *Georgie Porgie: Sexual Harassment in Everyday Life* (1988) with Sue Wise, and *Feminist Methodology* (forthcoming).

Ronnie Steinberg is an assistant professor of sociology and women's studies at Temple University. She is the author of *Wages and Hours: Labor and Reform in Twentieth Century America*, Editor of *Equal Employment Policy for Women* and coeditor of *Job Training for Women*. She edits a book series on "Women in the Political Economy" for Temple University Press. A pay equity advocate and technical expert for over a decade, she is writing a book on how reforms such as comparable worth come about.

Abigail J. Stewart has been a professor at the University of Michigan in psychology and women's studies since 1987. From 1975–87 she served on the faculty at Boston University. She was also a visiting professor at Wesleyan University and acting director of the Henry A. Murray Research Center at Radcliffe College, 1978–1980. Her major research interest is the study of change at the individual and social level.

Verta Taylor is an associate professor of sociology at The Ohio State University. She is coauthor, with Leila J. Rupp, of *Survival in the Doldrums: The American Women's Rights Movement, 1945 to the 1960s* and coeditor, with Laurel Richardson, of *Feminist Frontiers: Rethinking Sex, Gender, and Society*. Her teaching and research interests are in the sociology of gender and women's studies, social movements and collective behavior, and qualitative research methods.

Kathryn B. Ward is an associate professor of sociology at Southern Illinois University at Carbondale. Her articles (with Linda Grant) on the feminist critique of sociology have appeared in *The American Sociological Review, The Sociological Quarterly*, and *The American Sociologist*. Her other areas of research include women in the world-system, the debt crisis, and women's movements.

Sue Wise is an honorary research associate in the department of sociology at the University of Manchester. She is a social worker, teacher, and writer. Her publications include *Breaking Out: Feminist Consciousness and Feminist Research* and *Georgie Porgie: Sexual Harassment in Everyday Life* (both with Liz Stanley). Future publications include books on child abuse, social work, and equal opportunities policy.

INDEX